expressed, which should not be attributed to the grantors or to the University of Pennsylvania.

Philadelphia
January 1986

LABOR RELATIONS AND PUBLIC POLICY SERIES

No. 12

NLRB REMEDIES

FOR UNFAIR LABOR PRACTICES

(Revised Edition)

by

J. Freedley Hunsicker, Jr.
Jonathan A. Kane

and

Peter D. Walther, Jr.

Industrial Research Unit
The Wharton School, Vance Hall
University of Pennsylvania
Philadelphia, Pennsylvania 19104-6358
U.S.A.

Foreword

In 1968, the Industrial Research Unit inaugurated its Labor Relations and Public Policy Series as a means of examining issues and stimulating discussions in the complex and controversial areas of collective bargaining and the regulation of labor-management disputes. Thus far, twenty-nine monographs have been published in this series. Eleven of these deal with various policies and procedures of the National Labor Relations Board (NLRB). The other eighteen cover such significant issues as collective bargaining in the 1970s; welfare and strikes; opening the skilled construction trades to blacks; the Davis-Bacon Act; the labor-management situation in urban school systems; old age, handicapped, and Vietnam-era antidiscrimination legislation; the impact of the Occupational Safety and Health Act; the Landrum-Griffin Act; the effects of the AT&T-EEO consent decree; unions' rights to company information; employee relations and regulation; operating during strikes; union violence and the law; the impact of antitrust laws on employee relations; prevailing wage legislation; deregulation and union losses in trucking; and comparable worth theory and practice.

This study, *NLRB Remedies for Unfair Labor Practices*, No. 12 in the series, is a completely revised and updated version of the book, first published in 1976, and authored by Douglas S. McDowell and Kenneth C. Huhn. Terming the original edition "A comprehensive, well-organized treatment . . . issues are discussed factually and dispassionately . . . sophisticated enough for use in law schools . . .," *Choice*, June 1976, the journal of academic and research librarians chose it as one of their key academic publications of the year. The authors of the revised edition, J. Freedley Hunsicker, Jr., Jonathan A. Kane, and Peter D. Walther, Jr., are all practicing attorneys specializing in labor law, members of the Pennsylvania Bar, and partners in the Philadelphia law firm, Drinker Biddle & Reath. Mr. Walther also served for two years as a member of the National Labor Relations Board. Messrs. Walther, Hunsicker, and

Kane are very pleased to acknowledge the debt to the authors of the original edition, not only for their excellent analysis, but also for establishing the organizational framework for the book. They also wish to acknowledge the assistance of their partner John Markle, Jr., and associates D. Richard Powell, Jr., and Kevin C. Donovan for their effort and insight in the preparation of several chapters in the book, and to Dolores Hunt for her patience in the typing and preparation of the initial manuscript. Editing of the initial transcript was done by Mr. Hunsicker.

The decline in union membership and the seeming inability of organized labor to arrest this decline has occasioned much comment and analysis of the role of the National Labor Relations (Taft-Hartley) Act and of the National Labor Relations Board (NLRB) in protecting employees from unfair labor practices. Among the many suggestions made are that additional and more stringent penalties be assessed against employers who are found not to be in compliance with the Act. Often these proposed penalties include requiring the offending employer to bargain with a union that has not been selected by a majority of the employees involved. Under such an arrangement the rights of the employees would be sacrificed to punish the employer. The authors of this study understand these conflicts of rights and their public policy recommendations reflect a balance of the different interests. Most important, the facts and issues are set forth clearly and objectively before any recommendations are proposed.

The study was edited by the Wharton Industrial Research Unit's chief editor, Kate C. Bradford, and her associate editor, Barbara A. Kimmelman, who also prepared the index of cases. Support for the project came from a special grant made by the Alcoa Foundation, through the interest and courtesy of Frank A. Kramer, vice-president, Aluminum Company of America, and Earl L. Gadbery, secretary of the Foundation. Further support, and underwriting of publication costs, came from the generous annual grants of the J. Howard Pew Freedom Trust in support of the Labor Relations and Public Policy Series. The interest in our work by Robert I. Smith, president, Fred H. Billups, Jr., vice-president, Robert G. Dunlop, member, Board of Directors, of the Glenmede Trust Company, which administers the Pew foundations, is most heartening and appreciated. The Alcoa Foundation and a sister Pew foundation, the Pew Memorial Trust, also supported the first edition of this book.

As in all works published by the Industrial Research Unit, the authors are solely responsible for the research and for all opinions

TABLE OF CONTENTS

CHAPTER I

Introduction

Remedies under the Labor Management Relations (Taft-Hartley)
Act of 1947, which amended the National Labor Relations (Wagner)
Act of 1935, are of paramount importance because they are the
means by which Congress intended to address and rectify unfair
labor practices.[1] Congress delegated to the National Labor Relations
Board (NLRB) the task of devising remedies appropriate to protect
the rights of employees to engage freely in collective bargaining, to
select a bargaining representative of their choice, to engage in or
to refrain from engaging in concerted activities, and to protect
employers from improper conduct in relation to labor disputes.[2]

The Industrial Research Unit of the Wharton School published
its original study of NLRB remedies for unfair labor practices in
1976. In updating and rewriting the study, we were mindful that
the substantive labor law since 1976 has been marked by instability.
The Board in the 1970s and early 1980s significantly expanded the
reach of the labor law, often finding violations in situations where
they had not been found before. There were at least fourteen specific decisions that extended remedial action into uncharted areas.[3]
Consequently, the Board had to fashion remedies where it had not

---

[1] It has long been recognized that "the Act is essentially remedial." Republic Steel
Corp. v. NLRB, 311 U.S. 7, 9–11, 7 L.R.R.M. 287, 289 (1940).

[2] NLRB v. Pennsylvania Graylines, Inc., 303 U.S. 261, 271, 2 L.R.R.M. 600, 603
(1938); Amalgamated Local Union 355 v. NLRB, 481 F.2d 996, 83 L.R.R.M. 2849 (2d
Cir. 1973).

[3] Alleluia Cushion, 221 N.L.R.B. 999, 91 L.R.R.M. 1131 (1975); General Am. Trans.
Corp., 228 N.L.R.B. 808, 94 L.R.R.M. 1483 (1977); Torrington Constr. Co., 235 N.L.R.B.
1540, 98 L.R.R.M. 1135 (1978); W-I Canteen Servs., 238 N.L.R.B. 609, 99 L.R.R.M.
1571 (1978), enf't denied, 606 F.2d 738, 102 L.R.R.M. 2447 (7th Cir. 1979); Markle
Mfg. Co., 239 N.L.R.B. 1353, 100 L.R.R.M. 1125 (1979), enf't denied in part, 623 F.2d
1122, 105 L.R.R.M. 2500 (5th Cir. 1980); LOF Glass Co., 249 N.L.R.B. 428, 104 L.R.R.M.
1098 (1980); Kraft Foods, 251 N.L.R.B. 598, 105 L.R.R.M. 1233 (1980); PPG Indus.,
251 N.L.R.B. 1146, 105 L.R.R.M. 1434 (1980); Otis Elevator Co. (I), 255 N.L.R.B. 235,
106 L.R.R.M. 1343 (1981); TRW Bearings, 257 N.L.R.B. 442, 107 L.R.R.M. 1481 (1981);
Conair Corp., 261 N.L.R.B. 1189, 110 L.R.R.M. 1161 (1982), enf't denied in part, 721
F.2d 1355, 114 L.R.R.M. 3169 (D.C. Cir 1983); Materials Research, 262 N.L.R.B. 1010,
110 L.R.R.M. 1401 (1982); Propoco, 263 N.L.R.B. 136, 110 L.R.R.M. 1496 (1982),
enforced with unpublished nonprecedential opinion, Case No. 83-4058 (2d Cir. 1983);
Milwaukee Spring Division I, 265 N.L.R.B. 28, 111 L.R.R.M. (1496) (1982).

1

done so previously. The expansion met with resistance in the courts and in many of these decisions the courts denied enforcement.[4]

With the establishment of a Reagan-appointed majority in the late spring of 1983 under Chairman Dotson, the Board has recharted its course. The Board reversed all fourteen of the above-mentioned cases and restored the law to its form prior to its expansion in the 1970s and 1980s.[5]

This instability in the substantive law has been accompanied by the diminishing strength of the labor movement. More often than not employees rejected union appeals for collective organization. Members of the labor union movement and their academic and political partisans blamed the Board for this phenomenon. They have focused on the Board's remedies, which they say are largely ineffective, and have argued that stronger remedies might restore the movement's losses. The controversial Labor Reform Act of 1978, which proposed to provide more rigorous remedies, was a product of this thinking. Although the Labor Reform Act was killed by a filibuster in the Senate, the ideas behind it remain alive, and it is

---

[4] *See, e.g.,* W-I Canteen Servs., 238 N.L.R.B. 609, 99 L.R.R.M. 1571 (1978), *enf't denied,* 606 F.2d 738 (7th Cir. 1979); Markle Mfg., 239 N.L.R.B. 1353, 100 L.R.R.M. 1125 (1979), *enf't denied in part,* 623 F.2d 1122 (5th Cir. 1980); Conair Corp., 261 N.L.R.B. 1189, 110 L.R.R.M. 1161 (1982), *enf't denied in part,* 721 F.2d 1355, 114 L.R.R.M. 3169 (D.C. Cir. 1983); Krispy Kreme Doughnut Corp. v. NLRB, 635 F.2d 304 (4th Cir. 1980) (disapproving of *Alleluia Cushion*); Ontario Knife Co. v. NLRB, 637 F.2d 840 (2d Cir. 1980) (disapproving of *Alleluia Cushion*); NLRB v. Dawson Cabinet Co., 566 F.2d 1079 (8th Cir. 1977) (disapproving of *Alleluia Cushion*); Midwest Stock Exchange v. NLRB, 635 F.2d 1285 (7th Cir. 1980) (rejecting *per se* test of Board in *PPG Industries*); Graham Architectural Prods. v. NLRB, 697 F.2d 534 (3d Cir. 1983) (rejecting *PPG Industries*); E.I. DuPont de Nemours v. NLRB (DuPont I), 707 F.2d 1076, 113 L.R.R.M. 2931 (9th Cir. 1983) (rejecting *Materials Research*); *but see,* E.I. DuPont de Nemours Co. v. NLRB (DuPont II), 724 F.2d 1061, 115 L.R.R.M. 2153 (3d Cir. 1983), *vacated and remanded to Board,* May 14, 1984.

[5] Our Way Inc., 268 N.L.R.B. 394, 115 L.R.R.M. 1025 (1983) (overruling *T.R.W. Bearings*); Meyers Indus., Inc., 268 N.L.R.B. 493, 115 L.R.R.M. 1025 (overruling *Alleluia Cushion*), *remanded sub nom.* Prill v. NLRB, __ F.2d __, __ L.R.R.M. __ (D.C. Cir. 1985); United Technologies Corp., 268 N.L.R.B. 557, 115 L.R.R.M. 1049 (1984) (overruling *General Am. Trans. Corp.*); Olin Corp., 268 N.L.R.B. 573, 115 L.R.R.M. 1056 (1984) (overruling *Propoco, Inc.*); Milwaukee Spring Div. II, 268 N.L.R.B. 87, 115 L.R.R.M. 1065 (1984) (overruling *Milwaukee Spring Division I*); Otis Elevator II, 269 N.L.R.B. 891, 115 L.R.R.M. 1281 (1984); Rossmore House, 269 N.L.R.B. 1176, 116 L.R.R.M. 1025 (1984) (overruling *PPG Industries*); Gourmet Foods, Inc., 270 N.L.R.B. No. 113, 116 L.R.R.M. 1105 (1984) (overruling *Conair Corp.*); Buttersworth-Manning-Ashmore Mortuary, 270 N.L.R.B. No. 184, 116 L.R.R.M. 1193 (1984) (overruling *Torrington Constr. Co.*); Taracorp, 273 N.L.R.B. No. 54, 117 L.R.R.M. 1497 (1984) (overruling *Kraft Foods*); Indianapolis Power & Light Co., 273 N.L.R.B. No. 211, 118 L.R.R.M. 120 (1985) (overruling *W-I Canteen Services*); Sears Roebuck & Co., 274 N.L.R.B. No. 55, 118 L.R.R.M. 1329 (1985) (overruling *Materials Research Corp.*); Tri-Cast, Inc., 274 N.L.R.B. No. 59, 118 L.R.R.M. 1380 (1985) (overruling *LOF Glass*); American Thread Co., 274 N.L.R.B. No. 164, 118 L.R.R.M. 1499 (1985) (overruling *Markle Mfg.*).

apparent that they affected the actions of the Board in the late 1970s and early 1980s.[6]

Meanwhile, the Board's critics have intensified their attack. In a statement before the House Labor Subcommittee on Labor-Management Relations in June of 1984, Professor Dan H. Pollitt of the University of North Carolina stated bluntly that "the remedies at the end of a successful [Board] litigation are largely toothless." Even the *Gissel* bargaining order has been questioned. Professor Paul Weiler of Harvard University estimates that *Gissel* bargaining orders have led to meaningful and continuing collective bargaining less than 10 percent of the time.[7] (A history of the *Gissel* bargaining order is presented in Appendix A.)

Much of this criticism reflects the tendency to use the Board and its remedies as scapegoats.[8] The contention that the Board's remedies are responsible for the recent loss of labor influence simply does not wash. It should be remembered that the Board's remedies have not markedly changed over the fifty years of the Act's existence, and during the same period union influence (until recently) has continually increased. It would be as unfair to suggest that the Board's remedies in the 1940s, 1950s, and 1960s were the cause of labor's successes as it is to say today that they are the cause of its failures. The causes of the labor movement's losses can be referred to matters unrelated to Board remedies, and are beyond the scope of this book.

This is not to say, however, that some criticism of the Board's remedies is not due, particularly criticism relating to the unpredictability of Board bargaining orders and to delays in the processing of cases. Where appropriate, we shall not refrain from such criticism in this book.

---

[6] For example, in 1977 the Board launched a specific program to make greater use of §10(j) injunctions under the leadership of then-General Counsel, John Irving. This can be seen as a response to criticisms that the Board's processes were too slow. The following table of the number of applications for §10(j) injunctions covering the years 1975 through 1984, demonstrates the Board's increased activity in the §10(j) area:

1975	1976	1977	1978	1979	1980	1981	1982	1983	1984
21	20	45	46	62	50	45	53	51	30

[7] Weiler, *Promises to Keep: Securing Workers' Rights to Sell Organization Under the NLRA*, 96 HARV. L. REV. 1769, at 1795 n.94 (1983).

[8] Professor Bok has observed that "most of the professors and other critics who evaluate the law are likely to continue in their unwillingness and inability to study the actual impact of the laws upon workers, unions, and employers in ways that will identify rules that failed to achieve their intended result or rest upon fallible suppositions of human behavior." Bok, *Comparative Labor Laws*, 84 HARV. L. REV. 1394, 1462 (1971).

In discussing specific remedies in this revised study, we have examined both the remedies' factual context and the Board's theory of the substantive violation. This method will help readers who are unfamiliar with specific actions prescribed by the Labor Management Relations Act of 1947. One can never fully understand a Board remedy without comprehending the violation that the remedy is intended to correct.

This study, we hope, will provide an introduction for persons unfamiliar with the labor law, and will serve as a guide for those needing their knowledge refreshed. We have sought to provide the labor relations specialist, the personnel officer, the union official, and the labor law practitioner with a comprehensive reference to Board remedies. We have continued our predecessor's practice of elaborate footnotes in the hope of providing the practitioner with substantial research in readily usable form. Even though it is not possible to anticipate every legal issue, we have tried to provide a thorough explanation of basic principles and recurring issues which arise in labor litigation. Of course, practitioners are urged to supplement our work with independent research to satisfy themselves that the law has not changed significantly.

We have also noted areas of disagreement between the Board and the courts of appeals over the Board's exercise of its remedial authority, differences which incidentally have been markedly reduced by the Dotson Board. We hope that an explanation of these differences will not only provide aid in preparing cases, but also assist the reader in evaluating the effectiveness of the Board's remedial decisions; a Board order that has little chance for enforcement is a hollow one.

A discussion of potential modifications of NLRB remedies seems particularly timely because these issues have been the subject of strenuous oversight hearings conducted over the past year by the House Subcommittee on Labor-Management Relations and the Subcommittee on Manpower and Housing of the Committee on Education and Labor. These hearings, and the occasionally shrill criticism of the Board, have especially concerned employers who have flagrantly and repeatedly violated the Act.

In the concluding chapter, we will attempt to analyze these criticisms and examine the possibility of improvements in existing Board remedies and remedial procedures.

CHAPTER II

The Remedial Authority of the NLRB

Congress has granted to the National Labor Relations Board the sole authority to prevent the commission of unfair labor practices as described in section 8 of the National Labor Relations Act.[1] Section 10(c) of the Act states that should the Board find that an employer or union has engaged in or is engaging in such unfair labor practices, then

> the Board shall state its finding of fact and shall issue and cause to be served on such party an order requiring such person to cease and desist from such unfair labor practice, and to take such affirmative action including reinstatement of employees with or without back pay, as will effectuate the policies of the act . . .[2]

NLRB REMEDIAL DISCRETION

Within the limits specifically set forth (or as interpreted by the courts as intended) in the National Labor Relations Act, Congress has given the Board a relatively free hand in determining which remedies will best effectuate the policies of the Act.[3] The Supreme Court has cautioned the courts against substituting their judgment for that of the Board in determining how the effects of unfair labor practices may best be expunged. The relation of remedy to policy is a matter for administrative competence, and thus the "courts

---

[1] Section 10(a) of the Act (29 U.S.C. § 160(a)) provides that the "Board is empowered, as hereinafter provided, to prevent any person from engaging in any unfair labor practice affecting commerce. This power shall not be affected by any other means of adjustment or prevention that has been or may be established by agreement, law, or otherwise . . . ." See generally Garner v. Teamsters, 346 U.S. 485, 33 L.R.R.M. 2218 (1953); San Diego Building Trades Council v. Garmon, 353 U.S. 236, 43 L.R.R.M. 2838 (1957). However, in recognition of the compelling interest of the states in keeping the peace, an employer has the right to seek local judicial protection from tortious conduct during a labor dispute. E.g., Sears Roebuck & Co. v. Carpenters, 436 U.S. 180, 98 L.R.R.M. 2282 (1978).

[2] 29 U.S.C. § 160(c).

[3] See NLRB v. Mine Workers (P.M.W.), Local 403, 375 U.S. 396, 55 L.R.R.M. 2084 (1964); Republic Aviation Corp. v. NLRB, 324 U.S. 793, 16 L.R.R.M. 620 (1945); NLRB v. P. Lorillard Co., 314 U.S. 512, 9 L.R.R.M. 410 (1942). Fibreboard Paper Prods. Corp., 379 U.S. 203, 216, 57 L.R.R.M. 2609 (1964).

must not enter the allowable area of the Board's discretion and must guard against the danger of sliding unconsciously from the narrow confines of law into more specious domains of policy."[4] The Court in this decision, however, made it clear that the Board's purpose is not to adjudicate private rights but to effectuate declared public policy and that for there to be effective enforcement of the law, the Board must disclose the basis of its order in its decision.[5]

It is clear that Congress granted the Board exclusive remedial authority in order to take advantage of "expert judgment"[6] by "experienced officials with an adequate appreciation of the complexities of the subject...."[7] The Board is expected to exhibit its presumed expertise, and its order is not disturbed "unless it can be shown that the order is a patent attempt to achieve ends other than those which can fairly be said to effectuate the policies of the act."[8] On the other hand, it should be noted that the courts are not required to follow blindly the Board's holdings and remedial orders. The assumption that the Board possesses a unique expertise in the area of labor relations has not gone unchallenged and, in the eyes of some, is questionable in view of the actions of the courts over the years.[9]

EFFECTUATING THE POLICIES OF THE ACT

The Board's authority is limited by the statutory requirement that its orders must effectuate the policies of the Act. The relief granted by the Board must bear some rational relationship to the unfair labor practice committed and must serve the purpose it is expected to accomplish.[10] Whether the Board's remedy in fact effectuates the policies of the Act is often the issue in appeals from

---

[4] Phelps Dodge Corp. v. NLRB, 313 U.S. 177, 194, 8 L.R.R.M. 439, 446 (1941).

[5] For a discussion of cases where the courts have denied enforcement of Board orders because the Board has not adequately set forth the basis of its decision see Ch. III, *infra.*

[6] Machinists, Lodge 35 v. NLRB, 311 U.S. 72, 78, 7 L.R.R.M. 282, 287 (1940); NLRB v. 7-Up Bottling Co., 344 U.S. 344, 346, 31 L.R.R.M. 2237, 2238 (1953).

[7] Republic Aviation Corp. v. NLRB, 324 U.S. 793, 800, 16 L.R.R.M. 620, 624 (1945).

[8] Virginia Elec. & Power Co. v. NLRB, 319 U.S. 533, 540, 12 L.R.R.M. 739 (1943).

[9] *See, e.g.,* Getman & Goldberg, *The Myth of NLRB Expertise,* 39 U. CHI. L. REV. 681 (1972); and remarks by Judge Harry T. Edwards, D.C. Cir., before Oxford/BNA Symposium, 173 DAILY LAB. REP. D-1, at D-7 (1983). See also discussion at Ch. III, *infra.*

[10] Virginia Elec. & Power Co. v. NLRB, 319 U.S. 533, 540, 12 L.R.R.M. 739 (1943); NLRB v. MacKay Radio and Telegraph Co., 304 U.S. 333, 342, 2 L.R.R.M. 610, 615 (1938); NLRB v. 7-Up Bottling Co., 344 U.S. 344, 346, 31 L.R.R.M. 2237, 2238 (1938).

Board orders. Standing alone, the requirement that the order effectuate the policies of the act is obviously vague and gives scant assistance in determining the propriety of a Board remedy.

Pursuant to this declaration of policy and the provisions of section 7 establishing the "rights of employees,"[11] the Supreme Court has recognized that it was Congress's intent to accomplish three basic objectives through the Act: (1) free and unimpaired collective bargaining; (2) free choice in the selection of a bargaining representative; and (3) freedom to engage in, or refrain from, concerted activity for mutual aid and protection.[12] Board remedies, therefore, must accord with and further these statutory objectives, and will not stand if they represent "a patent attempt to achieve ends other than those which can fairly be said to effectuate the policies of the act."[13] The Board may not justify an order solely on the ground that it will deter future violations of the Act.[14] Further, the relief granted must not be in conflict with any other of the primary statutory objectives or the Constitution; and, where other established rights are in conflict with the remedy, the remedy normally must represent a balancing among those rights.[15]

The courts have rejected Board remedies that infringe upon employees' freedom of choice. In *Consolidated Edison Co. of New York v. NLRB*,[16] the Supreme Court refused to sanction an order that required an employer to abrogate nonexclusive collective bargaining agreements executed on behalf of employees who were members of an affiliated union which had not been certified as the employees' exclusive representative. There was no finding of domination or interference. The Court noted that the abrogation of the agreements would deprive the employees of the benefits of their representation. In *Local 57, ILGWU v. NLRB*,[17] the Board ordered a runaway New York employer, that had moved its operations to Florida, to bargain with the New York union in its new Florida plant. While recognizing that the Board was faced with a difficult remedial problem, the District of Columbia Court of Appeals denied enforcement because the remedy wrongfully deprived the Florida workers of their freedom to select their own bargaining representative.

---

[11] 28 U.S.C. §§ 151, 157.

[12] NLRB v. Pa. Greyhound Lines, Inc., 303 U.S. 261, 2 L.R.R.M. 599 (1938).

[13] NLRB v. 7-Up Bottling Co., 344 U.S. 344, 346, 31 L.R.R.M. 2237 (1953).

[14] Steelworkers v. NLRB, 646 F.2d 616, 106 L.R.R.M. 2573, 2583 (D.C. Cir. 1981); Florida Steel Corp. v. NLRB, 713 F.2d 825, 113 L.R.R.M. 3625 (D.C. Cir. 1983).

[15] See discussion at Ch. III, *infra*.

[16] 305 U.S. 197, 3 L.R.R.M. 645 (1938).

[17] 374 F.2d 295, 64 L.R.R.M. 2159 (D.C. Cir. 1967).

Two landmark Supreme Court decisions illustrate the complexity involved in implementing the congressional policy of promoting free collective bargaining. In *H.K. Porter Co. v. NLRB* [18] the Supreme Court declined to enforce a Board order, premised upon a refusal to bargain violation, which would have imposed a substantive contractual term on the employer contrary to its position in the bargaining and absent its agreement. The Court based its decision upon the primacy of the policy of free collective bargaining, stating:

> The Board's remedial powers under Section 10 of the Act are broad but they are limited to carry out the policies of the Act itself. One of the fundamental policies is freedom of contract. While the parties' freedom of contract is not absolute under the Act, allowing the Board to compel agreement when the parties themselves are unable to do so would violate the fundamental premises upon which the Act is based—private bargaining under governmental supervision of the procedure alone, without any official compulsion over the actual terms of the contract. [19]

The majority held that to rule otherwise would be to ignore the specific requirements of section 8(d) of the Act.

In *Fibreboard Paper Products Co. v. NLRB,* [20] the issue was whether the Board was empowered to direct an employer to resume a maintenance operation that had been subcontracted without prior bargaining with the union representing the maintenance employees. Finding that the Board's order was designed to promote collective bargaining by restoring the status quo prior to the unfair labor practice, the Court held that the remedy was within the Board's statutory authority to promote the policies of the Act. The fact that the remedy was clearly an imposition on management's right to conduct its business was held not to invalidate the order because the Board was engaged in effectuating a primary purpose of the Act. The decision, however, did suggest that the economic burden on the employer is a factor which might limit the Board's remedial authority in other circumstances. [21]

In a more recent decision interpreting *Fibreboard,* the Supreme Court has ruled that it is not a violation of the duty to bargain for an employer to refuse to bargain over the decision to shut down part of its business purely for economic reasons. [22] The Court's de-

---

[18] 397 U.S. 99, 73 L.R.R.M. 2561 (1970).

[19] 397 U.S. at 108, 73 L.R.R.M. at 2564.

[20] 379 U.S. 203, 57 L.R.R.M. 2609 (1964).

[21] For a discussion of cases where the Board balances sometimes-conflicting rights, see Ch. III, *infra.*

[22] First National Maintenance Corp. v. NLRB, 452 U.S. 666, 107 L.R.R.M. 2705 (1981).

cision was based on a balancing of the statutory rights of the union and the rights of the employer to freely manage its business. This balancing of the conflicting rights of labor organizations, employees, and employers under the Act and under the Constitution has become an increasingly recognized requirement of the Board and will be analyzed more fully in Chapter III below.

REMEDIAL V. PUNITIVE ORDERS

Another equally fundamental principle governing Board remedies is that the powers of the Board are remedial, not punitive, and the Board may not justify an order solely on the ground that it will deter future violations of the Act. The affirmative remedial power of the Board "is merely incidental to the primary purpose of Congress to stop and prevent unfair labor practice." [23]

> [W]e do not think the Congress intended to vest in the Board a virtually unlimited discretion to devise punitive measures, and thus to prescribe penalties or fines which the Board may think would effectuate the policies of the act.[24]

In devising remedies, the Board, drawing on its expertise in industrial relations, must attempt to create "a restoration of the situation as nearly as possible to that which would have obtained but for the unfair labor practice." [25] Consequently, Board orders are unenforceable to the extent that they are punitive rather than remedial.[26] In addition, the courts have refused to enforce Board orders seeking to ameliorate conditions that would have existed in any event, and, therefore, are not dependent upon the existence of the unfair labor practices.[27]

The Supreme Court has cautioned the courts not to engage in a semantic debate concerning what is "remedial" and what is "punitive":

> We prefer to deal with these realities and to avoid entering into the bog of logomachy, as we are invited to, by debate about what is "remedial" and what is "punitive." [28]

---

[23] International Union, UAW v. Russell, 356 U.S. 634, 643, 42 L.R.R.M. 2142, 2145 (1958).

[24] *Id.*

[25] NLRB v. J.H. Rutter-Rex Mfg. Co., 396 U.S. 258, 263, 72 L.R.R.M. 2881 (1969); Phelps Dodge Corp. v. NLRB, 313 U.S. 177, 194, 8 L.R.R.M. 439 (1941).

[26] Local 60, Carpenters v. NLRB, 365 U.S. 651, 47 L.R.R.M. 2900 (1961).

[27] Mountaineer Shaft & Tunnel Constr. Co. v. NLRB, 624 F.2d 50, 105 L.R.R.M. 2651 (6th Cir., 1980).

[28] NLRB v. 7-Up Bottling Co., 344 U.S. 344, 31 L.R.R.M. 2237 (1953); *see also* Steelworkers v. NLRB, 646 F.2d 616, 106 L.R.R.M. 2573 (D.C. Cir. 1981).

Sometimes, however, the Supreme Court has failed to follow its own advice. In *Local 60, Carpenters v. NLRB*,[29] the Board had ordered reimbursement of union dues deducted from the pay of a large group of long-standing union members. Although the contracts containing the deduction clauses were found to be illegal, the Court found that there was no evidence that the individuals were improperly induced to provide for the dues deduction. The Court, in denying enforcement, declared that where "no 'consequences of violation' are removed by the order compelling the union to return all dues and fees collected from its members; and no 'dissipation' of the effects of the prohibited action is achieved . . . [t]he order . . . becomes punitive and beyond the power of the Board." [30]

In *Republic Steel Corp. v. NLRB*,[31] the Supreme Court held that a Board order directing the employer to pay to appropriate government agencies an amount of money equal to that which had been earned by discriminatorily discharged employees who, during their back pay period, worked on "work relief projects," went beyond the Board's remedial authority. The payments had neither the effect of making whole the employees nor of assuring them of their rights to bargain collectively. Hence, the remedy served no statutory purpose. The Court concluded that such payments were in the nature of "an exaction" because the "work relief" payments constituted consideration for valuable services which the government received.[32] Further, the Court rejected the Board's argument that the remedy was permissible because it would have the effect of deterring others from violating the Act. The Court made clear its position that the Board was not permitted to impose remedies "solely" for the purpose of deterrence. The Court's holding reflects the well-established principle that a rational relationship must exist between the unlawful conduct and the relief ordered. This is especially true when the remedy purports to achieve ends other than those specifically contemplated by the Act. As the Court pointed out, an unfair labor practice is not a crime and the Board may not impose remedies to compensate the injuries it deems the body politic to have suffered.

In recent years, the Supreme Court has not faced the issue of punitive remedies to any meaningful extent. On the other hand, the circuit courts of appeals have done so on several noteworthy

---

[29] 365 U.S. 651, 47 L.R.R.M. 2900 (1961).
[30] 47 L.R.R.M. at 2901. *See also* Virginia Elec. & Power Co. v. NLRB, 319 U.S. 533, 340, 12 L.R.R.M. 739, 742 (1942); Containair Sys. Corp. v. NLRB, 521 F.2d 1166, 89 L.R.R.M. 2685 (2d Cir. 1975); Mountaineer Shaft & Tunnel Constr. Co. v. NLRB, 624 F.2d 50, 105 L.R.R.M. 2651 (6th Cir. 1980).
[31] 311 U.S. 7, 9–11, 7 L.R.R.M. 287, 289 (1940).
[32] 311 U.S. at 12–13, 7 L.R.R.M. at 290.

occasions. The D.C. Circuit, in one of the Florida Steel Corporation cases,[33] denied enforcement to a Board order granting access for the Steelworkers to all of the employer's plants. The court held that in order to grant access as a remedial measure, the "burden lies upon the Board to substantiate its conclusion that access is necessary to offset the consequences of an unlawful employer conduct." [34] The relevant "consequences" must be those that result from the violations found in that case.

In a case involving a pre-hire agreement in the construction industry, the Fifth Circuit denied enforcement of a Board order requiring the employer to apply the collective bargaining contract to construction projects that had not begun at the time of the unfair labor practices.[35] The court ruled that since the contracts were pre-hire agreements, and not binding upon the employer until the union had established its majority status at each succeeding job site, the Board could not properly direct enforcement of the contracts at job sites not in operation at the time of the unfair labor practice.

In another case, the Eighth Circuit refused to enforce a Board order requiring full reimbursement of the checkoff of assessments, even though it agreed that the checkoff of the assessment had been improper under the checkoff authorization cards signed by the 1,200 to 1,300 employees concerned.[36] The court held that the order was inappropriate to the extent that it required reimbursement to all of the employees because "in view of the technical nature of the violation such an order would be punitive." [37] Instead, the Court limited the reimbursement to those employees making written application for reimbursement of the $40 assessment within thirty days following posting of the notice and mailing of the notice to the last known address of eligible former employees.

---

[33] Steelworkers v. NLRB, 646 F.2d 616, 106 L.R.R.M. 2573 (D.C. Cir. 1981). The court did recognize the difficulty the Board would face in establishing that the exercise of employees' rights had been chilled in plants other than those in which the unfair labor practices, though minor, had been found to have been committed. The court stated that it would recognize that "the Board possesses an unmatched expertise in distilling and identifying the effects of unlawful employer conduct." In the return of the case to the D.C. Circuit, however, the court found that the Board had merely "repackaged its earlier decision" and denied enforcement of the access and extended notice remedies. Florida Steel Corp. v. NLRB, 713 F.2d 823, 113 L.R.R.M. 3625 (D.C. Cir. 1983).

[34] Steelworkers v. NLRB, 646 F.2d 616, 639, 106 L.R.R.M. 2573, 2590 (D.C. Cir. 1981).

[35] NLRB v. Haberman Constr. Co., 641 F.2d 351, 106 L.R.R.M. 2998 (5th Cir. 1981).

[36] Railway Carmen, Lodge 365 v. NLRB, 624 F.2d 819, 104 L.R.R.M. 3046 (8th Cir. 1980).

[37] *Id.* 104 L.R.R.M. at 3048.

On the other hand, the courts have found Board orders not to be punitive, in a number of cases, although the result might arguably exceed the status quo ante. The Seventh Circuit in *NLRB v. Keystone Consolidated Industries* [38] enforced an order requiring the restoration of all insurance benefits, and reimbursement of employees for any losses suffered as a result of a unilateral change in hospitalization insurance by the employer, and requiring continuation of the substitute hospitalization plan, even though the combined benefits exceeded those available under the original plan. In another case, the Fourth Circuit held that the Board had not abused its discretion in requiring an employer, which unlawfully had paid bonuses to employees who worked during a strike, to pay all employees the full bonus, whether or not they had worked during the strike.[39]

Regarding back pay, the Supreme Court has held in *Sure Tan, Inc. v. NLRB* that not only must the order not be punitive, but it "must be sufficiently tailored to expunge only the actual, and not merely speculative consequences of the unfair labor practice." [40] In *Sure Tan* the circuit court had amended the Board's remedial order, which had left open the provisions for back pay, and directed the employer to pay six months' back pay to the illegal alien employees he had turned in to the Immigration Service; as a result of which, they had been expelled from the country. The Supreme Court ruled that not only had the court overstepped the limits of its own reviewing authority as regards remedy, but that it had improperly directed the Board to apply a remedy it did not have the authority to direct, since back pay could only be directed for actual and not speculative losses resulting from the unfair labor practice, and the employer could not be required to pay back pay for a period of time that the employees were expelled from the country and, therefore, unable to mitigate the loss. The court's award of a minimum amount of back pay was not sufficiently tailored to the actual compensable injuries suffered by the employees and could not be enforced even if awarded by the Board.

The *Sure Tan* case is also interesting for the reason that the Supreme Court reversed the court of appeals in its direction that the employer must draft a notice in Spanish and ensure verification of receipt thereof by the individuals who had been expelled from

---

[38] 653 F.2d 304, 107 L.R.R.M. 3143 (7th Cir. 1981).

[39] NLRB v. Rubatex Corp., 601 F.2d 147, 101 L.R.R.M. 2660 (4th Cir. 1979).

[40] Phelps Dodge Corp., 313 U.S. 177, at 198, 8 L.R.R.M. 439 (1941); Sure Tan Inc. v. NLRB, __ U.S. __, 116 L.R.R.M. 2857 (1984).

the country. While the court notes that this did not appear as an objectionable remedy, it specified that that is the type of remedy which calls for the Board's superior expertise in remedial matters. As the Court notes, if the circuit court felt that the Board had erred in failing to impose such a requirement, the "appropriate course was to remand to the Board for a reconsideration."[41]

---

[41] 116 L.R.R.M. at 2866, citing NLRB v. Food Store Employees, 417 U.S. 1, 86 L.R.R.M. 2209 (1974).

Enforcement of Board Remedial Orders

Under the Act, the Board has authority to issue remedial orders within the statutory limitations discussed in the previous chapters. Board orders are not self-enforcing. If the respondent refuses to abide by the Board's order, the Board must obtain enforcement of that order in the appropriate circuit court of appeals.[1]

As already discussed, the Act has been interpreted as leaving to the discretion of the Board the determination of what constitutes an appropriate remedy in a given case, and the Board's remedial decision is not within the judgmental discretion of the courts of appeals on review. "It is for the Board, not the courts, to determine how the effects of prior unfair labor practices may be expunged."[2] The Supreme Court has made it clear that the statutory scheme left the question of remedies to "Board expertise." In *Phelps Dodge Corp. v. NLRB*,[3] the Supreme Court noted that Congress did not delimit or enumerate all of the remedies available to effectuate the policies of the Act.

> Congress met these difficulties by leaving the adaptation of means to end to the empiric process of administration. The exercise of the process was committed to the Board, subject to limited judicial review. Because the relationship of remedy to policy is particularly a matter for administrative competency, courts must not enter the allowable area of the Board's discretion and must guard against the dangers of sliding unconsciously from the narrow confines of law into the more spacious domain of policy. On the other hand, the power with which Congress invested the Board implies responsibility—the responsibility of exercising its judgment in employing the statutory powers.[4]

THE MYTH OF BOARD EXPERTISE

In exercising its expertise in fashioning remedies, the Board, as an administrative agency, is not confined to the record of a particular proceeding, but may take advantage of its cumulative expe-

---

[1] 29 U.S.C. §§ 160(e) and 160(f).
[2] IAM v. NLRB, 311 U.S. 72, 82, 7 L.R.R.M. 282 (1940).
[3] 313 U.S. 177, 8 L.R.R.M. 439 (1941).
[4] *Id.* at 194, 8 L.R.R.M. at 446.

rience.[5] When the Board "in the exercise of its informed discretion" issues a remedial order, the order "should stand unless it can be shown that the order is a patent attempt to achieve ends other than those which can fairly be said to effectuate the policies of the Act."[6]

In the area of remedies, the federal courts, therefore, are required to give "deference" to the National Labor Relations Board. While such deference is oftentimes recognized or espoused by the Supreme Court and the courts of appeals, the Board's enforcement statistics suggest that the principle is frequently ignored. The following tables show the Board's record in the last eleven years before the courts of appeals (see Table III-1) and the Supreme Court (see Table III-2).

These tables demonstrate that neither the Supreme Court nor the courts of appeals have shown any great deference to the Board. The Board's record before the Supreme Court in 1983 of 60 percent affirmation in full is almost identical with its total success rate before the Supreme Court since the Board's creation on July 5, 1935.[7]

Also, as pointed out by Judge Harry T. Edwards of the Court of Appeals for the District of Columbia, the Board's "affirmance in full" statistics include those cases in which the courts affirm Board decisions on grounds other than those relied upon by the Board.[8] Judge Edwards makes an interesting comparison of the Board's appellate success rate as compared to other agencies. For example, in 1981–82 the Board was reversed in approximately 35 percent of the cases, almost triple the percentage of reversals for all agencies before the courts of appeals. These figures give some credence to the view that judicial deference to Board expertise is more a myth than a reality. Also, the figures substantiate Judge Edwards' observation that "it seems clear that the Board has faired poorly"[9] at the hands of the Supreme Court.

As already discussed, the Courts require that the Board's orders effectuate the purposes of the Act, and not be punitive. There are

---

[5] NLRB v. 7-Up Bottling Co., 344 U.S. 344, 31 L.R.R.M. 2237 (1975).

[6] Virginia Elec. & Power Co. v. NLRB, 319 U.S. 533, 540, 12 L.R.R.M. 739 (1942).

[7] From the Board's creation in 1935 through 1984, its success ratio before the Supreme Court has been 146 cases of a total of 241, or 60.6 percent. While it may be early to evaluate the effect of the decisions of the Reagan Board, one interesting trend revealed in Table 1 is the steady reduction in the number of cases in the circuit courts since 1981.

[8] Also, the Board's statistics tend to overstate its appellate success, by including noncontested rulings such as consent decrees or formal settlements in which the Board requests and obtains enforcement.

[9] Remarks by Judge Harry T. Edwards before Oxford / BNA Symposium, 173 DAILY LAB. REP. D-1 (1983).

TABLE III-1
NLRB Cases Before the Courts of Appeals

	1984	1983	1982	1981	1980	1979	1978	1977	1976	1975	1974
Total Cases	259	338	424	479	449	361	353	260	250	261	298
Affirmed in Full	174	237	272	309	291	233	218	177	185	189	230
Percent Affirmed	67.2	70.1	64.3	63.9	64.8	64.6	65.5	68.1	74	72.4	77.2

Source: Annual Reports of National Labor Relations Board.

TABLE III-2
NLRB Cases Before the Supreme Court

	1984	1983	1982	1981	1980	1979	1978	1977	1976	1975	1974
Total Cases	4	5	3	2	3	4	5	2	2	7	6
Affirmed in Full	2	3	3	1	1	1	5	2	0	6	2
Percent Affirmed	50	60	100	50	33.3	25	100	100	0	86	33.3

Source: Annual Reports of National Labor Relations Board.

at least five other bases upon which the courts have denied enforcement of Board orders.

ASSUMPTION OF MAKING POLICY
PROPERLY LEFT TO CONGRESS

In *American Shipbuilding Co. v. NLRB*,[10] the Supreme Court reversed the Board's finding that an employer committed an unfair labor practice by temporarily locking out its employees after reaching an impasse in negotiations. The Supreme Court held that in such situations Congress had intended that both parties, employer and union alike, should be able to bring economic pressure to bear on each other should peaceful negotiations be unsuccessful. The Court rejected the Board's analysis of labor-management relations holding that the use of a lockout would unfairly tip the scales toward the employer. The Court noted that while "there is, of course, no question that the Board is entitled to the greatest deference in recognition of its special competency," it nonetheless stated, "the deference owed to an expert tribunal cannot be allowed to slip into a judicial inertia which results in the unauthorized assumption by an agency of major policy decisions properly made by Congress."[11] While the courts must recognize and defer to the Board's expertise, where a court finds that the Board had gone beyond the intent of Congress and invaded the policy decision-making area properly reserved for Congress, enforcement is denied.[12]

In *Conair Corp. v. NLRB*,[13] the Court of Appeals for the District of Columbia denied enforcement of a *Gissel* bargaining order where there was no majority demonstrated. The court agreed with the Board holding that the unfair labor practices were "outrageous" and "pervasive" within the standards or meaning of the Supreme Court in its *Gissel* decision. In *NLRB v. Gissel Packing Co.*[14] The Supreme Court had affirmed the Board's issuance of an order requiring the employer to bargain with a union based upon authorization cards signed by a majority of the employees where an employer's unfair labor practices have undermined the majority and have made the likelihood of a fair election impossible.

---

[10] 380 U.S. 300, 58 L.R.R.M. 2672 (1965).

[11] *Id.* at 318, 58 L.R.R.M. at 2679.

[12] *Id.*

[13] 721 F.2d 1355, 114 L.R.R.M. 3169 (D.C. Cir. 1983). *Contra,* United Dairy Farmers Coop. Ass'n v. NLRB, 633 F.2d 1054, 105 L.R.R.M. 3034 (3d Cir. 1980). The Court's theory in *Conair* was thereafter accepted by the Board in Gourmet Foods, Inc., 270 N.L.R.B. No. 113, 116 L.R.R.M. 1105 (1984).

[14] 395 U.S. 575, 77 L.R.R.M. 2481 (1969). For extended discussion of this see Ch. XII, *infra.*

In its consideration of remedies in the *Connair* case, the D.C. Circuit ruled that "non-majority bargaining orders are not within the NLRB's current remedial discretion." In analyzing the congressional intent, the court found that the only exception to a requirement of majority representation before bargaining is section 8(f) permitting nonmajority agreements in the construction industry. "Administrative 'expertise,' we note, does not appear to command great weight on the question of the Board's statutory authority to issue a non-majority bargaining order."[15] The court stated that if Congress wished, it could add to the construction industry exception and permit the Board to impose nonmajority bargaining orders with such qualifications as Congress may deem appropriate, to prevent the Board from veering too far from the freedom-of-choice majority rule premise upon which the statute is based. "Given the current shape of the statute, however, we believe Congress has not placed non-majority bargaining orders within the NLRB's remedial discretion."[16]

Deference to the Board's expertise thus does not prevent the courts from denying enforcement of Board orders where the courts, after analyzing the intent of Congress, find that the Board has gone beyond its delegated authority and made a policy decision which is properly left to Congress.

ARTICULATING THE BASIS OF ITS ORDER

While the Supreme Court early noted that Congress has left fashioning remedial policy to the Board's expertise, it also stated that this power in the Board "implies responsibility—the responsibility of exercising its judgment in employing the statutory powers."[17] The Supreme Court, in *NLRB v. Metropolitan Life Insurance Co.*,[18] further restricted the deference to be given to Board expertise:

> When the Board so exercises the discretion given it by Congress, it must 'disclose the basis of its order' and 'give clear indication that it has exercised the discretion with which Congress has empowered it.'[19]

In *NLRB v. Weingarten*[20] the Supreme Court, sustaining the Board's expansive construction of section 7 to require union rep-

---

[15] 721 F.2d at 1383, 114 L.R.R.M. at 3190. For further discussion of nonmajority bargaining orders, see Ch. XII, *infra*.
[16] *Id.*
[17] Phelps Dodge Corp. v. NLRB, 313 U.S. 177 at 194.
[18] 380 U.S. 438, 58 L.R.R.M. 2721 (1965).
[19] 380 U.S. at 443, 58 L.R.R.M. at 2723.
[20] NLRB v. Weingarten, Inc., 420 U.S. 251, 88 L.R.R.M. 2689, 2695 (1975).

resentation at disciplinary interviews, specifically found that "the Board has adequately explicated the basis of its interpretation."[21] Thus it is well established that the Board must clearly articulate the basis upon which it has reached its decision, especially when it applies a new or unusual remedy. The Board itself must articulate the basis, and cannot leave the articulation to its enforcement counsel.

> Although Board counsel, in his brief and argument before this court, has rationalized the different unit determinations and the variant factual situations of these cases on criteria other than a controlling effect being given to the extent of organization, the integrity of the administration process requires that "courts must not accept appellant counsel's post hoc rationalizations for agency action. . . . For reviewing courts to substitute counsel's rationale or their discretion for that of the Board is incompatible with the orderly function of the process of judicial review."[22]

The circuit court decisions following *Gissel* probably best exemplify the requirement that the Board must articulate the basis of its decision. In *NLRB v. Jamaica Towing, Inc.,*[23] the Second Circuit deferred to the Board's expertise on all the violations that the Board found. However, the court warned that the Board must do more than recite the magic words from *Gissel* to establish the need for a bargaining order. The court cautioned the Board to "explain in each case just what it considers to have precluded a fair election and why, and in what respect the case differs from others where it has reached an opposite conclusion."[24]

The Sixth Circuit, in *NLRB v. Marion Rohr Corp.,*[25] denied enforcement of a *Gissel* order because of "the absence of a reasoned factual analysis by the Board as to why a fair election cannot be held." The Sixth Circuit held that, when basing a remedial order upon the reasoning in the *Gissel* case, the Board must demonstrate that a fair election was no longer possible. The issues of the effects of employee turnover and the passage of time were left to the Board by the administrative law judge (ALJ), "which disposed of them in a cryptic and ambiguous footnote. This we will not accept."[26] The court noted that it could remand the case to the Board for further consideration, but "in full recognition of the Board's continuing failure to comply with our request for reasoned analyses, we de-

---

[21] 420 U.S. at 267, 88 L.R.R.M. at 2695.
[22] NLRB v. Metropolitan Life Ins. Co., 58 L.R.R.M. at 2723.
[23] 602 F.2d 1100, 101 L.R.R.M. 3011 (2d Cir. 1979). See discussion at Ch. XII, *infra.*
[24] 602 F.2d at 1103–5, 101 L.R.R.M. at 3014, *quoting from* NLRB v. General Stencils, Inc., 438 F.2d 894, 76 L.R.R.M. 2288 (2d Cir. 1971).
[25] 714 F.2d 228, 114 L.R.R.M. 2126 (6th Cir. 1983).
[26] *Id.* at 233, 114 L.R.R.M. at 2128.

cline."[27] The Third Circuit remanded a *Gissel* bargaining order case to the Board on a similar basis,[28] and the Fifth Circuit has taken the Board to task for its failure to live up to its "obligation" to "articulate its reasoning and to distinguish factually similar cases with contrary results."[29]

The Seventh Circuit has had a running battle with the Board concerning adequate findings to support issuance of a *Gissel* bargaining order. The court requires that the Board articulate reasons supporting a finding that "the unfair labor practices were so serious that employees would be intimidated from voting their true preferences in a new election,"[30] and makes clear that the Board must consider the possibility of dissipation[31] of the effects of the unfair labor practices during the period between the original election and a possible new election, including the effects of turnover. The court, despairing of the Board's failure to make adequate findings, now makes its own determination on these issues rather than remand the case.[32]

The Fifth Circuit, in *Mueller Brass v. NLRB*,[33] denied enforcement of a reinstatement and back-pay order based on the factual finding that an employee had been discharged in violation of the Act. The court made clear not only that the Board must articulate the basis of its decision, but also that that articulation must show that its reasoning is reasonable.

> We are literally shocked by the conclusion of the Board that Rogers was discharged in violation of the Act and that he is entitled to be reinstated.[34]

In *Service Employees Local 250 v. NLRB*,[35] the Court of Appeals for the District of Columbia similarly refused to enforce a Board

---

[27] *Id.* at 232, 114 L.R.R.M. at 2129.

[28] NLRB v. Armcor Indus., Inc., 535 F.2d 239, 92 L.R.R.M. 2374 (3d Cir. 1976).

[29] NLRB v. Gibson Prods. Co., 494 F.2d 762, 86 L.R.R.M. 2636 (5th Cir. 1973).

[30] NLRB v. Village IX, 723 F.2d 1360, 115 L.R.R.M. 2297, 2304 (7th Cir. 1983).

[31] NLRB v. Century Moving & Storage, Inc., 683 F.2d 1087, 1093, 110 L.R.R.M. 3298 (7th Cir. 1982); Red Oaks Nursing Homes, Inc. v. NLRB, 633 F.2d 503, 509, 105 L.R.R.M. 3028 (7th Cir. 1980); First Lakewood Assocs. v. NLRB, 582 F.2d 416, 423, 99 L.R.R.M. 2197 (7th Cir. 1978); NLRB v. Gruber's Super Market, Inc., 501 F.2d 697, 704, 87 L.R.R.M. 2037 (7th Cir. 1974); NLRB v. General Stencils, Inc., 472 F.2d 170, 173–75, 82 L.R.R.M. 2081 (2d Cir. 1972); Note, *Representative Bargaining Orders: A Time for Change,* 67 CORNELL L. REV. 950; 959–63 (1982); Comment, *A Reappraisal of the Bargaining Order: Toward a Consistent Application of NLRB v. Gissel Packing Co.,* 69 Nw. U.L. REV. 556, 565 (1974). *Cf.* discussion at Ch. XII.

[32] See, e.g., *NLRB v. Village IX,* 723 F.2d 1360, 115 L.R.R.M. 2297 (7th Cir. 1983); Walgreen Co. v. NLRB, 509 F.2d 1014, 1019, 88 L.R.R.M. 2401 (7th Cir. 1975).

[33] 544 F.2d 815, 94 L.R.R.M. 2225 (5th Cir. 1977).

[34] 94 L.R.R.M. at 2228.

[35] 600 F.2d 930 (D.C. Cir. 1979). *Also see* that court's decision in American Freight Systems, Inc. v. NLRB, 722 F.2d 828, 114 L.R.R.M. 3513 (D.C. Cir. 1983), discussed *infra* at notes 65–68 and accompanying text.

order because the result reached by the Board was inherently unreasonable. The Board had found a violation and ordered remedial
action where an employer had discharged thirteen employees for
leaving work contrary to instructions to attend a Board pre-election
hearing, absent a subpoena. The court found that the facts did not
establish that the presence of all the employees at the hearing was
required for any legitimate or necessary purpose. Therefore, the
Board requirement that the employer have the burden to come
forward with a substantial, legitimate business justification for prohibiting the employees to leave work en masse, beyond the obvious
reason that the employer would be required to shut down its production operations, was uncalled for. The court stated, "We cannot
sanction such a pronouncement even though we acknowledge the
Board's expertise in this field."[36]

FAILURE TO FOLLOW THE LAW OF THE CIRCUIT

Throughout its history, the Board on all-too-frequent occasions
has had disagreements with the courts concerning a specific theory,
policy, or exercise of the Board's expertise. Perhaps the longest
persisting disagreement involved the Board's application of its *Mid-
West Piping* theory.[37] During the almost thirty-five years that the
Board persisted in its *Mid-West Piping* theory until its reversal in
1982,[38] the Board was unable to persuade any circuit court to accept
it. It obtained enforcement only in a few cases where the court was
able to sustain the finding of a violation on some legal basis other
than that espoused by the Board. The differences of opinion between
the courts and the Board never contained any rancor or rose to a
level of strenuously expressed disagreement. While the courts denied enforcement of the Board orders, their strongest pronounce-
ments could be found in such statements as, "We do not believe
our result unduly limits the Board's discretion."[39] The Ninth Circuit,
in denying enforcement of a *Mid-West Piping* order, recognized that
"The Board's decision and order itself explicitly recognizes the con-

---

[36] 600 F.2d at 938. *See also* Krispy Kreme v. NLRB, ____ F.2d ____, 116 L.R.R.M.
2251 (6th Cir. 1984), in which the court refused to "rubber stamp" even a Board
credibility ruling it found unreasonable.

[37] Mid-West Piping and Supply Co., Inc., 63 N.L.R.B. 1060 (1945). The *Mid-West
Piping* theory is that an employer cannot recognize one union based upon a majority
card showing, if another union is seeking to organize the employees.

[38] Bruckner Nursing Home, 262 N.L.R.B. 955, 110 L.R.R.M. 1374 (1982).

[39] Modine Mfg. Co. v. NLRB, 453 F.2d 292, 79 L.R.R.M. 2109 (8th Cir. 1971).

flict between its decision and the great weight of authority in the Courts of Appeals."[40]

Since the late 1970s, however, although the Board has continued to "respectfully disagree" with the reversals it has suffered at the hands of the courts, the respectful attitude has not been mutual; the courts have become increasingly impatient with the Board. Several circuits have made it very clear that they will no longer accept the Board's refusal to abide by their decisions. For example, the First Circuit in 1979 lost patience with the Board for ignoring its "but for" rule in mixed motive discharge cases. "The Board's persistent disregard of the principles governing mixed motive cases ultimately led to our announcement that we would no longer rescue (it) if it does not both articulate and apply our rule." [41] This was followed shortly by the reprimand of the Board by the Third Circuit in the oft-quoted *Allegheny General Hospital v. NLRB* case.[42] The court stated: "We hold that the NLRB must respect the applicable decisions of this court," and continued:

> (T)he Board is not a court nor is it equal to this court in matters of statutory interpretation. Thus, a disagreement by the NLRB with a decision of this court is simply an academic exercise that possesses no authoritative effect .... Congress has not given to the NLRB the power or authority to disagree, respectfully or otherwise, with the decisions of this court .... For the board to predicate an order on its disagreement with this court's interpretation of a statute is for it to operate outside the law.[43]

The Seventh Circuit also lost patience in *Mary Thompson Hospital v. NLRB*,[44] which involved the appropriateness of a separate bargaining unit for maintenance employees of a hospital. The court reminded the Board of an earlier case denying enforcement in a separate maintenance unit in the health care industry, and admonished the Board for giving "mere lip-service" to the congressional mandate against proliferation of units in the health care industry. The court found the "flagrant omission by the Board to

---

[40] NLRB v. Inter-Island Resorts, Ltd., 507 F.2d 411, 87 L.R.R.M. 3075 (9th Cir. 1974).

[41] NLRB v. Eastern Smelting & Refining Corp., 598 F.2d 666, 672, 101 L.R.R.M. 2328, 2331 (1st Cir. 1979). The "but for" test of the First Circuit required a showing that the employer would not have discharged the employee but for the anti-union motive. The Board has subsequently adopted a "but for" standard, *Wright Line, Inc.,* 251 N.L.R.B. 1083, 105 L.R.R.M. 1169 (1980), *enforced,* 662 F.2d 899, 108 L.R.R.M. 2513 (1st Cir. 1981), *cert. denied,* 455 U.S. 989, 109 L.R.R.M. 2779 (1982).

[42] Allegheny General Hospital v. NLRB, 608 F.2d 965, 102 L.R.R.M. 2784 (3d Cir. 1979).

[43] 608 F.2d at 970, 102 L.R.R.M. at 2788–9.

[44] 621 F.2d 858, 862, 103 L.R.R.M. 2739 (7th Cir. 1980).

be fatal to its request for enforcement of its order . . . such flagrant disregard of judicial precedents must not continue." [45]

The Second Circuit, in denying enforcement of a Board order in a different area of the law, joined the many circuits citing *Allegheny General Hospital.* In *Ithaca College v. NLRB,*[46] the court scored the Board for refusing to accept its prior decision in *Yeshiva* and for its "consistent practice of refusing to follow the law of this Circuit unless it coincides with the Board's view. This is intolerable if the rule of law is to prevail." [47] The court went on to characterize the Board's actions as "arbitrary, capricious and unlawful." [48]

The Court of Appeals for the District of Columbia in *Suburban Yellow Taxi Co. of Minneapolis v. NLRB,*[49] admonished the Board for ignoring the court's prior decision. Senior Circuit Judge MacKinnon, in his opinion, chastised the Board for willfully disregarding prior judicial decisions of the circuit. The court recognized that the Board need not necessarily follow a single court decision reversing one of its theories or practices, but criticized the Board for continuing to espouse such a theory after reversal in several or more circuits. After extensive citation from the Third Circuit decision in *Allegheny General Hospital,* Judge MacKinnon wrote:

> We admonish the Board to halt its apparent *willful* defiance of long-established, controlling judicial precedents . . . . Should the board continue to act in defiance of well-established decisional law of this and other courts, we may be required to secure adherence to the rule of law by measures more direct than refusing to enforce its orders.[50]

The Reagan Board has reversed a number of expansive Board decisions that were issued in the latter half of the 1970s and early 1980s. In sixteen of those reversals, the Board noted that its purpose was to conform Board law with the law as set forth by the circuit courts.[51] Apparently, the Reagan Board's intent is to give "defer-

---

[45] 103 L.R.R.M. at 2742.

[46] 623 F.2d 224, 228, 104 L.R.R.M. 2493 (2d Cir. 1980).

[47] 104 L.R.R.M. at 2496.

[48] 104 L.R.R.M. at 2497.

[49] 721 F.2d 366, 114 L.R.R.M. 3060 (D.C. Cir. 1983).

[50] 114 L.R.R.M. at 3074.

[51] Milwaukee Spring II, 268 N.L.R.B. 601, 115 L.R.R.M. 1065 (1984); Meyers Indus., 268 N.L.R.B. 493, 115 L.R.R.M. 1025 (1984), *remanded sub nom.* Prill v. NLRB, _ F.2d _, 118 L.R.R.M. 2649 (D.C. Cir. 1985); Olin Corp., 268 N.L.R.B. 573, 115 L.R.R.M. 1056 (1984); Clear Pine Mouldings, 268 N.L.R.B. 1044, 115 L.R.R.M. 1113 (1984); Hotel & Rest. Employees, 269 N.L.R.B. No. 86, 115 L.R.R.M. 1249 (1984); Rossmore House, 269 N.L.R.B. No. 198, 116 L.R.R.M. 1025 (1984); Otis Elevator II, 269 N.L.R.B. No. 162, 115 L.R.R.M. 1281 (1984); American Navigation Co., 268 N.L.R.B. No. 62, 115 L.R.R.M. 1017 (1983); Benchmark Indus., 270 N.L.R.B. No. 8, 116 L.R.R.M. 1032 (1984); Gourmet Foods, 270 N.L.R.B. No. 113, 116 L.R.R.M. 1105 (1984); St. Francis Hospital II, 271 N.L.R.B. No. 160, 116 L.R.R.M. 1465 (1984); Taracorp., 273 N.L.R.B.

ence" to circuit court decisions reversing the Board, and will accept such decisions and attempt to comply with the demands and directions of the courts.[52] While most of these Board reversals do not relate directly to remedy issues, they signal a definite attempt on the part of the Board to initiate a new era of cooperation with the courts, and possibly to reestablish some "deference" to Board "expertise" for the future. If that is the Board's intent, it seems to be having some success. At this time the courts of appeals [53] and, seemingly, the Supreme Court[54] have commented favorably regarding eight of the Board's reversals. Only one of the court evaluations of the Board decisions can be considered at all unfavorable.[55]

FAILURE TO RESOLVE CONFLICTING BOARD DECISIONS

Since the mid-1970s, another basis upon which the courts have denied enforcement of Board orders is where the Board has failed, in the courts' view, to properly harmonize its own conflicting decisions.[56] The existence of conflicting Board decisions was an underlying factor in the Supreme Court's decision in *NLRB v. Metropolitan Life Insurance Co.,*[57] and in the decisions of the circuit courts denying enforcement of bargaining orders because of prior conflicting decisions.

This rationale for denying enforcement of a Board order was not specifically and forcefully articulated until 1975. In *Retail Clerks*

No. 54, 117 L.R.R.M. 1447 (1984); Harley-Davidson Trans., 273 N.L.R.B. No. 172, 118 L.R.R.M. 1201 (1985); Indianapolis Power & Light Co., 273 N.L.R.B. No. 211, 118 L.R.R.M. 1202 (1985); Sears Roebuck & Co., 274 N.L.R.B. No. 55, 118 L.R.R.M. 1329 (1985); United Artists, 274 N.L.R.B. No. 17, 118 L.R.R.M. 1375 (1985).

[52] *E.g.,* Jones Dairy Farms v. USCW Local P-1236, _ F.2d _, 118 L.R.R.M. 2841 (7th Cir. 1985), an arbitrator's decision based upon Milwaukee Spring I, notes that the latter decision was contrary to the law of the Seventh Circuit and was "repudiated by the board" in Milwaukee Spring II, 268 N.L.R.B. 601, 115 L.R.R.M. 1065 (1984).

[53] Bakery Workers v. NLRB, 730 F.2d 812, 115 L.R.R.M. 3390 (D.C. Cir. 1984) (approving *Olin Corp.*); A. Duie Pyle v. NLRB, 730 F.2d 119, 115 L.R.R.M. 3428 (3d Cir. 1984) (approving *Clear Pine Mouldings* which had adopted the Third Circuit standard for striker misconduct. See discussion at Ch. X *infra*); Newport News Shipbuilding Co. v. NLRB, 738 F.2d 1404, 116 L.R.R.M. 3042 (4th Cir. 1984) (approving *Clear Pine Mouldings*); United Sanitation Service v. NLRB, 737 F.2d 936, 116 L.R.R.M. 3302 (11th Cir. 1984) (approving *Rossmore House*); Pace Oldsmobile v. NLRB, 739 F.2d 108, 116 L.R.R.M. 3137 (2d Cir. 1984) (approving *Gourmet Foods, Inc.*).

[54] The Supreme Court remanded Georgia Kraft Co. v. NLRB, _ U.S. _, 115 L.R.R.M. 3296 (1984), and Catalytic Inc. v. NLRB, _ U.S. _, 117 L.R.R.M. 2144 (1984) to be determined under the *Clear Pine Mouldings* test.

[55] *See* Prill v. NLRB, _ F.2d _, 118 L.R.R.M. 2649 (D.C. Cir. 1985).

[56] Cross Baking Co. v. NLRB, 453 F.2d 1346, 78 L.R.R.M. 3059 (1st Cir. 1971); Walled Lake Door Co. v. NLRB, 472 F.2d 1010 (5th Cir. 1972); *also see* NLRB v. Eurodrive, Inc., 724 F.2d 556, 115 L.R.R.M. 2361 (6th Cir. 1984).

[57] 380 U.S. 438, 58 L.R.R.M. 2721 (1965).

Local 455 v. NLRB,[58] however, the D.C. Circuit lectured the Board on its decision-making responsibilities and criticized the Board for vacillating from prior positions without calling attention to the change, or worse, denying that it was changing positions and treating similar situations dissimilarly. The court said:

> (W)e decide to remand the case to the Board. If it wishes to overtly advance the proposition we suggest above, it should overrule *White Stores* and *Smith Management* and explicate why national labor policy requires 'additional store clauses' be held illegal. But the Board may not attempt, as it has done here, to establish this result through a process of statutory construction which purports to uphold the legality of 'additional store clauses' while silently nullifying them.[59]

In *Seafarers International Union v. NLRB,*[60] the D.C. Circuit severely scolded the Board for its continuing vacillation on the question of the independent contractor status of taxicab leasing drivers, and for its failure to reverse or overrule clear, contrary precedents. The court declared that "[w]hen it both fails to distinguish contrary decisions rendered in similar cases and also misinterprets accepted principles of law, it [the Board] errs doubly," and continued: "Because of this Board 'history of vacillation' in this area, 'it is inappropriate for this court to extend any great amount of deference to the Board's disposition of the problem.'" [61]

The same court again admonished the Board in *Suburban Yellow Taxi Company of Minneapolis v. NLRB,*[62] another decision on the status of leased taxi drivers. The court criticized the Board for its "thinly veiled defiance of the precedent established by our decision in *Seafarers.*" [63] In his concurring opinion, Judge Robert Bork stated that he could not concur with the court's strong criticism because be had not studied the Board's past conduct in necessary detail, but added: "that is not to say that I do not think some criticism warranted .... The Board appears less to have been seeking reconsideration of a legal issue than trying to achieve a desired result by a somewhat disingenuous treatment of the facts." [64]

More recently, the D.C. Circuit denied enforcement of a Board reinstatement and back-pay order in *American Freight System Inc.*

---

[58] (Kroger Co.), 510 F.2d 802, 88 L.R.R.M. 2592 (D.C. Cir. 1975).

[59] 88 L.R.R.M. at 2596.

[60] 603 F.2d 862, 99 L.R.R.M. 2903 (D.C. Cir. 1978).

[61] *Id.* at 872, 99 L.R.R.M. at 2909.

[62] 721 F.2d 366, 114 L.R.R.M. 3060 (D.C. Cir. 1983).

[63] 114 L.R.R.M. at 3073.

[64] *Id.* at 385, 114 L.R.R.M. at 3076.

v. NLRB.[65] In this case, the Board refused to defer to the award of a contractually-established arbitrator upholding the discharge of an employee for refusing to drive a vehicle that the employee felt was unsafe. The court noted that a few years before in *Bloom v. NLRB,*[66] it had sustained the Board in deferring to a similar arbitration decision sustaining the discharge of an employee who refused to take out a vehicle he felt was unsafe. The court stated, "It is difficult to comprehend why the Board refused to defer to the grievance committee decision in this case when it deferred in *Bloom* under nearly identical facts." [67] The court observed that the Board had attempted to distinguish *Bloom* on the basis that it had not analyzed whether the "statutory issue" in *Bloom* had been presented to and considered by the grievance panel, but that it was doing so in this case. The court stated that "[t]his argument is entirely unpersuasive and must fail." [68]

The Tenth Circuit recently denied enforcement to a bargaining order, disagreeing with the Board regarding the union's challenge to two "eligible" employees which the employer had inadvertently left off the Norris-Thermador list, because the Board had failed to follow its own precedents in this area of the law.[69] The court held that the Board had not validly or reasonably distinguished precedents, and applied prior Board precedents for the basis of its reversal of the Board's decision.

"BALANCING" CONFLICTING RIGHTS

The major device utilized by the Supreme Court in recent years for denying enforcement of certain Board remedial orders, even though such orders may effectuate the policies of the Act and not be punitive, has been its finding of the Board's failure to balance conflicting rights of unions, employers, and employees. The Court's critique is obviously result-oriented and reflective of its disagreement with the Board's decisions in particular cases. The first case remanded by the Supreme Court to the Board to balance conflicting

---

[65] 722 F.2d 828, 114 L.R.R.M. 3513 (D.C. Cir. 1983); *also see* Richmond Tank Car Co. v. NLRB, 721 F.2d 499, 115 L.R.R.M. 2165 (5th Cir. 1983), in which the court denied enforcement to a Board order declining to defer to an arbitrator's decision contrary to its own *Spielberg* standards.

[66] 603 F.2d 1015, 102 L.R.R.M. 2082 (D.C. Cir. 1979).

[67] 722 F.2d at 833, 114 L.R.R.M. at 3516.

[68] *Id.*

[69] Smith & Smith Aircraft Co. v. NLRB, __ F.2d __, 116 L.R.R.M. 2594 (10th Cir. 1984).

rights was *NLRB v. Babcock & Wilcox Co.,*[70] involving the right of
union access to employees where the means of effective communication may be absent, against the employer's property right. The
Court also recognized the need for balancing of conflicting rights
of managerial freedom as opposed to section 7 rights in the landmark *Fibreboard* case.[71]

In *Gissel Packing Co. v. NLRB,*[72] the Court authorized the Board
to balance the severity of the unfair labor practices which the employer had committed to undermine the majority strength and to
impede the election process, against the objective of employee free
choice of bargaining representative. If the Board finds that the effect
of the unfair labor practices is to make the possibility of a fair
election slight, "and that employee sentiment once expressed
through cards would, on balance, be better protected by a bargaining
order, then such an order should issue." [73]

The Supreme Court more recently has directed the Board, in
selecting the appropriate remedy, to weigh the duty of the employer
to supply relevant information to a union against the employer's
right to maintain security. In *Detroit Edison Co. v. NLRB,*[74] the
Court refused to enforce the Board order directing the employer to
provide certain test scores and results to the union, where release
of the results would make the test useless if it were in any way
disseminated to the employees. "It is obvious that the remedy selected by the Board does not adequately protect the security of the
tests . . . we hold that the Board abused its discretion in ordering
the company to turn over the test battery and answer sheets directly
to the union." [75] In ruling that the Board had abused its discretion,
the Supreme Court recognized the right of the employer to maintain
the validity and security of its tests through secrecy. In the same
decision, the Court also recognized the privacy rights of the employees or examinees who took the test, stating, "We agree with
the company that its willingness to disclose these scores only upon
receipt of consent from the examinees satisfied its statutory obligation under Section 8(a)(5)." [76]

---

[70] 351 U.S. 105, 38 L.R.R.M. 2001 (1956), involving the right of access to a plant
in the absence of the effective means of communication.
[71] Fibreboard Paper Prods. Co. v. NLRB, 379 U.S. 203, 57 L.R.R.M. 2609 (1964).
See discussion at Ch. II, *supra.*
[72] 395 U.S. 575, 71 L.R.R.M. 2481 (1969).
[73] 71 L.R.R.M. at 2496.
[74] 440 U.S. 301, 100 L.R.R.M. 2728 (1979).
[75] *Id.* at 315–17, 100 L.R.R.M. at 2733.
[76] *Id.* at 317, 100 L.R.R.M. at 2734.

The Board itself now has recognized the principle that individual employees have a right to privacy that can supersede the union's right to information necessary for the purpose of collective bargaining. The Board held in *Johns-Manville Sales* [77] that an employer did not have to make medical records of individual employees available to their union because the employees' interests in confidentiality outweighed the union's need. The employer's policy requiring the permission of employees before releasing such medical records was proper, the Board said, and provided a valid defense to the charge of refusing to supply the requested information. In *New Jersey Bell Telephone Co.,* [78] however, the Board found a violation in the employer's refusal to supply absentee records that included information regarding the medical reasons for absence, under a company policy prohibiting release of the records unless permission was given by the employees. The ALJ had dismissed the complaint, citing *Johns-Manville Sales,* because the grievance underlying the request had been settled and because of the union's "gamesmanship." The union had requested the absentee information, but when the employer requested the employees to sign waivers of the confidentiality policy, the union told the employees to refuse such permission, then filed the charges. The Board disagreed with the ALJ and held that this was not "gamesmanship." The Third Circuit denied enforcement,[79] in effect agreeing with the ALJ. The court found that the reasons given for absences were of an "intimate and highly personal nature" and weighed the compelling claims under the three factors outlined by the Supreme Court in *Detroit Edison:* the sensitive nature of the information; the minimal burden that employee consent places on the union; and the lack of evidence that confidentiality was being used to thwart the union. The court struck its balance in favor of confidentiality and the "laudable policy of protecting the employees' privacy rights." [80]

In a line of newspaper cases where the union demanded the salaries of nonunit employees who wrote editorials and articles for the papers, the Board found that the information was relevant and directed that it be furnished to the union, but ruled that the specific amounts paid to each individual who was not a member of the unit need not be made known, only the aggregate sum paid for editorial material from the editorial budget for such purposes. After remand

---

[77] 252 N.L.R.B. 368, 105 L.R.R.M. 1379 (1979).
[78] 265 N.L.R.B. 1382, 112 L.R.R.M. 1144 (1982).
[79] New Jersey Bell Tel. Co. v. NLRB, 720 F.2d 789, 114 L.R.R.M. 3337 (3d Cir. 1983).
[80] 114 L.R.R.M. at 3339.

from the circuit court,[81] which sought clarification regarding the
refusal to give the specifics of the information to the union, the
Board specifically ruled that its decision not only related to the
employer's interest in confidentiality, but also to the Board's concern for the obvious right to privacy of nonunit writers concerning
the amounts that they were paid.[82]

The Supreme Court also based its decision in *First National Maintenance Corp. v. NLRB* [83] on a balancing of conflicting rights theory.
The Court balanced the needs of the employer to make business
decisions "free from the constraints of the bargaining process"
against the union's interest in protecting the job security of the
employees. "[I]n view of an employer's need for unencumbered decision making, bargaining over management decisions that have a
substantial impact on the continued availability of employment
should be required only if the benefit, for labor-management relations and the collective bargaining process, outweighs the burden
placed on the conduct of the business." [84]

The case involved the right of the employer to close a part of its
business, necessarily resulting in the layoff of a group of employees,
and whether the employer was required to bargain the decision to
close. The Court noted that while the employer was required to
bargain the effects of such a closing, it was not required to bargain
the decision, since the factors in favor of the need for unencumbered
decision-making on the part of management outweighed the benefits
to the employees from bargaining over the decision. The Court held
that capital decisions that involve matters unrelated to collective
bargaining, while they may have an indirect effect on employment,
need not be bargained. Where there is a direct impact on employment, however, the Court requires that Board decisions balance
management's rights to decision-making and employees' interest in
their jobs.

In a recent decision, *Otis Elevator II*,[85] the Board accepted and
applied *First National Maintenance* in reversing its original decision
in *Otis Elevator I*.[86] In its unanimous four-member decision, the
Board nevertheless set forth conflicting theories as to when bargaining is required regarding decisions to transfer or close opera-

---

[81] Press Democrat Publ. Co. v. NLRB, 629 F.2d 1320, 105 L.R.R.M. 3046 (9th Cir.
1980).
[82] Newspaper Guild, Local 52, 258 N.L.R.B. 169, 250, 108 L.R.R.M. 1148; and Press
Democrat Publ. Co., 258 N.L.R.B. 1355, 108 L.R.R.M. 1149 (1981).
[83] 452 U.S. 666, 107 L.R.R.M. 2705 (1981).
[84] 107 L.R.R.M. at 2710.
[85] 269 N.L.R.B. No. 162, 115 L.R.R.M. 1281 (1984).
[86] 255 N.L.R.B. 235, 106 L.R.R.M. 1343 (1981).

tions. A two-member plurality decided that if, in fact, the management decision is a capital decision that involves management prerogatives, it is not necessary that any bargaining occur regardless of the effects the decision may have on the present employees. One concurring member took the position that the Board should first look to whether the problem might be susceptible to solution under collective bargaining; if so, the Board would then look to a balancing of the employer's need for a quick or a secret action against the interests of the employees, before determining whether bargaining is required. The fourth concurring member stated that the only test is whether or not in a particular case, collective bargaining might help resolve the problems that led to the need for a transfer of the work.

In *Bill Johnson's Restaurants v. NLRB,*[87] the Supreme Court used a balancing of conflicting rights theory in reversing the Board's enjoining of an employer's state court libel suit against an employee for statements made during picketing activities. The Court balanced the First Amendment right of access to the courts and the state's interest in regulating libel, against the statutory rights of employees to picket without interference. The Court recognized that the Board had the right to enjoin an unfair labor practice involving the prosecution of a baseless suit in retaliation for an employee's exercise of section 7 rights. On the other hand, the Court also recognized that the Board had no right to enjoin, as an unfair labor practice, a well-founded lawsuit even if it has been commenced as a result of the employer's desire to retaliate against an employee for exercising rights protected by the Act. The Court consequently ruled that the Board could not enjoin such a libel suit unless, under the facts presented at the hearing, it was clear that there was no basis on which a state court could possibly find any validity to the suit. The Court noted that the Board has no right to make a determination as to the validity of conflicting testimony in the suit and can enjoin the suit only if it is "frivolous."

In a subsequent decision, *Sure Tan, Inc. v. NLRB,*[88] the Supreme Court ruled, however, that the employer's First Amendment right to notify the Immigration and Naturalization Service that some of its employees who engaged in concerted activity were illegal aliens was not a defense to an unfair labor practice: the employer's zeal for the immigration laws followed shortly after a unionization effort. The *Sure Tan* opinion distinguished *Bill Johnson's Restaurants* in that there, the restaurant owner was asserting a personal interest

---

[87] 461 U.S. 731, 113 L.R.R.M. 2647 (1984).
[88] __ U.S. __, 116 L.R.R.M. 2857 (1984).

in his own reputation in the state court, but that the *Sure Tan* employer had not suffered any legally protected injury at the hands of the alien employees. Further, the Court noted that in *Bill Johnson's Restaurants* there were important issues of federalism involving federal-state relationships, which simply did not apply in *Sure Tan.*

In a related case, the Ninth Circuit sustained a Board back-pay award against a local union for requiring the discharge of an employee for failure to pay back dues.[89] The court, citing *Bill Johnson's Restaurants,* nevertheless declined to enforce the portion of the Board order enjoining the union from proceeding with a defamation suit, which it had filed in retaliation for the unfair labor practice charge filed by the discharged employee.

The District of Columbia Court of Appeals in *Passaic Daily News v. NLRB*[90] sustained the Board's finding of violation in the discriminatory acts against the employee. It refused, however, to enforce a portion of the board order that required the newspaper to reinstate the weekly column of the dischargee. The court stated that "the remedy mandating resumption of Stoddard's column must yield to the Company's First Amendment interest in retaining control of prospective editorial decisions. The Board does not have the power to disregard the First Amendment . . ."[91]

The Ninth Circuit has ruled that the balancing of conflicting rights is not applicable to a union's right to enforce rules against strikebreaking.[92] In reversing the Board, the court ruled that the Board had abused its discretion in balancing the union's right to restrict resignation, by a rule prohibiting employees from crossing a picket line after resigning, against the individual employee's right to refrain from engaging in concerted activity and to resign. The court ruled that both are rights "embedded" in the labor laws and neither can "impair" or "override" the other. The Seventh Circuit, on the other hand, earlier had agreed with the Board's balance of the conflicting rights in favor of the "overriding" employee right to choose whether to engage in concerted activity.[93] This conflict

---

[89] Sheet Metal Workers v. NLRB, 716 F.2d 1249, 114 L.R.R.M. 2569 (9th Cir. 1983).
[90] __ F.2d __, 116 L.R.R.M. 2721 (D.C. Cir. 1984).
[91] 116 L.R.R.M. at 2732.
[92] Machinists Local 1327 v. NLRB (Dalmo Victor), 725 F.2d 1212, 115 L.R.R.M. 2972 (9th Cir. 1984). The Board apparently has renounced any balancing tests in this area. *Cf.* Neufeld Porsche-Audi, 270 N.L.R.B. No. 209, 116 L.R.R.M. 1257 (1984), *reversing* Dalmo Victor II, 263 N.L.R.B. No. 984.
[93] Pattern Makers' League of N.A. v. NLRB, 724 F.2d 57, 115 L.R.R.M. 2264 (7th Cir. 1983), *cert. granted,* __ U.S. __.

between circuits will result in the Supreme Court deciding whether the theory of the balancing of conflicting rights is limited to only certain areas of the labor law or has permeated the labor law completely. A Supreme Court decision might result in a clear recital of the meaning, application, and effect of "balancing of conflicting rights" for the future.

CHAPTER IV

Cease and Desist Orders — The Appropriate Use of "Narrow" and "Broad" Orders

The most common NLRB remedial order is the "cease and desist" order. When the employer has violated section 8(a) of the Act—by interference with, restraint, or coercion of employees in the exercise of section 7 rights—the Board will normally order the employer to cease and desist from the conduct found unlawful in the particular case and, in addition, to cease and desist from violating the Act "in any like or related manner." This latter injunction is referred to as a "narrow order." Sometimes, however, the Board goes further and issues what is known as a "broad order," ordering the employer to cease and desist from violating the Act in "any other manner."

THE EXPRESS PUBLISHING DOCTRINE

In 1941, in *NLRB v. Express Publishing Co.*[1] the Supreme Court circumscribed the Board's authority to issue broad orders, holding that in fashioning the cease and desist order, the Board must consider the nature and seriousness of the unfair labor practices committed, the offender's past history of violations, and their probability of recurrence. In this case, the employer unlawfully refused to bargain. The Board's order not only directed the employer to cease and desist from refusing to bargain collectively but also ordered it to cease and desist from violating the Act in any manner. After the court of appeals modified the order, the Supreme Court granted certiorari to consider the breadth of the order. The Board argued that it could restrain future violations not only of the type committed, but any other unfair labor practices that infringe upon the section 7 rights of employees, because a violation of section 8(5) is also a technical violation of section 8(1), which in terms incorporates

---

[1] 312 U.S. 426, 8 L.R.R.M. 415 (1941).

all the rights enumerated in section 7.[2] The court rejected the Board's argument. It inferred from the Act's classification of separate unfair labor practices that Congress could not have intended that the commission of a particular unfair labor practice would justify an order restraining the commission of any unfair labor practice.[3] Since the Act had granted exclusive power to the Board to prevent unfair labor practices, it was apparent that "Congress did not contemplate that the Courts should, by contempt proceedings, try alleged violations . . . not in controversy and not found by the Board."[4] Rather, the Court treated the Board's authority to issue cease and desist orders as the federal court's authority to issue injunctions, i.e. since the federal courts were not permitted to enjoin conduct in violation of a statute that was neither like nor related to that committed, neither could the Board. Instead, the Court stated that

> [t]he breadth of the order, like the injunction of a court, must depend upon the circumstances of each case, the purpose being to prevent violations, the threat of which in the future is indicated because of their similarity or relation to those unlawful acts which the Board has found to have been committed by the employer in the past.[5]

For the Board to justify an order restraining violations other than those committed

> it must appear that they bear some resemblance to that which the employer has committed or that danger of their commission is to be anticipated from the course of his conduct in the past.[6]

The *Express Publishing* doctrine subjects the Board's order to two independent tests applicable on a case-by-case basis: (1) whether the violations restrained bear some resemblance to the violations found; and (2) whether there is a likelihood that the violator will engage in future unlawful practices.

The Board may justify a broad order where the conduct restrained bears some resemblance to the violations found. For example, in *Windsor Mfg. Co. v. NLRB*[7] the court enforced a broad order where, in addition to a section 8(5) violation, there were independent section

---

[2] *Id.* at 432–433, 8 L.R.R.M. at 418.

[3] *Id.* at 433–435, 8 L.R.R.M. at 418–419.

[4] *Id.* at 435, 8 L.R.R.M. at 419.

[5] *Id.* at 436, 8 L.R.R.M. at 419. *See* New York, N.H. & H.R. Co. v. Interstate Commerce Comm'n, 200 U.S. 361, 404 (1906); Swift & Co. v. United States, 196 U.S. 375 (1905).

[6] NLRB v. Express Publ. Co., 312 U.S. 426 at 437, 8 L.R.R.M. 415 at 420 (1941).

[7] 118 F.2d 486, 8 L.R.R.M. 566 (3d Cir. 1941). *See also* NLRB v. Entwistle Mfg. Co., 120 F.2d 532, 536, 8 L.R.R.M. 645, 650 (4th Cir. 1941) [§ 8(3) violation coupled with violations of § 8(1)].

8(1) violations. The likelihood of future violations might also justify a broad order. Such likelihood has been established by evidence of a pattern of numerous violations,[8] especially in the context of an unsuccessful union organizing drive, or by a past history of violations of the Act.[9]

The scope of the order is not necessarily limited to the proximate parties in the underlying dispute—usually the charging union and the employee. In *Marshfield Steel Co. v. NLRB*,[10] the Board ordered the employer to cease and desist from discouraging membership in the Steelworkers "or in any other labor organization." The employer challenged the scope of the order because it had not engaged in violations against unions other than the Steelworkers. The court enforced the Board's order, explaining that *Express Publishing* stood for the proposition that the Board could not restrain an employer from committing "other unfair labor practices in which it has not been found to be engaged. . . ." The Court then distinguished the order in the case at bar, which "merely restrains [the employer] from conducting against other labor organizations the same unfair labor practices in which it has been found to be engaged."[11] The court concluded that the order was fully within the guidelines of *Express Publishing* as the restrained violations resembled those which the employer had committed.

In an extension of this doctrine, the Board, in *West Coast Liquidators and Mrs. Gladys Selvin*,[12] issued a broad order not only

---

[8] Fremont Newspapers, Inc. v. NLRB, 436 F.2d 665, 76 L.R.R.M. 2049, 2056-2057 (8th Cir. 1970). The Board's order enjoining the employer from engaging in unlawful inducements and promises of benefits in violation of § 8(a)(1) was properly extended to "any other labor organization" since it was foreseeable that new efforts could be made at union organization attempts. Nevertheless, the court would not enforce the Board's order insofar as it enjoined the employer from violating the Act "in any other manner" because there was no evidence that the employer would have a proclivity to pursue unrelated unfair labor practices in the future. *See also* NLRB v. Circo Resorts, Inc. 646 F.2d 403, 107 L.R.R.M. 2608, at 2610 (9th Cir. 1981) where the court enforced a broad order based on a finding that the unfair labor practices committed manifested a "concerted effort to nip union organization in the bud."

[9] *See also* NLRB v. Great Atlantic and Pacific Tea Co., 406 F.2d 1173, 1175, 70 L.R.R.M. 2438 (5th Cir. 1969); Singer Company v. NLRB, 429 F.2d 172, 182, 74 L.R.R.M. 2669 (8th Cir. 1970); NLRB v. Kirk & Son, 154 F.2d 110, 18 L.R.R.M. 2177 (9th Cir. 1946) (per curiam) (general intent to violate all provisions of the Act warranted by specific findings of § 8(a)(1)–(3), (5), and § 9(a)–(b) violations). *See also* Kentucky Utilities Co., 76 N.L.R.B. 845, 849, 21 L.R.R.M. 1258, 1261 (1948).

[10] 324 F.2d 333, 54 L.R.R.M. 2648 (8th Cir. 1963).

[11] *Id.* at 339, 54 L.R.R.M. at 2653 (emphasis in original); *cf.* NLRB v. Morrison Cafeteria Co., 311 F.2d 534, 52 L.R.R.M. 2150 (8th Cir. 1963). *See also* Allegheny Pepsi-Cola Bottling Co. v. NLRB, 312 F.2d 529, 52 L.R.R.M. 2019 (3d Cir. 1962); General Motors Corp. v. NLRB, 512 F.2d 447, 89 L.R.R.M. 2431, 2432 (6th Cir. 1975).

[12] West Coast Liquidators and Mrs. Gladys Selvin, 205 N.L.R.B. 512, 517, 84 L.R.R.M. 1249 (1973), *enforced as modified*, NLRB v. Selvin, 527 F.2d 1273, 90

against the employer but also against a labor relations consultant representing the employer. The Board found that the consultant had engaged in a pattern of bad-faith bargaining while representing other employers which had resulted in numerous findings of section 8(a)(5) and section (1) violations. The Board ordered the consultant to cease and desist from "[r]efusing to bargain in good faith with any labor organization when she is agent for any employer subject to the jurisdiction of the Board, that has an obligation under the Act to bargain with said labor organization." The order also required the consultant to refrain from interfering "in any manner" with the section 7 rights of employees. The Ninth Circuit enforced the Board's order except for the "in any manner" provision, which it ordered deleted.

Generally, when faced with a challenge that a Board order is overly broad, the courts hold that "the order should not go beyond the evidence supporting unfair labor practices alleged."[13] Therefore, the courts will not enforce Board orders that restrain conduct unrelated to the unfair labor practices actually committed,[14] that restrain conduct beyond the threatened danger,[15] or where there is no evidence that future unfair labor practices are likely,[16] or no evidence from which the Board can infer a proclivity to violate the Act.[17]

L.R.R.M. 2829, 2832 (9th Cir. 1975); Chalk Metal Co. and Mrs. Gladys Selvin, 197 N.L.R.B. 1133, 80 L.R.R.M. 1516 (1972). *But see,* St. Francis Hospital, 263 N.L.R.B. 834, 111 L.R.R.M. 1153 (1982).

[13] NLRB v. Cleveland Cliffs Iron Co., 133 F.2d 295, 302, 12 L.R.R.M. 550, 555 (6th Cir. 1943). *See* NLRB v. American Rolling Mill Co., 126 F.2d 38, 42, 10 L.R.R.M. 389, 393 (6th Cir. 1942); *cf.* Morrison-Knudsen, Inc. v. NLRB, 270 F.2d 864, 865, 44 L.R.R.M. 2680, 2681 (9th Cir. 1959) (employer practice of conditioning employment upon union "clearance" through its hiring hall, even though unlawful, did not justify a broad § 8(a)(1) and (3) cease and desist order when other forms of encouragement of union membership and loyalty could not be fairly anticipated).

[14] *E.g.,* NLRB v. Walt Disney Productions, 146 F.2d 44, 50, 15 L.R.R.M. 691, 697 (9th Cir. 1944); NLRB v. Great Atlantic & Pacific Tea Co., 406 F.2d 1173, 70 L.R.R.M. 2438, 2439–2440 (5th Cir. 1969). *Cf.* NLRB v. Whitfield Pickle Co., 374 F.2d 576, 583, 64 L.R.R.M. 2656, 2661–2662 (5th Cir. 1967), wherein the court refused to enforce that part of the Board's order directing the employer to bargain collectively since the only reference to collective bargaining was a statement by a company official to the effect that he would not sign any agreement with the union. Although the statement violated § 8(a)(1), it did not violate § 8(a)(5), and therefore no bargaining order could be based upon it.

[15] Wyman-Gordon Co. v. NLRB, 394 U.S. 759, 70 L.R.R.M. 3345 (1969); NLRB v. Consolidated Machine Tool Corp., 163 F.2d 376, 379, 20 L.R.R.M. 2439, 2441 (2d Cir. 1947), *cert. denied,* 332 U.S. 824, 21 L.R.R.M. 2043 (1947).

[16] NLRB v. Beth Israel Hospital, 554 F.2d 477, 95 L.R.R.M. 2230 (1st Cir. 1977), *aff'd,* 437 U.S. 483, 98 L.R.R.M. 2727 (1978); NLRB v. Standard Metal Fabricating Co., 297 F.2d 365, 367, 49 L.R.R.M. 2309, 2310 (8th Cir. 1961).

[17] *E.g.,* Fremont Newspapers, Inc. v. NLRB, 436 F.2d 665, 675, 76 L.R.R.M. 2049, 2056 (8th Cir. 1970); Southwire Co. v. NLRB, 383 F.2d 235, 237, 65 L.R.R.M. 3042,

Moreover, courts are reluctant to enforce broad cease and desist orders to remedy "technical" unfair labor practices.[18] For example, an employer may not obtain direct appellate court review of NLRB election case rulings, since these rulings are not considered to be final orders as required by section 10(c) of the Act. Consequently, such employer must commit a "technical" section 8(a)(5) refusal to bargain violation to obtain court review.[19] In *May Department Stores Co. v. NLRB*,[20] the Supreme Court stated that:

> [A]lthough there is a violation of 8(1) as well as 8(5), the violation of 8(1) is so intertwined with the refusal to bargain with a unit asserted to be certified improperly that, without a clear determination by the Board of an attitude of opposition to the purposes of the Act to protect the rights of employees generally, the decree need not enjoin Company actions which are not determined by the Board to be so motivated.[21]

Accordingly, the Board has refused to issue broad orders in such cases.[22]

The Board has changed its practice of issuing broad orders in discriminatory discharge cases. In *Hickmott Foods, Inc.*,[23] the Board declared that in such cases the narrow order is generally more appropriate than the broad order, except in cases of repeat offenders or egregious violators of the Act.[24]

The importance of the Board's applying the proper scope to its cease and desist orders cannot be overestimated. The threat to an employer who must operate under broad order is formidable, since

---

3045 (5th Cir. 1967). The Board itself has narrowed the scope of an order recommended by a trial examiner on identical grounds; Central Rigging and Contracting Corp., 129 N.L.R.B. 342, 343 n.3, 46 L.R.R.M. 1548, 1549 (1960).

[18] NLRB v. Westinghouse Elec. Corp., 603 F.2d 610, 618, 101 L.R.R.M. 2870 (7th Cir. 1979).

[19] As the Fifth Circuit noted, the courts attach no opprobrium to the employer's refusal to bargain where it is the only means of challenging the Board's findings in an underlying representation case. NLRB v. Genesco, Inc., 406 F.2d 393, 70 L.R.R.M. 2252, 2253 (5th Cir. 1969).

[20] 326 U.S. 376, 17 L.R.R.M. 643 (1945).

[21] *Id.* at 392, 17 L.R.R.M. at 650.

[22] Southeastern Envelope Co., 206 N.L.R.B. 933, 84 L.R.R.M. 1577, 1580 (1973); Crucible Steel Co., 66 N.L.R.B. 1157, 1162, 17 L.R.R.M. 397, 398 (1946) (refusal to bargain undertaken on grounds that the determination of the appropriate bargaining unit was erroneous); *see also* United Fryer & Stillman, Inc., 139 N.L.R.B. 704 n.1., 51 L.R.R.M. 1385, 1386 (1962) (dispute as to appropriateness of multi-employer unit).

[23] 242 N.L.R.B. 1357, 101 L.R.R.M. 1342 (1979).

[24] *See, e.g.*, United Dairy Farmers Co-Op Ass'n v. NLRB, 633 F.2d 1054, 105 L.R.R.M. 3034 (3rd Cir. 1980); NLRB v. Blake Constr. Co., Inc., 663 F.2d 272, 108 L.R.R.M. 2136 (D.C. Cir. 1981); Hansa Mold, 243 N.L.R.B. 853, 102 L.R.R.M. 1021 (1979); Florida Steel Corp., 244 N.L.R.B. 395, 102 L.R.R.M. 1181 (1976); Valley West Welding Co., 265 N.L.R.B. No. 204, 112 L.R.R.M. 1344 (1983).

it may thereafter become the target of contempt proceedings for future violations of that order.[25]

As a matter of procedure, a litigant must raise timely objection to the scope of the order with the Board. The Supreme Court has held that the failure to do so bars a respondent from later raising the issue, absent extraordinary circumstances.[26] If the broad order is ordered *sua sponte* by the Board, apparently the respondent must request rehearing or reconsideration by the Board or it will be precluded from challenging the remedy before a court of appeals.[27] On the other hand, in *NLRB v. Cutting, Inc.,* the Seventh Circuit sustained an employer's challenge to a broad order even though it had not filed a motion for reconsideration with the Board, because the court's reversal of a major Board unfair labor practice finding *itself* provided the extraordinary circumstances excusing the employer for not filing such a motion.[28]

UNION VIOLATIONS OF SECTION 8(b)

The Taft-Hartley Act[29] and the Landrum-Griffin amendments[30] made labor organizations subject to unfair labor practice charges. As is the case with remedies for employer violations, the permissible scope of remedial orders enjoining union violations is tested under the guidelines enunciated in *Express Publishing*.

In *IBEW, Local 501 v. NLRB,*[31] the Supreme Court reviewed a broad order issued against a union that had violated section 8(b)(4)(A). The union's picketing had induced the employees of one construction project subcontractor (Deltorto) to engage in a strike to force the general contractor (Giorgi) to cease doing business with a nonunion subcontractor (Langer). On appeal, the union objected to the breadth of the Board's order, which in pertinent part ordered that the union

> [c]ease and desist from inducing or encouraging the employees of Nicholas Deltorto *or any employer,* by picketing . . . strike or a concerted refusal . . . to perform any services, where an object thereof is

---

[25] May Dep't Stores Co. v. NLRB, 326 U.S. 376, 388, 17 L.R.R.M. 643, 648 (1945); Red Oak Nursing Home v. NLRB, 633 F.2d 503, 105 L.R.R.M. 3028 (7th Cir. 1980).

[26] NLRB v. Ochoa Fertilizer Corp., 368 U.S. 318, 49 L.R.R.M. 2236 (1961); NLRB v. Proler Int'l Corp., 635 F.2d 351, 106 L.R.R.M. 2530 (5th Cir. 1981).

[27] NLRB v. Sambo's Restaurant, Inc., 641 F.2d 794, 107 L.R.R.M. 2332 (9th Cir. 1981) and cases cited therein.

[28] NLRB v. Cutting, Inc., 701 F.2d 659, 112 L.R.R.M. 3056 (7th Cir. 1983).

[29] 61 Stat. 136 (1947).

[30] 73 Stat. 541 (1959).

[31] 341 U.S. 694, 696–698, 28 L.R.R.M. 2115, 2116–2117 (1951).

to force or require Giorgi Construction Co. *or any other employer or person* to cease doing business with Samuel Langer.[32]

The union contended that the order was overly broad because it prohibited secondary activity directed not only at the employees of Deltorto but also at those of "any other employer," and because the condemned objective encompassed not only the business relationship between Giorgi and Langer, but also that between "any other employer" and Langer.[33] The court enforced the order, stating that if it were limited to Deltorto or Giorgi, it would expose Langer or any other employer doing business with him to the same type of unlawful pressure through other "comparable channels."[34] The court justified its decision on the principle that "when the purpose to restrain trade appears from a clear violation of law, it is not necessary that all of the untraveled roads to that end be left open and that only the worn one be closed."[35] This holding clearly falls within the *Express Publishing* test permitting restraint of future conduct which bears some resemblance to that for which the violation was found.

The Supreme Court in *Communication Workers v. NLRB*[36] subjected broad section 8(b) orders to the *Express Publishing* test. In that case, the union, in violation of section 8(b)(1)(A), had coerced employees of the Ohio Consolidated Telephone Company from exercising their section 7 right to refrain from striking. The Board ordered the union to cease and desist from violating the rights not only of the employees of Ohio Consolidated, but also the rights of employees of "any other employer" as well. In a *per curiam* opinion, the Supreme Court eliminated the words "or any other employer," from the order because there was no evidence that the union had violated the rights of the employees of any other employer; therefore, the order could not be justified on the principles of *Express Publishing*.[37]

In general, the *IBEW, Local 501* and *Communication Workers* cases require that the Board's order be directed only toward protecting the union's intended target and those with whom it does business,[38] not to other neutrals or primary employers unrelated to

---

[32] *Id.* at 698–699, 28 L.R.R.M. at 2117 (emphasis added).

[33] *Id.* at 705, 28 L.R.R.M. at 2120.

[34] *Id.* at 705–706, 28 L.R.R.M. at 2120.

[35] *Id.* at 706, 28 L.R.R.M. at 2120, *quoting from* International Salt Co. v. United States, 332 U.S. 392, 400 (1947).

[36] 362 U.S. 479, 46 L.R.R.M. 2033 (1960) (per curiam).

[37] *Id.* at 480–481, 46 L.R.R.M. at 2034.

[38] *Cf.* NLRB v. Carpenters Dist. Council (Kaaz Woodwork, Co.), 383 F.2d 89, 66 L.R.R.M. 2177 (8th Cir. 1967).

the participants in the dispute.[39] Yet, when the union's illegal conduct involves a multi-employer contract, the Board and the courts
are more likely to perceive the desirability of expanding the scope
of the Board's order beyond the immediate employer in the case.[40]

The aforementioned guidelines must be further qualified to take
into account other aspects of the *Express Publishing* doctrine. In
Local 469, Plumbers & Pipefitters (Howard C. Johnson),[41] the union,
in violation of section 8(b)(4)(A), had induced the employees of a
general contractor (Thomas) at a construction project to strike, with
the object of forcing Thomas to cease doing business with a nonunion
subcontractor (Johnson). In its initial hearing, the panel majority
held that, in light of the *Communication Workers* decision, a Board
order that restrained the union from inducing the employees of
Thomas "or any other employer" to engage in strikes directed at
terminating a business relationship with Johnson was too broad.
The evidence showed that the inducement was limited to the
Thomas-Johnson subcontract.[42] Member Rodgers dissented on the
grounds that the *Communication Workers* case was distinct because
it had involved only employee coercion, a violation of section
8(b)(1)(A), while the instant case involved a section 8(b)(4)(A) violation.[43] On the motion of the general counsel for reconsideration,
the Board amended its order and issued a supplemental decision
and order which, in effect, adopted the view of Member Rodgers.[44]

On the union's appeal, the Ninth Circuit refused to enforce the
extension of the order because of insufficient evidence under *Express*

---

[39] *See, e.g.,* Plumbers, Local 519 v. NLRB, 416 F.2d 1120, 70 L.R.R.M. 3300 (D.C.
Cir. 1969); NLRB v. Hatters Union (Korber Hats, Inc.), 286 F.2d 950, 47 L.R.R.M.
2752 (4th Cir. 1961); NLRB v. Carpenters Union (Midwest Homes, Inc.), 276 F.2d
694, 45 L.R.R.M. 3014 (7th Cir. 1960); NLRB v. Local 926, Operating Engineers, 267
F.2d 418, 44 L.R.R.M. 2200 (5th Cir. 1959); NLRB v. Int'l Hod Carriers, Local 1140,
285 F.2d 394, 396, 47 L.R.R.M. 2311 (8th Cir. 1960), and 285 F.2d 397, 404–405, 47
L.R.R.M. 2345 (8th Cir. 1960), *cert. denied,* 366 U.S. 903; NLRB v. Enterprise Ass'n,
Local Union No. 638, 285 F.2d 642, 47 L.R.R.M. 2189 (2d Cir. 1960); NLRB v. Local
Union No. 25, IBEW, 491 F.2d 838, 85 L.R.R.M. 2499, 2501 (2d Cir. 1974).

[40] *See* NLRB v. Local 294, Teamsters (Van Transport Lines, Inc.), 298 F.2d 105, 49
L.R.R.M. 2315, 2317 (2d Cir. 1961); NLRB v. Shuck Constr. Co., 243 F.2d 519, 39
L.R.R.M. 2322, 2326 (9th Cir. 1957), and cases cited therein; NLRB v. Sun Tent-
Leubbert Co., 151 F.2d 483, 17 L.R.R.M. 515, 521–522 (9th Cir. 1945) *cert. denied sub
nom.* Merchants & Mfgrs. Ass'n v. NLRB, 329 U.S. 714, 18 L.R.R.M. 2468; Milk
Drivers and Dairy Employees Union Local No. 471, Int'l Bro. of Teamsters (Ronco
Delivery), 209 N.L.R.B. 24, 86 L.R.R.M. 1239 (1974); Teamsters, Local Union No.
631, 154 N.L.R.B. 67, 70, 59 L.R.R.M. 1716 (1965); Milk Drivers and Dairy Employees,
Local Union No. 537 (Sealtest Foods), 147 N.L.R.B. 230, 237, 56 L.R.R.M. 1193 (1964).

[41] 129 N.L.R.B. 36, 46 L.R.R.M. 1483 (1960).

[42] *Id.* at 37 n.1, 46 L.R.R.M. at 1483–1484.

[43] *Id.,* 46 L.R.R.M. at 1484 (Member Rodgers, dissenting).

[44] Local 469, Plumbers & Pipefitters, 130 N.L.R.B. 1289, 47 L.R.R.M. 1484 (1961).

Publishing.[45] The court distinguished *IBEW, Local 501,* on the grounds that in that case the evidence showed a likelihood of further union secondary activity against the primary and secondary employers, whereas, in the case at bar, such evidence was lacking; hence, the Board failed to satisfy the requirements of *Express Publishing.*[46]

Nonetheless, when the evidence is sufficient to meet the *Express Publishing* guidelines of similarity or likelihood of recurrence, the courts have sanctioned broad orders against unions. For example, in *NLRB v. Brewery Drivers, Local 830,*[47] the court enforced an order prohibiting the union from violating not only the rights of the employees of five beer distributors at whose places of business the unlawful practices had occurred, but also the rights of employees of any other employer. In the same vein, the Court of Appeals for the Second Circuit sustained a broad order where the evidence established a generalized campaign of secondary pressure by the union. The court reasoned that an order limited solely to the employers involved would be an inadequate safeguard.[48]

For purposes of justifying a broad order, past violations are probative of a union's proclivity to violate the Act.[49] The Board also will consider a union's proclivity to engage in violence and threats of violence.[50] In a case involving unfair labor practices on the part

[45] NLRB v. Local 469, Plumbers & Pipefitters, 300 F.2d 649, 49 L.R.R.M. 2862 (9th Cir. 1962).

[46] *Id.; see, e.g.,* Local 69, Sheet Metal Workers (Wind Heating Co.), 209 N.L.R.B. 875, 85 L.R.R.M. 1481 (1974); Carpenters, Local 690 (Moore Constr. Co.), 190 N.L.R.B. 609, 77 L.R.R.M. 1271 (1971).

[47] 281 F.2d 319, 323, 46 L.R.R.M. 2732, 2735 (3d Cir. 1960).

[48] NLRB v. Local 25, IBEW, 383 F.2d 449, 454–455, 66 L.R.R.M. 2355, 2359 (2d Cir. 1967). *See also* NLRB v. Local 3, IBEW, 477 F.2d 260, 268–269, 82 L.R.R.M. 3190 (2d Cir. 1973).

[49] *See e.g.,* NLRB v. Teamsters, Local 327 (Whale, Inc.), 432 F.2d 933, 934, 75 L.R.R.M. 2435 (6th Cir. 1970); NLRB v. Teamsters, Local 327 (Hartmann Luggage Co.), 419 F.2d 1282, 1284, 73 L.R.R.M. 2199, 2200 (6th Cir. 1970); Teamsters, Local 70 (Morris Draying Co.), 195 N.L.R.B. 957, 79 L.R.R.M. 1601, 1602 (1972); NLRB v. Carpenters Dist. Council of Kansas City & Vic. (Kaaz Woodwork Co.), 383 F.2d 89, 96, 66 L.R.R.M. 2177 (8th Cir. 1967); NLRB v. Int'l Union of Operating Eng'rs, Local 571, 317 F.2d 638, 644, 53 L.R.R.M. 2294 (8th Cir. 1963); NLRB v. Milk Drivers & Dairy Emp. Local Union 584 (Old Dutch Farms, Inc.), 341 F.2d 29, 33, 58 L.R.R.M. 2290 (2d Cir. 1965); NLRB v. Local 282, Int'l Bro. of Teamsters, Local 282, 344 F.2d 649, 652–653, 58 L.R.R.M. 2065 (2d Cir. 1965); NLRB v. Local 810, Fabricators & Warehousemen, Int'l Bro. of Teamsters (Advance Trucking Corp.), 299 F.2d 636, 637, 49 L.R.R.M. 2433 (2d Cir. 1962); NLRB v. Local 542, Int'l Union of Operating Eng'rs, 329 F.2d 512, 515–516, 56 L.R.R.M. 2028 (3d Cir. 1964); Amalgamated Local Union 355 v. NLRB (Russell Motors, Inc.), 481 F.2d 996, 1008, 83 L.R.R.M. 2849 (2d Cir. 1973) and cases cited therein; NLRB v. Sequoia Dist. Council of Carpenters, etc., 499 F.2d 129, 86 L.R.R.M. 3001 (9th Cir. 1974).

[50] Teamsters Local 901 (Associated Federal Homes), 193 N.L.R.B. 591, 598, 78 L.R.R.M. 1377, 1379 (1971).

of a union, including incidents of threats and assaults (e.g., threatening employees with physical harm during recess at the Board
hearing), the Court of Appeals for the First Circuit affirmed a broad
order where the union had demonstrated a proclivity to violate
employees' rights and because the union had stated, at the hearing
and elsewhere, that it did not regard itself as subject to the authority
of the Act and had no obligation to conform to its requirements.[51]

As a matter of proof, judicial notice can be taken of past violations
of section 8(b)(4).[52] In *Teamsters, Local 70 (C&T Trucking Co.)*,[53]
however, the Board refused to issue a broad order against the union
despite the urgings of the general counsel. The Board, unlike the
trial examiner who would only receive evidence in connection with
the case at bar, recognized that prior decisions could be considered;
nonetheless, it refused to issue a broad order even though the particular Teamsters' local had a history of some eighteen prior unfair
labor practice dispositions against it.[54] Seventeen of these dispositions were discounted as having no probative value, and the eight-
eenth was deemed irrelevant. The decision is somewhat anomalous,
since the Board approached the problem of determining the proper
scope of its order in the same manner discredited by the Ninth
Circuit in *NLRB v. Local 469, Plumbers & Pipefitters*,[55] by "simply
. . . classifying the . . . case in one or another of the available statutory categories."[56]

Thus, even though the legal principles relating to the breadth of
Board orders are quite well established, it is not necessarily easy
to predict when the courts will agree with Board determinations
that similar past violations justify the issuance of a broad order.
Another illustration of this is found in a series of Board decisions
that were consolidated for court review in *San Francisco Local Joint*

---

[51] NLRB v. Trabajadores, 510 F.2d 1, 92 L.R.R.M. 3425 (1st Cir. 1976), *cert. denied*,
429 U.S. 1039, 94 L.R.R.M. 2201 (1977).

[52] *See* NLRB v. Local 85, Teamsters (Victory Transp. Service, Inc.), 454 F.2d 875,
879, 79 L.R.R.M. 2437, 2439 (9th Cir. 1972) (court had recently enforced broad order
against Local 85, noting its propensity for illegal secondary activities accompanied
by violence); NLRB v. Teamsters, Local 327 (Hartmann Luggage Co.), 419 F.2d 1282,
1284, 73 L.R.R.M. 2199, 2200 (6th Cir. 1970) (Board can take judicial notice of its
own case involving same local).

[53] 191 N.L.R.B. 11, 12, 77 L.R.R.M. 1336 (1971).

[54] In support of his request for a broad order based upon the union's penchant to
violate the Act, the General Counsel had cited thirteen settlement agreements, one
Board decision, one trial examiner's decision to which no exceptions were filed, and
another that was then pending before the Board, a civil and criminal contempt
adjudication in one case, and a preliminary injunction in another. 191 N.L.R.B. at
11, 77 L.R.R.M. at 1337.

[55] 300 F.2d 649, 49 L.R.R.M. 2862 (9th Cir. 1962).

[56] *Id.* at 654, 49 L.R.R.M. at 2866.

Executive Board of Culinary Workers v. NLRB.[57] There, the Board found in three separate cases that the union had picketed three employers with a recognitional object in violation of section 8(b)(7)(C), and ordered the union to refrain from so picketing "any other employer." Further, there was a similar fourth violation found in another unappealed Board decision. Despite this strong evidence of the union's tendency to violate this section of the Act, the court found that the union was not engaged in a general scheme to violate the Act. The court majority felt that since the union had a large membership in a major metropolitan area, its violations were "isolated instances."[58] Judge MacKinnon strongly dissented, writing that "the repeated illegal picketing against four different employers" satisfied the requirement of a generalized scheme to violate the Act.[59]

The uncertain fate of broad orders in the courts was highlighted by the next broad 8(b)(7)(C) order[60] against the same union that came before the District of Columbia Circuit. In all relevant aspects, this second case was identical to the previous one, except that the union had committed one more violation. The union challenged the broad order. The court enforced the Board's order in a *per curiam* opinion and did not even discuss the broad order issue that had so troubled the previous panel.[61]

BOARD ORDERS MUST CLEARLY INDICATE WHAT ACTIVITIES ARE PROHIBITED

In *Express Publishing*, the Supreme Court observed that Board orders may result in contempt proceedings. Therefore, an order must "state with reasonable specificity the acts which the [violator] is to do or refrain from doing."[62] Shortly thereafter, in *J. I. Case Co. v. NLRB*,[63] the Court reaffirmed this principle, stating:

> Questions of construction had better be ironed out before enforcement orders issue than upon contempt proceedings. A party is entitled to a definition as exact as the circumstances permit of the acts which he can perform only on pain of contempt of court.[64]

---

[57] 501 F.2d 794, 86 L.R.R.M. 2828, 2833–2834 (D.C. Cir. 1974).

[58] *Id.* at 802, 86 L.R.R.M. at 2834.

[59] *Id.*

[60] San Francisco Local Joint Exec. Board of Culinary Workers, *et al.*, 207 N.L.R.B. 199, 84 L.R.R.M. 1604 (1973).

[61] *See* San Francisco Local Joint Exec. Board of Culinary Workers v. NLRB (per curiam) (D.C. Cir., Docket No. 73–2259, 1975), 90 L.R.R.M. 2843.

[62] NLRB v. Express Publishing, 312 U.S. at 433, 8 L.R.R.M. 415, 418.

[63] 321 U.S. 332, 14 L.R.R.M. 501 (1944).

[64] *Id.* at 341, 14 L.R.R.M. at 505–506.

In *Express Publishing* the Court held that ". . . Congress did not
contemplate that the courts should, by contempt proceedings, try
alleged violations of the [Act] not in controversy. . . ."[65] Accordingly,
a party charged with contempt generally will receive a Board hearing.[66] This relieves a court of appeals, by virtue of its contempt
powers, from becoming a labor court of first instance.[67]

The Board's order must be limited to the facts of record. In *NLRB
v. Carpenters Union (Midwest Homes, Inc.)*,[68] the Board issued a
broad order prohibiting not only secondary activities directed at the
primary employer in the case before it, but also directed against
all other primary employers. Claiming that the Board lacked sufficient facts upon which to issue such an order, the Seventh Circuit
stated that the Board "merely announced a legal pattern, com-
manded 'Go and sin no more' and then washed its hands of the
matter."[69] The court objected that such an order "would impose
upon a court of appeals on a possible future hearing of contempt
charges, the duty of resolving factual issues . . . [concerning] a particular primary employer not named in the present proceeding."[70]
The court refused to undertake this because such determination
should be made by the Board prior to entering its order and because
Congress did not intend that the courts be involved in contempt
proceedings to remedy the deficiencies of Board orders.[71]

Similarly, the order should not be susceptible to possible miscon-
struction. For example, in *NLRB v. Stowe Spinning Co.*,[72] the Supreme Court denied enforcement of a Board order prohibiting the
employer, in a company town, from refusing to permit the union

---

[65] 312 U.S. at 435, 8 L.R.R.M. at 419.
[66] *See* Reliance Mfg. Co. v. NLRB, 125 F.2d 311, 322, 9 L.R.R.M. 536, 547 (7th Cir.
1941); *accord*, NLRB v. Ford Motor Co., 119 F.2d 326, 8 L.R.R.M. 656 (5th Cir. 1941);
NLRB v. Schill Steel Prods., Inc., 480 F.2d 586, 83 L.R.R.M. 2386, 2393 (5th Cir.
1973).
[67] Teamsters, Local 554 v. NLRB, 262 F.2d 456, 463, 43 L.R.R.M. 2197, 2202 (D.C.
Cir. 1958); *accord*, Morrison-Knudsen, Inc., 270 F.2d 864, 865, 44 L.R.R.M. 2680, 2681
(9th Cir. 1959).
[68] 276 F.2d 694, 45 L.R.R.M. 3014 (7th Cir. 1960).
[69] *Id.* at 699, 45 L.R.R.M. at 3017.
[70] *Id.*, 45 L.R.R.M. at 3017. See also NLRB v. Local 926, Operating Eng'rs, 267 F.2d
418, 421, 44 L.R.R.M. 2200, 2203 (5th Cir. 1959), wherein the court, recognizing the
discretionary authority of the Board to fashion remedies, stated:

> We consider more important, and basic to a fair administration of the Act,
> the hard-won principle of Anglo-American law that a judgment or order must
> find adequate support in the record. An order of a court or federal agency
> that goes beyond the record to penalize an offender smacks too much of
> attainder to be acceptable to this Court.

[71] 276 F.2d at 699, 45 L.R.R.M. at 3017; *see* text accompanying note 63, *supra*.
[72] 336 U.S. 226, 232–233, 23 L.R.R.M. 2371, 2374 (1949).

to use the company hall, when the Board had found that the company's refusal, in itself, was not an unfair labor practice, but that its denial was discriminatory. The court rejected contentions that implicit in the Board's decree was the word "reasonable" regarding the potential applicability of the decree to future violations. The Court noted that if "reasonable" were implied, then a court would have to review that decision in order to determine its appropriate scope. Since the Board should have determined the appropriate scope of the order originally, the Court concluded that a court review of the scope "makes the order itself a useless formality."[73]

In another case, *J. I. Case Co. v. NLRB*,[74] the Supreme Court cautioned the Board against ordering a violator "to desist from more on the theory that he may violate the literal language and then defend by resort to the Board's construction of it [since] Court's orders are not to be trifled with, nor should they invite litigation as to their meaning."[75] On the other hand, it has been held that a narrow order, requiring an offender to cease and desist from interfering with employee rights in any *like* or *related* manner, "is not subject to the construction of a scattergun charge subjecting [the offender] to the possibility of contempt proceedings for violations not substantially like or related to the subject matter specified in the Board's order."[76]

THE SCOPE OF THE REMEDY MAY VARY WITH THE SCOPE OF THE VIOLATOR'S OPERATIONS

Many employers have groups of plants and multi-state operations, and unions often operate on a regional or national basis. The Board has often ordered remedial action that extends beyond the unit or plant involved in the case. Thus, where it has been shown that the employer instituted a system-wide, centrally directed, and coordinated policy to commit unfair practices, the courts have found that the Board properly included all the employer's plants within its

---

[73] *Id.* at 233, 23 L.R.R.M. at 2374.

[74] 321 U.S. 332, 14 L.R.R.M. 501 (1944).

[75] *Id.* at 341, 14 L.R.R.M. at 506. *Cf.* NLRB v. United Wire & Supply Corp., 312 F.2d 11, 13, 52 L.R.R.M. 2110, 2112 (1st Cir. 1962) (order directing employer to cease and desist from creating an "impression of surveillance" overly broad without qualifying language setting forth the conduct which is specifically objected to and forbidden).

[76] NLRB v. Great Atl. & Pac. Tea Co., 277 F.2d 759, 765, 46 L.R.R.M. 2055, 2059 (5th Cir. 1960) (unlawful solicitation and distribution rules).

order.[77] The Board may properly infer that, if not deterred, the employer will pursue the same discriminatory policies at every unit within a certain geographic area, and therefore the Board may apply its cease and desist order to that entire area.[78] Moreover, when employers who have such a coordinated, system-wide policy commit flagrant unfair labor practices, the application of Board orders to plants other than those at which the violations occurred has been found to be appropriate.[79] When the employer controls several corporations, or one corporation with separate divisions, Board orders applicable to more than one division or corporation have also been upheld by the courts.[80]

On the other hand, it has been held inappropriate to extend orders to an employer's units that were not immediately involved in the unfair labor practices, in areas where the misconduct was not pervasive, occurred only at an individual plant, and did not affect employees in other units.[81] For example, in *NLRB v. Ford Motor*

---

[77] NLRB v. Salant & Salant, Inc., 183 F.2d 462, 465, 26 L.R.R.M. 2234, 2236 (6th Cir. 1950); *cf.* United Aircraft Co. v. NLRB, 440 F.2d 85, 100, 76 L.R.R.M. 2761, 2773 (2d Cir. 1971) (general pattern of union hostility and discriminatory conduct at five of company's six plants located in a compact geographical area justified order directing that notices be posted at all six plants); Decaturville Sportswear Co. v. NLRB, 406 F.2d 886, 889, 70 L.R.R.M. 2472, 2474 (6th Cir. 1969); *accord* United Aircraft Co. v. NLRB, 440 F.2d 85, 76 L.R.R.M. 2761, 2773 (2d Cir. 1971).

[78] NLRB v. Lummus Co., 210 F.2d 377, 33 L.R.R.M. 2513, 2516 (5th Cir. 1954); Texas Gulf Sulphur Co. v. NLRB, 463 F.2d 779, 80 L.R.R.M. 3171 (5th Cir. 1972).

[79] *See e.g.,* NLRB v. Great Atl. & Pac. Tea Co., 408 F.2d 374, 376, 70 L.R.R.M. 2829, 2830 (5th Cir. 1969) (per curiam); NLRB v. Great Atl. & Pac. Tea Co., 409 F.2d 296, 70 L.R.R.M. 3246, 3248 (5th Cir. 1969); J. P. Stevens & Co. v. NLRB, 388 F.2d 896, 65 L.R.R.M. 2829, 2838 (2d Cir. 1967); J. P. Stevens & Co. v. NLRB, 612 F.2d 881, 103 L.R.R.M. 2221 (4th Cir. 1979), *cert. denied,* 101 S. Ct. 315, 105 L.R.R.M. 2809 (1980); J. P. Stevens & Co. v. NLRB, 623 F.2d 322, 104 L.R.R.M. 2573 (4th Cir. 1980), *cert. denied,* 102 S. Ct. 3505, 106 L.R.R.M. 2136; and Florida Steel Corp. v. NLRB, 620 F.2d 79, 104 L.R.R.M. 2833 (5th Cir. 1980).

[80] NLRB v. Lipman Bros., 355 F.2d 1966, 61 L.R.R.M. 2193, 2197 (1st Cir. 1966) (three brothers were officers and directors of all corporations involved, were considered joint employers, and formulated and administered a common labor policy); NLRB v. Sunbeam Elec. Mfg. Co., 133 F.2d 856, 861, 11 L.R.R.M. 820, 826 (7th Cir. 1943) (broad order enforced, even though the distribution of illegal circulars was limited to one division, since a contemporaneous oral campaign directed at all employees had made them aware of the issues, placing them within the scope of the employer's propaganda campaign); Schramm & Schmieg Co., 67 N.L.R.B. 980, 993–994, 18 L.R.R.M. 1032, 1033 (1946) (employees of two factories, owned by a common employer and located in the same building, given notice since the individual found to have violated the Act was the superintendent of both factories).

[81] Dover Corp., 211 N.L.R.B. 955, 86 L.R.R.M. 1607, 1612 (1974); Albert's Inc., 213 N.L.R.B. 686, 87 L.R.R.M. 1682 (1974); United Mercantile Inc., 204 N.L.R.B. 663, 83 L.R.R.M. 1562 (1973); *but cf.* Kellwood Co., 199 N.L.R.B. 756, 82 L.R.R.M. 1015, 1016 (1972), wherein the Board denied the general counsel's request that Kellwood be enjoined from further § 8(a)(1) violations at all of its plants and that notices be posted for the fifty-one plants in the Kellwood complex, although the Board recognized the propensity of the employer to engage in unfair labor practices.

Co.,[82] the Board directed the employer to post notices in all of its plants even though the violations committed by the employer occurred only in its Dallas plant. The court found that the system-wide scope of the Board's order was too broad and held that the "Board was without jurisdiction to make the order operate as generally as it did."[83]

More recently, while enforcing a broad "in any other manner," order, the Court of Appeals for the District of Columbia would not enforce extraordinary remedies, such as company-wide mailing of the notice of violation to all employees and union access to any company plant to deliver a speech to employees if an election is scheduled.[84] In a scholarly opinion, Judge Edwards remanded the case to the Board to consider five factors: (1) the seriousness of the violation at issue; (2) knowledge of the violation at other plants; (3) distance between plants; (4) union activity at other plants, and (5) effect of the passage of time between accumulated violations.[85] In the second consideration of the case before a different panel, the Court of Appeals found that the Board failed to meet the requirements of the remand because it had relied solely on historical assumptions not supported by evidence in the record. The court denied enforcement of the requirements of the company-wide mailing and union access to plants.[86]

In *NLRB v. Haberman Construction Co.,*[87] the Fifth Circuit denied enforcement of the Board's company-wide order to enforce the prehire agreement at construction projects that had not yet begun at the time of the unfair labor practice, because the union was required

[82] 119 F.2d 326, 8 L.R.R.M. 656 (5th Cir. 1941).

[83] *Id.* at 330–331, 8 L.R.R.M. at 659. *See also* Reliance Mfg. Co. v. NLRB, 125 F.2d 311, 321–322, 9 L.R.R.M. 536, 547 (7th Cir. 1941), wherein the court, relying on *Ford Motor Co.,* refused to enforce an order requiring posting of notices in all of the plants operated by the employer (the original charges claimed violations at ten of thirteen plants; subsequently, the Board dismissed charges as to one plant for lack of evidence and severed as to another), holding that when a charge is filed complaining of violations at plants not included in the instant proceeding, the employer is entitled to a Board hearing. *Cf.* NLRB v. F. H. McGraw & Co., 206 F.2d 635, 641, 32 L.R.R.M. 2220, 2225 (6th Cir. 1953). *And see* NLRB v. Jack Smith Beverages, Inc., 202 F.2d 100, 102, 31 L.R.R.M. 2366, 2368 (6th Cir. 1953), *cert. denied,* 345 U.S. 995, 32 L.R.R.M. 2247 (1953). Where employer had violated § 8(a)(2) by rendering unlawful assistance to an incumbent union, the order was strictly limited by the court to apply to the one plant where the violations were found to have occurred on the rationale that to render a broad order on the basis of the *Express Publishing* doctrine would impose an unlawful restraint on the employees' freedom to choose their representatives in other plants within the system.

[84] Steelworkers v. NLRB, 646 F.2d 616, 106 L.R.R.M. 2573 (D.C. Cir. 1981); and Florida Steel Corp. v. NLRB, 713 F.2d 823, 113 L.R.R.M. 3625 (D.C. Cir. 1983).

[85] Steelworkers v. NLRB at note 84, *supra.*

[86] Florida Steel Corp. v. NLRB at note 84, *supra.*

[87] 641 F.2d 351, 106 L.R.R.M. 2998 (5th Cir. 1981).

to reestablish its majority status before the employer could be bound by the order.

In cases involving union violations, the relevant factors in determining whether to expand the scope of the remedy beyond the immediate parties involved were outlined in *Teamsters Local No. 386 (Valley Employers Ass'n)* [88] where the Board reversed the trial examiner and struck his recommendation that all of the members (numbering about 400) of the employers' association be required to post the notice to remedy the union's violation. The Board stressed that the member employers were engaged in various industries, many without union organization, and many were engaged only in intrastate commerce. Moreover, none of the other association members belonged to the industry group involved, none were covered by the same collective bargaining agreement, and most of them did not have a contract with the respondent union.

The courts have limited the scope of the Board's order to the "local" union in order to make it consonant with both the places and persons which have given rise to the litigation.[89] Thus, in *NLRB v. Teamsters, Local 327 (Hartmann Luggage Co.),*[90] the Sixth Circuit refused to enforce a Board order restraining the union from "coercing the employees of Hartmann Luggage Company *or the employees of any other employer within its jurisdictional* territory" in the exercise of their section 7 rights. The court opined that the order would violate the provisions of rule 65(d) of the Federal Rules of Civil Procedure,[91] in that it contained no limitation in time, was both too broad and too vague in relation to persons expected to obey it, and did not define the jurisdiction of Local 327, thus providing no means for ascertaining the individuals for whom protection was sought.[92]

Once again, regarding the scope of Board orders, one cannot easily predict how broad orders will fare at the hands of the courts. For

---

[88] 145 N.L.R.B. 1475, n. 1, 55 L.R.R.M. 1186 (1964).

[89] NLRB v. Brewery Drivers, Local 830, 281 F.2d 319, 323, 46 L.R.R.M. 2732, 2735 (3d Cir. 1960).

[90] 419 F.2d 1282, 1283, 73 L.R.R.M. 2199, 2200 (6th Cir. 1970) (per curiam).

[91] *See* Fed. R. Civ. P. 65(d), which provides in pertinent part that: "Every order granting an injunction . . . shall be specific in terms; shall describe in reasonable detail, and not by reference to the complaint or other document, the act or acts sought to be restrained. . . ."

[92] 419 F.2d at 1283, 73 L.R.R.M. at 2200. *See* NLRB v. Teamsters, Local 327 (Whale, Inc.), 432 F.2d 933, 934–935, 75 L.R.R.M. 2435, 2436 (6th Cir. 1970) (per curiam); *accord* NLRB v. Miscellaneous Drivers, Local 610 (Funeral Directors of Greater St. Louis, Inc.), 293 F.2d 437, 441, 48 L.R.R.M. 2816, 2820 (8th Cir. 1961) (court found an insufficient evidentiary basis to approve an order covering all other employers within the "territorial jurisdiction" of the union, but indicated such an order might be approved in a proper case).

example, in *Teamsters Local 554 (Clark Bros. Transfer Co.) v. NLRB,*[93] the District of Columbia Circuit found overly broad an order that was designed to protect not only the employers involved, but also "all other employers in the area over which the Union has jurisdiction." The court pointed out that no threat had been made to use illegal methods against all other employers. Moreover, since the basic function of the union was to unionize the area within its jurisdiction, the court felt that the broad order might conflict with the purpose of the Act to protect the right of the employees to organize and engage in collective bargaining. The next year, however, a similar Board order, based on similar violations, came before the District of Columbia Circuit in *Central States Drivers Council v. NLRB (Clark Bros. Transfer Co.).*[94] The Board's cease and desist order addressed the union's unlawful activity as it might affect the Clark Company "or any other similar carrier."[95] The union cited the court's earlier opinion and argued that the Board's order was too broad. The court disagreed, however, and enforced the Board's order, construing " 'any other similar common carrier' " to mean any "other 'nonunionized motor truck common carriers' " within the "jurisdiction" of the union.[96] The disposition of these two cases is confusing; the court in the second case approved the Board's order by construing its language to mean the same thing as the first Board order, which the court previously had found to be improper.

---

[93] 262 F.2d 456, 43 L.R.R.M. 2197, 2201–2202 (D.C. Cir. 1958).
[94] 267 F.2d 166, 168, 44 L.R.R.M. 2058, 2059 (D.C. Cir. 1959).
[95] *Id.* at 167, 44 L.R.R.M. at 2059.
[96] *Id.*

CHAPTER V

Isolated or Minor Violations
and the Necessity of an Order

The Board has processed many cases over the years where the violation has been isolated, insignificant, and not likely to recur. The general counsel has pursued administrative and judicial remedies against parties whose misconduct, if any, is of a minor nature. While these *de minimis* cases may or may not have contributed to the Board's backlog and consequent delay in the processing of important cases, there is little reason for expanding the limited administrative and judicial facilities and resources to decide cases in which no meaningful order is at stake.

DE MINIMIS *VIOLATIONS*

The Board has recognized that cases involving minor, innocuous, or isolated violations of the Act do not justify the issuance of an order, where doing so would not effectuate the purposes of the Act.[1] It initially had difficulty convincing the courts to accept a *de minimis* theory, however; neither could it convince itself. During the 1970s Board Members Fanning and Jenkins staunchly opposed the Board's *de minimis* decisions. Their argument was that section 10(c) requires a remedial order where a violation has been found, and that the Board has no discretion to dismiss the complaint or to refuse to issue a remedial order in such a case. The courts are now more favorably disposed to the refusal to issue orders in *de minimis* cases, and the Board seems fully committed to using the principle where appropriate.

---

[1] *See* Pepsi-Cola Allied Bottlers, Inc., 170 N.L.R.B. 1250, 67 L.R.R.M. 1603 (1968); Eaborn Trucking Serv., 156 N.L.R.B. 1370, 1372, 61 L.R.R.M. 1268, 1269 (1966); Bridwell Oil Co., 172 N.L.R.B. 1635, 69 L.R.R.M. 1382, 1383 (1968); Nehi-Royal Crown Corp., 178 N.L.R.B. 93, 94, 71 L.R.R.M. 1666, 1668–1669 (1969); Mallory Battery Co., 176 N.L.R.B. No. 108, 71 L.R.R.M. 1320 (1969).

Board Application of the De Minimis *Principle*

The Board initially refused to issue remedial orders in cases of a violation where the conduct was of an isolated or *de minimis* nature.[2] This policy was more than anything else a common sense approach to the administration of the Act, the conduct being viewed within its context.[3] For example, in *Country Cubboard Corp.,*[4] a supervisor-manager threatened to "write up" employees if they resorted to union help. Although the conduct violated section 8(a)(1), the Board affirmed the recommendation of the trial examiner that no remedy was necessary because the parties had a successful contractual collective bargaining relationship; the employer had been cooperative in administering the contract; there had been no actual or attempted use of the threatened "write up"; and the lack of any other unfair labor practices or any evidence that the employer had a propensity to interfere with the employees' rights under the Act— in short, the lack of any anti-union animus.

Similarly, where a supervisor has violated section 8(a)(1) by threatening an employee for filing a grievance, the Board has viewed such action within the framework of the give and take of the collective bargaining relationship. In so doing, the Board has rejected the notion that every isolated comment that can be deemed a threat should automatically require a finding that the Act has been violated.[5] In *International Harvester Co.,*[6] for example, a supervisor threatened to eliminate the job of an employee if "he did not stop bitching." The Board adopted the findings of the trial examiner, who recommended dismissing the complaint, noting that the grievance procedure would be "severely limited if the refinements of diplomatic language are required of factory personnel concerned

---

[2] *See, e.g.,* Decker Disposal, Inc., 171 N.L.R.B. 879, 880 n.1, 68 L.R.R.M. 1306, 1308 (1968) (unilateral change in starting time); Howell Refining Co., 163 N.L.R.B. 18, 19, 64 L.R.R.M. 1271, 1272 (1967) (coercion); Allied Chem. Corp., National Aniline Div., 143 N.L.R.B. 260, 263, 53 L.R.R.M. 1380, 1381 (1963) (interrogation); Frohman Mfg., Co., 107 N.L.R.B. 1308, 1315, 33 L.R.R.M. 1388, 1392 (1954) (veiled threat). It was not until the *Jimmy Wakely* case, *infra.* n.35, that the Board formally explicated its *de minimis* practice.

[3] Howell Refining Co., 163 N.L.R.B. 18, 19, 64 L.R.R.M. 1271, 1272 (1967); *cf.* Kohl Motors, Inc., 185 N.L.R.B. 324, 334, 76 L.R.R.M. 1747, 1748 (1970) (three unrelated instances of interrogation by a supervisor who was not otherwise improperly discussing a union campaign with a single employee); Pointsett Lumber & Mfg. Co., 147 N.L.R.B. 1197, 1201 n.5, 56 L.R.R.M. 1381, 1384 (1964) (alleged interrogation of employee while both he and a supervisor were socializing at a local tavern).

[4] 179 N.L.R.B. 53, 72 L.R.R.M. 1255 (1969).

[5] Consolidated Freightways Corp., 181 N.L.R.B. 856, 862, 74 L.R.R.M. 1038, 1039 (1970).

[6] 180 N.L.R.B. 1038, 73 L.R.R.M. 1331 (1970).

with the day-to-day operations of a collective bargaining agreement."[7]

In *International Paper Co.,*[8] a supervisor threatened a union stew-
ard for filing a grievance on behalf of another employee. The Board,
although finding a violation, held that a remedial order was not
warranted, because the statement by the supervisor was based on
a good faith belief that the contract did not permit stewards to file
grievances for others; the employer subsequently retracted its position; the evidence reflected an atmosphere of employee freedom
in voicing complaints and filing grievances; and the supervisor's
threat was an isolated incident.[9] Similarly, the Board has dismissed
a complaint where a supervisor engaged in an interrogation of a
union supporter, contrary to management's instructions.[10]

Consider another instance in which the *de minimis* rule is typically applied: where a supervisor who uttered an unlawful remark,
or an employee who heard, is no longer employed by the company
charged with the unfair labor practice. Does the departure of the
supervisor or employee make it unnecessary to issue an order? It
depends upon the context. For example, in *Leonard Refineries, Inc.*[11]
a supervisor violated section 8(a)(1) when he threatened several
employees that they would lose their Christmas bonus if the union
won the upcoming election. The trial examiner recommended that
no remedial order be issued because the supervisor's intervening
death eliminated the possibility of any recurrence of the violation,
because his remark was the only unlawful conduct during the pre-
election campaign, and because it was made to only a few employees.
The Board disagreed, pointing out that, in the context of the campaign, the Christmas bonus issue was of such a concern to the
employees that the supervisor's statement was likely to have received wide and prompt circulation. The Board held that the supervisor's death did not alter the effects of the violation.[12] On the

---

[7] 180 N.L.R.B. at 1039.

[8] 184 N.L.R.B. 351, 74 L.R.R.M. 1438 (1970).

[9] 184 N.L.R.B. at 353.

[10] *See* Craftsman's Elec. Prods., Inc., 179 N.L.R.B. 419, 72 L.R.R.M. 1345 (1969).

[11] 147 N.L.R.B. 488, 56 L.R.R.M. 1285 (1964).

[12] Id. at 489, 56 L.R.R.M., at 1285–86. In Consolidated Frieghtways Corp., 181
N.L.R.B. 856, 74 L.R.R.M. 1038 (1970) the Board refused, however, to issue a remedy
where the supervisor in question had left the employer. *See also* the refusal by the
Court of Appeals for the Fourth Circuit to enforce bargaining orders based on
statements made in an organizing campaign by a supervisor who had left the employer, Shulman's Inc. v. NLRB, 519 F.2d 498, 89 L.R.R.M. 2729 (4th Cir. 1975); and
by the Fifth Circuit because the supervisor who made the coercive statement had
died before the trial, and therefore the violation could not "by its very nature
reoccur," Hill-Behan Lumber Co. v. NLRB, 396 F.2d 807, 68 L.R.R.M. 2384 (5th Cir.
1968). *Cf.* R. E. WILLIAMS, P. A. JANUS & K. C. HUHN, NLRB REGULATION OF ELECTION

other hand, the Board has refused to issue a remedial order where the employee who was the object of the illegal conduct has either retired or quit.[13]

In *Bellinger Shipyards Inc.*,[14] the Board held that there was no violation of the Act where an employer removed an illegal no-solicitation rule and replaced it with a new, admittedly legal, rule one month before a complaint was issued.[15] The Board found that the employees were not adversely affected by the unlawful rule, and that the employer had not engaged in any other violation of the Act. The Board reasoned that voluntary compliance with the Act should be encouraged, and ruled that the misconduct involved was so minimal, and had been so substantially corrected by the subsequent voluntary conduct, that the entire situation was "one of little significance and there is no real need for a Board remedy."[16]

The *de minimis* reasoning had an uneven development in the 1970s.[17] The principle was the subject of stiff debate within the Board itself. Members Fanning and Jenkins insisted that the Board does not have the right to apply the *de minimis* theory to its decisions in unfair labor practice cases.[18] They argued that section

---

CONDUCT 244 (Lab. Rel. & Pub. Pol. Ser., Rep. No. 8, 1974). *See also* Advance Envelope Mfg. Co., 170 N.L.R.B. 1459, 1470 n.8, 68 L.R.R.M. 1023 (1968), wherein the Board, refusing to issue a bargaining order based on coercive statements prior to an election which the union subsequently lost, pointed out that another election is always available.

[13] Rosella's Fruit & Produce Co., 199 N.L.R.B. 633, 82 L.R.R.M. 1080 (1972); Craftsman's Elec. Prods., Inc., 179 N.L.R.B. 419, 72 L.R.R.M. 1345 (1969). *See also* Eaborn Trucking Serv., 156 N.L.R.B. 1370, 61 L.R.R.M. 1268 (1966), where the employer granted a unilateral wage increase to one employee during the pre-election period in violation of § 8(a)(1). The Board, however, held that no remedy was necessary when the union, upon winning the election, demanded union scale, and the employer, who was in dire economic circumstances, refused, whereupon all the employees quit their jobs. *Cf.* Braswell Motor Freight Lines, 107 N.L.R.B. 761, 33 L.R.R.M. 1243 (1954).

[14] 227 N.L.R.B. 620, 94 L.R.R.M. 1113 (1976). *Accord,* Deringer Mfg. Co., 201 N.L.R.B. 622, 82 L.R.R.M. 1607 (1973).

[15] *But see* IBEW, Local 1316, 271 N.L.R.B. No. 59, 116 L.R.R.M. 1416 (1984), wherein the Board rejected a *de minimis* argument where the respondent sought to cure the unlawful action after the issuance of the complaint, but never conceded the conduct was unlawful, and never publicized disavowal of the action.

[16] Bellinger Shipyards, 94 L.R.R.M. at 1114.

[17] *See, e.g.,* O'Neil Moving and Storage, Inc., 209 N.L.R.B. 713, 85 L.R.R.M. 1488 (1974); Fearn Int'l, Inc., Eggo Foods Div., 209 N.L.R.B. 237, 85 L.R.R.M. 1534 (1974); Walgreen Co. d/b/a Globe Shopping City, 203 N.L.R.B. 177, 83 L.R.R.M. 1059 (1973); American Federation of Musicians, Local 76 (Jimmy Wakely), 202 N.L.R.B. 620, 82 L.R.R.M. 1591 (1973).

[18] Members Fanning and Jenkins, who served twenty-five and twenty years respectively on the Board, steadfastly maintained this position until they left the Board in December 1982 and August 1983, respectively. The Board now is taking "a fresh look" at the *de minimis* principle to see if it would be advisable to utilize

10(c) obliges the Board to find an unfair labor practice where the evidence demonstrates one, however trivial, and to issue a cease and desist order in all such cases.[19] As previously discussed, the Board has the authority to order two types of relief: (1) a negative order directing that the party found guilty of the unfair labor practice "cease and desist" therefrom; and (2) an affirmative order directing the party guilty of the unfair labor practice to take such affirmative action to remedy the violation "as will effectuate the policies of this Act." The issue is whether Congress intended the language "as will effectuate the policies of this Act" to operate solely as a limitation on the affirmative remedies the Board has the right to direct, as Members Fanning and Jenkins argued, or whether it must be satisfied before either negative or affirmative relief can be directed by the Board, as those advocating a *de minimis* theory would suggest.

Judicial Evaluation of the De Minimis *Reasoning*

Until the 1970s, two circuits specifically had disapproved of the Board reasoning in *de minimis* cases. The Court of Appeals for the District of Columbia held in *Woodworkers Local 3-10 v. NLRB*[20] that if the Board finds that a violation has occurred, it must issue

---

it in cutting down the backlog. *See* Statement, Chairman Dotson before House Subcommittee on Manpower, Nov. 2, 1983.

[19] Carolina Am. Textiles, Inc., 219 N.L.R.B. 457, 90 L.R.R.M. 1074 (1975) (Chairman Murphy, dissenting); Interlake, Inc., 218 N.L.R.B. 1043, 89 L.R.R.M. 1794 (1975) (Member Kennedy, dissenting); Thermalloy Corp., 213 N.L.R.B. 129, 87 L.R.R.M. 1081, 1082 (1974) (Member Jenkins, dissenting); Triangle Publications, Inc., 204 N.L.R.B. No. 108, 83 L.R.R.M. 1382, 1384 (1973); Deringer Mfg. Co., 201 N.L.R.B. 622, 82 L.R.R.M. 1607, 1608 (1973). *And see* O'Neil Moving and Storage, Inc., 209 N.L.R.B. 713, 85 L.R.R.M. 1488, 1490-1491 (1974) (Members Fanning and Jenkins, dissenting); Las Vegas Sun, 209 N.L.R.B. 240, 85 L.R.R.M. 1536, 1538 (1974) (Member Fanning, dissenting); Fearn Int'l Inc., Eggo Foods Div., 209 N.L.R.B. 237, 85 L.R.R.M. 1534, 1535-1536 (1974) (Member Fanning, dissenting); Walgreen Co., d/b/a Globe Shopping City, 203 N.L.R.B. 177, 83 L.R.R.M. 1059, 1060-1061 (1973) (Member Fanning, dissenting). In each of these cases, Members Fanning and Jenkins would have issued a remedy, once a violation was found, regardless of its *de minimis* nature.

[20] 380 F.2d 628, 65 L.R.R.M. 2633 (D.C. Cir. 1967). Although the members of the Board who have opposed the *de minimis* principle also have frequently cited Eichleay Corp. v. NLRB, 206 F.2d 799, 32 L.R.R.M. 2628 (3d Cir. 1953), as an authority against the *de minimis* theory, it is very questionable whether it should serve as such. It is true the Third Circuit stated in *Eichleay* that the Board "*must* issue a cease and desist order once it has held a hearing and determined that the prohibited practice exists, but is allowed some discretion in ordering other affirmative action." The holding that it must issue an order where a violation has occurred was clearly *dicta* in that case, and the case has never been cited by either the Third Circuit or any other circuit court as precedent on the *de minimis* principle. Further, the Third Circuit appears to have adopted the *de minimis* theory in Champion Posts Rebuilders, Inc. v. NLRB, 709 F.2d 178, 113 L.R.R.M. 2922 (3d Cir. 1983).

a remedial order. The court distinguished cases involving misconduct of such a *"de minimis* character" that no unfair labor practice
finding could be predicated upon it.[21] The D.C. Circuit subsequently
moved away from this view, however. In *Dallas Mailers Union v.
NLRB,*[22] the court stated: "Infinitesimally small abstract grievances
must give way to actual and existing legal problems if courts are
to dispose of their heavy calendars."[23] And in *NLRB v. Columbia
Typographical Union,*[24] the court denied enforcement of an order
against a union which had improperly fined a supervisor $25 for
failing to notify the local union that he had performed work reserved
for members of the union, but later had returned the fine and taken
no further action. The court opined: "Under the circumstances, why
the General Counsel filed this charge and the Board persists in this
litigation is difficult to understand. We agree with Chairman Miller
of the Board dissenting from the Board's order on the grounds that
the issue in suit is moot."[25]

In 1970, the Sixth Circuit, in *UAW v. NLRB (Omni Spectra)*[26]
also ruled that once a violation has been found, a Board order must
be issued. The court, although not rejecting the *de minimis* principle, noted that the Act had delegated to the office of the general
counsel the discretion to determine whether charges were sufficiently meritorious to be brought to complaint and ruled: "We believe this indicates a Congressional intention that only the General
Counsel, not the Board, has the power to dismiss an alleged violation
as not warranting Board consideration."[27]

In contrast, the Second Circuit has stated that it "assumed, without deciding . . . [that] the Board in an appropriate case can balance
the detrimental effects of an order if issued on labor and management relations and refuse to issue one."[28] In *Catholic Medical Center
of Brooklyn v. NLRB*[29] the Second Circuit remanded the case to
the Board, stating that it considered the employer's withholding of

---

[21] *See, e.g.,* Caribe Gen. Elec., Inc. v. NLRB, 357 F.2d 664, 666, 61 L.R.R.M. 2513,
2514 (1st Cir. 1966); NLRB v. Clegg Mach. Works, 304 F.2d 168, 176, 50 L.R.R.M.
2524, 2530 (8th Cir. 1962); NLRB v. Grunwald-Marx, Inc., 290 F.2d 210, 47 L.R.R.M.
2940 (9th Cir. 1961); NLRB v. Mississippi Prods., Inc., 213 F.2d 670, 674, 34 L.R.R.M.
2431, 2343-2344 (5th Cir. 1954). *See also* UAW v. NLRB (Omni Spectra Inc.), 427
F.2d 1330, 1333 n.2, 74 L.R.R.M. 2481, 2483 (6th Cir. 1970).
[22] 445 F.2d 730, 76 L.R.R.M. 2247 (D.C. Cir. 1971).
[23] Id. at 733, 76 L.R.R.M. at 2249.
[24] 470 F.2d 1274, 81 L.R.R.M. 2668 (D.C. Cir. 1972).
[25] *Id.* at 1275, 81 L.R.R.M. at 2668.
[26] 427 F.2d 1330, 74 L.R.R.M. 2481 (6th Cir. 1970).
[27] 74 L.R.R.M. at 2483.
[28] Luxuray of NY v. NLRB, 447 F.2d 112, 114, 77 L.R.R.M. 2820, 2822 (2d Cir.
1971).
[29] 589 F.2d 1166, 100 L.R.R.M. 2225 (2d Cir. 1978).

a wage increase for three weeks during an election campaign, because it feared that the increase would violate the Act, to be an "inconsequential" violation and questioned whether it called for a remedial order. When the case was returned to the Second Circuit, the court adhered to its view that the violation was "inconsequential." Nevertheless, the court enforced the order, finding that the Board had correctly applied its own *de minimis* principle. In enforcing the Board order, the court stated: "The choice of whether or not to proceed with such trivia is for the General Counsel and the Board, rather than us." [30]

In strong language, the Fifth Circuit in *NLRB v. Big Three Industrial Gas Co.*[31] refused to enforce a Board order that was meant to remedy what the Board saw as a minimal violation of section 8(a)(3). The court stated:

> The maxim *de minimis non curat lex* is well known in the law and stands for the proposition that courts do not care for trifles. This *rede* is particularly applicable to the instant situation. The loss by two employees of a few dollars pay is simply to too picayune to warrant setting aside a long and costly election process involving hundreds of voters or, indeed, even to warrant a cease and desist and pay back order for the men involved. Conceding arguendo that the company's practice was discriminatory, it would be such a rank unfairness to the remaining electors and so clearly beneath the dignity of the Board's function, that we hold this triviality could not support any order.[32]

The Fourth Circuit in *NLRB v. Pilot Freight Carriers*[33] refused to enforce the Board's cease and desist order in a case involving a single incident of a management official interrogating an employee. The Fourth Circuit held that

> [i]n view of the absence of any other violation on the part of the company, the conversation with Hill becomes an isolated incident which does not require the entry of a formal cease and desist order . . .[34]

The leading Board decision involving the *de minimis* principle is *American Federation of Musicians, Local 76*,[35] better known as the *Jimmy Wakely* case. Here the Board sought, in response to court criticism, to articulate a *de minimis* theory. In this case, the union, in violation of section 8(b)(1)(B), interfered with management's right

---

[30] 620 F.2d 20, 104 L.R.R.M. 2186 (2d Cir. 1980).
[31] 441 F.2d 774, 77 L.R.R.M. 2120 (5th Cir. 1971).
[32] *Id.* at 778, 77 L.R.R.M. at 2123.
[33] 558 F.2d 205, 95 L.R.R.M. 2900 (4th Cir. 1977).
[34] *Id.* at 214, 95 L.R.R.M. at 2908.
[35] 202 N.L.R.B. 620, 82 L.R.R.M. 1591 (1973).

to select its supervisors or representatives in dealing with the union
by engaging in a temporary refusal to work. Declining to issue a
remedial order, the Board pointed out that "the alleged misconduct
... is of such an obviously limited impact and significance that we
ought not to find that it raises to the level of constituting a violation
of our act." [36] The Board quoted extensively from the two District
of Columbia Circuit cases which had signalled a greater willingness
to accept a *de minimis* theory. The Board stated that the case before
it involved a small and abstract grievance. Although conceding that
the evidence may have established a technical violation of the Act,
the Board dismissed the complaint noting the importance of disposing of its heavy backlog.[37]

For a brief period subsequent to the *Jimmy Wakely* ruling, the
Fanning-Jenkins strict constructionist view on *de minimis* was as-
cendant. In *Regency at the Roadway Inn*,[38] the administrative law
judge (ALJ), citing *Jimmy Wakely*, found the challenged interrogation to be only "a technical violation" of the Act and recommended dismissal of the complaint, because the respondent
committed no other violations; the record did not show that more
than one employee had heard the interrogation; the remarks had

---

[36] *Id.* at 622, 82 L.R.R.M. at 1593. *But see* Georgia Hosiery Mills, 207 N.L.R.B. 781,
85 L.R.R.M. 1067 (1973), wherein the Board distinguished the *Jimmy Wakely* case
as pertaining to a single, isolated threat that was rescinded before any action was
taken and hence was substantially remedied before the complaint was even issued.

[37] 202 N.L.R.B. at 622, 82 L.R.R.M. at 1593. The two District of Columbia Circuit
cases were: NLRB v. Columbia Typographical Union, 470 F.2d 1274, 81 L.R.R.M.
2668 (D.C. Cir. 1972); and Dallas Mailer's Union, Local 143 v. NLRB, 445 F.2d 730,
76 L.R.R.M. 2247 (D.C. Cir. 1971), where Judge Tamm in reluctantly enforcing the
Board's order wrote:

> Now [this case] has finally come to rest in the bosoms of three judges, who
> must pick their way through a quagmire of grammar totaling almost 300
> pages of briefs, documents, and transcripts that will presumably aid us in
> determining whether Colston's manner was too overbearing or Cantrell's skin
> too thin.
>
> At a time when this court is confronted with an all-time high in caseload and
> backlog, it is most unfortunate that three of its judges must conscientiously
> spend the necessary time to do justice to a dispute that should have been
> settled long ago within the Company and Union family. We see no hope for
> the expeditious determination of appeals unless an effective method of weeding
> out cases of this sort is established to prevent others like it from receiving so
> much unearned attention. It seems elementary to the very existence of our
> judicial machinery that infinitesimally small abstract grievances must give
> way to actual and existing legal problems if courts are to dispose of their
> heavy calendars. We mention this only to encourage other members of the
> legal community to constructively think of ways to alleviate the problem. Any
> step in the right direction would be a giant service to us and the public at
> large. (76 L.R.R.M. at 2249.)

[38] 255 N.L.R.B. 961, 107 L.R.R.M. 1030 (1981).

not had any effect on the concerted activity of the employees; and the supervisor had later been discharged by the employer. The three-member Board panel of Fanning, Jenkins, and Zimmerman ruled that the factors relied on by the ALJ were not sufficient to sustain his finding, and were indeed irrelevant.

In *Holladay Park Hospital*,[39] the same three-member panel ruled that the ALJ was wrong in applying the *de minimis* reasoning to a hospital rule proscribing the wearing of yellow ribbons to show support for the union. The panel did not specifically reverse or overrule *Jimmy Wakely*, however; the only reference to that ruling was contained in a footnote setting forth that Members Fanning and Jenkins disagreed with the *de minimis* principle.

Despite several twists and turns, it is apparent that with the departure of the members who steadfastly opposed it, the *de minimis* principle is a reasonably well-established Board policy. One can also expect that if the Board applies this principle in accordance with the *Jimmy Wakely* case, it will be affirmed by most, if not all, of the circuit courts.[40] This is true regardless of whether or not the General Counsel continues to refuse to apply the *de minimis* principle in determining whether to issue a complaint. The caseloads of both the Board and the courts have reached such proportions that it has become almost mandatory that both seriously consider and apply the *de minimis* principles where applicable.[41]

MOOTNESS

In one of its early decisions relating to the National Labor Relations Act, the Supreme Court held in *NLRB v. Pennsylvania Greyhound Lines, Inc.*[42] that an order of the Board "lawful when made, does not become moot because it is obeyed or because changing circumstances indicate the need for it to be less than when made."[43] Observing that "[t]he Act does not require the Board to play hide and seek with those guilty of unfair labor practices," the Court

---

[39] 262 N.L.R.B. 278, 110 L.R.R.M. 1305 (1982).

[40] In fact, the only circuit court that at this point would show any potential opposition thereto would be the Sixth Circuit because *Omni Spectra* is still the law of that circuit.

[41] More and more authorities and interested parties are following the lead of the New York City Bar Association in suggesting that the General Counsel should actively screen out *de minimis* or isolated violations to reduce the case load and help improve case processing. Report, *Improved Enforcement of the National Labor Relations Act*, 27 Record of N.Y.C.B.A. 523, 530 (1972).

[42] 303 U.S. 261, 2 L.R.R.M. 600 (1938).

[43] 303 U.S. at 271, 2 L.R.R.M. at 603. *Cf.* Consolidated Edison Co. of N.Y. v. NLRB, 305 U.S. 197, 230, 3 L.R.R.M. 646, 653 (1938).

added in a later case that compliance with a Board order does not render it moot.[44]

The rationale for enforcing Board orders, even though enforcement may be contrary to accepted common law doctrines,[45] is that under the Act, the violation is of a continuing nature [46] and hence "... enforcement of the order provides an incentive for continued compliance through the possible sanction of contempt proceedings for violations." [47] Thus, for example, a refusal to sign an agreement is violative of the duty to bargain in good faith and requires a negative order [48] but will not be affirmatively remedied—i.e., by an order to sign—when the agreement has expired under its terms.[49] Since determining whether a matter has been successfully concluded, thereby obviating the need for enforcement, lies within the discretionary authority of the Board,[50] private agreements between parties which purport to constitute a final settlement of the dispute are not considered binding by the Board.[51]

---

[44] NLRB v. Mexia Textile Mills, 339 U.S. 563, 567–568, 26 L.R.R.M. 2123, 2125 (1950). See NLRB v. Carpenters, District Council of Kansas City, 184 F.2d 60, 63, 26 L.R.R.M. 2480, 2483 (10th Cir. 1950), where the court pointed out that an order does not become moot because of compliance, changing circumstances, or discontinuance of the unfair practice, thereby depriving the Board of its right to secure enforcement. Accord G & W Electric Specialty Co. v. NLRB, 360 F.2d 873, 874, 62 L.R.R.M. 2085 (7th Cir. 1966).

[45] See, e.g., NLRB v. Pac. Gas & Elec. Co., 118 F.2d 780, 789, 8 L.R.R.M. 848, 857 (9th Cir. 1941). In this case, the court rejected the equitable (equity will not enjoin completed transactions) and constitutional (no case or controversy within the meaning of Article III of the Constitution) contentions of the offender, citing the statement of the Supreme Court in IAM, Lodge 35 v. NLRB, 311 U.S. 72, 82, 7 L.R.R.M. 282, 287 (1940) that it "is for the Board not the courts to determine how the effect of prior unfair labor practices may be expunged." See also NLRB v. Ford Motor Co., 119 F.2d 326, 329, 8 L.R.R.M. 656, 658 (5th Cir. 1941) (rejection of equitable argument that injunctions will not be issued to prevent practices that have not only been discontinued but of which there is no reasonable likelihood of recurrence).

[46] See, e.g., NLRB v. Jones & Laughlin Steel Corp., 331 U.S. 416, 20 L.R.R.M. 2115 (1947). See also NLRB STATEMENTS OF PROCEDURE, Series 8, as amended, § 101.13.

[47] NLRB v. Southern Household Prods. Co., 449 F.2d 749, 750, 78 L.R.R.M. 2597, 2598 (5th Cir. 1971); accord, NLRB v. Raytheon, 398 U.S. 25, 27, 74 L.R.R.M. 2177, 2178 (1970); NLRB v. Marsh Supermkts., Inc., 327 F.2d 109, 111, 55 L.R.R.M. 2017, 2018 (7th Cir. 1963), cert. denied, 377 U.S. 944, 56 L.R.R.M. 2288 (1964); Modine Mfg. Co., 500 F.2d 914, 86 L.R.R.M. 3197, 3199 n.4 (8th Cir. 1974); NLRB v. Unoco Apparel, Inc., 508 F.2d 1368, 88 L.R.R.M. 2956, 2958 (5th Cir. 1975).

[48] E.g., Henry I. Siegel Co. v. NLRB, 340 F.2d 309, 310–311, 58 L.R.R.M. 2182, 2183 (2d Cir. 1965).

[49] See NLRB v. Painters Union, Local 1385, 334 F.2d 729, 732, 56 L.R.R.M. 2648, 2650 (7th Cir. 1964); NLRB v. Cosmopolitan Studios, Inc., 291 F.2d 110, 112, 48 L.R.R.M. 2398, 2399 (2d Cir. 1961); NLRB v. Local 19, Longshoremen (AFL-CIO), 286 F.2d 661, 664, 47 L.R.R.M. 2420, 2422 (7th Cir. 1961), cert. denied, 368 U.S. 820, 48 L.R.R.M. 3110 (1961).

[50] NLRB v. T.W. Phillips Gas & Oil Co., 141 F.2d 304, 14 L.R.R.M. 509 (3d Cir. 1944).

[51] See NLRB v. Prettyman, d/b/a Ann Arbor Press, 117 F.2d 921, 7 L.R.R.M. 469

Conditions Pertaining to Mootness

The Supreme Court in *NLRB v. Raytheon Co.*[52] rejected the employer's mootness argument, and held that an intervening election did not bar enforcement of a section 8(a)(1) order because there was nothing in the record to show that the specific acts complained of had not been repeated or would not be repeated in the future. It is important that the Court acknowledged situations where an enforcement proceeding will become moot because a party can establish that "there is no reasonable expectation that the wrong will be repeated."[53]

On rare occasions, the courts, reversing the Board, have ruled that changed conditions have made the remedy moot. In *Soule Glass and Glazing Co. v. NLRB*,[54] the Court of Appeals for the First Circuit reversed the Board's findings that the employer had bargained in bad faith and converted an economic strike into an unfair labor practice strike, and consequently refused to enforce the reinstatement order. Furthermore, the permanent employment of strike replacements, and other related facts, dictated a finding that the union no longer held status as bargaining agent. The court sustained the Board's finding that the employer had violated the Act by unilaterally transferring work and by refusing to provide requested information to the union, and sustained the cease and desist order, but denied the affirmative remedial order of returning the employees to work and providing the information. The court reasoned that these "corresponding affirmative remedial measures to restore the *status quo ante* ... are and will remain moot unless the union regains its status as bargaining agent."[55] While it recognized that this imposed "limited sanctions" with "little practical impact," the court concluded that this was the result of the unsuccessful economic strike.

(6th Cir. 1941); NLRB v. Gen. Motors Corp., 116 F.2d 306, 7 L.R.R.M. 506 (7th Cir. 1940); Jerstedt Lumber Co., 209 N.L.R.B. 662, 85 L.R.R.M. 1460 (1974); Finishline Indus., Inc., 181 N.L.R.B. 756, 74 L.R.R.M. 1654 (1970); Superior Coach Corp., 175 N.L.R.B. 200, 70 L.R.R.M. 1514 (1969). Additionally, § 10(a) of the Act confers upon the Board the statutory authority "to prevent any person from engaging in any unfair labor practice (listed in Section 8) affecting commerce" and further provides that this "power shall not be affected by any other means of adjustment ... that has been ... established by agreement."

[52] 398 U.S. 25, 27, 74 L.R.R.M. 2177, 2178 (1970), *citing* NLRB v. Jones & Laughlin Steel Corp., 331 U.S. 416, 428, 20 L.R.R.M. 2115 (1947), and United States v. W.T. Grant Co., 345 U.S. 629, 633.

[53] 74 L.R.R.M. at 2178.

[54] 652 F.2d 1055, 1072 L.R.R.M. 2781 (1st Cir. 1981).

[55] 107 L.R.R.M. at 2818.

Discontinuance of Unlawful Practices. In *Consolidated Edison Co. of N.Y., Inc. v. NLRB,*[56] the Supreme Court enforced a Board order barring an employer from spying on the union's attempts to organize its employees, even though the employer's practice had been voluntarily discontinued. The Supreme Court held that the Board possessed the authority to have its order enforced. Its brief opinion has spawned the doctrine denying mootness as a defense in these circumstances.[57] The courts accept that a Board order may have a preventative as well as a remedial purpose and, therefore, the fact that the illegal activity has been discontinued will not render moot the need for remedial action. For example, voluntary discontinuance of an unlawful no-distribution rule,[58] and discontinuance of the use of questionnaires soliciting respective employees' union membership,[59] do not render moot a Board order prohibiting such practices in the future. Nor does a substantial lapse of time after the unfair labor practices have been abandoned and enforcement is sought operate as laches against the Board.[60]

After the Taft-Hartley Amendments, the Board held that the discontinuance of unlawful activity, a defense unavailable to employers, was equally invalid as a union defense.[61] Thus, a union claim that a primary dispute has been settled,[62] or that it has abolished its illegal hiring practice,[63] does not render the controversy moot and a Board order may be properly issued and enforced. Unions, however, have had limited success, in section 10(1) injunction proceedings, in persuading district courts to refrain from issuing temporary injunctions on the grounds that the danger of

---

[56] 305 U.S. 197, 3 L.R.R.M. 646 (1938).

[57] *See, e.g.,* NLRB v. Oertel Brewing Co., 197 F.2d 59, 30 L.R.R.M. 2236 (6th Cir. 1952).

[58] United Aircraft, 67 N.L.R.B. 594, 18 L.R.R.M. 1009 (1946).

[59] NLRB v. F.H. McGraw & Co., 206 F.2d 635, 32 L.R.R.M. 2200 (6th Cir. 1953); Clark Printing Co., 146 N.L.R.B. 121, 58 L.R.R.M. 2169 (1964). *But see* National Freight, Inc., 154 N.L.R.B. 621, 633, 59 L.R.R.M. 1789, 1792 (1965), where the Board held that no remedial order was necessary since the use of such application forms was discontinued when the employer learned that it might be in violation of the Act, and where there was no evidence that the employer intended to use the form again.

[60] NLRB v. Sewell Mfg. Co., 172 F.2d 459, 23 L.R.R.M. 2323 (5th Cir. 1949); *cf.* NLRB v. Pool Mfg. Co., 339 U.S. 577, 580–582, 26 L.R.R.M. 2127, 2128 (1950).

[61] Teamsters Local 145 (Harland Dry Goods Co.), 85 N.L.R.B. 1037, 1038 n.1, 24 L.R.R.M. 1513, 1515 (1949), *enforced,* 191 F.2d 65, 28 L.R.R.M. 2450 (2d Cir. 1950).

[62] *E.g.,* NLRB v. Local 751, Carpenters (Mengel Co.), 285 F.2d 633, 638, 47 L.R.R.M. 2425, 2429 (9th Cir. 1960); Teamsters, Local 688 (Acme Paper Co.), 121 N.L.R.B. 702, 703, 42 L.R.R.M. 1416, 1418 (1958). *See also* Local 1976, Carpenters v. NLRB (San Door & Plywood Co.), 357 U.S. 93, 97 n.2, 42 L.R.R.M. 2243, 2245 (1958).

[63] Funeral Directors of Greater St. Louis, Inc., 125 N.L.R.B. 241, 243, 45 L.R.R.M. 1103, 1104 (1959).

recurrence has abated because of the union's abandonment of illegal acts.[64] On the other hand, courts have ruled that even a written assurance by the party union that it will not engage again in the unlawful conduct is not sufficient since it was Congress's intent, in framing the Act, that illegal secondary activity, once proved, obligates the court to issue a temporary injunction.[65]

Compliance with Board Orders. In most cases, compliance with a Board order by an employer [66] or a labor organization [67] does not render moot an order for enforcement purposes. In *NLRB v. Mexia Textile Mills, Inc.,*[68] the Supreme Court stated:

> [T]he employer's compliance with an order of the Board does not render the cause moot, depriving the Board of its opportunity to secure enforcement from an appropriate court. . . . A Board order imposes a continuing obligation; and the Board is entitled to have the resumption of the unfair practice barred by an enforcement decree.[69]

---

[64] Vincent v. Local 106, Operating Eng'rs, 207 F. Supp. 414, 417, 50 L.R.R.M. 2879, 2881–2882 (N.D. N.Y. 1962); *see also* Reliance Mfg. Co. v. NLRB, 125 F.2d 311, 321–322, 9 L.R.R.M. 536, 547 (7th Cir. 1941), wherein the court, relying on *Ford Motor Co.*, refused to enforce an order requiring posting of notices in all of the plants operated by the employer (the original charges claimed violations at ten of thirteen plants; subsequently the Board dismissed charges as to one plant for lack of evidence and severed as to another), holding that when a charge is filed complaining of violations at plants not included in the instant proceeding, the employer is entitled to a Board hearing. *Cf.* NLRB v. F.H. McGraw & Co., 206 F.2d 635, 641, 32 L.R.R.M. 2220, 2225 (6th Cir. 1953). *And see* NLRB v. Jack Smith Beverages, Inc., 202 F.2d 100, 102, 31 L.R.R.M. 2366, 2368 (6th Cir. 1953), *cert. denied,* 345 U.S. 995, 32 L.R.R.M. 2247 (1953). The employer had violated § 8(a)(2) by rendering unlawful assistance to an incumbent union. The order was strictly limited by the court to apply to the one plant where the violations were found to have occurred, on the rationale that to render a broad order on the basis of the *Express Publishing* doctrine would impose an unlawful restraint on the employees' freedom to choose their representatives in other plants within the system.

[65] Green v. Bangor Bldg. Trades Council, 165 F. Supp. 902, 906, 42 L.R.R.M. 2713, 2716 (N.D. Me. 1958).

[66] *E.g.,* NLRB v. Mexia Textile Mills, Inc., 339 U.S. 563, 26 L.R.R.M. 2123 (1950). *Cf.* NLRB v. Crompton-Highlands Mills, 337 U.S. 217, 225, 24 L.R.R.M. 2088, 2091 (1949); G&W Elec. Specialty Co. v. NLRB, 360 F.2d 873, 874, 62 L.R.R.M. 2085, 2086 (7th Cir. 1966).

[67] *See* NLRB v. Elevator Constructors, Local 8, 465 F.2d 794, 975–976, 81 L.R.R.M. 2091, 2093 (9th Cir. 1972); NLRB v. Teamsters, Local 364 (Light Co.), 274 F.2d 19, 25, 45 L.R.R.M. 2393, 2397 (7th Cir. 1960); NLRB v. Local 926, Operating Eng'rs, 267 F.2d 418, 420, 44 L.R.R.M. 2200, 2202 (5th Cir. 1959). *But cf.* NLRB v. Columbia Typographical Union, 470 F.2d 1274, 1275, 81 L.R.R.M. 2668 (D.C. Cir. 1972), where the court found the issue in the suit moot where the respondent union had vacated its alleged unlawful action and ended the dispute before the complaint, and considered that it was once again presented with one of those "infinitesimally small abstract grievances [that] must give way to actual and existing legal problems if the courts are to dispose of their heavy calendars," *citing* Dallas Mailers Union, Local No. 143 v. NLRB, 445 F.2d 730, 733, 76 L.R.R.M. 2247, 2249 (D.C. Cir. 1971).

[68] 339 U.S. 563, 26 L.R.R.M. (1950).

[69] *Id.* at 567, 26 L.R.R.M. at 2125.

Moreover, compliance is generally considered to be a matter reserved for Board determination, and not for appellate enforcement proceeding.[70] Thus, in seeking enforcement of a bargaining order, the Board is under no obligation to show that subsequent to the issuance of its remedial order, an employer declined to bargain at the union request.[71] Since a Board order has a preventive, as well as remedial purpose, it is clear that enforcement of the negative (cease and desist) portion of the order is best left to the discretion of the Board. To do otherwise would, in effect, give the violator "a second bite at the apple" before the Board could bring contempt proceedings against him for further violations. Some controversy has arisen concerning whether a court should enforce the affirmative sections of a Board order when the violator has already complied.

Although the Supreme Court in *Mexia Textile Mills* stated broadly that an "employer's compliance with an order of the Board does not render the cause moot," the order in that case merely enjoined the employer from further refusals to bargain in good faith—no affirmative duty was required.[72] Thereafter, the Court of Appeals for the Fifth Circuit denied enforcement to the portion of a Board order in *NLRB v. Caroline Mills, Inc.*[73] which required reinstatement of one employee, because the employee had not only already been reinstated but had been given a better job. The Fifth Circuit subsequently adopted a *pro forma* order which required an employer to do only such things as have been left undone.[74] Similarly, the Court of Appeals for the Third Circuit in *NLRB v. National*

---

[70] Solo Cup Co. v. NLRB, 332 F.2d 447, 449, 56 L.R.R.M. 2383 (4th Cir. 1984) and cases cited therein.

[71] *See, e.g.,* NLRB v. Rippee, d/b/a Pacific Multiforms Co., 339 F.2d 316, 58 L.R.R.M. 2054, 2055 (9th Cir. 1964) (rejecting employer's contention that it stands ready, willing, and able to bargain with union at any time upon the latter's request); NLRB v. Dworkin Electroplaters, 323 F.2d 934, 9 L.R.R.M. 2427 (3d Cir. 1963) (per curiam); NLRB v. Lettie Lee, 140 F.2d 243, 13 L.R.R.M. 782 (9th Cir. 1944); NLRB v. C.E. Hobbs Co., 132 F.2d 249, 11 L.R.R.M. 742 (1st Cir. 1942).

[72] NLRB v. Mexia Textile Mills, Inc., 339 U.S. 563, 566–567, 26 L.R.R.M. 2123, 2125 (1950). In a similar vein, although the courts will not enforce an order requiring an employer or labor organization to execute an agreement that has expired by its terms, they will enjoin any further bad faith bargaining. *See* NLRB v. Painters Local 1385, 334 F.2d 729, 56 L.R.R.M. 2648 (7th Cir. 1964); NLRB v. Local 19, Longshoremen (AFL-CIO), 286 F.2d 661, 47 L.R.R.M. 2420 (7th Cir. 1961), *cert. denied,* 386 U.S. 820, 84 L.R.R.M. 3110 (1961); Proctor & Gamble Mfg. Co. v. NLRB, 663 F.2d 133, 108 L.R.R.M. 2177 (4th Cir. 1981).

[73] NLRB v. Caroline Mills, Inc., 167 F.2d 212, 214, 21 L.R.R.M. 2542, 2543 (5th Cir. 1948).

[74] *See* NLRB v. Davis Lumber Co., 172 F.2d 225, 23 L.R.R.M. 2380 (5th Cir. 1949) (per curiam); *accord,* NLRB v. American Thread Co., 188 F.2d 161, 162, 28 L.R.R.M. 2004, 2005 (5th Cir. 1951) (per curiam). *But see* NLRB v. Patterson Menhaden Corp., d/b/a Gallant Man, 389 F.2d 701, 67 L.R.R.M. 2545 (5th Cir. 1968).

Biscuit Co.[75] drew a clear distinction between the "negative" and "affirmative" parts of a Board order, stating that although the decision in *Mexia Textile Mills* required it to enforce the injunction against the employer's unfair labor practices, it would not enter a decree "requiring the [employer] to do things which it has already done." On the other hand, the Court of Appeals for the Ninth Circuit has taken a *per se* approach, holding that compliance with a Board order, whether negative or affirmative, is no defense against court enforcement nor does it render the order moot.[76]

The courts have also held that an enforcement proceeding initiated by the Board is not moot when the violator has claimed that he has complied fully with the recommendation of the trial examiner.[77] In so deciding, the Ninth Circuit in *NLRB v. Oregon Worsted Co.*[78] reasoned as follows:

> The remedy of the statute . . . is in the orders of the Board . . . [while t]he recommendations of the trial examiner are not more than recommendations to the Board as to its action . . . [which t]he Board may accept or reject . . .
> While performance of all the recommendations by the examiner covering every phase of the complaint may lead the Board, in its administrative discretion, to dismiss the petition, such performance gives no right to the respondent to insist on such dismissal.[79]

Similarly, an order of the Board entered upon stipulation may not be denied enforcement on the grounds that an offender has neither violated, nor intends to violate, the order.[80]

Congress, in enacting sections 10(c) and 10(e), granted the Board discretionary authority to seek enforcement.[81] Consequently, when a violator has fully complied with the Board's order and has no

---

[75] 185 F.2d 123, 124, 27 L.R.R.M. 2086, 2087 (3d Cir. 1950).

[76] *See* NLRB v. Trimfit of Cal., Inc., 211 F.2d 206, 208, 33 L.R.R.M. 2705, 2706 (9th Cir. 1954); NLRB v. Ronney & Sons Furniture Mfg. Co., 206 F.2d 730, 32 L.R.R.M. 2635 (9th Cir. 1953), *cert. denied,* 346 U.S. 937, 33 L.R.R.M. 2394 (1954).

[77] *See* NLRB v. Hamel Leather Co., 135 F.2d 71, 72–73, 12 L.R.R.M. 655, 657 (1st Cir. 1943).

[78] 94 F.2d 671, 1A L.R.R.M. 638 (9th Cir. 1938).

[79] *Id.* at 672, 1A L.R.R.M. at 639 (emphasis added).

[80] NLRB v. Fickett-Grown Mfg. Co., 140 F.2d 883, 884–885, 13 L.R.R.M. 811, 812 (5th Cir. 1944).

[81] *See also* NLRB v. Local 926, Operating Eng'rs 267 F.2d 418, 420, 44 L.R.R.M. 2200, 2202 (5th Cir. 1959); NLRB v. Newspaper & Mail Deliverer's Union, 246 F.2d 62, 65, 40 L.R.R.M. 2295, 2297 (3d Cir. 1957). *See* NLRB v. Marland One-Way Clutch Co., 520 F.2d 856, 89 L.R.R.M. 2721, 2725 (7th Cir. 1975), where the court observed that circumstances may arise where an enforcement proceeding will become moot because a party can establish that there is no reasonable expectation that a wrong will be repeated, but then declined to speculate on the issue in order to await Board compliance proceedings.

history of serious unfair labor practices, or when there is no showing
of a concerted or implacable position in defiance of the Act, the
Board should carefully consider whether to seek enforcement. Recognizing that voluntary compliance with the Board's order, pursuant to *Mexia Textile Mills,* is no defense to enforcement, a
discriminating use of appellate litigation resources by the Board
seems desirable in order to husband the resources of the Board and
the courts. Even though enforcement has some preventive value in
that it subjects the violator to contempt proceedings should further
unlawful acts occur, in many cases compliance by the violator may
indicate an intention to abide by the Act, albeit under the duress
of a potential enforcement proceeding. The Court of Appeals for the
Sixth Circuit in *NLRB v. United States Gypsum* [82] alluded to this
problem when it refused to enforce a Board order concerning a
minor and subsequently remedied violation, and concluded that
"under the facts . . . this is a case in which a minimum amount of
investigation by the Board would have avoided pursuing the enforcement petition on the heavily congested docket of this Court." [83]
In short, when the likelihood of future violations is small and when
voluntary compliance has occurred, the Board might do well to
exercise its discretion and not continue further with enforcement
proceedings.

Changing Conditions of Operation

Employers have frequently argued that a Board order is moot if
the business is sold or dissolved. In *Southport Petroleum Co. v.
NLRB,* [84] the Supreme Court was faced with a situation in which,
three days after an employer executed a stipulation of obedience
to the Board's order, it distributed all of its assets to its four stockholders as a liquidating dividend. Two of the stockholders who received the Texas City refinery (the subject of the Board's order)
conveyed their shares to a newly organized Delaware corporation
whose remaining stockholders at no time had any interest in the
Texas corporation. Implicit in the Board's order, which had provided
for reinstatement, was a condition of ongoing operations by the
employer. The court affirmed the Board's order, but held that the
offender could present additional evidence to determine whether
there was a *bona fide* discontinuance and true change of ownership,

---

[82] 393 F.2d 883, 68 L.R.R.M. 2253 (6th Cir. 1968).
[83] *Id.* at 884, 68 L.R.R.M. at 2254.
[84] 315 U.S. 100, 103, 9 L.R.R.M. 411, 412 (1942).

thereby terminating the duty of reinstatement.[85] In so holding, the Court rejected the employer's contention that changed conditions— i.e., the liquidation and distribution of the assets—*per se* rendered moot the Board's order requiring reinstatement.[86]

Reorganization, Merger, and Retrenchment. The courts have held that the fact that a violator has been reorganized in a chapter XI bankruptcy proceeding resulting in new management and ownership,[87] has been placed in receivership,[88] or is insolvent and awaiting liquidation,[89] does not render a Board order moot. Nor does a mere change in the form of ownership bar enforcement.[90] Moreover, even *after* dissolution, state statutes that preserve the corporate entity for a period of years prevent an offender from urging his changed conditions as a defense to a Board order.[91]

The courts have not ignored the practical problems involved when an employer has ceased doing business or has become insolvent and is ordered to reinstate discriminatorily discharged employees, pay make-whole orders, or post notices. Under the principle of *Southport*

---

[85] *Id.* at 106, 9 L.R.R.M. at 413–414. *Cf.* Regal Knitwear Co. v. NLRB, 324 U.S. 9, 15 L.R.R.M. 882 (1945), wherein the Court held that a successor could be held liable for the acts of his predecessor where there was an identity of interest between the employers.

[86] *See* NLRB v. Nat'l Car Rental Systems, 672 F.2d 1191, 109 L.R.R.M. 2839 (3d Cir. 1982) and cases cited therein: NLRB v. West Coast Casket Co., 469 F.2d 871, 81 L.R.R.M. 2857, 2859 (9th Cir. 1972); NLRB v. Family Heritage Home, Inc., 491 F.2d 347, 350–351, 85 L.R.R.M. 2545, 2546–2547 (7th Cir. 1974); NLRB v. Autotronics, Inc., 434 F.2d 651, 652, 76 L.R.R.M. 2121 (8th Cir. 1970); Cap Santa Vue, Inc. v. NLRB, 424 F.2d 883, 886, 73 L.R.R.M. 2224 (D.C. Cir. 1970).

[87] NLRB v. Autotronics, Inc., 434 F.2d 651, 652, 76 L.R.R.M. 2121, 2122 (8th Cir. 1970) (per curiam).

[88] NLRB v. Coal Creek Coal Co., 204 F.2d 579, 580, 32 L.R.R.M. 2098, 2099 (10th Cir. 1953).

[89] NLRB v. Somerset Classics, Inc., 193 F.2d 613, 616, 29 L.R.R.M. 2331, 2334 (2d Cir. 1952), *cert. denied,* 344 U.S. 816, 30 L.R.R.M. 2711 (1952); NLRB v. Acme Mattress Co., 192 F.2d 524, 528, 29 L.R.R.M. 2079, 2083 (7th Cir. 1951).

[90] *See, e.g.,* De Bardeleben v. NLRB, 135 F.2d 13, 14, 12 L.R.R.M. 685, 686 (5th Cir. 1943), where the employer contended that a Board order was invalid when it was rendered after the dissolution of the corporation in question, and was not applicable to the subsequent partnership since it was based on findings of illegal practices on the part of the corporation. Pointing out that the corporation was still liable pursuant to a state saving statute and that the partnership was clearly a successor, the court held that the changing conditions did not render the order moot.
See also NLRB v. Adel Clay Prods. Co., 134 F.2d 342, 346, 12 L.R.R.M. 634, 637 (8th Cir. 1943) (partnership took over business and assets of corporation with same management and employees); NLRB v. William Tehel Bottl'g Co., 129 F.2d 250, 255, 10 L.R.R.M. 791, 796 (8th Cir. 1942) (death of partner in co-partnership where business being carried on by the survivors); *accord,* NLRB v. Colten, d/b/a Kiddie Kover Mfg. Co., 105 F.2d 179, 183, 4 L.R.R.M. 638, 641 (6th Cir. 1939).

[91] NLRB v. Weirton Steel Co., 135 F.2d 494, 498, 12 L.R.R.M. 693, 698 (3d Cir. 1943) (Delaware statute); De Bardeleben v. NLRB, 135 F.2d 13, 14, 12 L.R.R.M. 685, 686 (5th Cir. 1943) (Alabama statute); NLRB v. Timken Silent Automatic Co., 114 F.2d 449, 450, 6 L.R.R.M. 763, 764 (2d Cir. 1940) (Michigan statute).

Petroleum, enforcement of the order is granted and the case is then remanded to the Board to consider the possibilities of compliance.[92] Because an employer cannot be forced to do the impossible, during a subsequent compliance hearing a Board determination that overlooks the changed circumstances may be tested by the court if contempt proceedings are instituted.[93]

Not all courts, however, have been content to enforce Board orders and then allow subsequent Board compliance proceedings to determine whether an employer's sale of equipment and assets renders the order moot and unenforceable. Indeed, the Sixth Circuit views such an approach as "put[ting] the proverbial cart before the horse,"[94] and has required the Board itself to determine whether there exits a functioning employer against whom a court decree could be enforced before the Board comes to the court seeking enforcement.[95]

Similarly, the Fifth Circuit in *NLRB v. Highview, Inc.*[96] denied enforcement of an order that would have left the issues of rein-

---

[92] Southport Petroleum Co. v. NLRB, 315 U.S. 100, 106, 9 L.R.R.M. 411, 414 (1942); Bel Air Chateau Hosp., Inc. v. Jonas, 611 F.2d 1248, 104 L.R.R.M. 2976 (9th Cir. 1979); NLRB v. Autotronics, Inc., 434 F.2d 651, 652, 76 L.R.R.M. 2121, 2122 (8th Cir. 1970) (per curiam); NLRB v. Kostilnik, d/b/a Pac. Baking Co., 405 F.2d 733, 735, 70 L.R.R.M. 3102, 3104 (3d Cir. 1969); NLRB v. Ephraim Haspel, 228 F.2d 155, 156, 37 L.R.R.M. 2218, 2219 (2d Cir. 1955); NLRB v. Acme Mattress Co., 192 F.2d 524, 528, 29 L.R.R.M. 2079, 2083 (7th Cir. 1951).

The same rationale has been applied where the changed conditions involved the abolishment of a department within the company. Wallace Corp. v. NLRB, 159 F.2d 952, 19 L.R.R.M. 2311, 2314, 2315 (4th Cir. 1947).

[93] NLRB v. West Coast Casket Co., 469 F.2d 871, 873, 81 L.R.R.M. 2857, 2859 (9th Cir. 1972); NLRB v. Somerset Classics, Inc., 193 F.2d 613, 616, 29 L.R.R.M. 2331, 2334 (2d Cir. 1952), *cert. denied,* 344 U.S. 816, 30 L.R.R.M. 2711 (1952); *cf.* NLRB v. New York Merchandise Co., 134 F.2d 949, 12 L.R.R.M. 578 (2d Cir. 1943). *See also* NLRB v. Caroline Mills, Inc., 167 F.2d 212, 214, 21 L.R.R.M. 2542, 2543 (5th Cir. 1948), where the court, pointing out that it would not hold the employer in contempt for failing to reinstate an employee when the company had ceased doing business, stated that, "the Board cannot . . . require that an employer stay in business merely in order to give employment."

But see American Needle & Novelty Co., 206 N.L.R.B. 534, 84 L.R.R.M. 1526 (1973), in which the owner of a three-plant operation, who had transferred production work from its Chicago plant to one of its other plants, was ordered to restore the *status quo ante* by resuming production activities at the Chicago facilities. The Board felt that no undue hardship was involved since the Chicago plant was still in existence, under the same management, and continued to perform much the same functions, with the exception of production, that it had performed prior to the transfer. *See also* NLRB v. Jackson Farmers, 457 F.2d 516, 79 L.R.R.M. 2909 (10th Cir. 1972).

[94] NLRB v. Schnell Tool & Die Corp., 359 F.2d 39, 62 L.R.R.M. 2091, 2094 (6th Cir. 1966).

[95] NLRB v. Armitage Sand & Gravel, Inc., 495 F.2d 759, 86 L.R.R.M. 2245, 2246 (6th Cir. 1974); NLRB v. Schnell Tool & Die Corp., 359 F.2d 39, 62 L.R.R.M. 2091 (6th Cir. 1966).

[96] 590 F.2d 174, 100 L.R.R.M. 2829 (5th Cir. 1979), *modified because of changed facts,* 595 F.2d 339, 101 L.R.R.M. 1387.

statement and backpay to compliance proceedings, and instead remanded the case to the Board for a determination of the effect of the changed conditions. The County Commissions (exempt from Board jurisdiction) had decided to dissolve and take over operation of the privately-run home from the original employer, Highview. The Fifth Circuit recognized that in some circumstances compliance was the procedure to be followed,[97] but remanded this case because of solicitude for the county and intergovernmental relations, and fear of a contempt order, which would be the penalty in future litigation arising after the compliance stage.

The following instances of "changed circumstances" have not been found to bar enforcement: payment of backpay to the estate of a discriminatorily discharged employee who had died;[98] a turnover in Board membership that had resulted in an alleged change of policy;[99] a complete turnover of the supervisory personnel who had engaged in the unlawful conduct;[100] and the completion of a construction project against which the union had engaged in illegal secondary activities.[101] In like fashion, the holding of a rerun election and the certification of a union did not moot the enforcement of a Board order predicated on findings that the employer engaged in unfair labor practices during the first election campaign.[102]

On the other hand, changed circumstances that have led circuit courts to deny enforcement of affirmative portions of a Board order include: an order of reinstatement of three building engineers to jobs which were no longer available as a result of automation and where no substantial equivalent positions existed in the bargaining

---

[97] NLRB v. Lamar Creamery Co., 246 F.2d 8, 10, 40 L.R.R.M. 2275 (5th Cir. 1957); NLRB v. Cordele NFGR Co., 172 F.2d 225, 226, 23 L.R.R.M. 2380 (5th Cir. 1949); NLRB v. West Coast Casket Co., 469 F.2d 871, 873, 81 L.R.R.M. 2857 (9th Cir. 1972); NLRB v. Autotronics, Inc., 434 F.2d 651, 652, 76 L.R.R.M. 2121 (8th Cir. 1970).

[98] NLRB v. Atlantic Towing Co., 179 F.2d 497, 498, 25 L.R.R.M. 2313, 2314 (5th Cir. 1950), *judgment set aside on other grounds*, 180 F.2d 726, 25 L.R.R.M. 2480 (5th Cir. 1950) (backpay made to employee's estate). *But cf.* Loveman, Joseph & Loeb v. NLRB, 146 F.2d 769, 771, 15 L.R.R.M. 858, 860 (5th Cir. 1945) (order for reinstatement of employee denied where employee was dead). *See also* Estate of Edward Bryan Moritz d/b/a E. B. Moritz Foundry, 220 N.L.R.B. 1247, 90 L.R.R.M. 1540 (1975) (estate responsible for the unfair labor practices of deceased employer).

[99] NLRB v. Trimfit of Cal., Inc., 211 F.2d 206, 210, 33 L.R.R.M. 2705, 2707–2708 (9th Cir. 1954).

[100] Dixie Highway Express, Inc., 153 N.L.R.B. 1224 n.2, 59 L.R.R.M. 1624, 1626 (1965).

[101] NLRB v. Local 74, Carpenters (Watson's Specialty Store), 341 U.S. 707, 715, 28 L.R.R.M. 2121, 2124 (1951).

[102] NLRB v. Raytheon, 398 U.S. 25, 27, 74 L.R.R.M. 2177, 2178 (1970); NLRB v. Metalab-Labcraft (Div. Metalab Equip. Co.), 367 F.2d 471, 63 L.R.R.M. 2321, 2322 (4th Cir. 1966); NLRB v. Marsh Supermkts., Inc., 327 F.2d 109, 55 L.R.R.M. 2017 (7th Cir. 1963), *cert. denied* 377 U.S. 944, 56 L.R.R.M. 2288 (1964); NLRB v. Clark Bros. Co., 163 F.2d 373, 20 L.R.R.M. 2436 (2d Cir. 1947).

unit;[103] a Board order of reinstatement of illegally terminated employees to jobs in an operation that had lawfully closed;[104] and a Board order to cease and desist from refusing to sign a collective bargaining agreement, where the agreement had terminated by its own terms.[105] In *NLRB v. Fort Vancouver Plywood Co.*,[106] the Ninth Circuit, although holding that the Board's finding of unfair labor practices was supported by substantial evidence, denied enforcement of an order against a worker-owned corporation to reinstate seventy-two nonshareholder employees, and remanded the case to the Board for a determination of whether changed circumstances resulted in there being no employment positions for the seventy-two employees. The Board found that with the advent of the union organizing campaign the board of directors determined to fire all seventy-two nonshareholder employees as a result of anti-union sentiments, and refused thereafter to recognize the nonshareholder's union. The court refused to enforce the remedial order requiring the rehiring of all seventy-two nonshareholder employees. The employer contended that eventually it would have eliminated or drastically reduced the nonshareholder workforce, regardless of the question of unionization. The court agreed, stating:

> [T]he Board has a duty to consider how many employees, if any, the company would have continued but for the unfair labor practices, and for how long. The record indicates that ... the board in review gave no consideration to whether some or all of the temporary employees eventually would have lost their jobs for acceptable business reasons.[107]

The court rejected the Board's argument that the exact terms of reinstatement are properly left for subsequent determination during the compliance proceedings and do not effect the order's enforceability. The court noted that the order required the reinstatement not just of those among the nonshareholders for whom work was available, but of exactly seventy-two discharged workers. Because of its specificity, the Board order denied "the company an opportunity to show that fewer than 72 jobs would have been available regardless of its unfair labor practice."[108]

---

[103] NLRB v. Doug Neal Mgt. Co., 620 F.2d 1133, 104 L.R.R.M. 2045 (6th Cir. 1980).

[104] NLRB v. Townhouse T.V. & Appliances, Inc., 531 F.2d 826, 91 L.R.R.M. 2636 (7th Cir. 1976).

[105] Proctor & Gamble Mfg. Co. v. NLRB, 663 F.2d 133, 108 L.R.R.M. 2177 (4th Cir. 1981).

[106] 604 F.2d 596, 102 L.R.R.M. 2232 (9th Cir. 1979), *cert. denied*, 445 U.S. 915, 103 L.R.R.M. 2628 (1980).

[107] 604 F.2d at 602.

[108] *Id.* at 603.

In *NLRB v. Grace Co.*,[109] the employer contested a Board order directing it to bargain with the union and post notices because it had permanently closed the plant in question. Objecting to being called upon to "rubber stamp" the Board's order when the facts showed that it was inoperative and impossible to enforce, the Eighth Circuit denied enforcement and remanded the case to the Board to determine whether the plant had been permanently closed.[110] The court distinguished *Grace* from *Southport* and its progeny on the basis that *Grace* did not involve an order that was partially enforceable, nor did it involve a successor employer who could be bound by the Board's order.[111]

The Board itself has recognized that in a situation in which the workforce, during the backpay period, has declined to a point where the employees would have been laid off if they had not been illegally terminated, reinstatement will not be ordered.[112]

Illegal Closing. The Board's normal remedy for violations involving an illegal closing of an operation by an employer is to order it to restore the *status quo ante* unless it can establish that the normal remedy "would endanger its continued viability." [113] These cases usually involve a company that operated a manufacturing plant, had closed down and contracted out a division, department, or production line to another location, but still had a functioning operation at the location involved. In a situation where a complete plant operation has been closed down, the Board normally will not order reopening if to do so would cause an undue burden upon the

---

[109] 184 F.2d 126, 26 L.R.R.M. 2536 (8th Cir. 1950).

[110] *Id.* at 131, 26 L.R.R.M. at 2540. The court also refused to consider the Board's petition for enforcement as withdrawn without prejudice upon the N.L.R.B.'s report that the employer's plant had indeed closed. NLRB v. Grace Co., 189 F.2d 258, 28 L.R.R.M. 2320 (8th Cir. 1951).

Cf. NLRB v. U.S. Trailer Mfg. Co., 184 F.2d 521, 523–524, 26 L.R.R.M. 2658, 2660 (8th Cir. 1950), wherein the Eighth Circuit distinguished *Grace* from the instant case on the grounds that the rights of employees to reimbursement for lost wages were involved.

[111] NLRB v. Grace Co., 184 F.2d 126, 131, 26 L.R.R.M. 2536, 2540. *See also* NLRB v. Reynolds Corp., 155 F.2d 679, 681–682, 18 L.R.R.M. 2087, 2089 (5th Cir. 1946) (order by Board directing employer to cease and desist interfering with organizational and bargaining rights of its employees denied enforcement where plant in question was only operated by Reynolds as a wartime munitions manufacturer and was turned over to Navy at end of war); Cambridge Dairy Inc., 404 F.2d 866, 70 L.R.R.M. 2218, 2219 (10th Cir. 1968) (order held unwarranted since employer had completely closed his business).

[112] Castleman & Bates, 228 N.L.R.B. 1504, 96 L.R.R.M. 1104 (1977).

[113] *See* Wood Indus. Inc. and its wholly owned subsidiary, BNA Transp., Inc., 248 N.L.R.B. 597, 103 L.R.R.M. 1540 (1980); Lion Uniform, Janesville Apparel Div., 247 N.L.R.B. 992, 103 L.R.R.M. 1264 (1980).

employer. In *Great Chinese American Sewing Co.*,[114] the employer
operated several plants under different companies, and for an eight-
month period had been suffering substantial economic losses in the
operation of the GCA plant and had been urged by its accountant
to close that operation. The Board found, however, that the employer
did not decide to close the plant until the advent of the union, and
that the closure and the termination of the employees violated
section 8(a)(3) of the Act. The majority held that "compliance with
such order under the facts of this case would likely be unduly
burdensome,"[115] and declined to order the reopening of the plant.
However, the Board did order backpay until substantial employment had been obtained by the employees elsewhere, and the back-
pay order was held appropriate under the circumstances and
enforced by the circuit court.

Since *Great Chinese American Sewing Co.*, the Board in two cases
has ordered the reopening of an entire manufacturing operation,
not merely part of an otherwise existing operation.[116] But in both
cases, the employer had failed to file an answer to the complaint,
so no hearing was held and no evidence was introduced to indicate
that the reopening would have been unduly burdensome.

On the other hand, in a case involving the illegal closing of a
plant of a subsidiary of a larger parent company, the court enforced
a Board order and, while not requiring reopening of the illegally
shut plant, ordered the employer to offer their illegally terminated
employees employment at the other employer-controlled facility in
the area of the closed plant.[117] In this case, the employer had unlawfully closed its plant following a strike by the union over the
employer's refusal to bargain. No backpay was ordered because the
strikers had not made unconditional offers to return to work within
a reasonable time following the end of the strike. However, the
court sustained the Board in its decision directing the employer to
bargain with respect to the closing of the plant; to bargain with the
union concerning the manner, terms, and conditions of employment
at subsidiary employers' facilities in the area; to offer reinstatement
at such facilities to the employees; and to pay moving expenses to
those who accept employment at these other facilities.

---

[114] 227 N.L.R.B. 1670, 95 L.R.R.M. 1594; *enforced,* Great Chinese American Sewing
Co. v. NLRB, 578 F.2d 251, 99 L.R.R.M. 2347 (9th Cir. 1977).

[115] *Id.*

[116] Handi-Bag Co., 267 N.L.R.B. 221, 114 L.R.R.M. 1056 (1983); and APD Transport
Corp., and its alter ego, National Book Consolidators, Inc., 253 N.L.R.B. 468, 105
L.R.R.M. 1675 (1980).

[117] Royal Typewriter Co. v. NLRB, 533 F.2d 1030, 92 L.R.R.M. 2013 (8th Cir. 1976),
enforcing Royal Typewriter Co., 209 N.L.R.B. 1006 (1974).

CHAPTER VI

Obligations of the Successor Employer

A change in corporate structure or ownership, liquidation of a business, or distribution of its assets ordinarily will not render moot a Board order, and that order will stand against a new employer who is "merely a disguised continuance of the old employer."[1] Under our enterprise system there are, of course, a large number of bona fide instances in which one corporation will either purchase, acquire, or merge with another. Often the employer who relinquishes his business (the predecessor) will have an established bargaining relationship or collective bargaining agreement with a union which represents his employees. When such a relationship exists, questions may arise concerning the responsibility of the acquiring employer (the successor) to recognize or bargain with the union and to remedy unfair labor practices committed by the predecessor.

THE BURNS INTERNATIONAL STANDARDS

The Supreme Court in *NLRB v. Burns International Security System, Inc.*[2] held that, where the bargaining unit remains unchanged and a majority of the employees hired by the new employer are represented by the union which represented those of the former employer, the successor employer must bargain with the incumbent union. Burns and the Wackenhut Corporation, both engaged in the business of providing security services, bid against each other to provide security service for Lockheed Aircraft Corporation under a new contract replacing a prior one under which Wackenhut had provided these services. Burns won the bid and decided to employ twenty-seven of the forty-two guards that had been employed by Wackenhut and represented by a union under a collective bargaining agreement. The union demanded that Burns recognize it and honor its collective agreement; when Burns refused, it filed unfair labor practice charges. The Board ordered Burns to bargain with

---

[1] Southport Petroleum Co. v. NLRB, 315 U.S. 100, 106, 9 L.R.R.M. 411, 414 (1942). *See also* NLRB v. Family Heritage Home, Inc., 491 F.2d 347, 85 L.R.R.M. 2545, 2546–2547 (7th Cir. 1974), and cases cited therein.
[2] 406 U.S. 272, 280–281, 80 L.R.R.M. 2225 (1972).

the union and to honor the agreement.[3] The Supreme Court reaffirmed the view that, absent unusual circumstances, a mere change in ownership does not relieve the new employer from bargaining where the unit remains unchanged and a majority of the employees hired are represented by the incumbent union. However, even though a successor like Burns was bound to bargain with the union, the Supreme Court reversed the Board and held it was not bound to honor the predecessor's collective bargaining agreement, to which it had not agreed.[4] This is subject to the exception that the successor may be required to arbitrate under the predecessor's arbitration agreement if there is a substantial continuity of identity in the business enterprise and workforce[5] and the new employer expressly or implicitly assumes the arbitration agreement.[6] For example, a successor will be obliged to honor the predecessor's agreement if it is an "alter ego." The Board test is that an "alter ego" exists where the predecessor and successor enterprises have "substantially identical management, business purposes, operation, equipment, customers, and supervision, as well as ownership."[7] The courts have

---

[3] Burns Int'l Detective Agency, 182 N.L.R.B. 348, 74 L.R.R.M. 1098 (1970). The Board's holding that Burns had to honor the predecessor's agreement, itself subsequently reversed by the Supreme Court, reversed prior cases. The Board relied on Wiley & Sons v. Livingston, 376 U.S. 543, 55 L.R.R.M. 2769 (1969), holding that the duty to arbitrate may survive a merger where there was a substantial continuity of identity in the business enterprise before and after the change of ownership.

[4] 406 U.S. at 281–291, 80 L.R.R.M. at 2228–2232. This view followed from the Court's decision in H.K. Porter, Inc. v. NLRB, 397 U.S. 99, 73 L.R.R.M. 2561 (1970) holding that § 8(d) of the Act precludes the Board from ordering a party to agree to any substantive contractual provision. See discussion *supra*, at Chapter II, text accompanying and following n.18.

[5] While the threshold criterion to successorship after *Burns* is the majority in the continuing workforce, a finding of successorship may be negated if there are substantial changes in the business, in cases, for example, where there is a long hiatus in the resumption of operations [*e.g.*, Spencer Foods, Inc. 268 N.L.R.B. 1483, 115 L.R.R.M. 1251 (1984)], a different location, or differences in customers, products, or markets. *See e.g.*, Radiant Fashions, Inc., 202 N.L.R.B. 938, 82 L.R.R.M. 1742 (1973); Norton Precision, Inc., 199 N.L.R.B. 1003, 81 L.R.R.M. 1383 (1972); Galis Equip. Co., 194 N.L.R.B. 799, L.R.R.M. 1073 (1972).

[6] Howard Johnson Co. v. Detroit Local Joint Exec. Bd., Hotel and Rest. Employees and Bartenders Int'l Union, AFL-CIO, 417 U.S. 249, 86 L.R.R.M. 2449 (1974); John Wiley & Sons v. Livingston, 376 U.S. 543, 55 L.R.R.M. 2769 (1964); Teamsters, Local 249 v. Bill's Trucking, Inc., 493 F.2d 956, 85 L.R.R.M. 2713 (3d Cir. 1974); Boeing Company v. Int'l Ass'n of Machinists and Aerospace Workers, AFL-CIO, 504 F.2d 307, 87 L.R.R.M. 2865 (5th Cir. 1974).

[7] Crawford Door Sales Co., Inc., 226 N.L.R.B. 1144, 94 L.R.R.M. 1393 (1976). *Cf.*, Howard Johnson Co., 417 U.S. at 259 n.5, where the Supreme Court noted that an "alter ego" represents "a mere technical change in the structure or identity of the employing entity, frequently to avoid the effect of the labor laws, without any change in its ownership or management. In these circumstances the courts have had little difficulty holding that the successor is in reality the same employer and is subject to the legal and contractual obligations of the predecessor."

accepted these standards; indeed, they require the Board to meet them. In *Meat Cutters, Local 567 v. NLRB,*[8] the District of Columbia Court of Appeals overruled the Board's alter ego finding in an asset purchase case where the "identity of ownership" element was missing. Prior to the sale the store manager was the minority stockholder, owning 18 percent of its stock. After the sale he continued as stock manager and owned 30 percent of the new company. Since he had held only an 18 percent interest in the predecessor, the court found that there was a substantial change in ownership, and that the sale was not a paper transaction without impact upon ownership or operation. Consequently, the successor was not an alter ego, and therefore not bound to the collective bargaining agreement of the predecessor.

The Board rendered an interesting decision in *Spencer Foods, Inc.,*[9] a case involving new ownership of the same corporation. In October 1977, the corporation lawfully closed down one of its plants, which had a union, and the plant remained closed for sixteen months. The corporation eventually sold its stock, but not its assets. The corporation, under new ownership and management, reopened the plant sixteen months later. Approximately one-third of its employees were former unit members. The Board held that the corporation was not a successor and not obligated to bargain with the union as the new business was not a substantial continuation of the old business because of changes in the corporate structure, operations, and customers, and because of the sixteen-month hiatus. On the other hand, the Board did find that the corporation had committed an unfair labor practice in refusing to hire many of the former employees. The Board, however, refused to use this finding to establish a constructive majority which would have required a bargaining relationship. To this extent the decision appears to be in conflict with prior Board decisions which had been enforced by the Ninth Circuit Court of Appeals.[10]

THE PERMA VINYL *DOCTRINE*

Once successorship is established under the *Burns* standards, the extent of the successor's obligation to remedy unfair labor practices committed by the predecessor has been formulated in the now well-

---

[8] 663 F.2d 223, 106 L.R.R.M. 2187 (D.C. Cir. 1980).
[9] 268 N.L.R.B. 1483, 115 L.R.R.M. 1251 (1984).
[10] Kalman v. NLRB, 640 F.2d 1094, 107 L.R.R.M. 2011 (9th Cir. 1981); *and* NLRB v. Nevis Indus., 647 F.2d 905, 107 L.R.R.M. 2890 (9th Cir. 1981).

established *Perma Vinyl*[11] doctrine. Under this doctrine, the successor is required to remedy the predecessor's unfair labor practices if it acquires and operates the business in an essentially unchanged form and under circumstances which charge it with notice of the unfair labor practice. The Board also held that the bona fide purchaser is entitled to a hearing to determine whether it is a successor responsible for the predecessor's unfair labor practices. The successor also is afforded a hearing concerning the enforcement of any order issued against him.[12]

The Board's *Perma Vinyl* decision was enforced by the Fifth Circuit in *United States Pipe and Foundry Co. v. NLRB*,[13] where the court pointed out that United States Pipe had purchased Perma Vinyl with notice of the unfair labor practice proceedings but continued the same operation with regard to the jobs in question. The court saw this as a "sufficient basis for requiring [U.S. Pipe] to offer reinstatement to the employees on the successorship theory."[14]

The Supreme Court adopted *Perma Vinyl* in *Golden State Bottling Co. v. NLRB*,[15] holding that the bona fide purchaser of a business,

---

[11] Perma Vinyl Corp., 164 N.L.R.B. 968, 65 L.R.R.M. 1168 (1967). The Board relied on its remedial authority to frame such orders "as will effectuate the policies of the Act and achieve the objectives of 'national labor policy.' " 164 N.L.R.B. at 969, 65 L.R.R.M. at 1169.

[12] *Id.* If the new employer is not deemed a successor, there is no duty to remedy the unfair labor practices of the former employer. Bellingham Frozen Foods, Inc. v. NLRB, 626 F.2d 674, 105 L.R.R.M. 2404 (9th Cir. 1980) *enforcing in part* 237 N.L.R.B. 1450, 99 L.R.R.M. 1270 (1978).

[13] 398 F.2d 544, 68 L.R.R.M. 2913 (5th Cir. 1968).

[14] *Id.* at 548, 68 L.R.R.M. at 2915. *But see* Wheeler (Northern Virginia Sun, Inc.) v. NLRB, 382 F.2d 172, 65 L.R.R.M. 2921 (D.C. Cir. 1967), where the court held that *Perma Vinyl* did not require the Board to order reinstatement by a second successor employer where that employer did not assume the obligations of the prior employers' unfair labor practices. The two prior employers had settled differences concerning back pay with the employees, and there was no privity between the original employer and the second successor. The validity of *Wheeler* is questionable, however, in light of the rationale of the Supreme Court in *Golden State Bottling Co. (see infra*, note 15). *See also* Ramada Inns, Inc., 171 N.L.R.B. 1060, 68 L.R.R.M. 1209, 1212 (1968) (*Perma Vinyl* not applicable where the successor was a remote purchaser with no knowledge of the unfair labor practices and there was substantial turnover in the employee complement).

[15] 414 U.S. 168, 84 L.R.R.M. 2839 (1973). Early in the administration of the Act, the Board adopted a remedial formula which ordered not only a particular respondent, but also its officers, agents, successors and assigns, to cease and desist from the unfair labor practices found by the Board. The wording of the formula was approved by the Supreme Court in Regal Knitwear Co. v. NLRB, 324 U.S. 9, 15 L.R.R.M. 882 (1945). The Court, however, by no means held that such language would have broad application to successor employers; rather, the Court indicated that it was not deciding under what circumstances any kind of successor or assign would be liable for a violation of a Board order. 324 U.S. at 15, 15 L.R.R.M. at 882. The Court did indicate that the order would bind those who operate as "merely a disguised continuance of the old employer" and "those to whom the business may have been

who acquires and continues the business with knowledge that his predecessor has committed an unfair labor practice in the discharge of an employee, may be ordered to reinstate the employee with back pay. The Court explained that:

> ... [w]hen a new employer ... has acquired substantial assets of its predecessor and continued, without interruption or substantial change, the predecessor's business operations, those employees who have been retained will understandably view their job situations as essentially unaltered. Under these circumstances, the employees may well perceive the successor's failure to remedy the predecessor employer's labor practices arising out of an unlawful discharge as a continuation of the predecessor's labor policies. To the extent that the employees' legitimate expectation is that the unfair labor practices will be remedied, a successor's failure to do so may result in labor unrest as the employees engage in collective activity to force remedial action. Similarly, if the employees identify the new employer's labor policies with those of the predecessor but do not take collective action, the successor may benefit from the unfair labor practices. Moreover, the Board's experience may reasonably lead it to believe that employers intent on suppressing union activity may select for discharge those employees most actively engaged in union affairs, so that a failure to reinstate may result in a leadership vacuum in the bargaining unit. Cf. Phelps Dodge Corp. v. NLRB, 313 U.S. 177, 193, [8 L.R.R.M. 439] (1941). Further, unlike Burns, where an important labor policy opposed saddling the successor employer with the obligations of the collective-bargaining agreement, there is no underlying congressional policy here militating against the imposition of liability.[16]

Section 10(c)'s broad grant of discretion to the Board to fashion relief that would effectuate the policies of the Act was found not to limit the Board's remedial powers to the "actual perpetrator of any unfair labor practice."[17]

---

transferred whether as a means of evading the judgment or *for other reasons.*" 324 U.S. at 14, 15 L.R.R.M. at 884, *citing from* Southport Petroleum Co. v. NLRB, 315 U.S. 100, 106, 9 L.R.R.M. 411 (1942).

[16] 414 U.S. at 184–185, 84 L.R.R.M. at 2845.

[17] 414 U.S. at 176, 180, 84 L.R.R.M. at 2842 and 2844. Simply because a predecessor has sold his business does not mean that he then may move to be dismissed from further proceedings; there may be "tag ends" to the proceeding that would make advisable his continuance as a party, for the order against the original employer may still prove to be the indispensable basis for imposing liability against successors and assigns. *See* Cap Santa Vue, Inc. v. NLRB, 424 F.2d 883, 73 L.R.R.M. 2224, 2226 (D.C. Cir. 1970). The *Perma Vinyl* decision may not be used by the Board as a justification for adding the dollar volume both of the predecessor and successor in order to satisfy the Board's $500,000 minimum for asserting jurisdiction. Thus, for the Board to assert jurisdiction over either enterprise, each must, on its own, satisfy these dollar volume standards. *See* Martin J. Baker, d/b/a Galaxy Theater, 210 N.L.R.B. No. 118, slip op. p. 5 & n.8, 86 L.R.R.M. 1191 (1974).

It is apparent, therefore, that under *Perma Vinyl* and *Golden State,* a successor employer who knows of pending unfair labor practice charges against the predecessor has a fairly broad responsibility to remedy those violations of the Act. In both decisions, the successor employers were required to reinstate unlawfully discharged employees and found to be jointly and severally liable for any back pay owed to the discriminatees.[18] Both the predecessor and successor may be held responsible for back pay; this does not mean, however, that their back-pay liabilities will necessarily cover the same time periods. In *Southeastern Envelope Co.,*[19] the predecessor was held responsible for back pay until the discriminatees had secured substantially equivalent employment, while the successor's back-pay liability was limited to the period from the date of discrimination until the date of purchase of the enterprise.

FURTHER CONDITIONS PERTAINING TO SUCCESSOR LIABILITY

The Board has held that where the successor does not have substantially the same workforce as the predecessor, the successor will not be required to offer full and immediate reinstatement to the discriminatees. Rather, the successor is obligated merely to place the former employees on a preferential hiring list and offer them reemployment as jobs become available, and before other employees are hired for such work.[20] Additionally, where a successor employer unlawfully refused to bargain with the union after hiring a workforce of which a majority had been the predecessor's employees, the Board held that employees who were engaged in an economic strike against the predecessor did not become unfair labor practice strikers entitled to reinstatement. The Board reasoned that the strikers who were not rehired never became the successor's employees, and that there was no evidence that any of these employees ever tendered an unconditional offer to return to work.[21] On the other hand, the

---

[18] *See also* Riley Aeronautics Corp., 178 N.L.R.B. 495, 499, 74 L.R.R.M. 1543 (1969).

[19] 206 N.L.R.B. 933, 934, 84 L.R.R.M. 1577 (1973).

[20] *Id.* The Ninth Circuit agreed with the Board in one instance that the hiring of 90 out of 125 of the predecessor's employees would not support a finding that the successor had hired "substantially" or "essentially" the same workforce. In those circumstances, both the Board and court agreed that it would be inappropriate to order the successor to provide back pay or offer reinstatement to the discriminatees. *See* Thomas Engine Corp., d/b/a Tomadur, Inc., 179 N.L.R.B. 1029 & n.4, 73 L.R.R.M. 1289 (1969), *enforced sub nom.* UAW v. NLRB, 442 F.2d 1180, 77 L.R.R.M. 2401, 2403 (9th Cir. 1971).

[21] United Maintenance & Mfg. Co., 214 N.L.R.B. 529, 87 L.R.R.M. 1469, 1476–1477 (1974).

Board has required full reinstatement of employees under *Perma Vinyl* over the objection of a successor who argued that, since it had contractually agreed to assume all of its predecessor's financial obligations for section 8(a)(3) violations, this contract should be construed to limit his remedial obligations to monetary damages, and exclude the reinstatement remedy.[22]

In addition to offering reinstatement and back-pay reimbursements, the successor may also be required to post a notice to employees stating that the successor will undertake the remedies previously prescribed.[23] As with back pay and reinstatement, however, the cease and desist and notice requirements placed upon a successor employer may differ significantly from those which would have been required of the prior owner. Thus, shortly after the *Perma Vinyl* decision, the Board in *Tomadur*[24] deleted from a notice language which would have required the successor to promise the employees that it would cease and desist from the unfair labor practices committed by his predecessor. Subsequently, in *Golden State* the Supreme Court noted that, as in *Tomadur,* there was no requirement that the bona fide purchaser cease and desist from the illegal activity found.[25] Justice Brennan noted that this approach seemed consistent with the fact that the successor's remedial obligations arise out of another employer's unfair labor practices and not its own. Accordingly, the Board will not enter a cease and desist order against the successor employer.[26]

The Board has also held that a successor employer, who succeeds to the assets free and clear of all liens, claims, and encumbrances through bankruptcy purchase is still responsible for back-pay obligations of the predecessor.[27] Further, the Second Circuit in *NLRB v. Hot Bagels and Donuts*[28] enforced a Board order against a successor formed after the bank had foreclosed on a loan to the predecessor, and which leased back all of the company's equipment in an arrangement with the bank. The court sustained the Board's

---

[22] Emerson Elec. Co., 176 N.L.R.B. 744, 71 L.R.R.M. 1297, 1298 (1969).

[23] *See, e.g.,* Ocomo Foods Co., 186 N.L.R.B. 697, 702, 75 L.R.R.M. 1537 (1970).

[24] Thomas Engine Corp., d/b/a Tomadur, Inc., 179 N.L.R.B. 1029, 73 L.R.R.M. 1289 & n.4 (1969), *enforced sub nom.* UAW v. NLRB, 442 F.2d 1180, 77 L.R.R.M. 2401, 2403 (9th Cir. 1971). The Board held that it was significant that the successor's obligation in *Perma Vinyl* was restricted to an affirmative reinstatement order and there was no requirement that he cease and desist from either the § 8(a)(1) or the § 8(a)(3) violations of the predecessor. 77 L.R.R.M. at 2402–2403.

[25] *See* Golden State Bottling Co. v. NLRB, 414 U.S. at n.4, 84 L.R.R.M. at 2842–2843 n.4.

[26] *See, e.g.,* NLRB v. East Side Shopper, Inc., 498 F.2d 1334, 86 L.R.R.M. 2817, 2818 n.1 (6th Cir. 1974); Southeastern Envelope Co., 206 N.L.R.B. at 934.

[27] International Technical Prods., 249 N.L.R.B. 1301, 104 L.R.R.M. 1294 (1980).

[28] 622 F.2d 1113, 104 L.R.R.M. 2963 (2d Cir. 1980).

finding that the successor, after only a very short hiatus, operated with virtually the same line of goods in the same location and with the same equipment, with a high percentage of the same employees and with basically the same ownership, as the original company.

UNIONS AS SUCCESSOR EMPLOYERS

It is also well established (although there have been few such cases before the Board or the courts) that a labor union can be an alter ego or successor and, consequently, responsible for its predecessor labor organization's unfair labor practices. However, a labor union will not be considered a successor and therefore liable for back pay owed to employees by reason of an unfair labor practice committed by the predecessor, even though there is some connection in statements being made by individuals related to the successor union, where the statements were not clear positions of officers or paid employees of the successor union; where there was no evidence that the two unions did, in fact, merge; where many of the officers are, in fact, different; and where there is evidence that the predecessor still, in fact, exists.[29]

In *NLRB v. Lathers, Local 46*,[30] the Second Circuit sustained the Board's holding that the international union was jointly liable with the local union for unlawful disciplinary action taken against three members, but denied enforcement of the Board's order that the successor international union was secondarily liable. While the president of the original international was employed by the successor, the court ruled two-to-one that the Board could not impute his knowledge of the unlawful conduct to the successor international under common-law agency principles.

---

[29] Security Personnel Union, 267 N.L.R.B. 974, 114 L.R.R.M. 1161 (1983).
[30] __ F.2d __, __ L.R.R.M. __ (2d Cir. 1984).

CHAPTER VII

Notification: Disseminating the Board's Order Among Employees

The usual Board remedy in an unfair labor practice case generally includes an affirmative requirement covering the posting of notices, in addition to the negative, or cease and desist, provisions. Compliance with the affirmative order usually requires that, for a period of sixty days, the respondent employer or union will post, and maintain in a conspicuous location, a signed notice that sets forth the terms and conditions of the cease and desist order.[1] In the case of unfair labor practices committed by a union, copies of the order, signed by appropriate union officials, must be furnished to the Board's regional director, who will transmit the notice to the employer for posting if the employer so desires.[2]

At the very least, the notice is a useful means of informing employees that Board action has been taken to remedy activities found to be in violation of employees' rights under the Act.[3] In many cases, however, the notice requirement is especially important because it may be the only affirmative action which the respondent is directed to undertake.[4]

The notice must be both accessible and understandable. Thus, an employer who claimed literal compliance with an order directing him to post notices in his plant did not fulfill his obligations when the posting occurred during a time period in which his employees were on strike and, therefore, unable to read the notice.[5] In some instances, the Board has ruled that because a plant employs a bilingual workforce, the posted notice must be both in English and

---

[1] NLRB FIELD MANUAL, § 10752.1; see NLRB v. Express Publishing Co., 312 U.S. 426, 8 L.R.R.M. 415 (1941), wherein the Supreme Court upheld the power of the Board to require posting of its orders.

[2] Von's Grocery Co., 91 N.L.R.B. 504, 26 L.R.R.M. 1528 (1950).

[3] Cf. NLRB v. Douglas & Lomason Co., 443 F.2d 291, 295, 77 L.R.R.M. 2449, 2451 (8th Cir. 1971).

[4] See, e.g., National Maritime Union, 78 N.L.R.B. 971, 22 L.R.R.M. 1289 (1948).

[5] American Newspapers, Inc., 22 N.L.R.B. 899, 6 L.R.R.M. 251 (1940).

the appropriate second language.[6] Also, the courts of appeals have cautioned the Board against the use of superfluous or ambiguous language,[7] or wording that "smacks" of punitive action, in the sense that innuendos in the notice suggest that the respondent is basically untrustworthy and reliable only under duress.[8]

SPECIAL NOTIFICATION CONDITIONS

Generally, the provisions covering notification simply stipulate that the notice be posted in conspicuous places, such as bulletin boards, time clocks, department entrances, meeting hall entrances, or dues payment windows. Under certain circumstances, however, the Board has fashioned special notification conditions, which conform to the requirement that the remedy bear some rational relationship to the type of industry involved and to the unfair labor practice which has been committed.

In *Proctor & Gamble Mfg. Co. v. NLRB*,[9] the Court of Appeals for the Fourth Circuit enforced the Board's order requiring the employer to post the notice at all four plants where the employees affected by the unfair labor practices worked or where employees

---

[6] Cosmetic Components Corp., 257 N.L.R.B. 1335, 108 L.R.R.M. 1085 (1981); John F. Cuneo, 152 N.L.R.B. 929, 59 L.R.R.M. 1226 (1965); Teamsters Local 901 (F.F. Instrument Corp.), 210 N.L.R.B. No. 153, 86 L.R.R.M. 1286 (1974); Pollack Elec. Co., 219 N.L.R.B. No. 195, 90 L.R.R.M. 1335 (1975); *cf.* General Iron Corp., 218 N.L.R.B. No. 109, 89 L.R.R.M. 1783 (1975).

[7] NLRB v. Douglas & Lomason Co., 443 F.2d 291, 77 L.R.R.M. 2449, 2451 (8th Cir. 1971). *Cf.* NLRB v. Priced-Less Discount Foods, Inc., 407 F.2d 1325, 70 L.R.R.M. 2743 (6th Cir. 1969) (Board did not adequately inform employees that they had a right to decertify the union as their representative by bald statement that, pursuant to § 9(c)(1), the employees may petition the NLRB for an election). *See* NLRB v. Laney & Duke Storage Warehouse Co., 369 F.2d 859, 63 L.R.R.M. 2552 (5th Cir. 1966), wherein the Board's order against the employer had provided, *inter alia*, that "We [the employer] will not promise to restore the raises which our employees used to get every year before they joined the union." Assuming that the proscription was aimed at unlawful promises of benefit, the court observed that as it stood, it doubted that "the employees will greet this restriction with enthusiasm." *See also* Ch. III, *supra*, for additional discussion of ambiguous orders.

[8] *E.g.*, NLRB v. Douglas & Lomason Co., 443 F.2d 291, 77 L.R.R.M. 2449 (8th Cir. 1971) (court replaced words indicating that the Board had ordered the employer to promise with the words "we promise"); Love Box Co. v. NLRB, 422 F.2d 232, 235, 73 L.R.R.M. 2746, 2749 (10th Cir. 1970) (court deleted language indicating that the Board had ordered the employer to keep its word, and inserted the words "we intend to carry out the order . . . and abide by the following . . ."); Unit Drop Forge Div., Eaton, Yale & Towne, Inc. v. NLRB, 412 F.2d 108, 111, 71 L.R.R.M. 2519 (7th Cir. 1969) (same); Amalgamated Local Union 355 (Russell Motors, Inc.) v. NLRB, 481 F.2d 996, 83 L.R.R.M. 2849 (2d Cir. 1973), *enforcing as modified* 198 N.L.R.B. No. 58, 80 L.R.R.M. 1757 (1973) (court modified the Board's order to read that the union had entered into a "collusive" contract, rather than a "sweetheart" contract).

[9] 658 F.2d 968, 108 L.R.R.M. 2177 (4th Cir. 1981).

knew about the unfair labor practices committed even though the unfair labor practice itself occurred at only one of those plants. Similarly, the Fifth Circuit affirmed a Board order requiring notice posting at seventeen stores of the employer in a single metropolitan area, although the unfair labor practices involved supervisory employees at only two stores and affected employees at a third. The court found that the close association of all stores required affirmation in order to better serve the ends of the Act.[10]

In industries such as construction, where the job site is highly mobile, the Board may require that its notices be posted at the respondent's offices [11] and job sites for sixty days,[12] or at all projects where work is begun by the respondent within a specified period of time commencing from the first date of compliance.[13] For seasonal operations such as the packing or canning industries, the NLRB notice must be posted for sixty days commencing from the date the plant is in full operation: the so-called peak of the season.[14]

---

[10] NLRB v. Delchamps Inc., 653 F.2d 225, 107 L.R.R.M. 3324 (5th Cir. 1981). *See also* Winn-Dixie Stores, 236 N.L.R.B. 1547, 98 L.R.R.M. 1437 (1978), where the Board required that the notice be posted in all Miami operations of the employer and published in the two largest Miami newspapers at least once a week for three weeks.

[11] Building & Constr. Trades Council (Phila. & Vicinity) (Fisher Constr. Co.), 149 N.L.R.B. 1629, 58 L.R.R.M. 1001 (1964); *cf.* Swinerton and Walberg Co., 94 N.L.R.B. 1079, 28 L.R.R.M. 1148 (1951), *enforced,* 202 F.2d 511, 31 L.R.R.M. 2384 (9th Cir. 1953). Reflecting the notion that the scope of the order must bear some relationship to the unfair labor practices committed, the employer in this case was not ordered to post notices in his New York office when the misconduct occurred in San Francisco. The New York office was deemed too far removed from the offending locality and, furthermore, its major operations were confined to manufacturing, whereas the San Francisco operation concerned machinery installation.

[12] Utah Constr. Co., 95 N.L.R.B. 196, 28 L.R.R.M. 1300 (1951).

[13] *Compare* J.R. Cantrall Co., 96 N.L.R.B. 786, 28 L.R.R.M. 1588 (1951), *enforced,* 201 F.2d 853, 31 L.R.R.M. 2332 (9th Cir. 1953), *cert. denied,* 345 U.S. 996, 32 L.R.R.M. 2247 (1953) (within six months), *with* Swinerton and Walberg Co., 94 N.L.R.B. 1079, 28 L.R.R.M. 1148 (1951), *enforced,* 202 F.2d 511, 31 L.R.R.M. 2384 (9th Cir. 1953) (within one year). The difference in the time allotted for notification to commence is attributable to the fact that the *Cantrall* case involved a traditional construction contractor, while the *Swinerton* case involved only isolated instances of machinery installation, the performance of which was dependent upon sales of machinery by the parent company to California purchasers.

See also Wyoming Valley Bldg. & Constr. Trades Council (Altemose Constr. Assoc.), 211 N.L.R.B. 1049, 87 L.R.R.M. 1394 (1974), where the Board fashioned several methods of notification in order to reach construction employees who were members of a local that had no regular meeting place.

[14] *See* Wade & Paxton, 96 N.L.R.B. 650, 28 L.R.R.M. 1559 (1951); Charbonneau Packing Corp., 95 N.L.R.B. 1166, 28 L.R.R.M. 1428 (1951); Southern Fruit Distribs., Inc., 81 N.L.R.B. 259 (1949). This particular remedy reflects the Board's overall policy for dealing with seasonal industries in matters affecting the entire bargaining unit at the height of operations. For example, representation elections among employees of seasonal employers are held at the "peak of the season." *See e.g.,* WILLIAMS, NLRB REGULATION OF ELECTION CONDUCT 492–494 (Lab. Rel. & Pub. Policy Ser., Rep. No. 8, rev. ed. 1985) for an extended discussion of this subject.

Peculiar or unusual conditions affecting employment may cause the Board to rule that a simple posting is inadequate and that additional notification is required. For example, in instances where the plant has closed down, the project has been completed, or the workforce has been reduced, the Board has directed the respondent to mail a copy of the notice to each employee discriminated against and to each employee employed at the time of the shutdown, completion, or reduction.[15]

The Board has also held that "flagrant and gross" unfair labor practices may warrant extraordinary notification provisions in addition to the normal posting requirements. In an attempt to neutralize the effect of aggravated unfair labor practice conduct, the Board may rule that the respondent must mail a copy of the notice to each employee.[16] In a case of unfair labor practices by an employer, the Board may require that his bulletin boards be made available to the union for a specified period of time.[17] The Board has itself denied union access to the bulletin boards, however, or been denied enforcement of its order of access to bulletin boards in the Circuit Court of Appeals, in situations where the unfair labor practices are not clear and flagrant violations.[18]

The Board, in addition to requiring access to bulletin boards, has on several occasions required the employer to permit access by union officials to the employer's property so that they could directly communicate with employees in nonwork areas during nonwork periods.[19] Similar provisions may be ordered in cases in which the

---

[15] Southland Mfg. Corp., 157 N.L.R.B. 1356, 61 L.R.R.M. 1552 (1966) (shutdown); Interboro Contrs., Inc., 157 N.L.R.B. 1295, 61 L.R.R.M. 1537 (1966) (completion); Clement Bros., Inc., 170 N.L.R.B. 1327, 68 L.R.R.M. 1086 (1968) (reduction).

[16] Betra Mfg. Co., 233 N.L.R.B. 1126 (1979), aff'd, NLRB v. Betra Mfg. Co., 106 L.R.R.M. 2365 (9th Cir. 1980); H.W. Elson Bottling Co., 155 N.L.R.B. 714, 60 L.R.R.M. 1381 (1965), enforced on this ground, NLRB v. H.W. Elson Bottling Co., 379 F.2d 223, 65 L.R.R.M. 2673 (6th Cir. 1967); NLRB v. Teamsters Local 294 (August Bohl Contracting Co. and Cooley Contracting Co.), 470 F.2d 57, 81 L.R.R.M. 2920 (2d Cir. 1972), enforcing 193 N.L.R.B. 920, 78 L.R.R.M. 1479 (1971).

[17] Conair Corp., 261 N.L.R.B. 1189, 110 L.R.R.M. 1161 (1981); modified, Conair Corp. v. NLRB, 721 F.2d 1355, 114 L.R.R.M. 3169 (D.C. Cir. 1983); Great Lakes Screw Corp., 164 N.L.R.B. 149, 65 L.R.R.M. 1236 (1967); Heck's Inc., 191 N.L.R.B. 886, 77 L.R.R.M. 1513 (1971), enforced as amended sub nom. Meat Cutters, Local 347 v. NLRB, 476 F.2d 546, 82 L.R.R.M. 2955 (1973), cert. denied, 414 U.S. 1069, 84 L.R.R.M. 2835 (1973); J.P. Stevens and Co. v. NLRB, 461 F.2d 490, 80 L.R.R.M. 2609 (4th Cir. 1972); J.P. Stevens and Co. v. NLRB, 417 F.2d 533, 72 L.R.R.M. 2433 (5th Cir. 1969).

[18] Clements Wire & Mfg. Co., Inc., 257 N.L.R.B. 1058 (1981); NLRB v. Florida Steel Corp., 648 F.2d 233, 107 L.R.R.M. 3443 (5th Cir. 1981).

[19] Conair Corp., 261 N.L.R.B. 1189, 110 L.R.R.M. 1161 (1981); modified, Conair Corp. v. NLRB, 721 F.2d 1355, 114 L.R.R.M. 3169 (D.C. Cir. 1983); United Supermkts., Inc., 261 N.L.R.B. 1291, 110 L.R.R.M. 1173 (1982), in which the Board ordered two years' reasonable access based on extensive and serious unfair labor practices; International Union of Elec. Workers (Scott's Inc.) v. NLRB, 383 F.2d 230, 66 L.R.R.M.

unlawful conduct involved individual contact between the respondent and the employee(s).[20]

Finally, the Board may order that respondent or an agent of the Board read the contents of the notice to the employees if circumstances such as illiteracy [21] or widespread and flagrant violations of the Act [22] deem it necessary. Some courts have refused to enforce Board orders requiring the employer to read the notice to his employees. These courts have considered that a public reading by the employer would be humiliating and degrading to the employer and would have a lingering effect on future relations between the company and union.[23] On occasion, the Board has even required a designated representative of the employer to sign the notice because

---

2081 (D.C. Cir. 1967); *cf.* Heck's Inc., 191 N.L.R.B. 886, 77 L.R.R.M. 1513 (1971), *enforced as amended sub nom.* Meat Cutters, Local 347 v. NLRB, 476 F.2d 546, 82 L.R.R.M. 2955 (1973), *cert. denied* 414 U.S. 1069, 84 L.R.R.M. 2835 (1973); Loray Corp., 184 N.L.R.B. 557, 74 L.R.R.M. 1513 (1970). However, on several occasions the Board has refused to grant requests for notice mailing, bulletin board access, or company time to appeal to employees. *See, e.g.,* Dee Knitting Mills, 214 N.L.R.B. No. 138, 88 L.R.R.M. 1273 (1974); Moore Mill & Lumber Co., 212 N.L.R.B. No. 27, 86 L.R.R.M. 1545 (1974). For a full treatment of NLRB policies concerning requests for extraordinary remedies to deal with flagrant unfair labor practices see Chapter XIV, *infra.*.

[20] *See, e.g.,* J.I. Case Co. v. N.L.R.B., 321 U.S. 332, 14 L.R.R.M. 501 (1944) (individual notice to employees who had entered into individual employment contracts); Reed & Prince Mfg. Co., 96 N.L.R.B. 850, 28 L.R.R.M. 1608 (1951), *enforced,* 205 F.2d 131, 32 L.R.R.M. 2225 (1st Cir. 1953) (individual notice to each unfair labor practice striker who had been threatened by his employer in soliciting a return to work); U.S. Automatic Corp., 57 N.L.R.B. 124, 14 L.R.R.M. 214 (1944) (individual notice to each employee with whom the employer had bargained individually concerning his grievances); Atlas Bag and Burlap Co., 1 N.L.R.B. 292, 1 L.R.R.M. 385 (1936) (individual notice to each employee who had entered into unlawful "yellow dog" contract of employment). Significantly, in each of these cases, notices were ordered sent only to those employees who had actual contact with their employer and not to the entire bargaining unit.

[21] NLRB v. Bush Hog, Inc., 405 F.2d 755, 70 L.R.R.M. 2070, 2072 (5th Cir. 1968); Marine Welding & Repair Works v. NLRB, 439 F.2d 395, 76 L.R.R.M. 2660, 2663 (8th Cir. 1971) and cases cited therein.

[22] Conair Corp. v. NLRB, 721 F.2d 1355, 114 L.R.R.M. 3169 (D.C. Cir. 1983); United Dairy Farmers Coop. Ass'n, 242 N.L.R.B. 1026, 101 L.R.R.M. 1278 (1979), *remanded on other grounds,* 633 F.2d 1054, 105 L.R.R.M. 3034 (3d Cir. 1980); Sterling Aluminum Co., 163 N.L.R.B. 302, 64 L.R.R.M. 1354 (1967); J.P. Stevens and Co. v. NLRB, 417 F.2d 533, 72 L.R.R.M. 2433 (5th Cir. 1969); International Union of Elec. Workers (Scott's Inc.) v. NLRB, 383 F.2d 230, 66 L.R.R.M. 2081 (D.C. Cir. 1967); Heck's Inc., 191 N.L.R.B. 886, 77 L.R.R.M. 1513 (1971), *enforced as amended sub nom.* Meat Cutters, Local 347 v. NLRB, 476 F.2d 546, 82 L.R.R.M. 2955 (1973), *cert. denied,* 414 U.S. 1069, 84 L.R.R.M. 2835 (1973).

[23] Teamsters Local 115 v. NLRB (Haddon House), 640 F.2d 392, 106 L.R.R.M. 2462 (D.C. Cir. 1981); *see* International Union of Elec. Workers (Scott's Inc.) v. NLRB, 383 F.2d 230, 66 L.R.R.M. 2081, 2082–2083 (D.C. Cir. 1967), and cases cited therein at n.5; NLRB v. Laney and Duke Storage Co., 369 F.2d 859, 869, 63 L.R.R.M. 2552 (5th Cir. 1966); *but see* NLRB v. Bush Hog, Inc., 405 F.2d 755, 70 L.R.R.M. 2070, 2072 (5th Cir. 1968).

that person was identified with the employer's unlawful conduct. Without such person's signature, the employees might not recognize that the usual notice contains a bona fide commitment by the employer to refrain from committing similar unfair labor practices in the future.[24]

POSTING REQUIREMENTS IN UNION VIOLATIONS

In situations involving a union's unfair labor practices, the Board, where appropriate, has ordered the union to post notices at more than one location, and to supply copies for posting at more than one plant.[25] Similarly, where the union's unfair labor practices are considered of a more serious nature, or infringe upon its members' protected activities, the Board has required the union to mail a copy of the remedial notice to each member of the union or to each affected employee.[26]

In secondary boycott cases, the Board has also ordered that the union mail signed copies of the notice to all employees of the charging party.[27] Also, where the misconduct involved the use of mails in the issuance of coercive statements, such as the sending of letters,[28] leaflets,[29] or postcards,[30] the Board has ordered that notices be mailed to the employees.

---

[24] United Supermkts., Inc., 261 N.L.R.B. 1291, 110 L.R.R.M. 1173 (1982); Southern Athletic Co., 157 N.L.R.B. 1051, 61 L.R.R.M. 1051 (1966); Paymaster Corp., 162 N.L.R.B. 123, 63 L.R.R.M. 1508, 1509 (1966).

[25] Mego Corp., 254 N.L.R.B. 300, 106 L.R.R.M. 1198 (1981); Masters, Mates & Pilots, 224 N.L.R.B. 1626, 92 L.R.R.M. 1617 (1976), enforced, 575 F.2d 896, 97 L.R.R.M. 3083 (D.C. Cir. 1978).

[26] Plumbers & Pipefitters Local Union No. 403, 261 N.L.R.B. 257, 110 L.R.R.M. 1039 (1982); see, e.g., International Union of Operating Engineers, Local 18, AFL-CIO, 205 N.L.R.B. 901, 84 L.R.R.M. 1349 (1973), enforced per curiam Docket No. 73-2140 (6th Cir. 1974); NLRB v. Local 294, Teamsters, 470 F.2d 57, 64, 81 L.R.R.M. 2920 (2d Cir. 1972), citing Philadelphia Moving Picture Mach. Operators' Union, Local No. 307, I.A.T.S.E. v. NLRB, 382 F.2d 598, 600, 65 L.R.R.M. 3020, 3022 (3d Cir. 1967).

[27] Teamsters, Local 901 (F.F. Instrument Corp.), 210 N.L.R.B. No. 153, 86 L.R.R.M. 1286, 1288 (1974). Cf., Union de Tronquistas de Puerto Rico, Local 901 (Lock Joint Pipe & Co. of Puerto Rico), 202 N.L.R.B. 399, 82 L.R.R.M. 1525 (1973); Union de Tronquistas de Puerto Rico, Local 901 (Hotel La Concha), 193 N.L.R.B. 591, 78 L.R.R.M. 1377 (1971).

[28] Operating Eng'rs, Local 12, 270 N.L.R.B. No. 175, 116 L.R.R.M. 1277 (1984); Clark Bros., Inc., 70 N.L.R.B. 802, 18 L.R.R.M. 1360 (1946), enforced, 163 F.2d 373, 20 L.R.R.M. 2436 (2d Cir. 1947).

[29] NLRB v. American Laundry Mach. Co., 152 F.2d 400, 17 L.R.R.M. 685 (2d Cir. 1945).

[30] Yoder Co., 47 N.L.R.B. 557, 12 L.R.R.M. 30 (1943).

If the announcement of a course of action which the Board subsequently finds violative of the Act appears in either an employer [31] or union [32] controlled publication, or because of the nature of the violation,[33] the Board has required that a copy of its notice be similarly published.

THE D.C. CIRCUIT COURT DECISIONS

Perhaps the best and most up-to-date analysis of the entire area of the law involving access, unusual notice posting, and required reading of the notice by a company official can be found in three decisions of the District of Columbia Court of Appeals. The first two decisions of the court arise out of the same case involving Florida Steel Corporation. The case first came to the court for enforcement on the appeal of the union. Judge Harry T. Edwards did a masterful analysis of the complete law in this area before setting forth the standards and findings the Board must satisfy in order to obtain enforcement of such remedies, and then remanding the matter to the Board.[34] Thereafter, the matter returned to the court on appeal of the respondent. A different panel again analyzed the factors as set forth in the original decision of that court and the reasons why the Board had failed to satisfy the requirements of the decision and, generally speaking, denied enforcement of the access and mailing remedies.[35]

The third D.C. Circuit case is *Conair Corp. v. NLRB*,[36] in which the Court, while denying the Board's right to remedy outrageous and pervasive unfair labor practices with a bargaining order without

---

[31] Meier & Frank Co., 89 N.L.R.B. 1016, 26 L.R.R.M. 1081 (1950) (department store, which had announced invalid no-solicitation rule in company bulletin, ordered to publish notice of its decision and also a facsimile of the Board's order in the same publication).

[32] Typographical Union (American Newspaper Publs. Ass'n), 86 N.L.R.B. 951, 25 L.R.R.M. 1002 (1949) (union, which had announced the adoption of a bargaining strategy to avoid the impact of the Taft-Hartley restrictions on closed shops and had engaged in widespread publication of its policy through its internal bulletins, ordered to publish Board's notice); Variety Artists (Harrah's Club), 195 N.L.R.B. 416, 79 L.R.R.M. 1345 (1972), *supplementing* 176 N.L.R.B. 580, 71 L.R.R.M. 1275 (1969); Musicians Local 368 (Harrah's Club), 195 N.L.R.B. 1104, 79 L.R.R.M. 1650 (1972), *supplementing* 178 N.L.R.B. 707, 72 L.R.R.M. 1284 (1969).

[33] Plumbers & Pipefitters Local 403, 261 N.L.R.B. 300, 110 L.R.R.M. 1039 (1982).

[34] Steelworkers v. NLRB, 646 F.2d 616, 106 L.R.R.M. 2573 (D.C. Cir. 1981).

[35] Florida Steel Corp. v. NLRB, 713 F.2d 823, 113 L.R.R.M. 3625 (D.C. Cir. 1983).

[36] 721 F.2d 1355, 114 L.R.R.M. 3169 (D.C. Cir. 1983).

evidence of majority status, *did* enforce more unusual remedies such as access to bulletin boards; union official access in order to talk to workers on company property; equal time whenever management engages in any speeches; thirty minutes to speak prior to any scheduled election; and requiring the employer to specifically read the notice to the employees.

CHAPTER VIII

Back Pay and Reimbursement

Correlative with the Board's authority to order reinstatement under section 10(c) of the Act is its authority to order that such reinstatement be "with or without back pay, as will effectuate the policies of the Act."[1] In the typical discrimination case, involving an employer's violation of section 8(a)(3) of the Act by discharging an employee for union activity, the Board orders reinstatement of the employee with back pay. The purpose of back-pay orders is to make the employee whole, to restore the earnings he or she lost because of the discriminatory discharge, layoff, or refusal to reinstate.[2] Although most often used in situations involving loss of work, the Board may also order back pay following an unlawful change in the employee's job status, such as demotion,[3] transfer,[4] or pay reduction.[5]

Just as the Board has authority to order affirmative relief against employer violators of section 8(a) of the Act, it also has the authority to order the union violator of section 8(b) of the Act to reimburse employees for illegally exacted dues, fines, or other losses.[6]

The Board's power to devise and to compute monetary remedies is broad. The courts regard this power as primarily a function of the Board and its expertise[7] and consequently will enforce Board back-pay and reimbursement orders unless they conclude that the

---

[1] 29 U.S.C. § 160(c)(1976). Further explanation of the NLRB back-pay procedures can be found in McGuiness, How to Take a Case Before the NLRB, ch. 18 (4th ed. 1976).

[2] Republic Steel v. NLRB, 311 U.S. 7, 7 L.R.R.M. 287 (1940); Phelps Dodge Corp. v. NLRB, 313 U.S. 177, 8 L.R.R.M. 439 (1941).

[3] Tan-Tar-A Resort, 198 N.L.R.B. 81, L.R.R.M. 1200 (1972); Walker-Electric Co., 219 N.L.R.B. 481, 90 L.R.R.M. 1171 (1975).

[4] Hall Elec. Co., 111 N.L.R.B. 68, 35 L.R.R.M. 1414 (1955); 170 N.L.R.B. 1079, 68 L.R.R.M. 1077 (1968).

[5] Standard Generator Serv. Co., 186 F.2d 606, 27 L.R.R.M. 2274 (8th Cir. 1951); Cascade Employers Ass'n, 126 N.L.R.B. 1014, 45 L.R.R.M. 1426 (1960); Zim's Food Liner v. NLRB, 496 F.2d 18, 85 L.R.R.M. 3019 (7th Cir. 1974).

[6] See discussion at notes 118–134, infra; and Chapter XI, infra.

[7] NLRB v. Seven-Up Bottling Co., 344 U.S. 7, 7 L.R.R.M. 2237 (1953); NLRB v. J.H. Rutter-Rex Mfg. Co., 393 U.S. 1117, 70 L.R.R.M. 2828 (1969), reversing 399 F.2d 356, 68 L.R.R.M. 2916 (1968); Shepard v. N.L.R.B., 459 U.S. 344, 112 L.R.R.M. 2369 (1983).

order is a "patent attempt to achieve ends other than those which can be fairly said to effectuate the policies of the Act." [8] As the Act is essentially remedial, courts will not enforce monetary orders that are punitive in nature.[9]

Although the typical Board order in a section 8(a)(3) case combines reinstatement with back pay, the two remedies are not necessarily automatically issued. The Board has, on occasion, awarded back pay to a discharged employee but denied reinstatement. Thus, if after his discriminatory discharge an employee engages in serious misconduct that would be cause for his termination, the Board may deny reinstatement.[10] Similarly, if subsequent to the discharge an employer learns of a discharged employee's earlier misconduct, which conduct independently would have been cause for termination, the Board may deny reinstatement. In such instances, however, the Board usually awards back pay but limits it to the period from the discharge to the date the employer learned of the employee's supervening misconduct [11] or up to the time when the employee has become unavailable because of his or her arrest.[12] Similarly, the Board may order back pay without reinstatement where an employee does not want to be reinstated and so indicates,[13] or where

---

[8] Virginia Elec. & Power Co. v. NLRB, 319 U.S. 533, 12 L.R.R.M. 739 (1943); NLRB v. J.H. Rutter-Rex Mfg. Co., 393 U.S. 1117, 70 L.R.R.M. 2828 (1969), *reversing* 399 F.2d 356, 68 L.R.R.M. 2916 (1968).

[9] Republic Steel Corp. v. NLRB, 311 U.S. 7, 7 L.R.R.M. 287 (1940); *see also* Chapter II, *supra*, at text accompanying n.23 *et seq.*

[10] Section 10(c) of the Act provides in part: "No order of the Board shall require the reinstatement of any individual ... if such individual was suspended or discharged for cause." See Chapter IX, *infra*, at text accompanying n.7 *et. seq.*

[11] East Island Swiss Prods., 220 N.L.R.B. 175, 90 L.R.R.M. 1206 (1975) (employer learned of employee's previous discharge and conviction for misappropriating funds); Banker's Club, Inc., 218 N.L.R.B. 22, 89 L.R.R.M. 1812 (1975) (employee who would have been replaced because of poor attendance record awarded thirty days' back pay but reinstatement denied); Gifford-Hill & Co., 188 N.L.R.B. 337, 76 L.R.R.M. 1349 (1971) (since Board hearing, employee convicted of five armed robberies and sentenced to serve fifteen years in prison); O.R. Cooper & Son, 220 N.L.R.B. 287, 90 L.R.R.M. 1267 (1975) (employees intentionally destroyed employer's property); Montgomery Ward & Co., 254 N.L.R.B. 826, 106 L.R.R.M. 1148 (1981) (employee stole property, Board denied reinstatement but awarded back pay to date he admitted theft); Service Garage, Inc., 256 N.L.R.B. 931, 107 L.R.R.M. 1345 (1981) (employee falsification of original employment application warranted waiver of right to reinstatement and back pay); Colorado Forge Corp., 260 N.L.R.B. 25, 109 L.R.R.M. 1261 (1982) (back pay tolled at point employee made misrepresentation to lending institution that he was still employed and forged signature of employer official).

[12] East Island Swiss Prods., 220 N.L.R.B. 175, 90 L.R.R.M. 1206 (1975); *but see* Hillside Ave. Pharmacy, 265 N.L.R.B. No. 205, 112 L.R.R.M. 1073 (1982), where the Board denied reinstatement to an employee who had a violent confrontation with the employer's president who was himself partially responsible. The Board awarded back pay until the discriminatee obtained substantially equivalent employment elsewhere.

[13] Phelps Dodge Corp. v. NLRB, 313 U.S. 177, 8 L.R.R.M. 439 (1941).

the employer is no longer in business, if it can be shown that the operation was discontinued for economic reasons and not to evade remedying an unfair labor practice.[14] The Board, in its discretion, may also order that an employee be reinstated without back pay.[15]

THE WOOLWORTH *FORMULA*

The amount of the back-pay award is the sum of the wages, benefits, and overtime pay the employee would have earned but for the discriminatory discharge, less the amount earned by the employee in the interval, in an amount computed under what is known as the *Woolworth* formula.[16]

Prior to *Woolworth,* the Board had subtracted an employee's interim earnings from the gross back pay owed over the entire period between the discharge and the offer of reinstatement.[17] If over the entire period the employee's interim earnings exceeded the gross back pay, no back pay was awarded. Upon reconsideration in *Woolworth,* the NLRB determined that its formula adversely affected the companion remedy of reinstatement. For example, if an employee, following discriminatory discharge, had obtained a better-paying job, it would have profited the employer to delay an offer

---

[14] Riley Aeronautics Corp., 178 N.L.R.B. 495, 74 L.R.R.M. 1543 (1969); Arnold Graphics v. NLRB, 505 F.2d 257, 87 L.R.R.M. 2753, 2756 (6th Cir. 1974) (no back pay where employer lawfully shut down operation at one location and transferred to another); Mastell Trailer Corp. v. NLRB, 682 F.2d 753, 110 L.R.R.M. 3193 (8th Cir. 1982); Castleman & Bates, Inc., 228 N.L.R.B. 1504, 96 L.R.R.M. 1419 (1977). *But see* cases where Board has rejected employer defense that discriminatees would have been laid off: Midwest Hanger Co., 221 N.L.R.B. 911, 91 L.R.R.M. 1218 (1975); Jobbers Supply, Inc., 236 N.L.R.B. 112, 98 L.R.R.M. 1208 (1978); United Contractors, Inc., 238 N.L.R.B. 893, 99 L.R.R.M. 1683 (1978); Sparkle Mills, Inc., 246 N.L.R.B. 473, 102 L.R.R.M. 1597 (1979); Neely's Car Clinic, 255 N.L.R.B. 1420, 107 L.R.R.M. 1157 (1981); Quick Find Co., 259 N.L.R.B. 1051, 109 L.R.R.M. 1079 (1982); A&W Prods. Co., 261 N.L.R.B. 166, 110 L.R.R.M. 1023 (1982). For special remedial problems where there is an unlawful shutdown or a "runaway shop" see Ch. XIII *infra*, text beginning at n.56.

[15] Republican Publishing Co., 174 F.2d 474, 24 L.R.R.M. 2052 (1st Cir. 1949), *adj'g in contempt* 180 F.2d 437, 25 L.R.R.M. 2559 (1st Cir. 1950). *Cf.* where an employer has violated its duty under § 8(a)(5) of the Act to bargain in good faith over the effects of its decision to go out of business completely, the Board will order back pay under a period beginning five days after the Board's decision to continue until the exhaustion of its duty to bargain, but in no event are employees to receive less than two weeks' back pay. Transmarine Navigation Corp., 170 N.L.R.B. No. 43, 67 L.R.R.M. 1419 (1963); Contris Packing Co., 268 N.L.R.B. No. 7, 114 L.R.R.M. 1250 (1983). *See discussion*, Ch. IX, *infra*, text beginning at n.7.

[16] F.W. Woolworth Co., 90 N.L.R.B. 289, 26 L.R.R.M. 1185 (1950); NLRB v. Seven-Up Bottling Co., 344 U.S. 7, 7 L.R.R.M. 2237 (1953). *See* NLRB FIELD MANUAL, § 10530.2.

[17] NLRB v. Pennsylvania Greyhound Lines, Inc., 1 N.L.R.B. 1, 51 L.R.R.M. 303 (1935), *enforced*, 303 U.S. 261, 2 L.R.R.M. 599 (1938).

of reinstatement as long as possible, as each day the employee worked on the new job would *pro tanto* reduce the employer's back-pay liability. In addition, the old formula encouraged the employee to waive reinstatement, since such would prevent further reduction of the sum of the back-pay award. Consequently, the *Woolworth* computation treats each quarter of the calendar year as a separate period. If interim earnings exceed back pay in any quarter, this will negate back pay for that quarter only; the net back pay figure will be unaffected by computations in other quarters.

In many cases it may be difficult to determine precisely the amount of back pay owed. Where such difficulty arises, the Board will estimate the amount, and may adopt reasonable formulae designed to achieve that end. The courts will not interfere with such formulae unless it can be shown that they are arbitrary or unreasonable in the circumstances of the particular case.[18]

ELIGIBILITY AND MITIGATION

Although the finding of an unfair labor practice and discriminatory discharge is presumptive proof that some back pay is owed, in 1941 the Supreme Court in *Phelps Dodge v. NLRB*[19] established that the principles of mitigation applied in back-pay proceedings; that is, a claimant has a duty to minimize back pay by seeking or accepting other employment. Thus, the Board may subtract willfully incurred losses of earnings from an award of back pay.

The Sure Tan *Ruling*

The Supreme Court in *Sure Tan Inc. v. NLRB*[20] held that the back-pay remedy must be tailored to expunge only actual, not speculative losses. In that case, the employer's response to the election of a union was to call the Immigration and Naturalization Service (INS) to report that its employees were illegal aliens. As a result of the INS investigation, five employees left the country to avoid being deported. The Board held the employer's actions to be in violation of section 8(a)(3) and ordered its conventional remedy of

---

[18] NLRB v. Brown & Root, Inc., 311 F.2d 447, 452, 52 L.R.R.M. 2115 (8th Cir. 1963); NLRB v. Charley Toppino & Sons, Inc., 358 F.2d 94, 97, 61 L.R.R.M. 2655 (5th Cir. 1966); NLRB v. Carpenters Union, Local 180, 433 F.2d 934, 935, 75 L.R.R.M. 2560 (9th Cir. 1970).

[19] 313 U.S. 177, 8 L.R.R.M. 439 (1941).

[20] __ U.S. __, 116 L.R.R.M. 2857 (1984).

reinstatement and back pay.[21] The Board declined the recommendations of the administrative law judge (ALJ) that the employer keep the reinstatement offer open for six months and provide a minimum four-weeks' back pay to provide some measure of relief to the employees and to deter future violations of the Act. The Board held the ALJ's analysis of the remedy to be unnecessarily speculative, thereby leaving to a compliance hearing the question of whether the employees were available for work.

On appeal, the Court of Appeals for the Seventh Circuit enforced the Board's order subject to modification. The court concluded that reinstatement would be a proper remedy only if the employees were present and free to be employed in the United States, and held the reinstatement offer to be inadequate since they did not provide a reasonable time to allow the employees to make arrangements for legal reentry. The court therefore ordered the reinstatement offers to remain open for four years.[22] Although the court recognized that the employees would not likely be lawfully available for employment and not likely to receive any back pay, it suggested a minimum of six months' back pay.

The Supreme Court affirmed the Board's finding of an unlawful constructive discharge but reversed the remedies modified by the Court of Appeals. It held that the Seventh Circuit had impermissibly interfered with the Board's discretion in fashioning remedies and also had compelled the Board to issue an order it did not have the authority to issue, stating that the back pay should cover only actual, not speculative, loss.[23] The Court agreed that the employees probably would never be entitled to back pay.

> We share the Court of Appeals' uncertainty concerning whether any of the discharged employees will be able either to enter the country lawfully to accept the reinstatement offers or to establish at the compliance proceedings that they were lawfully available for employment during the backpay period. The probable unavailability of the Act's more effective remedies in light of the practical workings of the immigration laws, however, simply cannot justify the judicial arrogation of remedial authority not fairly encompassed within the Act. Any perceived deficiencies in the NLRA's existing remedial arsenal can only be addressed by Congressional action.[24]

---

[21] Sure Tan Inc., 234 N.L.R.B. 1187, 97 L.R.R.M. 1439 (1978). The Board also ordered the employees to notify the INS of their employees' status because of support for the union.

[22] 672 F.2d 592 (7th Cir. 1972). The court also ordered that the offers be in Spanish and delivered so as receipt could be verified.

[23] 116 L.R.R.M. at 2866.

[24] *Id.* at 2866. The Court declined to opine on the claim that any minimum back pay awards are punitive and thus beyond the Board's authority. *Id.* at n.14.

General Eligibility Criteria

To qualify for the remedial benefits of back pay, an employee must remain in the labor market, diligently search for alternative work, accept substantially equivalent employment if available, and not voluntarily quit alternative employment without good reason.[25] For example, in 1982 the Board held in *Medline Industries, Inc.*[26] that an unlawfully discharged employee incurred willful loss of earnings at various times during the back-pay period by quitting jobs without any prospect of getting another job, by quitting to become a full-time student, and by rejecting jobs which he did not believe were commensurate with his abilities. If the employee leaves a new job because of reasons which would not have prompted leaving the old position, or if the employee would have left the original job to take the new position, back pay will be tolled at that date.[27]

Prior to 1956, registration with a government employment service constituted conclusive proof that a reasonable search for employment had been made.[28] In *Southern Silk Mills* and subsequent decisions involving willfully incurred earning losses, however, the Board has held that the sufficiency of the search effort would be determined in light of all of the circumstances of the case and the individual's experience.[29] A claimant is not required, in the first instance, to seek work outside the general geographic area of pre-discrimination employment,[30] but may be found to have incurred a willful loss of earnings upon relinquishing a job outside the area.[31] Nor is a claimant obliged to seek or accept employment that is dangerous, distasteful, or essentially different from the original job.[32]

---

[25] NLRB v. Mastro Plastics Corp., 354 F.2d 170, 178, 60 L.R.R.M. 2578 (2d Cir. 1966), *cert. denied*, 384 U.S. 972, 62 L.R.R.M. 2292 (1966); NLRB v. Madison Courier, Inc., 472 F.2d 1307, 80 L.R.R.M. 3377 (D.C. Cir. 1972) and cases cited therein.

[26] 261 N.L.R.B. 1329, 110 L.R.R.M. 1286 (1982).

[27] *But see* Johnson Nursing Home, 266 N.L.R.B. No. 215, 113 L.R.R.M. 1106 (1983), where Board held that leaving interim employment to care for a sick child did not toll back pay.

[28] Harvest Queen Mill & Elevator Co., 90 N.L.R.B. 320, 26 L.R.R.M. 1189 (1950).

[29] NLRB v. Southern Silk Mills, Inc., 242 F.2d 697, 39 L.R.R.M. 2647 (6th Cir. 1957), *cert. denied*, 355 U.S. 821, 40 L.R.R.M. 2680 (1957); Missouri Transit Co, Inc., 125 N.L.R.B. 1316, 45 L.R.R.M. 1267 (1959); Ozark Hardwood Co., 119 N.L.R.B. 1130, 41 L.R.R.M. 1243 (1957), *remanded on other grounds*, 282 F.2d 1, 46 L.R.R.M. 2823 (8th Cir. 1960); McCann Steel Co., 224 N.L.R.B. 607, 93 L.R.R.M. 1365, *enforced*, 570 F.2d 652, 97 L.R.R.M. 2921 (6th Cir. 1978).

[30] American Bottling Co., 116 N.L.R.B. 1303, 38 L.R.R.M. 1465 (1956); NLRB v. Mastro Plastics Corp., 354 F.2d 170, 60 L.R.R.M. 2578 (2d Cir. 1966), *cert. denied*, 384 U.S. 972, 62 L.R.R.M. 2292 (1966).

[31] Ozark Hardwood Co., 119 N.L.R.B. 1130, 41 L.R.R.M. 1243 (1957), *remanded on other grounds*, 282 F.2d 1, 46 L.R.R.M. 2823 (8th Cir. 1960).

[32] Florence Printing Co. v. NLRB, 376 F.2d 216, 65 L.R.R.M. 2047 (4th Cir.), *cert.*

The failure to work overtime during an interim job will not be considered a willful loss of earnings.[33] Self-employment is treated as interim employment and the profits as interim earnings.[34] Furthermore, an employee's participation in union activities, such as picketing or attendance at training sessions, does not of itself show insufficient effort in the search for interim employment. The union activity must interfere with the employee's ability to seek alternative employment before the Board will consider such activity as mitigating the back-pay liability.[35] After an employee has unsuccessfully sought equivalent employment for a reasonable period of time,[36] he or she may be required to look for suitable work at a rate of pay lower than the one earned prior to the discharge.[37]

The Board does not award back pay to a striking employee, even where a strike is precipitated by the employer's unfair labor practice. Back pay will be assessed only if the employer, upon receipt of the striker's unconditional application for reinstatement, refuses reinstatement because of protected activity.[38] On the other hand, if an employee participates in a strike which began after the date of discharge, back-pay eligibility is unaffected.[39] In the case where a striker makes an unconditional offer to return to work, the Board allows a five-day grace period before back pay will begin to accrue.[40]

---

denied, 389 U.S. 840, 66 L.R.R.M. 2307 (1967); Mooresville Cotton Mills v. NLRB, 110 F.2d 179, 6 L.R.R.M. 780 (4th Cir. 1940). *But see* Knickerbacker Plastic Co., 132 N.L.R.B. 1209, 48 L.R.R.M. 1505 (1961), where the Board found that it was incumbent upon a claimant to seek work for which he had extensive experience.

[33] McCann Steel Co., 224 N.L.R.B. 607 (1976).

[34] Heinrich Motors, Inc. v. NLRB, 403 F.2d 145, 69 L.R.R.M. 2613 (2d Cir. 1965); McCann Steel Co., 203 N.L.R.B. No. 115, 83 L.R.R.M. 1175 (1973), *enforcement denied pending factual clarification,* McCann Steel Co. v. NLRB, 489 F.2d 1328, 85 L.R.R.M. 2302 (6th Cir. 1974).

[35] NLRB v. Madison Courier, Inc., 472 F.2d 1307, 80 L.R.R.M. 3377 (D.C. Cir. 1972).

[36] NLRB v. Moss Planning Co., 256 F.2d 653, 42 L.R.R.M. 2393 (4th Cir. 1958) (three months' search found reasonable).

[37] NLRB v. Southern Silk Mills, 242 F.2d 697, 39 L.R.R.M. 2647 (6th Cir. 1957), *cert. denied,* 355 U.S. 821, 40 L.R.R.M. 2680 (1957); NLRB v. Madison Courier, Inc., 472 F.2d 1307, 80 L.R.R.M. 3377 (D.C. Cir. 1972).

[38] Phelps Dodge Corp. v. NLRB, 313 U.S. 177, 8 L.R.R.M. 439 (1941); NLRB v. Thayer Co., 213 F.2d 748, 34 L.R.R.M. 2250 (1st Cir. 1954), *cert. denied,* 348 U.S. 883, 35 L.R.R.M. 2100 (1954), *suppl'd on remand,* 115 N.L.R.B. 1591, 38 L.R.R.M. 1142 (1956).

[39] East Texas Steel Castings Co., 116 N.L.R.B. 1336, 38 L.R.R.M. 1470 (1956), *enforced,* 255 F.2d 284, 42 L.R.R.M. 2109 (5th Cir. 1958).

[40] Tiny Town Togs, Inc., 7 N.L.R.B. 54, 2 L.R.R.M. 236 (1938); Roosevelt Roofing & Sheet Metal Works, 204 N.L.R.B. No. 110, 83 L.R.R.M. 1614 (1973); NLRB v. Crosby Chems., 188 F.2d 91, 27 L.R.R.M. 2541 (5th Cir. 1951); Artim Transp. Systems, Inc., 166 N.L.R.B. 795, 68 L.R.R.M. 2388 (1967). *See also* discussion of rule in Drug Package Co., 228 N.L.R.B. 108, 94 L.R.R.M. 1570 (1977); *cf.,* a union's back-pay liability tolls five days after its has advised the employer it has no objections to reinstatement. See n.87 *infra.*

The Board also will allow for reasonable delays where the striker's offer comes at the close of the strike and pre-strike operations have not yet been restored. In these circumstances, the back-pay period may run from the date that work becomes available.[41]

In *Abilities and Goodwill, Inc.,*[42] the Board overruled its long-standing policy regarding when an employer's back-pay liability to an unlawfully discharged striker begins. The Board held that a discharged striker no longer has to request reinstatement to trigger an employer's back-pay obligation. The Board also held that unlawfully discharged strikers are entitled to back pay from the date of their discharge to the date of the employer's offer to reinstate them, placing unlawfully discharged strikers on a par with other discriminatorily discharged employees.

CIRCUMSTANCES PERTAINING TO BACK-PAY CASES

The Board and the courts, in interpreting the labor law, have developed various procedures and standards for determining technical factors pertaining to back-pay cases.

The Back-Pay Period

The back-pay period runs from the date of the unlawful discharge[43] or, in the case of a striking employee, from the date of the striker's unconditional offer to return to work until the date reinstatement is offered.[44] It does not include intervening periods in which the employee was unavailable for work for reasons such as military service,[45] college attendance,[46] pregnancy,[47] or a dis-

---

[41] Volney Felt Mills, 70 N.L.R.B. 908, 18 L.R.R.M. 1422 (1946), *enforced,* 162 F.2d 204, 20 L.R.R.M. 2195 (2d Cir. 1947).

[42] 241 N.L.R.B. 27, 100 L.R.R.M. 1470 (1979), *enforcement denied on unrelated grounds,* 612 F.2d 6, 103 L.R.R.M. 2029 (11th Cir. 1979); *accord* B.N. Beard Co., 248 N.L.R.B. 198, 103 L.R.R.M. 1560 (1980).

[43] When an employer discharges strikers, back pay runs from the date the employer mailed the notices, not the date of their receipt by the strikers. Inta-Roto, 267 N.L.R.B. No. 167, 114 L.R.R.M. 1079 (1983).

[44] Richard W. Kaase Co. (Local 219, American Bakery & Confectionery Workers), 141 N.L.R.B. 245, 52 L.R.R.M. 1306 (1963), *enforced in pertinent part,* 364 F.2d 24, 59 L.R.R.M. 2290 (6th Cir. 1965); American Mfg. Co., 167 N.L.R.B. 520, 66 L.R.R.M. 1122 (1967); Associated Transp. Co. of Texas, 194 N.L.R.B. 62, 78 L.R.R.M. 1678 (1971).

[45] NLRB v. Gluek Brewing Co., 144 F.2d 847, 14 L.R.R.M. 912 (8th Cir. 1944).

[46] Two Wheel Corp., 218 N.L.R.B. 486, 89 L.R.R.M. 1405 (1975); J.L. Holtzendorff Detective Agency, Inc., 206 N.L.R.B. 483, 84 L.R.R.M. 1479 (1973).

[47] NLRB v. Mastro Plastics Corp. 354 F.2d 170, 60 L.R.R.M. 2578 (2d Cir. 1966); Avon Conval. Ctr., 219 N.L.R.B. 1210, 90 L.R.R.M. 1264 (1975).

ability,[48] or times when the back-pay claimant would not have worked regardless of discrimination.[49] If, however, the discriminatee's inability to work was attributable to environmental factors which would not have been encountered absent the discrimination, back pay will be awarded.[50] As shown, the pivotal point of the back-pay period is the date of the employer's reinstatement offer.

In 1962, the Board established the policy of awarding back pay for the entire period from the discharge to the offer of reinstatement in instances where the ALJ's proposed dismissal of the unfair labor practice charge is reversed by the Board. In *A.P.W. Products*,[51] the Board held that unless such action is taken, the respondent benefits at the expense of the discriminatee. Similarly, the back-pay period is not tolled where the Board, on remand from an appellate court, reverses a finding of no violation. As before, the back-pay period runs for the entire period from the discharge to the offer of reinstatement.[52]

Offsets and Additions

In the terminology of the back-pay hearing, the amount of the back-pay award is determined by subtracting the sum of the "interim earnings less expenses" from the "gross back-pay." The Board's back-pay philosophy is to "make whole" the discriminatorily discharged employee and not to punish the party liable for the discrimination, nor to reward the individual subjected to the unfair labor practice.[53]

"Gross back-pay" is the amount the employee would have earned during the back-pay period absent discrimination. The sum includes not only the wages for that period,[54] but also other sums of money

---

[48] Miller, 204 N.L.R.B. No. 165, 83 L.R.R.M. 1716 (1973), *reh'g denied*, 87 L.R.R.M. 3276 (7th Cir. 1974).

[49] NLRB v. Carolina Mills, 190 F.2d 675, 28 L.R.R.M. 2323 (4th Cir. 1951). *But see* Johnson Nursing Home, 266 N.L.R.B. No. 215, 113 L.R.R.M. 1106 (1983).

[50] American Mfg. Co., 167 N.L.R.B. 520, 66 L.R.R.M. 1123 (1967); Associated Transp. Co. of Texas, 194 N.L.R.B. 62, 78 L.R.R.M. 1678 (1971). For a more complete and detailed analysis of what constitutes an offer of reinstatement, see Ch. IX, *infra*, text accompanying n.20 and following; and Ch. X *infra*.

[51] 137 N.L.R.B. 25, 50 L.R.R.M. 1042 (1962), *enforced*, 316 F.2d 899, 53 L.R.R.M. 2055 (2d Cir. 1963).

[52] Golay & Co., 447 F.2d 290, 77 L.R.R.M. 3041 (7th Cir. 1971). *And see* Graphic Arts Union, Local 245, 217 N.L.R.B. 1112, 89 L.R.R.M. 1376 (1975).

[53] Republic Steel v. NLRB, 311 U.S. 7, 7 L.R.R.M. 287 (1940); NLRB v. Stilley Plywood Co., 199 F.2d 319, 31 L.R.R.M. 2014 (4th Cir. 1942), *cert. denied*, 344 U.S. 933, 31 L.R.R.M. 2347 (1953).

[54] In determining the wages the employee would have earned, the Board takes into account such things as the union rate, New England Tank Indus., Inc., 147 N.L.R.B. 598, 56 L.R.R.M. 1253 (1964); change of status, Golden State Bottling Co.

or the equivalent that would have been received, such as bonuses,[55] raises,[56] overtime pay,[57] vacation pay,[58] and tips.[59] Deductions from gross pay may be made for employees with a long history of absenteeism; the Board has held that an employer may assume that the absences would have continued if the employee had not been discharged.[60] The Board may also order the employer to include in the back pay total the contributions it would have made to pension plans, insurance programs, or to hospitalization policies, or to pay hospital expenses that would have been covered by a lapsed policy.[61] From this gross amount, interim earnings are subtracted.

Interim earnings are the wages the back-pay claimant actually earned from self-employment or alternative employment during the back-pay period. While the Board includes severance pay,[62] early retirement benefits,[63] and money earned from working on government relief projects [64] as interim earnings, it does not include wages obtained from a second or additional job held prior to the discrim-

---

v. NLRB, 414 U.S. 168, 84 L.R.R.M. 2839, 2846 (1973), *aff'g*, 467 F.2d 164, 81 L.R.R.M. 2097 (9th Cir. 1972); and the hours the employee's replacement worked, American Casting Serv. Inc., 177 N.L.R.B. 104, 73 L.R.R.M. 1524 (1969); *but see* Central Freight Lines, 266 N.L.R.B. No. 31, 112 L.R.R.M. 1289 (1983), where calculation was based on full-time work, not the hours of replacement.

[55] Story Oldsmobile, Inc., 145 N.L.R.B. 1647, 55 L.R.R.M. 1217 (1964); Hickman Garment Co., 196 N.L.R.B. 383, 80 L.R.R.M. 1684 (1972).

[56] NLRB v. Condensor Corp. of Am., 128 F.2d 67, 10 L.R.R.M. 483 (3d Cir. 1942).

[57] Controlled Alloy, Inc., 208 N.L.R.B. 882, 85 L.R.R.M. 1494 (1974); Merchants Home Delivery Serv., Inc., 234 N.L.R.B. 1040, 97 L.R.R.M. 1419 (1978); J/B Indus., Inc., 245 N.L.R.B. 538, 102 L.R.R.M. 1500 (1979); Wayne Trophy Corp., 254 N.L.R.B. 881, 106 L.R.R.M. 1460 (1981).

[58] Barberton Plastics Prods., Inc., 146 N.L.R.B. 393, 55 L.R.R.M. 1337 (1964); Sioux Falls Stock Yards Co., 236 N.L.R.B. 543, 98 L.R.R.M. 543 (1978); Marlene Indus. Corp., 255 N.L.R.B. 1446, 107 L.R.R.M. 1346 (1981).

[59] Home Restaurant Drive-In, 127 N.L.R.B. 635, 46 L.R.R.M. 1065 (1960).

[60] Mooney Aircraft, Inc., 164 N.L.R.B. 1102, 65 L.R.R.M. 1349 (1967); *but see* Marine Welding & Repair Works, Inc., 202 N.L.R.B. 553, 82 L.R.R.M. 1676 (1973).

[61] NLRB v. Rice Lake Creamery Co., 365 F.2d 888, 62 L.R.R.M. 2332 (D.C. Cir. 1966); Shell Oil Co., 218 N.L.R.B. 87, 89 L.R.R.M. 1534 (1975); Ace Tank & Heater Co., 167 N.L.R.B. 663, 66 L.R.R.M. 1129 (1967) (Board ordered the company to reimburse the employee for a substantial amount of what he would have received under cancelled hospitalization policy); Stoughton Trailers, Inc., 245 N.L.R.B. 190, 102 L.R.R.M. 1458 (1979); Hillside Ave. Pharmacy, 265 N.L.R.B. No. 205, 112 L.R.R.M. 1073 (1982) (back pay included disability); Capitol City Lumber Co. v. NLRB, 721 F.2d 546, 114 L.R.R.M. 3429 (6th Cir. 1983) (Board required contributions to health and welfare plans even after collective bargaining agreement expired). *But see* Triangle Sheet Metal Works, 267 N.L.R.B. No. 111, 114 L.R.R.M. 1189 (1983) (employer did not have to make contributions to health and welfare plan where the claimants had no medical claims during period).

[62] United Nuclear Corp., 156 N.L.R.B. 691, 61 L.R.R.M. 1186 (1966), *enforced*, 381 F.2d 972, 66 L.R.R.M. 2101 (10th Cir. 1967).

[63] Shell Oil Co., 218 N.L.R.B. 87, 89 L.R.R.M. 1534 (1975).

[64] Republic Steel Corp. v. NLRB, 311 U.S. 7, 7 L.R.R.M. 287 (1940).

ination,[65] unemployment compensation, strike or picketing benefits,[66] or voluntary contributions from company employees.[67]

Difficulties occasionally arise over whether to include workers'
compensation. In *American Manufacturing Co.,*[68] the Board held
that only that portion of the compensation which was reparation
for physical damage should be excluded from interim earnings. The
portion representing actual wages should be included. When cal-
culating interim earnings, the Board subtracts expenses the employee incurred in seeking and holding alternative employment that
would not have been incurred had the discrimination not occurred.
Examples of such expenses are employment agency fees, transportation costs, room and board, and family moving costs.[69] If an employee's alternative work requires him or her to join a union and
pay registration and membership dues, the Board will also deduct
these expenses.[70]

Where a discriminatee has willfully concealed interim earnings,
the Board normally has denied back pay,[71] except where the discriminatee belatedly admits earlier concealment.[72] In *American
Navigation Co.*[73] the Board modified this policy, holding that discriminatees found to have willfully concealed their interim employment from the Board would be denied back pay for those
quarters in which they engaged in the employment so concealed.
The Board stated that to reward full back pay to those who willfully
conceal earnings would reward perfidy [74] and might encourage de-
ceit by claimants because they will have nothing to lose by con-
cealing employment. On the other hand, the Board did not want to
provide the employer with an unjustified windfall. Consequently,
the Board will deny back pay on a quarter-by-quarter basis.

---

[65] Golay & Co., Inc., 447 F.2d 290, 77 L.R.R.M. 3041 (7th Cir. 1971).

[66] NLRB v. Gullet Gin Co., 340 U.S. 361, 27 L.R.R.M. 2230 (1951); NLRB v. Laidlaw
Corp., 507 F.2d 1381, 87 L.R.R.M. 3216 (7th Cir. 1974).

[67] Hyster Co., 220 N.L.R.B. 1230 (1975).

[68] 167 N.L.R.B. 520, 66 L.R.R.M. 1123 (1967).

[69] NLRB v. Brown & Root, Inc., 311 F.2d 447, 52 L.R.R.M. 2115 (8th Cir. 1963);
Southern Household Prods., Co., 203 N.L.R.B. No. 138, 83 L.R.R.M. 1247 (1973);
Graphic Arts Union, Local 245, 217 N.L.R.B. No. 162, 89 L.R.R.M. 1376 (1975);
Harvest Queen Mill & Elevator Co., 90 N.L.R.B. 320, 26 L.R.R.M. 189 (1950).

[70] NLRB v. Miami Coca-Cola Bottling Co., 360 F.2d 569, 62 L.R.R.M. 2155 (5th Cir.
1966).

[71] Great Plains Beef Co., 255 N.L.R.B. 1410 (1981); M.J. McCarthy Motor Sales Co.,
147 N.L.R.B. 605 (1964).

[72] Big Three Industrial Gas, 263 N.L.R.B. 1189 (1982); Flite Chief, 246 N.L.R.B.
407, *enforcement denied in pertinent part,* 640 F.2d 989 (9th Cir. 1981). The Ninth
Circuit found that awarding back pay in this case was rewarding "perfidy."

[73] 268 N.L.R.B. 426 (1983).

[74] *See* Flite Chief, 246 N.L.R.B. 407, *enforcement denied in pertinent part,* 640 F.2d
989 (9th Cir. 1981).

Prior to 1962, the Board had refused to add interest to back-pay awards, noting that such action would neither effectuate the policies of the Act nor be appropriate.[75] In *Isis Plumbing*,[76] however, the NLRB established the policy of awarding back pay with interest at 6 percent annually on the amount found due for each quarter. In *Florida Steel Corporation*[77] the Board abandoned its fixed 6 percent rate and adopted the sliding scale used by the Internal Revenue Service for charging interest on underpayment of federal taxes. In *Olympic Medical Corp.*,[78] the Board reaffirmed the *Florida Steel* formula, rejecting the argument that interest be calculated according to the fluctuating Treasury Bill rate. The Board reasoned that tying the back-pay interest rate to the Treasury Bill rate would substitute a highly volatile formula of fluctuating rates for the stability and predictability of the *Florida Steel* formula.

Burden of Proof

As noted above, the "finding of an unfair labor practice ... is presumptive proof that some back-pay is owed."[79] The allocation of the burden of proof in back-pay proceedings was set forth in *NLRB v. Brown & Root, Inc.* by the Eighth Circuit:

> ... in a back pay proceeding the burden is upon the General Counsel to show the gross amounts of back pay due. When that has been done, however, the burden is upon the employer to establish facts which would negate the existence of liability to a given employee or which would mitigate that liability.[80]

Under the Board's *Rules and Regulations*,[81] the General Counsel serves the parties with what is called a "back-pay specification." The specification details for each employee, by calendar quarter, the gross back pay and the interim earnings, expenses, and any other relevant information. This serves as the basis of the Board's *prima facie* case. It is also the practice of the General Counsel to include an approximate net back pay, by deducting mitigating fac-

---

[75] Sifers Candy Co., 92 N.L.R.B. 1220, 27 L.R.R.M. 1232 (1951).

[76] 138 N.L.R.B. 1221, 511 L.R.R.M. 1122 (1962).

[77] 231 N.L.R.B. 651, 96 L.R.R.M. 1070 (1977).

[78] 250 N.L.R.B. 146, 104 L.R.R.M. 1325 (1980). The Board calculates interest on the gross amount due, including portions payable as taxes and social security. Inta-Roto, 267 N.L.R.B. No. 167, 114 L.R.R.M. 1079 (1983).

[79] NLRB v. Mastro Plastics Corp., 354 F.2d 170, 178, 60 L.R.R.M. 2578 (2d Cir. 1966), *cert. denied*, 384 U.S. 972, 62 L.R.R.M. 2292 (1966).

[80] NLRB v. Brown & Root, 311 F.2d 447, 454, 52 L.R.R.M. 2115 (8th Cir. 1963). *See also* NLRB v. Ohio Hoist Mfg. Co., 496 F.2d 14, 86 L.R.R.M. 2135, 2136–2137 (6th Cir. 1974).

[81] NLRB Rules and Regulations, Series 8 (29 C.F.R.), §§ 102.52 and 102.53.

tors discovered through investigation. By including this information, however, the General Counsel does not assume the burden of proving all matters in mitigation. Once the General Counsel has shown the amount of gross back pay due, the employer must prove any mitigating factors which would provide an affirmative defense and permit a deduction from or offset to back pay.[82]

LIABILITY OF EMPLOYERS, UNIONS, AND SUCCESSOR EMPLOYERS

The Board's back-pay order will hold the employer, the union, or both, liable for making whole the employee. If the employer is the sole respondent, the order will stipulate that in addition to paying the amount of back pay due, the employer must report and pay the full tax and social security payments on the award.[83] The Board will usually not hold the president or sole owner of a company personally liable unless there is evidence that the individual had committed some act to justify piercing the corporate veil.[84] The Board on one occasion, however, did hold an employer association liable for the action of a company that discharged a nonunion employee. Although the company itself was not a member of the association, its president was, and the Board found that membership was maintained through the agency of its president.[85]

If a union alone is liable, the Board will require it to "remove the barrier it has erected" by notifying both the employer and the employee that it no longer has any objection to immediate rein-

---

[82] NLRB v. Madison Courier, Inc., 472 F.2d 1307, 80 L.R.R.M. 3377, 3383 (D.C. Cir. 1972); NLRB v. Mooney Aircraft, 366 F.2d 809, 813, 63 L.R.R.M. 2208 (5th Cir. 1966); NLRB v. Mastro Plastics Corp., 345 F.2d 170, 178, 60 L.R.R.M. 2578 (2d Cir. 1966), *cert. denied,* 384 U.S. 972, 62 L.R.R.M. 2292 (1966). If an employee dies before the back-pay proceeding, back pay usually will be awarded to the deceased's estate. The Board is expected to make available for the employer's cross-examination such evidence as it may reasonably obtain. Although the evidence submitted might be hearsay in a civil action, it is the burden of the employer to disprove that a diligent search for alternative employment was made by the employee before his or her death.

[83] NLRB FIELD MANUAL, § 10694.1.

[84] Chef Nathan Sez Eat Here, 201 N.L.R.B. 343, 82 L.R.R.M. 1265 (1973); NLRB v. I.U.O.E., Local 925, AFL-CIO, 460 F.2d 589, 80 L.R.R.M. 2398, 2409 (5th Cir. 1972); Metropolitan Bureau of Investigation, Inc., 246 N.L.R.B. 544, 102 L.R.R.M. 1615 (1979). *But see* Concrete Mfg. Co. of Dekalb, 262 N.L.R.B. 727, 110 L.R.R.M. 1353 (1982), where the Board held the bankrupt employee's president and plant manager personally liable. The two were also members of the Board who ordered that the surplus of the retirement be paid out to the beneficiaries at a time when they knew of Board's back-pay order for two discriminatees.

[85] NLRB v. Shuck Constr. Co., 243 F.2d 519, 39 L.R.R.M. 2322 (9th Cir. 1957).

statement.[86] Until 1981, compliance with this stipulation would toll the period of the union's liability for back pay.[87] However in *Sheet Metal Workers Union Local 355 (Zinsco Electrical Products)*,[88] the Board held that where a union alone was liable for a discharge, its back-pay liability would continue until the claimant obtained substantially equivalent employment.

A union, unlike an employer, is not required to make social security or tax payments.[89] In *Teamster Union, Local 249*,[90] the Board noted that the Commissioner of Internal Revenue has held that back-pay awards by a labor organization cannot legally be treated as wages paid by or on behalf of the employer.[91]

If both the employer and the union are liable, the back-pay order will direct both parties to remit to the Internal Revenue Service a deduction for income tax and will direct the employer to make the appropriate deductions and contributions for social security.[92] The order, however, will not stipulate the portion that each must pay. The fact that section 10(c) of the Act states that "either one or the other would be responsible for back pay, but not both" does not bar the Board from holding the employer and the union jointly and severally liable. In *Union Starch and Refining Co. v. NLRB*,[93] the court held that Congress had manifested no intent to restrict the remedial powers of the Board, but instead had sought to preserve its broad authority to dissipate the effects of an unfair labor practice.

In some instances, the Board will distinguish between primary and secondary liability. In *NLRB v. Lexington Electric Products Co.*,[94] the Third Circuit found that it would be "patently inequitable

---

[86] Pen and Pencil Workers, Local 19593 (Parker Pen Co.), 91 N.L.R.B. 883, 888–889, 26 L.R.R.M. 1583 (1950). In Radio Officers' Union v. NLRB, 347 U.S. 17, 54–55, 33 L.R.R.M. 2417, 2431–2432 (1954), *Pen and Pencil Workers* was approved insofar as the Board's policy of holding that the absence of the employer in a proceeding against a union for a § 8(b)(2) violation did not preclude a back-pay order running solely against the union. *See also* discussion in Chapter IX, *infra*, at text accompanying n.62 *et. seq.*

[87] Local Union 595, Int'l Ass'n of Bridge and Iron Workers (R. Clinton Constr. Co.), 109 N.L.R.B. 73, 34 L.R.R.M. 1285 (1954). Pursuant to current NLRB practice, the union's back-pay liability is terminated five days after the receipt by an employer of a notice withdrawing all objection to the reemployment of a discriminatee. *E.g.,* Local 1311, Carpenters (American Riggers, Inc.), 193 N.L.R.B. 995, 78 L.R.R.M. 1450 (1971); Loft Painting Co., 267 N.L.R.B. No. 23, 113 L.R.R.M. 1143 (1983).

[88] 254 N.L.R.B. 773, 106 L.R.R.M. 1337 (1981).

[89] NLRB FIELD MANUAL, § 10694.2

[90] 116 N.L.R.B. 399, 38 L.R.R.M. 1254 (1956).

[91] *Id.* at 400, 38 L.R.R.M. at 1255.

[92] NLRB FIELD MANUAL, §§ 10692.2 and 10694.1.

[93] 186 F.2d 1008, 27 L.R.R.M. 2342 (7th Cir. 1951), *cert. denied*, 342 U.S. 815, 28 L.R.R.M. 2625 (1951).

[94] 283 F.2d 54, 46 L.R.R.M. 3028 (3d Cir. 1960), *cert. denied*, 315 U.S. 485, 47 L.R.R.M. 2752 (1961).

that the employer be more than secondarily responsible for back pay," since the employer had yielded to economic coercion only after unsuccessfully invoking the normal legal remedy against an unfair labor practice strike. The circumstances of the case and the court's subsequent findings of an unfair labor practice by the union did not prevent the employer's coerced action from being another unfair labor practice. The court, however, reasoned that the Act would be fully effectuated "by imposing primary liability to the injured employees upon the union alone, and at the same time holding the employer liable to make the employees whole, should the union fail to do so." [95]

Prior to 1973, the Board pursued a rather uneven course in its treatment of a successor employer's liability to remedy unfair labor practices committed by its predecessor. In *Golden State Bottling Co.,*[96] however, the Supreme Court held that a successor employer who purchases an enterprise with notice of unremedied wrongs may be considered in privity with the former employer. Agreeing with the Board, the Court believed that the public would not benefit by permitting the violator to shed all responsibility simply by disposing of the business. Furthermore, by holding both employers jointly and severally liable, the employee is protected from the possible insolvency either of the predecessor or successor employer.[97]

EFFECT OF PRIVATE SETTLEMENT AGREEMENTS

A private[98] settlement by the parties in an unfair labor practice case does not prevent the Board from issuing its own back-pay order.[99] Instead, the Board looks to see whether the agreement

---

[95] 46 L.R.R.M. at 3030; *accord,* NLRB v. Bulletin Co., 443 F.2d 863, 77 L.R.R.M. 2599 (3d Cir. 1971), *cert. denied,* 404 U.S. 1018, 79 L.R.R.M. 2183 (1972); Alberici-Fruin-Colnon, 226 N.L.R.B. 1315, 94 L.R.R.M. 1159 (1976); Wismer and Becker, 228 N.L.R.B. 779, 96 L.R.R.M. 1571 (1977); Loft Painting Co., 267 N.L.R.B. No. 23, 113 L.R.R.M. 1143 (1983).

[96] Golden State Bottling Co. v. NLRB, 414 U.S. 168, 84 L.R.R.M. 2839 (1973), *accord,* Zim's Foodliner, Inc. v. NLRB, 496 F.2d 18, 85 L.R.R.M. 3019, 3028–3029 (7th Cir. 1974). This subject is treated fully in Chapter VI, *supra.*

[97] *See also* Gateway Serv. Co., 209 N.L.R.B. 1166, 86 L.R.R.M. 1115 (1974).

[98] A "private" or "informal" settlement is accomplished where, after the issuance of a complaint, the charging party and the respondent agree on a withdrawal of the unfair labor practice charge. By definition the General Counsel is not a party to the settlement. In formal proceedings the General Counsel will not approve a settlement unless it provides at least 80 percent of back pay.

[99] The Board has the power to disregard private settlements. Section 10(a) of the Act specifically states that the Board's power to prevent unfair labor practices "shall not be affected by any other means of adjustment or prevention that has been or may be established by agreement, law or otherwise." *E.g.,* Panoramic Indus., Inc., 267 N.L.R.B. No. 14, 113 L.R.R.M. 1152 (1983).

contains provisions that specifically reimburse the employees for monetary losses stemming from the discriminatory action. Thus, in *Great Atlantic & Pacific Tea Co.*,[100] the Board did not grant back pay where the parties had explicitly agreed to a salary increase to compensate for the employees' monetary losses resulting from a lockout.

On the other hand, where the Board has found that wage increases were not negotiated to compensate for wages lost or that the employees were not fully reimbursed, it has ordered back pay despite the existence of a settlement agreement.[101] Typical of the Board's view is *Community Medical Services of Clearfield, Inc. d/b/a Clearhaven Nursing Home*,[102] where the ALJ approved a private settlement between the parties after a long strike in which the union had waived back pay in return for full reinstatement rights of employees. The General Counsel filed a request with the Board for special permission to appeal the ALJ's ruling, arguing that the private settlement agreement did not effectuate the purposes of the Act. The General Counsel was prepared to prove violations of both sections 8(a)(1) and 8(a)(3). The Board granted the General Counsel's request, noting that the agreement allowed the employer to escape $60,000 in back-pay liability. The Board noted also that once a complaint had been filed, the General Counsel acted not in vindication of private rights but as a representative of the public with the duty of enforcing the public statutory rights,[103] and held: "we find it inconceivable that the public interest in the vindication of statutory rights will be advanced or the underlying purposes and policies of the Act effectuated by acceptance of a settlement agreement that trades off employees' rights to be made whole for a wrongdoer's agreement to execute a contract." [104] Regarding the fact that in a union vote, the employees had voted sixty to fourteen to approve the contract and to forego back pay, the Board ruled "statutory rights are not, and cannot be, a matter for referendum vote." [105] This is because "there is an overriding public interest in the effectuation of statutory rights which cannot be cut off or circumvented at the whim of individual discriminatees." [106] Members

---

[100] 145 N.L.R.B. 361, 54 L.R.R.M. 1384 (1963).
[101] Safeway Stores, Inc., 148 N.L.R.B. No. 76, 57 L.R.R.M. 1043 (1964); NLRB v. Trinity Valley Iron and Steel Co., 410 F.2d 1161, 71 L.R.R.M. 2067 (5th Cir. 1969); NLRB v. Laidlaw Corp., 507 F.2d 1381, 87 L.R.R.M. 3216 (7th Cir. 1974).
[102] 236 N.L.R.B. 853, 98 L.R.R.M. 1314 (1978).
[103] *Id.* at 853.
[104] *Id.* at 854.
[105] *Id.* at 855.
[106] *Id.*

Murphy and Penello dissented, arguing that the Board paternalistically had denied the employees the right to regain their jobs, albeit at a cost of back pay, a tradeoff which had been fully explained to them before they voted on it. The dissenters noted: "we regard the employees as adults who, with the assistance of their union representatives, are well qualified to make decisions affecting their future." [107]

The courts are split as to whether the Board's skeptical attitude towards enforcing private settlement agreements is justified. In *Roadway Express Limited, Inc. v. NLRB*,[108] the issue was whether the Board should have deferred to a voluntary settlement agreement in which the union and the employer agreed to settlement of an employee's grievance by reinstating him with full seniority, but without back pay. The court held that the Board improperly had refused to defer to the voluntary settlement agreement. It noted that in the case of private settlement agreements, as in the case of Board deferral to arbitration agreements, the question was "whether the settlement voluntarily arrived at by the parties covering all the pertinent issues effectuates the policies of the Act." [109] In this case there was no evidence of anti-union animus and the court concluded that "deferring to the settlement ... effected by the union's representative acting with the full approval of (the respondent) would not be repugnant to the national labor policy of respecting agreements freely made between an employee and an employer [where the union representative is present]." [110]

In *Hotel Holiday Inn De Iola Verde v. NLRB* [111] the First Circuit remanded a case to the Board to determine whether a private settlement reinstating an employee without back pay should have been enforced. The ALJ and the Board had refused to defer to the agreement on the theory that an individual's right to reinstatement could not be infringed. The Court noted that neither the ALJ nor the Board considered that as of the date of the settlement the employee had no right to reimbursement, as such could only be determined after a Board hearing, and that the Board's approach left no incentive for an employer to bargain in a reinstatement issue.

[107] *Id.* at 859. The Board will not accept an employer's financial inability to pay as a reason to reduce back-pay liability. *See, e.g.,* Star Grocery Co., 245 N.L.R.B. 196, 102 L.R.R.M. 1227 (1979); Schnadig Corp., 265 N.L.R.B. No. 147, 112 L.R.R.M. 1331 (1982); Columbia Eng'rs Int'l, 268 N.L.R.B. 337, 114 L.R.R.M. 1274 (1983).
[108] 647 F.2d 415, 107 L.R.R.M. 2155 (4th Cir. 1981).
[109] 107 L.R.R.M. at 2159.
[110] *Id.* at 2163.
[111] 723 F.2d 169, 115 L.R.R.M. 2188 (1st Cir. 1983).

On the other hand, in *Schaefer v. NLRB*,[112] the employer laid off six employees and the union initially filed section 8(a)(1) and 8(a)(5) charges. Pursuant to a private agreement the union withdrew the section 8(a)(5) charges. The ALJ ruled, however, that neither he nor the Board could be bound by any such private agreement to withdraw the section 8(a)(5) charge and ordered a cease and desist order and back pay. Although the employer claimed that the union, in the collective bargaining agreement, had waived back pay for all discriminatees, the ALJ ruled that it had always been the Board's position that back pay could not be waived since "it is not a private right which attaches to the discriminatees but is, indeed, a public right which only the Board or the Regional Director may settle." [113] The Board agreed. On appeal, the Third Circuit affirmed the Board's order, reasoning that "given the higher scrutiny required by the Board in cases involving Section 7 rights, the absence of a formal arbitration, and the absence of any information as to what scrutiny was given to the claimed violations in the two private settlements . . . we cannot hold the Board abused its discretion in entertaining the unfair labor practice claims and in awarding back pay." [114]

MITIGATION OF BACK-PAY LIABILITY

In *NLRB v. J.H. Rutter-Rex Mfg. Co.*,[115] the Supreme Court ruled that delay on the part of the Board should have no effect on the mitigation of the respondent's liability. Reversing a lower court's decision to toll the back-pay period, the Court held that the Fifth Circuit had exceeded the narrow scope of review provided for the Board's remedial orders when it shifted the cost of the delay from the company to the employees. The lower court, arguing that the Board had been guilty of "inordinate" delay and was in violation of the Administrative Procedure Act, concluded that the purpose of the back-pay award was to deter unfair labor practices and that a substantial award would be sufficient to achieve this effect. Thus, it tolled the employer's liability on an arbitrary date. The Supreme Court reversed this, basing its holding on its prior decision in *NLRB v. Electric Cleaner Co.*,[116] which had held that the Board is not

---

[112] 697 F.2d 558, 112 L.R.R.M. 2609, (3d Cir. 1980).

[113] 112 L.R.R.M. at 2610. There is some appellate authority that the Board's Spielberg-Collyer doctrine of deferral to arbitration should be recognized in private settlements. Roadway Express Limited, Inc. v. NLRB, 647 F.2d 415, 107 L.R.R.M. 2155 (4th Cir. 1981).

[114] 112 L.R.R.M. at 2612.

[115] 396 U.S. 258, 72 L.R.R.M. 2881 (1969).

[116] 315 U.S. 685, 698, 10 L.R.R.M. 501 (1942). *Accord,* NLRB v. Katz, 369 U.S. 736, 748, n.16, 50 L.R.R.M. 2177 (1962).

required to place the consequences of its own delay, even if inordinate, on the wronged employees to the benefit of the respondent. Furthermore, it reasoned that even if the delay was in violation of the Administrative Procedure Act, the full back-pay remedy was not an abuse of the Board's discretion.[117]

REIMBURSEMENT OF ILLEGALLY EXACTED UNION DUES, FEES, AND FINES

In 1956, the NLRB adopted the *Brown-Olds* [118] remedy in a case where a union violated the Act by maintaining and enforcing an unlawful closed shop agreement, and by incorporating into a collective bargaining agreement workrules and regulations requiring employees to obtain union clearance before seeking employment. The NLRB ordered the union to reimburse employees for dues and assessments collected under the illegal agreement, even though the complaint did not allege that the monies were unlawfully collected. The Board reasoned that the order was necessary to expunge the effects of the unfair labor practice.

The *Brown-Olds* remedy was limited substantially by the Supreme Court in *Local 60, Carpenters v. NLRB*.[119] The Court held that the Board did not have the authority to order a union to reimburse employees for union dues and fees paid under an unlawful hiring agreement unless there was a showing that specific individual employee membership had been induced, obtained, or retained in violation of the Act.[120] If there were no individual coercion, the Court reasoned that the reimbursement order would not be designed to remove the "consequences of the violation" [121] and would then be punitive and beyond the power of the Board.

In accordance with the principles set forth in *Carpenters, Local 60*, the Board has ordered that coerced employees be reimbursed for union dues and fees exacted from them through illegal union

---

[117] Subsequent to the Supreme Court decision, J.H. Rutter-Rex Mfg. Co. filed a suit against the NLRB to recover damages allegedly occasioned by the Board's delay. The Fifth Circuit held that the company could not collect under the Federal Tort Claims Act. J.H. Rutter-Rex Mfg. Co. v. U.S., 515 F.2d 97, 89 L.R.R.M. 2811 (1975).

[118] Plumbing and Pipefitters Local 231 (Brown-Olds Plumbing & Heating Corp.), 115 N.L.R.B. 594, 37 L.R.R.M. 1360 (1956).

[119] 365 U.S. 651, 47 L.R.R.M. 2900 (1961).

[120] *Accord*, Local 357, Teamsters v. NLRB, 365 U.S. 667, 47 L.R.R.M. 2906 (1961) which was decided in tandem with *Local 60, Carpenters,* and held that the Board may not order reimbursement of dues and fees under an illegal hiring-hall agreement, where there is no evidence that any employees had been individually coerced.

[121] Local 60, Carpenters, 365 U.S. at 651, 47 L.R.R.M. at 2901.

security clauses,[122] check-off agreements,[123] and prehire agreements.[124] Where both the employer and union are found to share responsibility for the illegal exaction, the Board has ordered that they be held jointly and severally liable for reimbursing the employees.[125] Fees and dues will not be reimbursed to members who joined the union voluntarily or who were members of the union when hired.[126]

In cases previously discussed, the Board has ordered reimbursement where employers had coerced employees into making unlawful payments to the union through check-off authorizations or otherwise. Conversely, where an employer has breached an agreement to check off employee dues, and the union has requested that the Board order the employer to reimburse dues which it has not received from any source, the Board's general rule is that it will order an employer to pay membership dues to the union only for those employees who have authorized the employer to deduct dues from

---

[122] NLRB v. Booth Servs., Inc., 516 F.2d 949, 89 L.R.R.M. 3122 (5th Cir. 1975); NLRB v. Hi-Temp, Inc., 503 F.2d 583, 87 L.R.R.M. 2437 (7th Cir. 1974); Crown Cork and Seal Co., 182 N.L.R.B. No. 96, 76 L.R.R.M. 1713, (1970); NLRB v. Jan Power, Inc., 421 F.2d 1058, 73 L.R.R.M. 2350 (9th Cir. 1970); NLRB v. Midtown Serv. Co., 425 F.2d 665, 73 L.R.R.M. 2634 (2d Cir. 1970); NLRB v. District 12, United Mine Workers of Am., 76 L.R.R.M. 2828 (7th Cir. 1971); Teamsters Local 705 (Gasoline Retailers Ass'n), 210 N.L.R.B. 210, 86 L.R.R.M. 1011 (1974); Hermet, Inc., 222 N.L.R.B. 29, 91 L.R.R.M. 1268 (1976); Hudson River Aggregates, Inc., 246 N.L.R.B. 192, 102 L.R.R.M. 1524 (1979); Baine Serv. Sys., Inc., 248 N.L.R.B. 563, 103 L.R.R.M. 1518 (1980). Further discussion of reimbursement remedies where the employer violates § 8(a)(2) by illegally dominating or assisting a labor organization can be found in Chapter XI, *infra*, text accompanying n.29 *et. seq.*

[123] Paramount Plastic Fabricators, Inc., 190 N.L.R.B. 170, 77 L.R.R.M. 1089 (1971) (reimbursement ordered if dues were not otherwise collected by union); NLRB v. American Beef Packers, Inc., 438 F.2d 331, 76 L.R.R.M. 2530 (10th Cir. 1971); Ogle Protection Serv., 183 N.L.R.B. 682, 76 L.R.R.M. 1715 (1970), *enforced*, 444 F.2d 502, 77 L.R.R.M. 2832 (6th Cir. 1971); Railway Carmen, Lodge 365 v. NLRB, 624 F.2d 819, 104 L.R.R.M. 3046 (8th Cir. 1980); Peninsula Shipbldrs. Ass'n v. NLRB, 663 F.2d 488, 108 L.R.R.M. 2400 (4th Cir. 1981); General Instrument Corp., 262 N.L.R.B. No. 149, 111 L.R.R.M. 1017 (1982). *But see* American Geriatric Enterprises, 235 N.L.R.B. 1532, 98 L.R.R.M. 1220 (1978) (Board did not order reimbursement because the payments were owing to the union under the agreement).

[124] Luke Constr. Co., 211 N.L.R.B. No. 91, 87 L.R.R.M. 1087 (1974); R.J.E. Leasing Corp., 262 N.L.R.B. 373, 110 L.R.R.M. 1313 (1982).

[125] NLRB v. Hi-Temp, Inc., 503 F.2d 583, 87 L.R.R.M. 2437 (7th Cir. 1974); Sheraton-Kaui Corp. v. NLRB, 429 F.2d 1352, 74 L.R.R.M. 2933 (9th Cir. 1970). *But cf.*, Kinney Nat'l Maintenance Servs. v. NLRB, 468 F.2d 953, 81 L.R.R.M. 2733 (9th Cir. 1972) (court refused to order employer to reimburse dues from illegal check-off, since that would compel the employer to pay twice; union which had the money was required to reimburse the employees); and NLRB v. Mears Coal Co., 437 F.2d 502, 76 L.R.R.M. 208 (3d Cir. 1970) (employer not ordered to reimburse dues deductions, since union which had received the money was not a party to the Board's proceedings); American Geratric Enterprises, 235 N.L.R.B. 1532, 98 L.R.R.M. 1220 (1978).

[126] Booth Servs., Inc., 206 N.L.R.B. 862, 84 L.R.R.M. 1598 (1973); Komatz Constr., Inc. v. NLRB, 458 F.2d 317, 80 L.R.R.M. 2005 (8th Cir. 1972).

their wages.[127] The purpose of this rule is to protect the employee's right to choose the manner by which his or her union dues will be paid, whether through check-off or by some other means.

Unions that violate the Act will be ordered to reimburse illegally exacted fines and fees to employees. For example, the Board may order that union fines of members who work behind a union's illegal picket line be returned to the employees.[128] Similarly, where a union violated section 8(b)(1)(A) by conditioning the right of the employer's unit employees to obtain picket line passes during a strike upon the payment of one-third of their wages to the union, the Board ordered the union to return these payments to the employees.[129] Also, a union that runs a hiring hall in an illegal manner by obtaining excessive fees from nonmembers as a condition of referring them for employment will be ordered to reimburse that portion of the fees which is beyond the value of the union's hiring hall services.[130]

In the case of contributions arising out of unlawful hot cargo clauses, there is some authority for the proposition that the Board order the union to reimburse the employer for illegally extracted deductions and fees. However, in *Shepard v. NLRB,*[131] a section 8(e) case, the Board approved the ALJ's cease and desist order but refused to approve his make-whole reimbursement order, which ordered the union and contractors to reimburse operators for illegal payments made to the union in connection with an illegal hot cargo provision in the collective bargaining agreement. The Supreme Court, in an opinion by Justice Rehnquist, affirmed that the Board was not *required* to order a make-whole remedy in a section 8(e) case, citing the broad discretionary remedial powers of the Board under section 10(c). The opinion, however, put the following gloss

---

[127] Allied Mills, Inc., 218 N.L.R.B. 281, 89 L.R.R.M. 1891 (1975); Southland Dodge, Inc., 205 N.L.R.B. 276 n.1, 84 L.R.R.M. 1231 (1973); Ogle Protection Serv., Inc., 183 N.L.R.B. 682, 689–690 (1970) *enforced,* 444 F.2d 502, 504, 77 L.R.R.M. 2832 (6th Cir. 1971); NLRB v. Shen-Mar Food Prods., Inc., 557 F.2d 396, 95 L.R.R.M. 2721 (4th Cir. 1977); Cummins Component Plant, 259 N.L.R.B. 456, 109 L.R.R.M. 1005 (1981). Even if back pay is due the employees, the Board will order union dues deducted from the back-pay award. Ogle Protection, 183 N.L.R.B. 682.

[128] Bricklayers, Local 2 (Weidman Metal Masters), 166 N.L.R.B. 117, 65 L.R.R.M. 1433 (1967); Carpenters Local 1620 (David M. Fisher Constr. Co.), 208 N.L.R.B. 94, 85 L.R.R.M. 1271 (1974). *See generally,* NLRB v. Granite State Joint Board, Textile Workers, Local 1029, AFL-CIO (Int'l Paper Box Mach. Co.), 409 U.S. 213, 81 L.R.R.M. 2853 (1972); NLRB v. Boeing Co., 412 U.S. 84, 83 L.R.R.M. 2183 (1973).

[129] National Cash Register Co. v. NLRB, 466 F.2d 945, 81 L.R.R.M. 2001 (6th Cir. 1972).

[130] NLRB v. Local 138, Operating (J.J. Hagerty, Inc.), 385 F.2d 874, 66 L.R.R.M. 2703 (2d Cir. 1967); NLRB v. H.K. Ferguson Co., 337 F.2d 205, 57 L.R.R.M. 2213 (5th Cir. 1964).

[131] 51 U.S.L.W. 4087, 112 L.R.R.M. 2369 (1983).

on the NLRB's discretionary decision not to order reimbursement in this case, a gloss which indicated that in particularly egregious cases of union coercion, a reimbursement remedy might be in order:

> In this case, we think that the sense of the Board's explanation is that it has decided to treat cases in which there is no finding of 'actual' coercion differently from cases in which there is such a finding . . . it can scarcely be doubted that the Board could properly conclude that a remedy such as reimbursement should be reserved for especially egregious situations.[132]

Nevertheless, the Court reaffirmed the Board's broad discretionary power to fashion appropriate remedies in section 8(e) cases, as in any other unfair labor practice case. "We find nothing in the language or structure of the Act that requires the Board to reflexively order that which a complaining party may regard as 'complete relief' for every unfair labor practice."[133]

In *Joint Council of Teamsters v. NLRB (California Dump Truck Owners Association)*,[134] another section 8(e) case, the Board, citing *Shepard*, held (on facts much like those in *Shepard*) that it was in its discretion to deny reimbursement of initiation fees and union dues to contractors who had lost and/or been denied work because of an illegal hot cargo provision.

BACK PAY FOR WAGES LOST BECAUSE OF UNION STRIKE VIOLENCE

The Board has refused to award back pay to employees who are coerced into joining a strike by threats of union violence.[135] The Board has reasoned that other adequate remedies exist which would not interfere with the right to strike; relief from violence can be sought through court injunction under section 10 (j) of the Act, and if the injunction is ignored, effective contempt action is available.[136] This suggestion is perhaps a hollow one, as the General Counsel has seldom used section 10 (j) injunctions against union violence. Furthermore, the Board has reasoned that if unions were forced to provide back pay where a few of its members engaged in misconduct, few unions could afford to establish a picket line.

---

[132] 112 L.R.R.M. at 2371.

[133] *Id.* at 2372.

[134] 702 F.2d 168, 113 L.R.R.M. 2252 (9th Cir. 1983).

[135] *See, e.g.,* Union de Tronquistas de Puerto Rico, Local 901, Teamsters (Lock Joint Pipe & Co. of Puerto Rico), 202 N.L.R.B. 399, 82 L.R.R.M. 1525 (1973); Meat Cutters Local 222, 233 N.L.R.B. 839, 97 L.R.R.M. 1078 (1977).

[136] See discussion of § 10 (j) injunctions Chapter XIV, *infra.*

Thus, the Board has reversed an ALJ's recommendation which would have ordered a union to provide back pay to employees who were kept from work as a result of the labor organization's picket line violence, threats, and assaults.[137] There, the union not only engaged in threats, criminal assaults, and industrial sabotage, but defied a court injunction and proclaimed that it did "not recognize the authority of the laws or of the Board that administers the law." [138] Thirty-nine employees were trapped inside the plant for a fifteen-day period, and attempts by employees who were not engaged in the strike activity to go to work were repulsed by both threats and violence. As Member Kennedy noted in his dissent, "It is difficult to conceive of a situation in which back pay orders could be more appropriate," and he went on to say, "We are dealing with a labor organization which denounces the laws applicable to its conduct and which systematically threatens the lives of any and all individuals who dare to act in any manner contrary to its self-interest." [139] The majority of the Board disagreed, holding that "the only new argument we perceive in our colleague's dissent is that he is shocked by respondent union's expressed contempt for the law and the Board. . . . This argument appears to call not so much for remedy as for punishment. That, of course, is not part of our statutory function." [140]

The Board's holding ignores the settled principle that Board orders are considered punitive only when they go beyond remedying the effects of the particular unfair labor practice found.[141] The remedy advanced by the ALJ and Member Kennedy is directly related to the loss of work occasioned by the union's unlawful acts, and would be of the same nature as traditional back-pay remedies for other violations. The failure of the Board to order back pay in such an instance results in innocent employees bearing the burden of the respondent's unlawful acts. This was not, after all, a case of a few union members engaging in conduct unsanctioned by the union's leaders. Rather, the union had adopted widespread and repeated violence as its own policy. As in other employee misconduct cases,[142] the Board has misapplied a legal principle designed to deal with lesser instances of misconduct, and has, in effect, sanctioned reprehensible conduct, thereby detracting from the proper exercise of its remedial functions.

---

[137] Union Nacional de Trabajadores, 219 N.L.R.B. 414 (1975).
[138] *Id.* at 419 (Member Kennedy, dissenting in part).
[139] *Id.* at 420.
[140] *Id.* at 414.
[141] See Chapter II, *supra.*
[142] See Chapter X, *infra,* text accompanying n.54 *et seq.*

EXPUNGEMENT OF PERSONNEL RECORDS

The Board has recently been supplementing back pay and reinstatement remedies with a new remedy which requires an employer to expunge the record of any discriminatee if the references in the disciplinary record arose out of an underlying unfair labor practice.

In *Sterling Sugars*,[143] upon finding that an employer violated section 8(a)(3) of the Act when it discharged a janitor for failing to report to work as a substitute, the Board held that the real reason he had been discharged had been anti-union animus. The Board so reasoned because only two weeks previously the janitor had asked management to provide the union representative with a list of any new employees. As a remedy, the Board ordered reinstatement plus expungement of his disciplinary record, as well as a written notice to him that his record had been expunged. The rationale in this case was that although expungement has not typically been part of an unlawful discharge remedy, it nevertheless has been a traditional remedy for lesser forms of discipline, such as warnings. The Board noted: "We see no purpose in distinguishing between these two types of cases, for in either situation the individual affected by any unlawful discipline should be protected from the subsequent use of files pertaining to such misconduct. Accordingly, we shall henceforth routinely include such an affirmative expungement remedy in all cases of unlawful discipline." [144]

---

[143] 261 N.L.R.B. 472, 110 L.R.R.M. 114 (1982).

[144] *Accord,* Marine Grand Prix Motors, 261 N.L.R.B. 1156, 110 L.R.R.M. 1206 (1982); Foodarama, 260 N.L.R.B. 298, 109 L.R.R.M. 1195 (1982); Riley-Beaird, Inc., 259 N.L.R.B. 1339, 109 L.R.R.M. 1120 (1982); *But see,* Tressler Lutheran Home for Children, 263 N.L.R.B. 651, 111 L.R.R.M. (1982), where Board denied expungement of those warnings which in themselves were not discriminatorily motivated. Unions guilty of unfair labor practices have also been ordered to expunge. International Brotherhood of Boilermakers, 266 N.L.R.B. 602, 113 L.R.R.M. 1014 (1983); Operating Engineers, Local 450, 267 N.L.R.B. 775, 114 L.R.R.M. 1201 (1983).

CHAPTER IX

Reinstatement of Discriminatorily Discharged Employees

Section 10(c) of the Act authorizes the Board "to take such affirmative action including *reinstatement* of employees . . . as will effectuate the policies of this Act." [1] Reinstatement orders are used as remedies in two general contexts: (1) upon a discriminatory discharge, layoff, or refusal to hire; [2] and (2) upon the offer of a striking employee to return to work. The reinstatement rights of discriminatorily discharged employees are usually automatic. The reinstatement rights of strikers, however, generally do not accrue until they have unconditionally applied for reinstatement. Once an application has been tendered on behalf of the striking employees, they are normally entitled to reinstatement subject to separate rules that depend upon whether they are deemed economic strikers or unfair labor practice strikers. [3]

Discriminatory discharges or layoffs may be attributable either to an employer or a labor organization. An employer's obligation to reinstate an employee is fulfilled only when it makes an unconditional offer to reinstate the employee to his or her former position or a substantially equivalent one. To be valid, such an offer must be extended for a reasonable period of time and be readily interpretable by the employee as a disavowal of the employer's previous misconduct. Under special circumstances, the Board may order an employer to reinstate supervisory employees, even though they are not defined as employees for purposes of the Act.

When the employee's discharge is initiated by the union, reinstatement will be ordered if both the employer and the labor organization are jointly responsible for the unfair labor practices. When only the union is charged, however, a reinstatement order is not issued by the Board. Instead, the offending labor organization

---

[1] 29 U.S.C. § 160(c) (1976) (emphasis added).

[2] Very early in the history of the Act, the Supreme Court approved the Board's extension of the reinstatement remedy to the hiring of new applicants. Phelps Dodge v. NLRB, 313 U.S. 177, 8 L.R.R.M. 439 (1941).

[3] *See* Ch. X, *infra.*

need only give notice to the employer and employee that it is no longer opposed to the latter's employment.

Although an employee might be otherwise entitled to reinstatement, within certain bounds the Board may refuse to order reinstatement if the employee has engaged in serious misconduct, unless, however, it is shown that the employer has condoned the misconduct.

EMPLOYER-INITIATED DISCRIMINATORY DISCHARGES

Since 1935, section 8(a)(3) of the Act has made it an unfair labor practice for an employer "by discriminating in regard to *hire* or *tenure* of employment or any term or condition of employment to encourage or discourage membership in a labor organization." [4] Even where union activities are not involved, an employer may not discriminate in hiring or tenure of employment when such discrimination would interfere with employee rights under sections 7 and 8(a)(1) to "engage in concerted activities for the purpose of collective bargaining or other mutual aid or protection." [5]

---

[4] 29 U.S.C. § 158(a)(3) (1976) (emphasis added). *Cf.* Radio Officers' Union v. NLRB, 347 U.S. 17, 42–43, 33 L.R.R.M. 2417, 2430 (1954).

[5] 29 U.S.C. §§ 157, 158(a)(1). *See* NLRB v. Washington Aluminum Co., 370 U.S. 2, 12, 50 L.R.R.M. 2235 (1962); Morrison-Knudsen Co. v. NLRB, 358 F.2d 411, 61 L.R.R.M. 2625 (9th Cir. 1966); Socony Mobil Oil Co. v. NLRB, 357 F.2d 662, 61 L.R.R.M. 2553 (2d Cir. 1966); Walls Mfg. Co. v. NLRB, 321 F.2d 753, 53 L.R.R.M. 2428 (D.C. Cir. 1963), *cert. denied*, 375 U.S. 923, 54 L.R.R.M. 2576 (1963). The majority of the following material concerns discharges connected with union activities, but § 7 protection also extends to concerted activity unrelated to union activities. The notion of protected concerted activity unrelated specifically to union activities has had a turbulent recent history. In Meyers Indus., Inc., 268 N.L.R.B. 493, 115 L.R.R.M. 1025 (1984), *remanded sub nom.* Prill v. NLRB, __ F.2d __, 118 L.R.R.M. 2649 (D.C. Cir. 1985) the Board readopted an "objective" standard for determining concerted activity and held that to be concerted the activity will require that the activity be "engaged in with or on the authority of other employees," overruling Alleluia Cushion Co., 221 N.L.R.B. 999, 91 L.R.R.M. 1131 (1975), where the Board had held that a lone employee's invocation of rights under a state safety law was concerted activity, under the rationale that as such laws benefitted other employees the protest would be construed to be a collective one. The Court of Appeals for the District of Columbia remanded *Meyers Industries* to the Board, finding erroneous the Board's interpretation that the Act mandated its *Meyers* decision. The Court suggested that the Board had the discretion to interpret concerted activity. Other courts of appeals had previously rejected the *Alleluia Cushion* test. NLRB v. Dawson Cabinet Co., 566 F.2d 1079 (8th Cir. 1979); Krispy Kreme Doughnut Corp. v. NLRB, 635 F.2d 304, 310 (4th Cir. 1980); Ontario Knife v. NLRB, 637 F.2d 840 (2d Cir. 1980). Compare with decisions holding that an individual's invocation of a right under a collective bargaining agreement is concerted even if alone. Interboro Contractors, 157 N.L.R.B. 1295, *enforced*, 388 F.2d 495 (2d Cir. 1967); City Disposal Systems, 256 N.L.R.B. 451 (1981), *enforcement denied*, 683 F.2d 1005 (6th Cir. 1982), *rev'd*, 104 S.Ct. 1505, 115 L.R.R.M. 3193 (1984); *cf.* Mushroom Transp. Corp. v. NLRB, 330 F.2d 683, 685 (3d Cir. 1964). On the other hand, such activity may lose its protection if it is not for mutual aid

While not as flexible a remedy as back pay,[6] reinstatement is not an absolute right. Accordingly, our analysis will concern the circumstances in which reinstatement may be denied: the "for cause" defense, the rejection of an employer's unconditional offer of reinstatement, changed circumstances, and special cases.

Suspension or Discharge "for Cause" as a Bar to Reinstatement

Indicative of the strong emotions which had arisen in Congress prior to the passage of the Taft-Hartley Amendments, the House Report characterized the "for cause" proviso to section 10(c) as being:

> ... intended to put an end to the belief, now widely held and certainly justified by the Board's decisions, that engaging in union activities carries with it a license to loaf, wander about the plants, refuse to work, waste time, break rules, and engage in uncivilities and other disorders and misconduct.[7]

Although these sentiments did not appear in the final Conference Report, there is no doubt that Congress intended to place some check on the NLRB. The Board's authority to direct the reinstatement of employees who had engaged in some form of misconduct was diminished when Congress prohibited the Board from ordering the "reinstatement of any individual as an employee who has been suspended or discharged . . . for cause." [8]

Essentially, the drafters of the "for cause" limitation codified prior court decisions limiting the applicability of the Board's reinstatement authority to unfair labor practice situations only. For example, in 1942, the Court of Appeals for the Third Circuit in *NLRB v. Condensor Corp.*[9] had observed that an employee "may be discharged by the employer for a good reason, a poor reason, or no

---

and protection, if it contravenes another section of the Act or another statute, or if it concerns a matter over which the employer has no control *(Meyers Industries)*. *See also* G&W Elec. Supply Specialty Co. v. NLRB, 360 F.2d 873, 62 L.R.R.M. 2085 (7th Cir. 1966); NLRB v. C&I Air Conditioning, 486 F.2d 977, 84 L.R.R.M. 2625 (9th Cir. 1973).

[6] *See* discussion of back pay in Ch. VIII, *supra. See also* Walter S. Johnson Bldg. Co., 209 N.L.R.B. 428, 86 L.R.R.M. 1368 (1974), where the discharged employee worked as a laborer at a construction project completed prior to the Board's order. Since an order directing the employer to offer the discriminatee reinstatement was considered inappropriate because of the project's completion, the Board ordered the employer to notify both the employee and his union that he would be eligible for employment in the future at any of the employer's projects. *Cf.* NLRB v. Interboro Contrs., Inc., 388 F.2d 495, 67 L.R.R.M. 2083 (2d Cir. 1967).

[7] H.R. Rep. No. 245, 80th Cong., 1st Sess. 42 (1947).

[8] 29 U.S.C. § 160(c). *See also* NLRB v. Electrical Workers, Local No. 1229, 346 U.S. 464, 33 L.R.R.M. 2183 (1953).

[9] 128 F.2d 67, 10 L.R.R.M. 483 (3d Cir. 1942); *cited with approval in* Meyers Indus., Inc., 268 N.L.R.B. at 497, n.23.

reason at all, so long as the terms of the statute are not violated."[10]
In cases decided subsequent to Taft-Hartley, the courts have indicated that implicit in the statutory amendment is the requirement
that the Board's jurisdiction to entertain discharge questions is
limited to those situations which involve a violation of the Act.[11]
Therefore, the complaint must reflect the results of an investigation
that attributes the discharge either to an employer's attempt to
discourage or encourage union membership or to an act of reprisal
against employees who have engaged in protected concerted activities.[12] Without such evidence, the merit or fairness of a particular
discharge is irrelevant.[13]

Many section 8(a)(3) discussions have noted that employee participation in union activity is no bar to termination provided that
the discharge is not predicated upon the employer's desire to encourage or discourage union membership.[14] Nonetheless, when an
employer raises just cause as a defense, its motive is put at issue.
In its 1980 decision in *Wright Line*,[15] the Board borrowed from the
Supreme Court's decision in *Mt. Healthy City School District Bd.
of Ed. v. Doyle*,[16] and established a shifting burden of proof in mixed
motive cases. The General Counsel has the burden of establishing
that anti-union animus contributed to the decision to discharge. The
employer must then show by a preponderance of evidence that the
employee would have been discharged even if he or she had not
been involved in union activity. This "but for" test has stabilized
an area of dispute between the Board and the courts.[17]

---

[10] 128 F.2d at 75, 10 L.R.R.M. at 489.

[11] *Cf.* Radio Officers' Union v. NLRB, 347 U.S. 17, 33 L.R.R.M. 2417 (1954).

[12] Indiana Metal Prods. Corp. v. NLRB, 202 F.2d 613, 31 L.R.R.M. 2490 (7th Cir.
1953); *cf.* NLRB v. Montgomery Ward & Co., 157 F.2d 486, 19 L.R.R.M. 2009 (8th
Cir. 1946).

[13] In addition to cases already cited at n.12, *see also* NLRB v. McGahey (Columbus
Marble Works), 233 F.2d 406, 38 L.R.R.M. 2142 (5th Cir. 1956); NLRB v. Northern
Metal Co., 440 F.2d 881, 76 L.R.R.M. 2958 (3d Cir. 1971); Indiana Gear Works v.
NLRB, 371 F.2d 273, 64 L.R.R.M. 2253 (7th Cir. 1967); Illinois Ruan Transp. Corp.
v. NLRB, 404 F.2d 274, 69 L.R.R.M. 2761 (8th Cir. 1968); NLRB v. Commonwealth
Foods, 506 F.2d 1065, 87 L.R.R.M. 2609 (4th Cir. 1974) (despite coincidence of the
discharges and employees' union activity, case was remanded for a determination
of whether employees' admissions of thefts were true; if so, reinstatement was to be
denied). For a full examination of an employer's right to deny reinstatement because
of employee misconduct, see Chapter X, *infra*, at test accompanying n.54 *et. seq.*,
discussed with the analogous issue of striker misconduct.

[14] *E.g.*, Tompkins Motor Lines, Inc. v. NLRB, 337 F.2d 325, 57 L.R.R.M. 2337 (6th
Cir. 1964); NLRB v. Williams Lumber Co., 195 F.2d 669, 29 L.R.R.M. 2633 (4th Cir.
1952), *cert. denied*, 344 U.S. 834, 30 L.R.R.M. 2712 (1952).

[15] 251 N.L.R.B. 1083 (1980).

[16] 429 U.S. 274 (1977).

[17] Wright Line, 251 N.L.R.B. 1083 (1980), *enforced*, 662 F.2d (1st Cir. 1981), *cert.
denied*, 455 U.S. 989. The Supreme Court approved the *Wright Line* test in NLRB

Reinstatement Offers

Unlike the unconditional applications for reinstatement required of economic strikers,[18] the Board has long held that a discriminatee has no duty to apply for reemployment in order to protect his or her reinstatement rights, on the theory that the Board would not require a vain act.[19] On the other hand, once an employer makes an unconditional offer of reinstatement to a discriminatee the employer's back-pay liability "is tolled (1) on the date of the actual reinstatement, (2) on the date of rejection of the offer, or (3) in the case of discriminatees who did not reply on the date of the last opportunity to accept the offer of reinstatement." [20] Reinstatement is also inappropriate where the employee has refused a prior reinstatement offer.[21]

Timing. Although each of the foregoing conditions may be objectively measured after the fact, the Board does not require that the employees accept or reject an offer of reinstatement within a definite time period.[22] Instead, the Board has held that the employer's offer must be kept open for a "reasonable" period of time.[23] The courts at times have disagreed with the Board over the duty of the employer to keep its offer open. They have occasionally found

---

v. Transp. Mgt. Corp., 462 U.S. 393, 113 L.R.R.M. 2857 (1983). While the employer's motivation is important in determining whether § 8(a)(3) has been violated, no such inquiry is necessary when analyzing a discharge that has been alleged to violate § 8(a)(1), as that section only requires that the employer's action tends to interfere with, restrain, or coerce employees in exercising their § 7 rights.

[18] *See* Chapter X, *infra.*

[19] *E.g.*, Morristown Knitting Mills, 80 N.L.R.B. 731, 23 L.R.R.M. 1138 (1948); Macomb Block and Supply, Inc., 223 N.L.R.B. 1285, 92 L.R.R.M. 1124 (1976); Mason City Dressed Beef, Inc., 231 N.L.R.B. 735, 97 L.R.R.M. 1215 (1977); Abilities and Good Will, Inc., 241 N.L.R.B. 27, 100 L.R.R.M. 1470 (1979).

[20] American Mfg. Co. of Texas, 167 N.L.R.B. 520, 521, 66 L.R.R.M. 1122 (1967); *accord,* Issac and Vinson Security Services, Inc., 208 N.L.R.B. 47, 85 L.R.R.M. 1517 (1973). *See* Chapter VIII, *supra;* Kenston Trucking Co. v. NLRB, 547 F.2d 159, 93 L.R.R.M. 2958 (2d Cir. 1976). The Board holds that notification of the offer is the burden of the employer, which has the obligation to remedy its unlawful action by "seeking out the employees and offering reinstatement." Southern Greyhound Lines, 169 N.L.R.B. 627, 628, 67 L.R.R.M. 1368 (1968); Hickory's Best, 267 N.L.R.B. No. 199, 114 L.R.R.M. 1145–1146 (1983).

[21] NLRB v. Winchester Elec., Inc., 295 F.2d 288, 292, 49 L.R.R.M. 2013 (2d Cir. 1961).

[22] *See* Ordman, *The National Labor Relations Act: Current Developments,* 24 N.Y.U. CONF. ON LAB. 115, 124 (1972), which points out that the situations which give rise to a reinstatement right have been delineated, but acknowledges that "the outer limits, how long the reinstatement rights continue, remains yet to be defined."

[23] *See* Refaire Refrig. Corp., 207 N.L.R.B. 523, 84 L.R.R.M. 1535 (1973); Southern Household Prods. Co., 203 N.L.R.B. 881, 83 L.R.R.M. 1247 (1973); Penco Enterprises, Inc., 216 N.L.R.B. 734, 88 L.R.R.M. 1621 (1975); Freehold AMC-Jeep Corp., 230 N.L.R.B. 903, 95 L.R.R.M. 1419 (1977); NLRB v. W.C. McQuaide, Inc., 552 F.2d 519, 94 L.R.R.M. 2950 (3d Cir. 1977).

it incumbent upon the employee, not the employer, to take affirmative action ensuring a prompt response to any offer by the employer
entailing a specified time limitation.[24] Perhaps the most definitive
statement that can be made is that offers which condition reemployment upon a one or two day time limit [25] are much less likely
to be viewed as valid offers of reinstatement than those which allow
a week or more.[26]

The "Clear and Definite" Standard. The employer must make
an offer that is bona fide,[27] and it must also be made both clearly
and definitively so that the employees are able to interpret it as
indicative of their employer's willingness to abide by the provisions
of the Act.[28] It follows that when the offer is not communicated to
the employee by the employer, but rather by the employer's agent,
it is invalid unless the employee has knowledge that the agent
possesses the requisite authority to tender the offer.[29] As long as
nothing in the offer suggests a change in the employee's former
rights and privileges, the clear and definite standard does not re-

---

[24] E.g., NLRB v. Betts Baking Co., 428 F.2d 156, 74 L.R.R.M. 2714 (10th Cir. 1970);
NLRB v. Harrah's Club, 403 F.2d 865, 69 L.R.R.M. 2775 (9th Cir. 1968); NLRB v.
Izzi, 395 F.2d 241, 68 L.R.R.M. 2197 (1st Cir. 1968). In each of these cases, the court
disagreed with the Board's conclusion that the employer bore sole responsibility of
ensuring a reasonable time for consideration of an offer of reinstatement. Instead,
the courts observed that in weighing the reasonableness of any given offer, the
responsibility for any alleged lack of time shifts to the employee when the delay is
directly attributable to the employee's own actions.

[25] E.g., Refaire Refrig. Corp., 207 N.L.R.B. 523, 84 L.R.R.M. 1535 (1973) (one day).
Woodland Supermkt., 240 N.L.R.B. 295, 100 L.R.R.M. (1979), supp. is instructive.
The Board in its original decision [237 N.L.R.B. 1481, 99 L.R.R.M. 1206 (1978)] deemed
the employer's telegraphic offer of reinstatement to be invalid because the acceptance
time was two days after the date of the telegram. On reconsideration the Board
found that the telegram to the employees had actually been sent eight days before
the deadline and reversed itself, finding the eight-day offer reasonable.

[26] See NLRB v. Betts Baking Co., 428 F.2d 156, 74 L.R.R.M. 2714 (10th Cir. 1970)
(one week); Elling Halvorsen, Inc., 222 N.L.R.B. 534, 91 L.R.R.M. 1179 (1976) (one
week); Southern Household Prods. Co., 203 N.L.R.B. 881, 83 L.R.R.M. 1247 (1973)
(ten days); American Mfg. Co. of Texas, 167 N.L.R.B. 520, 66 L.R.R.M. 1122 (1967)
(ten days). And see Freehold AMC-Jeep Corp., 230 N.L.R.B. 903, 95 L.R.R.M. 1419
(1977), where the Board held a four-day offer unreasonably short.

[27] A bona fide offer of reinstatement is one which places the employees within
their former or substantially equivalent position, without prejudice to seniority and
other rights and privileges they possessed prior to discharge.

[28] Compare B&Z Hosiery Prods. Co., 85 N.L.R.B. 633, 24 L.R.R.M. 1441 (1949),
enforced, 180 F.2d 1021, 25 L.R.R.M. 2529 (3d Cir. 1950) (offer must be made by
employer, not fellow employee), with Barr Packing Co., 82 N.L.R.B. 1, 23 L.R.R.M.
1527 (1949) (offer must not be posed as hypothetical question); also Big Sky Sheet
Metal Co., 266 N.L.R.B. 21, 112 L.R.R.M. 1267 (1983) (offer must not be made through
a friend of employee).

[29] Refaire Refrig. Corp., 207 N.L.R.B. 523, 84 L.R.R.M. 1535 (1973). Cf., Hickory's
Best, 267 N.L.R.B. No. 199, 114 L.R.R.M. 1145.

quire that all the rights and privileges of the employee be literally specified [30] nor does it require that the offer be made in writing.[31]

To be clear and definite, the reinstatement offer must be made to the employees in language that is understandable to them. Nevertheless, in *General Iron Corp.*,[32] the Board refused to accept the conclusion of the administrative law judge (ALJ) that reinstatement offers in English were not *bona fide* when the employer knew that the discharged employees spoke only Spanish. The Board said that they knew of no case suggesting that the language of the land is an inappropriate means for communicating with employees.[33] This reasoning appears inconsistent with the Board's policy that bilingual ballots in elections be used upon a valid request,[34] and that unfair labor practice notices be in a language the employees are likely to understand.[35]

Conditionality. An offer of reinstatement must be unconditional,[36] and must not contain either affirmative or implicit limitations. For example, in *Art Metalcraft Plating Co.*,[37] the employer ordered all of its employees who had supported union representation to leave the plant. The employees declared that they could not accept a subsequent offer of reinstatement because they were union members. The Board found that the failure of the employer to respond to the employees' declaration indicated that the offer had been conditional upon abandonment of the union; the employer could have explained that he was disavowing his previous policy against employing union adherents.[38] Furthermore, the employer may not,

---

[30] Eastern Die Co., 142 N.L.R.B. 601, 604, 53 L.R.R.M. 1103, 1106 (1963), *enforced,* 340 F.2d 607, 58 L.R.R.M. 2255 (1st Cir. 1965), *cert. denied,* 381 U.S. 951, 59 L.R.R.M. 2432 (1965); *cf.* American Enterprises, Inc., 200 N.L.R.B. 114, 81 L.R.R.M. 1491 (1972).

[31] Rental Uniform Serv., 167 N.L.R.B. 190, 66 L.R.R.M. 1019 (1967); Adams Book Co., 203 N.L.R.B. 761, n.39, 83 L.R.R.M. 1475 (1973); Hickory's Best, 267 N.L.R.B. 1274, 114 L.R.R.M. 1145 (1983).

[32] 218 N.L.R.B. 770, 89 L.R.R.M. 1788, 1789 (1975).

[33] *Id.* at 770.

[34] *E.g.,* NLRB v. Lowell Corrugated Container Corp., 431 F.2d 1196, 75 L.R.R.M. 2346 (1st Cir. 1970); General Dynamics Corp., 187 N.L.R.B. 679, 76 L.R.R.M. 1540 (1971). *See also* WILLIAMS, NLRB REGULATION OF ELECTION CONDUCT, 482–484 (Lab. Rel. & Pub. Pol. Ser., Rep. No. 8, rev. ed. 1985).

[35] John F. Cuneo, 152 N.L.R.B. 929, 59 L.R.R.M. 1226 (1965); Teamsters Local 901 (F.F. Instrument Corp.), 210 N.L.R.B. No. 153, 86 L.R.R.M. 1286 (1974); Pollack Elec. Co., 219 N.L.R.B. 1237, 90 L.R.R.M. 1335 (1975); *see also* Chapter VII *supra.*

[36] *See* NLRB v. Quest-Shon Mark Brassiere Co., 185 F.2d 285, 27 L.R.R.M. 2036 (2d Cir. 1950), *cert. denied,* 342 U.S. 812, 28 L.R.R.M. 2625 (1951) (offer to reinstate employees at another plant without notice that their original jobs no longer existed constituted conditional offer since it was premised on accepting employment at different location).

[37] 133 N.L.R.B. 706, 48 L.R.R.M. 1701 (1961), *enforced,* 303 F.2d 478, 50 L.R.R.M. 2254 (3d Cir. 1962).

[38] 133 N.L.R.B. at 707–708, 48 L.R.R.M. at 1703–1704.

for example, offer to reinstate an employee "if everything cools down," [39] or condition the offer upon an employee's refraining from future pursuit of his statutory rights, [40] or upon the employee's bringing back a customer that the employee was responsible for losing. [41] Nevertheless, an employer is not required to accompany the reinstatement offer with the restoration of accrued back pay. [42]

Changed Circumstances and the Reinstatement Offer Requirement

Under special circumstances, the Board has recognized that changed circumstances have rendered impractical the requirement of an unconditional offer of reinstatement. [43] For example, where subsequent economic changes eliminate the former position of a discriminatee, the remedy may be limited to reimbursing back pay until the time that the employee would have been discharged for economic reasons. [44]

Thus, even though the Board may order that illegally discharged employees be reinstated, reinstatement may never occur because their jobs have been eliminated for legitimate economic reasons. An employer will be permitted to show that such permissible economic changes have intervened and whether or not the former jobs remain available. As stated by the Fifth Circuit, "discrimination by the Employer does not compel it to make work for these persons. Such discrimination does not require the Employer to discharge or layoff others to provide jobs for these discriminatees." [45] This situation often occurs where the discrimination was directed against temporary employees. Where the employer in such cases can show that these temporary employees would not have retained their employment, the Board's remedy will be limited to back pay. [46] If, however, there is a possibility of future employment, the employer

---

[39] K. & E. Bus Lines, Inc., 255 N.L.R.B. 137, 107 L.R.R.M. 1239 (1981).

[40] Tri-State Truck Serv., Inc., 241 N.L.R.B. 225, 100 L.R.R.M. 1479 (1979).

[41] Genova Express Lines, Inc., 245 N.L.R.B. 229, 102 L.R.R.M. 1602 (1979).

[42] Moro Motors Ltd., 216 N.L.R.B. 192, 88 L.R.R.M. 1211 (1975).

[43] *See* Walter S. Johnson Bldg. Co., 209 N.L.R.B. 428, 86 L.R.R.M. 1368 (1974).

[44] NLRB v. Transamerican Freight Lines, 275 F.2d 311, 45 L.R.R.M. 2864 (7th Cir. 1960); *cf.* Franklin Homes, Inc., 187 N.L.R.B. 389, 76 L.R.R.M. 1412 (1970), *enforced,* 461 F.2d 847, 80 L.R.R.M. 2932 (5th Cir. 1972).

[45] NLRB v. Biscayne Television Corp., 289 F.2d 338, 48 L.R.R.M. 2021, 2022 (5th Cir. 1961). *Cf.* NLRB v. McMahon, 428 F.2d 1213, 74 L.R.R.M. 2684 (9th Cir. 1970).

[46] Armstrong Rubber Co. v. NLRB, 511 F.2d 741, 89 L.R.R.M. 2100, 2101–2102 (5th Cir. 1975); NLRB v. Corning Glass Works, 293 F.2d 784, 48 L.R.R.M. 2759, 2760– 2761 (1st Cir. 1961); Combustion Eng'g, Inc., 130 N.L.R.B. 184, 47 L.R.R.M. 1301 (1961); Two Wheel Corp., 218 N.L.R.B. No. 87, 89 L.R.R.M. 1405 (1975) (no reinstatement of student who planned to return to school).

may be ordered to place such employees on a preferential hiring list for reinstatement when jobs become available.[47]

In other instances, when employees have become physically disabled during the period between discharge and the Board's reinstatement order, some form of back pay will be granted.[48] Reinstatement may be offered, although the Board may condition reinstatement upon receipt of a certificate of physical fitness from a physician.[49]

Reinstatement of Supervisory Employees

Despite specific statutory language declaring that supervisory employees are not to be considered as employees for purposes of the Act,[50] an interesting body of case law involving the reinstate-

---

[47] Waukesha Lime & Stone Co., 145 N.L.R.B. 973, 55 L.R.R.M. 1103 (1964), *enforced,* 343 F.2d 504, 58 L.R.R.M. 2782 (7th Cir. 1955); Myers Ceramic Prods. Co., 140 N.L.R.B. 232, 51 L.R.R.M. 1605 (1962); Ventre Packing Co., 163 N.L.R.B. 540, 64 L.R.R.M. 1414 (1967). There are special remedies crafted by the Board to redress the problem of the runaway plant, or the violation of § 8(a)(3) by a discriminatory discontinuance of operations. In one early case, the Board ordered the employer to pay moving expenses to the new location or transportation expenses at the option of the employee. J. Klotz & Co., 13 N.L.R.B. 746, 4 L.R.R.M. 344 (1939); *but see* New Madrid Mfg. Co., 104 N.L.R.B. 117, 32 L.R.R.M. 1059 (1953), *enforced,* 215 F.2d 908, 34 L.R.R.M. 2844 (8th Cir. 1954), where the Board ordered moving expenses only. In another case where an employer discontinued manufacturing the Board ordered reinstatement should there be a resumption of manufacturing. Bonnie Lass Knitting Mills, Inc., 126 N.L.R.B. 1396, 45 L.R.R.M. 1477 (1960). See discussion at Ch. XIII, *infra,* at text accompanying n.56 *et. seq.*

[48] *See* American Mfg. Co. of Texas, 167 N.L.R.B. 520, 66 L.R.R.M. 1122 (1967). If the discharged employee has become disabled through a job-related injury arising from interim employment, only the amount of money constituting lost wages received under a subsequent workmen's compensation award may be deducted from the back pay order. *See* Chapter VII, *supra.*

[49] Phelps Dodge Corp., 28 N.L.R.B. 442, 7 L.R.R.M. 138 (1940), *cf.* Shawnee Milling Co., 82 N.L.R.B. 1266, 24 L.R.R.M. 100 (1949), *enforcement denied on other grounds,* 184 F.2d 57, 26 L.R.R.M. 2462 (10th Cir. 1950); Niles Firebrick Co., 30 N.L.R.B. 426, 8 L.R.R.M. 61 (1941), *enforced,* 128 F.2d 258, 10 L.R.R.M. 642 (6th Cir. 1942). *But cf.,* Lipman Bros. Inc., 147 N.L.R.B. 1342, 56 L.R.R.M. 1420, 1427 (1964), where the Board ordered the reinstatement of a physically disabled employee whose prior job had been eliminated. The employee, though disabled, had performed that job satisfactorily and the Board reasoned that the employer should be required to reinstate him within the unit to another job suitable to his physical condition.

[50] 29 U.S.C. § 152(3) (1976). Pursuant to the Wagner Act, the Supreme Court had sustained the Board's interpretation of the term employee as including supervisory employees. *See* Packard Motor Car Co. v. NLRB, 330 U.S. 485, 19 L.R.R.M. 2397 (1947). The subsequent Taft-Hartley Amendments, however, expressly excluded supervisors from being considered as employees under the Act. *See also* § 14(a) of the Act, [29 U.S.C. § 164(a)] which provides, inter alia, that ". . . no employer subject to the Act shall be compelled to deem individuals defined herein as supervisors as employees for the purpose of any law, either national or local, relating to collective bargaining." *Cf.* Beasly v. Food Fair of North Carolina, Inc., 415 U.S. 907, 86 L.R.R.M. 2196 (1974).

ment of supervisors has arisen. Since supervisory employees clearly do not possess any specific statutory right to reinstatement, the Board's authority to grant relief must constitute a discretionary judgment that the reinstatement of supervisors is necessary to effectuate some fundamental policy of the Act. On occasion, the Board has determined that where a supervisor's discharge intimidates nonsupervisory employees in the exercise of their section 7 rights, the employer commits a violation of section 8(a)(1).[51] The ensuing reinstatement order is derived from the Board's authority to protect employees in the exercise of their statutory rights.

Section 8(a)(4) Discrimination

Section 8(a)(4) makes it an unfair labor practice for an employer "to discharge or otherwise discriminate against an employee because he has filed charges or given testimony under this Act."[52] Until 1972, there had been some confusion as to whether the mere presence at a formal Board hearing of an employee who does not testify, although prepared to do so, entitles the employee to the protection afforded by section 8(a)(1).[53] In terms of the actual substantive relief granted an employee who had been either discharged or discriminated against in retaliation for participation, the distinction between actual and preparatory participation was virtually meaningless. A reinstatement order in such a case could be issued

---

[51] *Compare* NLRB v. Better Monkey Grip Co., 243 F.2d 836, 40 L.R.R.M. 2027 (5th Cir. 1957), *cert. denied*, 355 U.S. 864, 41 L.R.R.M. 2007 (1957), *with* NLRB v. Talledega Cotton Factory, Inc., 213 F.2d 209, 34 L.R.R.M. 2196 (5th Cir. 1954) (discharge of supervisor for giving testimony adverse to employer's position in Board proceeding); NLRB v. Electro Motive Mfg. Co., 389 F.2d 61, 67 L.R.R.M. 2513, 2514 (4th Cir. 1968) (reinstatement of a supervisor discharged for giving a Board agent a signed statement admitting that he had unlawfully threatened employees); Gainesville Publishing Co., 150 N.L.R.B. 602, 58 L.R.R.M. 1128 (1964) (violation by reducing foreman's pay rate when he refused to cooperate in antiunion drive); *see also* General Eng'g Inc., 131 N.L.R.B. 648, 48 L.R.R.M. 1105 (1961), *enforcement denied on other grounds*, 311 F.2d 570, 52 L.R.R.M. 2277 (9th Cir. 1962) (supervisor refused to assist in discriminatory discharge of employee); see also NLRB v. Dewey Bros., Inc., 80 L.R.R.M. 2112 (4th Cir. 1972). *But cf.*, NLRB v. Brookside Indus., Inc., 308 F.2d 224, 51 L.R.R.M. 2148 (4th Cir. 1962), *denying enforcement to* Brookside Industries, Inc., 135 N.L.R.B. 16, 49 L.R.R.M. 1420 (1962) (court refused to reinstate a supervisor who was discharged for refusing to engage in antiunion activities). The court based its decision on the conflict of interest that would result because supervisor was also the wife of a nonsupervisory employee; however, back pay was awarded.
[52] 29 U.S.C. § 158(a)(4)(1970). *See, e.g.*, Big Three Indus. Gas & Equip. Co., 212 N.L.R.B. No. 115, 87 L.R.R.M. 1543 (1974).
[53] *Compare* Ogle Protection Serv., Inc., 149 N.L.R.B. 545, 57 L.R.R.M. 1337 (1964) [planning to file charges or to testify not within § 8(a)(4)] *with* Thomas J. Aycock, d/b/a Vita Foods, 135 N.L.R.B. 1357, 49 L.R.R.M. 1723 (1962), *enforced*, 328 F.2d 314, 55 L.R.R.M. 2575 (5th Cir. 1964) [fact that employee who was prepared to testify did not actually do so was immaterial to finding a violation of § 8(a)(4)].

upon the basis of a section 8(a)(1) or 8(a)(3) violation in either circumstance.[54]

Nevertheless, the Supreme Court in *NLRB v. Scrivener, d/b/a AA Electric Co.,*[55] held that an employer also violated section 8(a)(4) of the Act when it discharged employees who had given sworn written statements to Board agents during an investigatory stage of an unfair labor practice charge. The employees involved had neither filed charges with the Board, nor actually given testimony in a Board hearing.[56] Similar to remedies for other violations, reinstatement orders in section 8(a)(4) cases are not limited to actual discharges, but may encompass refusals to hire applicants who have filed previous charges against the employer.[57]

Weingarten *Violations and Reinstatement*

Under *NLRB v. Weingarten* [58] it is a violation of section 8(a)(1) of the Act for an employer to deny an employee's request that a union representative be present at an investigatory interview. When such an illegal interview takes place and results in obtaining evidence supporting a finding of cause for discharge, the Board has recently concluded in *Taracorp Industries* [59] that reinstatement is not an appropriate remedy in view of section 10(c) of the Act prohibiting reinstatement for employees discharged for cause.[60] *Taracorp* overruled a series of Board cases ordering reinstatement.[61]

---

[54] *See* NLRB v. Ritchie Mfg. Co., 354 F.2d 90, 61 L.R.R.M. 2013 (8th Cir. 1965).

[55] 405 U.S. 117, 79 L.R.R.M. 2587 (1972).

[56] *See also* NLRB v. King Louie Bowling Corp., 472 F.2d 1192, 82 L.R.R.M. 2576 (8th Cir. 1973); Sinclair Glass Co. v. NLRB, 465 F.2d 209, 80 L.R.R.M. 3082 (7th Cir. 1972). *But see* Rock Road Trailer Parts and Sales, 204 N.L.R.B. 1136, 83 L.R.R.M. 1467 (1973) (employee fired immediately after engaging in phone conversation with Board representative was not discriminatorily discharged but was fired for cause, since employee had conducted phone conversation in loud and belligerent voice in front of employer's customers and had threatened to put employer out of business); Nachman Corp. v. NLRB, 337 F.2d 421, 57 L.R.R.M. 2217 (7th Cir. 1964); Beiser Aviation Corp., 135 N.L.R.B. 433, 49 L.R.R.M. 1512 (1962).

[57] Central Rigging & Contracting Corp., 129 N.L.R.B. 342, 46 L.R.R.M. 1548 (1960). *See also* Southern Bleachery & Print Works, Inc., 118 N.L.R.B. 299, 40 L.R.R.M. 1174 (1957), *enforced,* 257 F.2d 235, 42 L.R.R.M. 2533 (4th Cir. 1958), *cert. denied,* 359 U.S. 911, 43 L.R.R.M. 2576 (1959); Underwood Machinery Co., 79 N.L.R.B. 1287, 22 L.R.R.M. 1506 (1948), *enforced,* 179 F.2d 118, 25 L.R.R.M. 2195 (1st Cir. 1949). *Cf.,* Phelps Dodge Corp. v. NLRB, 313 U.S. 177, 8 L.R.R.M. 439 (1941) (policy regarding the extension of reinstatement orders to include job applicants in § 8(a)(3) situations).

[58] 420 U.S. 251, 88 L.R.R.M. 2689 (1975).

[59] 273 N.L.R.B. No. 54, 117 L.R.R.M. 1497 (1984).

[60] *See text accompanying* nn.7-16, *supra.*

[61] Kraft Foods, 251 N.L.R.B. 598 (1980); Illinois Bell Tel. Co., 251 N.L.R.B. 932 (1980); Ohio Masonic Home, 251 N.L.R.B. 606 (1980); *cf.* Chromalloy Am. Corp., 263 N.L.R.B. 244 (1982).

UNION-INITIATED DISCRIMINATORY DISCHARGES

Pursuant to section 8(b)(2), it is an unfair labor practice for a labor organization, *inter alia,* "to cause or attempt to cause an employer to discriminate against an employee in violation of subsection 8(a)(3)." [62] The Board usually remedies an attempt to cause employer discrimination by directing the union to cease and desist and to post a notice of the NLRB order.[63] When discrimination has actually occurred—i.e., when an employee is discharged or a job applicant denied hire as a result of union initiative—a reinstatement and back-pay order may be issued.[64] Reinstatement, however, will be ordered only if both the union and employer have been jointly charged with violations. If the union's discrimination was responsible for the discharge, reinstatement will not usually be ordered. Rather, the union merely will be required to notify both the employer and employee that it has no objection to the employee's immediate reinstatement.[65]

The Board's policy of refusing to order reinstatement where only a labor organization is charged with an unfair labor practice poses serious questions as to the adequacy of the discharged employee's relief. In such cases, the Board's affirmative remedy has been limited to orders directing the union to tender back pay to the employee and notify both the employer and the discharged employee that it has withdrawn its objections to the discriminatee's future employment.[66]

In *Pen and Pencil Workers, Local 19593 (Parker Pen Co.),*[67] the Board first faced the problem of fashioning an affirmative order where the union alone had been charged with an unfair labor practice. The Board claimed that, in the absence of a charge against the employer, its authority to remedy a discriminatory discharge was limited to a certain degree. The Board concluded, therefore, that the most it could do for the discharged employee was to direct the

---

[62] 29 U.S.C. § 158(b)(2) (1976).

[63] *See* MORRIS, THE DEVELOPING LABOR LAW 1682 (2d ed. 1983).

[64] *E.g.,* Acme Mattress Co., 91 N.L.R.B. 1010, 26 L.R.R.M. 1611 (1950), *enforced,* 192 F.2d 524, 29 L.R.R.M. 2079 (7th Cir. 1951). Of course, a reinstatement order will also be accompanied by a cease and desist provision and affirmative requirements such as notice posting and back pay.

[65] Pen and Pencil Workers, Local 19593 (Parker Pen Co.), 91 N.L.R.B. 883, 26 L.R.R.M. 1583 (1950). *But see* discussion at Ch. VIII *supra.*

[66] UAW, Local 291 (Timken-Detroit Axle Co.), 92 N.L.R.B. 968, 27 L.R.R.M. 1188 (1950), *enforced,* 194 F.2d 698, 29 L.R.R.M. 2433 (7th Cir. 1952); *cf.* NLRB v. Local 57, Operating Eng'rs, 201 F.2d 771, 31 L.R.R.M. 2344 (1st Cir. 1953).

[67] 91 N.L.R.B. 883, 26 L.R.R.M. 1583 (1950).

union "to remove the barrier which it has erected" to reemployment by requiring the offending labor organization to notify both the employee and the employer that it no longer had any objection to immediate reinstatement.[68] The Board added, however, that "[a]s the employer, who is not a respondent, has sole control over the employment of its employees, we cannot order that the [discriminatee] be reinstated." [69]

As a half measure, this truncated form of relief is unfair not only to the employee, but may also prove so to the employer. Since an employee must prove that both the employer and union have violated the Act in order to ensure his reinstatement rights,[70] the rule encourages the employee to bring charges against the employer regardless of the circumstances or the employer's culpability. Once the employer is charged with discrimination, he cannot defend his actions as the result of union coercion. In *Acme Mattress Co.,*[71] decided in the same year as *Pen and Pencil Workers,* the Board rejected union coercion as an employer defense and held the union and employer jointly and severally liable for a discriminatory discharge. In this case, however, the unlawful discharge had been exacted by the union from the employer as its price for terminating an existing strike. According to the majority, a remedial policy was necessary as a means of introducing an economic incentive to help an employer resist unlawful union demands.[72]

---

[68] *Id.* at 888–889, 26 L.R.R.M. at 1585–1586.

[69] *Id.* at 888, 26 L.R.R.M. at 1585.

[70] *See* Union Starch & Refining Co. v. NLRB, 186 F.2d 1008, 27 L.R.R.M. 2342 (7th Cir. 1951), *cert. denied,* 342 U.S. 815, 28 L.R.R.M. 2625 (1951).

[71] 91 N.L.R.B. 1010, 26 L.R.R.M. 1611 (1950), *enforced,* 192 F.2d 524, 29 L.R.R.M. 2079 (7th Cir. 1951).

[72] *See* 91 N.L.R.B. at 1015–1016, 26 L.R.R.M. at 1615–1616, for a statement of the majority view:

Our policy of assessing liability for back pay jointly against both the employer and the union, even where the discrimination would not have been effected but for pressures brought by the union, is founded upon a basic principle well established. . . . Whatever the situation may be, the fact remains that, in the ultimate analysis, it is the employer, and only the employer, who *controls* the hiring and discharge of his employees. Recognizing this, this Board and the courts have frequently held that it is the duty of an employer to resist the usurpation of his control over employment by any group that seeks to utilize such control for or against any labor organization, and that the Act affords no immunity because the employer believes that the exigencies of the moment require that he capitulate to the pressures and violate the statute (emphasis in original).

Cf. NLRB v. Pinkerton's Nat'l Det. Agency, 202 F.2d 230, 31 L.R.R.M. 2336 (9th Cir. 1953).

A few years later, the Supreme Court, in *Radio Officers' Union v. NLRB*,[73] approved the Board's policy of holding that the absence of a joinder of the employer in a proceeding against a union for violation of section 8(b)(2) does not preclude entry by the Board of a back pay order against the union.

---

[73] 347 U.S. 17, 54–55, 33 L.R.R.M. 2417, 2431–2432 (1954).

CHAPTER X

Reinstatement Rights of Strikers

In assessing the reinstatement rights of a striking employee who has made an unconditional offer to return to work, the threshold question is whether the employee was engaged in an economic or unfair labor practice strike. Generally, the economic striker's right to immediate reinstatement depends upon whether his job is available—i.e., whether or not his job has been filled by a permanent replacement. If it has, the striker is not entitled to immediate reinstatement but is placed upon a preferential rehire list. On the other hand, the unfair labor practice striker has the right to immediate reinstatement even if permanently replaced,[1] unless he or she has engaged in misconduct which would be cause for discharge.

ECONOMIC STRIKERS

The Act provides that "the term 'employee' . . . shall include any individual whose work has ceased as a consequence of, or in connection with, any current labor dispute . . . and who has not obtained any other regular and substantially equivalent employment."[2] Thus, the same protection given to regular employees is extended to strikers. Under the terms of the Act, the reinstatement rights of economic strikers are not premised upon any inherent rights acquired upon by entering into an employment relationship; rather their rights are predicated upon their section 7 right to join and participate in labor organizations and to engage in protected con-

---

[1] This right to reinstatement assumes that there is a job available to which the unfair labor practice striker may be reinstated. Because business fluctuations may render a Board's order impossible to implement, reemployment is effectuated under the following set of priorities: 1) all replacements must be discharged, Sunshine Hosiery Mills, 1 N.L.R.B. 664, 1 L.R.R.M. 49 (1936); 2) available jobs are to be distributed to those affected on a nondiscriminatory basis such as seniority, Timken Silent Automatic Co., 1 N.L.R.B. 335, 1 L.R.R.M. 30 (1936); 3) any remainder are to be placed on a preferential hiring list, Tiny Town Togs, Inc., 7 N.L.R.B. 54, 2 L.R.R.M. 236 (1938).

[2] 29 U.S.C. § 152(3).

certed activities in general.[3] Consequently, an employer's refusal to reinstate an economic striker who has unconditionally offered to return to work is presumed to be an unfair labor practice[4] unless the employer presents a legitimate and substantial business justification for its refusal to reinstate, such as the unavailability of substantially equivalent work, whether the result of hiring permanent replacements[5] or of a bona fide change in economic circumstances.[6]

Limitations on Reinstatement Rights of Economic Strikers

As indicated above, the reinstatement rights of an economic striker are conditional. The employer has the right to replace an economic striker in order to keep its operation functioning, and is under no obligation to discharge the replacement when the striker offers to return to work.[7] This limitation was approved by the Supreme Court in one of its first Wagner Act decisions, *NLRB v. Mackay Radio & Telegraph Co.,*[8] on the grounds that:

> [A]n employer, guilty of no act denounced by the statute, has [not] lost the right to protect and continue his business by supplying places left vacant by strikers. And he is not bound to discharge those hired

---

[3] Any other rationale is untenable as the Board's remedial authority to fashion relief is dependent upon the commission of an unfair labor practice. Without the necessary unfair labor practice, the Board is without jurisdiction, and an employer's treatment of its employees is entirely its prerogative.

[4] NLRB v. Fleetwood Trailer Co., 389 U.S. 375, 378, 66 L.R.R.M. 2737, 2738 (1967); NLRB v. Great Dane Trailers, 388 U.S. 26, 34, 65 L.R.R.M. 2465 (1967).

[5] NLRB v. MacKay Radio & Telegraph Co., 304 U.S. 333, 345-6, 2 L.R.R.M. 610 (1938).

[6] The participation of employees in a strike which is economically oriented, but conducted by illegal means or for an unlawful objective, is also considered a legitimate business reason excusing the employer of any duty to reemploy such strikers pursuant to the "for cause" proviso of § 10(c). *E.g.,* St Regis Paper Co. v. NLRB, 105 L.R.R.M. 2652 (6th Cir. 1980); Oneita Knitting Mills, Inc. v. NLRB, 375 F.2d 385, 64 L.R.R.M. 2724 (4th Cir. 1967); American News Co., 55 N.L.R.B. 1302, 14 L.R.R.M. 64 (1944). See also discussion at n.55 and accompanying text, *infra.*

[7] In hiring permanent replacements, an employer commits an unfair labor practice if it offers inducements which have the effect of discriminating in the terms of employment between strikers and nonstrikers. *See* NLRB v. Erie Resistor Corp., 373 U.S. 221, 53 L.R.R.M. 2121 (1963). *But see* Belknap, Inc. v. Hale, 463 U.S. 491, 113 L.R.R.M. 3057 (1983), where the Supreme Court held that a lawsuit brought by the replacements under Kentucky law alleging a promise by the employer that they would not lose their jobs at the end of the strike was not preempted by federal law. A replacement employee is one actually hired before an employer has received an unconditioned offer to turn to work by a striker. NLRB v. Cutting, Inc., 112 L.R.R.M. 3056 (7th Cir. 1983).

[8] 304 U.S. 333, 2 L.R.R.M. 610 (1938).

to fill the places of strikers, upon the election of the latter to resume their employment, in order to create places for them.[9]

The ruling in *Mackay*, however, did not resolve the issue of whether an economic striker was entitled to the next available job opening. Initially, the Board, in *Brown & Root, Inc.,*[10] treated the replaced economic striker on the same nondiscriminatory basis afforded new job applicants. In *Brown & Root*, several replaced strikers sought back pay retroactive to the date that openings first occurred in their job classifications. The employer's hiring was not tinged with anti-union animus. In denying the award of back pay, the Board held:

> [W]e reject the theory urged by the General Counsel, to the effect that the 13 strikers were entitled to appropriate vacancies as they arose.... In the circumstances of this case, we hold that Respondents had no obligation to seek out or prefer the 13 IAM strikers for vacancies which opened up after their application.[11]

The Board's *Brown & Root* policy was subsequently rendered untenable by two Supreme Court decisions. In *NLRB v. Great Dane Trailers*[12] the Court held that independent proof of anti-union animus is not essential to a finding that an employer violated section 8(a)(3) by failing to reinstate a striking employee. The Court stated that "if it can reasonably be concluded that an employer's discriminatory conduct was inherently destructive of important employee rights," no proof of animus is needed, and a violation can be found "even if the employer introduces evidence that the conduct was motivated by business considerations."[13] Additionally, even where the harm to employees' rights is not inherently destructive but "comparatively slight," animus need be proved only "if the employer has come forward with evidence of legitimate and substantial business justifications for the conduct."[14] This holding, of course, undercut the anti-union animus requirement of *Brown & Root*.

---

[9] *Id.* at 345–346, 2 L.R.R.M. at 614. Economic strikers cannot be refused reemployment, however, if their jobs have been filled only on a temporary basis. Cyr Bottle Gas Co. v. NLRB, 497 F.2d 900, 87 L.R.R.M. 2253 (6th Cir.1974). *Cf.* NLRB v. International Van Lines, 409 U.S. 48, 81 L.R.R.M. 2595 (1972).

[10] 132 N.L.R.B. 486, 48 L.R.R.M. 1391 (1961), *enforced*, 311 F.2d 447, 52 L.R.R.M. 2115 (8th Cir. 1963).

[11] 132 N.L.R.B. at 494, 48 L.R.R.M. at 1394. *Accord*, Flint Glass Workers (Bartlett-Collins Co.), 110 N.L.R.B. 395, 35 L.R.R.M. 1006 (1954), *aff'd*, 230 F.2d 212, 37 L.R.R.M. 2409 (D.C. Cir. 1956), *cert. denied*, 351 U.S. 988, 38 L.R.R.M. 2238 (1956). *Cf.*, NLRB v. Plastilite Corp., 375 F.2d 343, 64 L.R.R.M. 2741 (8th Cir. 1967).

[12] 388 U.S. 26, 65 L.R.R.M. 2465 (1967).

[13] *Id.* at 33–34, 65 L.R.R.M. at 2469.

[14] *Id.*

In *NLRB v. Fleetwood Trailer Co.*,[15] the Court held that economic strikers' reinstatement rights do not depend upon job availability as of the moment when they make unconditional application for reinstatement. On the contrary, their status as employees and their right to reinstatement continue until they have obtained other regular and substantially equivalent employment.[16] Thus, under *Fleetwood*, an economic striker is entitled to return to work "[i]f and when a job for which the striker is qualified becomes available."[17] The Court noted that these rights are not absolute, and that an employer will not violate the Act by refusing to reinstate economic strikers if it can show that its action was due to "legitimate and substantial business justifications." Such justification is found when either (1) "the jobs which the strikers claim are occupied by workers hired as permanent replacements during the strike in order to continue operations," or (2) "the striker's job has been eliminated for substantial and bona fide reasons."[18] *Fleetwood* also emphasized that the burden is not on the NLRB General Counsel but on the employer to show that jobs are unavailable.[19]

The Laidlaw *Doctrine*

In 1968, the Board in *Laidlaw Corp.*[20] overruled *Brown & Root.* Relying upon *Fleetwood Trailer,* the Board reasoned that its prior policy of treating an economic striker

> as a new employee or an employee with less than rights accorded by full reinstatement (such as denial of seniority) was wholly unrelated to any of [an employer's] economic needs, could only penalize [the employee] for engaging in concerted activities, was inherently destructive of employee interests, and thus was unresponsive to the requirements of the statute.[21]

Accordingly, the Board announced that strikers who have been permanently replaced at the time of their application for reinstatement

> (1) remain employees; and (2) are entitled to full reinstatement upon the departure of replacements unless they have in the meantime acquired regular and substantially equivalent employment, or the

---

[15] 389 U.S. 375, 66 L.R.R.M. 2737 (1967).
[16] *Id.* at 381, 66 L.R.R.M. at 2739.
[17] *Id.*
[18] *Id.* at 379, 66 L.R.R.M. at 2738.
[19] *Id.* at 378–379 n.4, 66 L.R.R.M. at 2738 n.4.
[20] 171 N.L.R.B. 1366, 68 L.R.R.M. 1252 (1968), *enforced,* 414 F.2d 99, 71 L.R.R.M. 3054 (7th Cir. 1969), *cert. denied,* 397 U.S. 920, 73 L.R.R.M. 2537 (1970).
[21] 171 N.L.R.B. at 1368, 68 L.R.R.M. at 1256.

employer can sustain his burden of proof that the failure to offer full reinstatement was for legitimate and substantial business reasons.[22]

Laidlaw was enforced by the Seventh Circuit,[23] and has received substantial approval in other circuits.[24] *Laidlaw* requires an employer to maintain a preferential hiring list of economic strikers entitled to reinstatement and to notify them when substantially equivalent jobs become available. Responding to complaints that this might be onerous, the Seventh Circuit in *Laidlaw* stated:

> We do not view the employer's duty to seek out replaced economic strikers to be a severe burden in practice. Employers, who presumably retain the addresses and phone numbers of the strikers, should not find it overly burdensome to give them notice that a position has fallen vacant. 82 Harv. L. Rev. 1777, 1779 (1969).[25]

The Seventh Circuit noted, however, that *Laidlaw* did not resolve the question of when a striker's right to reinstatement might expire.[26] After *Laidlaw*, employers complained that it would be onerous to require them to keep current applications indefinitely.[27] For example, in *American Machinery Corp. v. NLRB*[28] the Fifth Circuit rejected the employer's contention that the difficulty of finding the replaced strikers was a "legitimate and substantial business reason" for not contacting them when vacancies arose.[29] Nonetheless, the court indicated that it was not totally unreceptive to some limitation of the *Laidlaw* doctrine, and suggested that the duration of the employer's duty to extend reinstatement privileges to permanently

---

[22] *Id.* at 1370, 68 L.R.R.M. at 1258 (enumeration in original). *See* Colour TV Corp., 202 N.L.R.B.44, 82 L.R.R.M. 1477 (1973), where the Board found that an employer successfully demonstrated "legitimate and substantial business reasons" for refusing to reemploy an economic striker where the employer had suffered a decline in business and the employee had previously demonstrated only marginal productivity in comparison to fellow employees who had been retained.

[23] Laidlaw Corp. v. NLRB, 414 F.2d 99, 71 L.R.R.M. 3054 (7th Cir. 1967), *cert. denied*, 397 U.S. 920, 73 L.R.R.M. 2537 (1970).

[24] H & F Binch Co. v. NLRB, 456 F.2d 357, 79 L.R.R.M. 2692, 2697 (2d Cir. 1972); Little Rock Airmotive, Inc. v. NLRB, 455 F.2d 163, 79 L.R.R.M. 2544 (8th Cir. 1972); NLRB v. Anvil Prods., 496 F.2d 94, 86 L.R.R.M. 2822, 2824 (5th Cir. 1974); American Mach. Corp. v. NLRB, 424 F.2d 1321, 73 L.R.R.M. 2977 (5th Cir. 1970); NLRB v. Johnson Sheet Metal, Inc., 442 F.2d 1056, 1061, 77 L.R.R.M. 2245 (10th Cir. 1971); NLRB v. Hartmann Luggage Co., 453 F.2d 178, 79 L.R.R.M. 2139 (6th Cir. 1971); C.H. Guenther & Son, Inc. d/b/a Pioneer Flour Mills v. NLRB, 427 F.2d 983, 74 L.R.R.M. 2343 (5th Cir. 1979), *cert. denied*, 400 U.S. 942, 75 L.R.R.M. 2752 (1970); NLRB v. Transport Co. of Texas, 438 F.2d 258, 76 L.R.R.M. 2482 (5th Cir. 1971).

[25] 414 F.2d at 105, 71 L.R.R.M. at 3059 n.2.

[26] 414 F.2d 105, 71 L.R.R.M. at 3059.

[27] *E.g.*, NLRB v. Hartmann Luggage Co., 453 F.2d 178, 79 L.R.R.M. 2139, 2141 (6th Cir. 1971).

[28] 424 F.2d 1321, 73 L.R.R.M. 2977 (5th Cir. 1970).

[29] *Id.* at 1327–1329, 73 L.R.R.M. at 2981–2982.

replaced strikers might be regulated by reasonable rules which the Board may devise.[30]

Modifications to Laidlaw

Acting upon the Fifth Circuit's suggestion, the Board instituted several modifications. In *Brooks Research & Mfg.,*[31] the Board held that an employer might ask replaced strikers from time to time to advise the employer whether they wished to remain on the preferential hiring list. The Board explained that

> [u]nder the agreement reached by the parties herein, the Respondent's burden is slight. Thus, when a vacancy arises recall is to be by telephone with confirmation by letter or telegram. Respondent is required only to use the last known addresses and telephone numbers on file with it. The recalled employee has only three working days to report after being notified to return. If an employee refuses an offer of reinstatement or does not respond, his name may be deleted from the list.
>
> Therefore, contrary to its contention, Respondent does not have to maintain the entire preferential hiring list indefinitely. In addition, there may be other means by which Respondent can cope with its alleged burden. For example, although we find it unnecessary to consider at this time, we note that the Fifth Circuit suggested in *American Machinery,* supra:
>
> " . . . he might notify the strikers when they request reinstatement of a reasonable time during which their applications will be considered current and at the expiration of which they must take affirmative action to maintain their current status." [32]

In *Brooks,* the employer contended that a contractual provision limiting the recall rights of laid-off employees to a period of six months was also applicable to former strikers awaiting reinstatement. In deciding otherwise, the Board stated:

> We reject the [employer's] contention that economic strikers should be equated with laid-off employees. The reinstatement rights of economic strikers under *Fleetwood Trailer* and *Laidlaw* are statutory as distinguished from the rights of laid-off employees.[33]

In *Bio-Science Laboratories,*[34] the Board rejected its General Counsel's contention that replaced strikers awaiting reinstatement under

---

[30] *Id.* at 1328, 73 L.R.R.M. at 2981. The court observed that "a reasonable rule would not contravene Fleetwood's assertion that '[t]he right to reinstatement does not depend upon technicalities relating to application.'" *Accord,* NLRB v. Hartmann Luggage Co., 453 F.2d 178, 79 L.R.R.M. 2139, 2141 (6th Cir. 1971).

[31] 202 N.L.R.B. 634, 82 L.R.R.M. 1599 (1973).

[32] *Id.* at 636, 82 L.R.R.M. at 1602.

[33] *Id.,* 82 L.R.R.M. at 1601.

[34] 209 N.L.R.B. 796, 85 L.R.R.M. 1568 (1974).

Laidlaw must be recalled to work in the same order as they would be recalled from a layoff under the terms of an existing collective bargaining agreement. The administrative law judge (ALJ), whose decision the Board adopted, repeated that economic strikers cannot be equated with laid-off employees. The ALJ concluded that unless the parties have specifically agreed upon an order of reinstatement, the employer may use any method of recalling former strikers "as long as it is not shown to have been unlawfully motivated or inherently destructive of employee rights."[35]

In *United Aircraft Corp.*[36] the Board established the principle that the reinstatement rights of permanently replaced economic strikers might be modified or terminated by an agreement between the employer and the union. In so deciding, the Board reversed its trial examiner, who had found that, despite the employer-union agreement, the employer had violated the Act by abandoning its preferential recall list upon the expiration of a negotiated waiting period. The Board held that this neither violated the spirit of *Laidlaw,* nor did it contravene the Supreme Court's *Fleetwood* decision, which had expressly reserved the question of whether a labor organization could waive the right of strikers to reinstatement before the hiring of new employees.[37] The Board stated that it approved of the settlement agreement because it was bargained in good faith;[38] there was no evidence that the employer had sought to undermine the union's status; the recall period (approximately four-and-one-half months) was not unreasonably short; and there was no evidence of discriminatory intent or objective by either party in the negotiation or implementation of the agreement.

---

[35] *Id.* at 804.

[36] 192 N.L.R.B. 382, 77 L.R.R.M. 1785 (1971), *aff'd on other grounds,* Machinists v. United Aircraft Corp., Lodges 743 and 1746, IAM v. NLRB, 90 L.R.R.M. 2272 (2d Cir. 1975).

[37] *Id.* at 386, 77 L.R.R.M. at 1790–1791. In *Fleetwood,* 389 U.S. at 381, 66 L.R.R.M. at 2739 n.8, the Court had noted:

> The respondent contends that the Union agreed to a nonpreferential hiring list and thereby waived the rights of the strikers to reinstatement ahead of the new applicants. The Board found that the Union, having lost the strike, merely "bowed to the [respondent's] decision." The Court of Appeals did not rule on this point or on the effect, if any, that its resolution might have upon the outcome of this case. Upon remand, the issue will be open for such consideration as may be appropriate.

[38] The union's representative authority enables it to bargain for the job rights of the individual employee. The establishment of a negotiated cut-off date for recall is analogous to impact bargaining engaged in by unions and employers when a change in operations necessitates job elimination. *See generally* Chapter XIII, *infra,* at n.57 *et seq.* and accompanying text.

In a companion case, *Laher Spring & Corp.*,[39] the Board found
that an employer had violated section 8(a)(3), despite the existence
of a strike settlement agreement. The Board pointed to the substantial increase in overtime work and to an unexplained failure
to fill positions during preferential recall period followed immediately by a dramatic increase in new hires. The Board concluded
that the employer had entered into the accord as part of a scheme
to delay or avoid rehiring the strikers.[40]

An employer's obligation to reemploy an economic or unfair labor
practice striker arises immediately upon the striker's filing of an
unconditional application for reinstatement. Assessing back-pay liability against an employer from the date upon which such an
application is tendered encourages, or should encourage, prompt
compliance by the employer. Just as the employer must make an
unconditional offer of reinstatement to discriminatorily discharged
employees,[41] the striker's reinstatement application may not attach
conditions other than requesting reemployment to his former position or to one which is substantially equivalent.[42] Furthermore,
it is not necessary that strikers' applications for reinstatement be
made individually; an offer by the employees to return as a group
is sufficient.[43] It follows that the employees may designate a labor
organization to act as their spokesman, as long as the chosen union
represents a majority of the employees in the bargaining unit.[44]

UNFAIR LABOR PRACTICE STRIKERS

A work stoppage that has been initiated in whole or in part by
an employer unfair labor practice is an unfair labor practice strike.[45]
An employer must reinstate unfair labor practice strikers to their

---

[39] 192 N.L.R.B. 464, 77 L.R.R.M. 1800 (1971).

[40] *Id.* at 466, 77 L.R.R.M. at 1802.

[41] *See* Ch. IX, *supra,* at n.17 *et seq.* and accompanying text.

[42] *Cf.* NLRB v. Textile Mach. Works, 214 F.2d 929, 34 L.R.R.M. 2535 (3d Cir. 1954);
NLRB v. Pecheur Lozenge Co., 209 F.2d 393, 33 L.R.R.M. 2324 (2d Cir. 1953), *cert.
denied,* 347 U.S. 953, 34 L.R.R.M. 2027 (1954).

[43] *See* Draper Corp., 52 N.L.R.B. 1477, 13 L.R.R.M. 88 (1943), *enforcement denied
on other grounds,* 145 F.2d 199, 15 L.R.R.M. 580 (4th Cir. 1944). *But cf.* Southwestern
Pipe, Inc., 179 N.L.R.B. 364, 72 L.R.R.M. 1377 (1969), *enforced in part,* 444 F.2d 340,
77 L.R.R.M. 2317 (5th Cir. 1971). In *Southwestern Pipe,* the Board reversed its previous policy concerning the back-pay liability incurred by employers who refuse to
reinstate unfair labor practice strikers upon the receipt of a group application.
Although the reinstatement rights of such individuals remain intact, the back-pay
liability is terminated for those employees who refuse reinstatement.

[44] Electric Auto Lite Co., 80 N.L.R.B. 1601, 23 L.R.R.M. 1268 (1948).

[45] *See* NLRB v. Mackay Radio & Telegraph Co., 304 U.S.333, 2 L.R.R.M. 610 (1938).
But cf. Southwestern Pipe, Inc. v. NLRB, 179 N.L.R.B. 364, 72 L.R.R.M. 1377 (1969),

former jobs,[46] even though it must fire replacements to make room for them.[47]

An economic strike may be converted into an unfair labor practice strike by the employer's subsequent commission of unfair labor practices,[48] if such practices prolong the strike. Here too, the employer must reinstate the strikers and, if necessary, discharge replacements hired after the date of conversion.[49] A conversion may occur where the employer illegally initiates a back-to-work movement among striking employees.[50] For example, a conversion of an economic to an unfair labor practice strike was found where the employer bypassed a certified bargaining representative and dealt with the employees directly.[51] An employer is even likelier to be

enforced in part, 444 F.2d 340, 77 L.R.R.M. 2317 (5th Cir. 1971); Clinton Foods, Inc., 122 N.L.R.B. 239, 36 L.R.R.M. 1006 (1955). In order to be considered an unfair labor practice strike, there must be a causal relationship between the work stoppage, or the prolongation of an existing strike, and the employer's violation of the Act. *See* Allied Indus. Workers, Local 289 (Cavalier Div. of Seeburg Corp.) v. NLRB, 476 F.2d 868, 883, 82 L.R.R.M. 2225 (D.C. Cir. 1972), and cases cited therein. The unfair labor practices must be shown to be a "sole or substantial contributing cause" of the strike's continuation. General Drivers and Helpers, Local 662 v. NLRB, 302 F.2d 908, 911, 50 L.R.R.M. 2243 (D.C. Cir. 1962), *cert. denied,* 371 U.S. 827, 61 L.R.R.M. 2222 (1962).

[46] NLRB v. Fotochrome, 343 F.2d 631, 58 L.R.R.M. 2844 (2d Cir. 1964), *cert. denied,* 382 U.S. 833, 60 L.R.R.M. 2234 (1965); Kitty Clover, Inc. v. NLRB, 208 F.2d 212, 33 L.R.R.M. 2177 (8th Cir. 1953).

[47] Mastro Plastics Corp. v. NLRB, 350 U.S. 270, 37 L.R.R.M. 2587 (1956); NLRB v. Jones & Laughlin Steel Corp., 301 U.S. 1, 1 L.R.R.M. 703 (1937); NLRB v. Sunrise Lumber and Trim Corp., 241 F.2d 620, 625, 39 L.R.R.M. 2441 (2d Cir. 1957), *cert. denied,* 355 U.S. 818, 40 L.R.R.M. 2680 (1957); Colecraft Mfg. Co. v. NLRB, 385 F.2d 998, 1004–1005, 66 L.R.R.M. 2677 (2d Cir. 1967) although unfair labor practice strikers may not be permanently replaced, an employer may use temporary replacements during the strike.

[48] *See* NLRB v. Pecheur Lozenge Co., 209 F.2d 393, 33 L.R.R.M. 2324 (2d Cir. 1953), *cert. denied,* 347 U.S. 953, 34 L.R.R.M. 2027 (1954).

[49] *Id.* at 404–405, 33 L.R.R.M. at 2333. *See also* NLRB v. Remington Rand, Inc., 130 F.2d 919, 11 L.R.R.M. 575 (2d Cir. 1942).

[50] *E.g.,* Coast Radio Broadcast Corp. d/b/a Radio Station KPOL, 166 N.L.R.B. 359, 65 L.R.R.M. 1538 (1967).

[51] *E.g.,* Great Western Mushroom Co., 27 N.L.R.B. 352, 7 L.R.R.M. 72 (1940) (forcing employees to sign no-strike pledges). Coercive strike preparation may also provide the catalyst in applying the conversion doctrine. *See* Southland Cork Co., 146 N.L.R.B. 906, 55 L.R.R.M. 1426 (1964), *modified,* 342 F.2d 702, 58 L.R.R.M. 2555 (4th Cir.1965). In *Southland Cork,* the employer had "far exceeded the reasonable necessities of the situation"—preparing to hire replacements in anticipation of a strike—when it conspicuously canvassed the local neighborhood for job applicants, who were then paraded through the plant while the original employees were still there. The Board held that because the employer's actions were the immediate cause of the strike, the displaced employees would be treated as unfair labor practice strikers in determining their reinstatement rights. *But see* Hot Shoppes, Inc., 146 N.L.R.B. 802, 55 L.R.R.M. 1419 (1964), a companion case of *Southland Cork,* where no violation or conversion occurred where the management used standard procedures in attempting to locate job replacements prior to an impending strike. Consequently, it is not

found prolonging the strike when it conditions a reemployment offer on abandonment of the employees' union activities.[52]

In *NLRB v. International Van Lines*,[53] however, the Supreme Court found the conversion issue irrelevant and ordered the unconditional reinstatement of employees regardless of whether they were economic or unfair labor practice strikers. The employees had refused to cross a union's organizational picket line. The employer informed the employees that because they had failed to work, they were permanently replaced. At the time of the discharge, however, the employees had not been replaced. The court of appeals ruled that they were economic strikers and not entitled to unconditional reinstatement. The Supreme Court reversed the lower court, holding that the initial discharges were illegal and reinstatement was required regardless of the nature of the strike.[54] The Court reasoned that the timing of the notice implicitly proved the employer's intent to discriminate against employees for engaging in protected activity.

Nevertheless, the employer must reinstate unfair labor practice strikers who have made an unconditional application for reinstatement unless the striker has engaged in misconduct that would provide the employer legitimate cause for refusing to reemploy him.

EMPLOYEE MISCONDUCT AS A BAR TO REINSTATEMENT

As indicated in Chapter IX, section 10(c) of the Act prohibits the Board from ordering the "reinstatement of any individual as an employee who has been suspended or discharged ... for cause."[55] The right of employers to refuse to reinstate economic strikers who have participated in strike misconduct or have been discharged for cause was recognized by the Supreme Court in *NLRB v. Fansteel Metallurgical Corp.*[56] In *Fansteel* the employer discharged employees who had participated in the seizure and retention of the com-

---

preparation which is forbidden but rather the use of preparation to coerce employees from exercising their rights that constitutes a violation.

[52] *Compare* W.T. Rawleigh Co., 90 N.L.R.B. 1924, 26 L.R.R.M. 1421 (1950) (employer solicitation followed by refusal to reinstate although vacancies existed) *with* Samuel Bingham's Son Mfg. Co., 80 N.L.R.B. 1612, 23 L.R.R.M. 1266 (1948) (employer told solicited employees that it would not meet with union "until Hell freezes over"). *But see* American Steel & Pump Corp., 121 N.L.R.B. 1410, 42 L.R.R.M. 1564 (1958).

[53] 409 U.S. 48, 81 L.R.R.M. 2595 (1971). *See also* NLRB v. United States Cold Storage Corp., 203 F.2d 924, 32 L.R.R.M. 2024 (5th Cir. 1953), *cert. denied,* 346 U.S. 818, 32 L.R.R.M. 2750 (1953).

[54] 409 U.S. at 53, 81 L.R.R.M. at 2596–2597.

[55] 29 U.S.C. § 160(c). *See* Ch. IX, supra, n.7 *et seq.* and accompanying text; *see also* NLRB v. Electrical Workers, Local No. 1229, 346 U.S. 464, 33 L.R.R.M. 2183 (1953).

[56] 306 U.S. 240, 4 L.R.R.M. 515 (1939).

pany's buildings during a sitdown strike. The Board ordered the employer to reinstate the employees. Before the Supreme Court, the Board defended its order as within its discretion to effectuate the policies of the Act.[57] The Court, however, refused to construe the Act to compel employers to retain persons in their employ regardless of their unlawful conduct,[58] and noted that such a remedial policy would tend to insulate employees engaged in unlawful acts from discharge merely because their illegal conduct occurred within the context of a labor dispute.[59] Finally, the Court chided the Board for defending its order as necessary to effectuate the policies of the Act, concluding that the Board's position could be regarded as counterproductive to those very policies which it seeks to invoke:

> There is not a line in the statute to warrant the conclusion that it is any part of the policies of the Act to encourage employees to resort to force and violence in defiance of the law of the land. On the contrary, the purpose of the Act is to promote peaceful settlements of disputes by providing legal remedies for the invasion of the employees' rights. . . . We are of the opinion that to provide for the reinstatement or reemployment of employees guilty of the acts [plant seizure] which the Board finds to have been committed . . . would not only not effectuate any policy of the Act but would directly tend to make abortive its plan for peaceable procedure.[60]

The Thayer *Doctrine*

To determine whether misconduct of unfair labor practice strikers should bar their reinstatement, additional analysis may be required. Thus, the Board must also consider the impact of the employer's unfair labor practice. Under the *Thayer* doctrine,[61] the misconduct of both employer and employee must be balanced to determine if

---

[57] *Id.* at 253, 4 L.R.R.M. at 519.

[58] *Id.* at 255, 4 L.R.R.M. at 519.

[59] *Id.* at 256, 4 L.R.R.M. at 519. *Fansteel* is not the only case in which the Court has exhibited concern about the exercise of the Board's remedial powers where discharged employees were fired during the pendency of a labor dispute. *See* NLRB v. Local 1229, IBEW (Jefferson Std. Broadcasting Co.), 346 U.S. 464, 33 L.R.R.M. 2183 (1953).

[60] 306 U.S. at 257–258, 4 L.R.R.M. at 520.

[61] *See* NLRB v. H.N. Thayer Co., 213 F.2d 748, 34 L.R.R.M 2250 (1st Cir. 1954), *cert. denied,* 348 U.S. 883, 35 L.R.R.M. 2100 (1954); Blades Mfg. Corp., 144 N.L.R.B. 561, 54 L.R.R.M. 1087 (1963), *enforcement denied,* 344 F.2d 998, 59 L.R.R.M. 2210 (8th Cir. 1965); Fairview Nursing Home, 202 N.L.R.B. 318, 82 L.R.R.M. 1566 (1973), *enforced* 486 F.2d 1400, 84 L.R.R.M. 3010 (5th Cir. 1973); Local 833, UAW v. NLRB (Kohler Co.), 300 F.2d 699, 49 L.R.R.M. 2485 (D.C. Cir. 1962), *cert. denied,* U.S. 911, 50 L.R.R.M. 2326 (1962); Golay & Co. v. NLRB, 447 F.2d 290, 77 L.R.R.M. 3041, 3043 (7th Cir. 1971).

the employer has cause for refusing to reinstate the employee. As stated by the *Thayer* court:

> On the other hand where, as in the instant case, the strike was caused by the unfair labor practice the power of the Board to order reinstatement is not necessarily dependent upon a determination that the strike activity was a "concerted activity" within the protection of § 7. Even if it was not, the National Labor Relations Board has power under § 10(c) to order reinstatement if the discharges were not "for cause" and if such an order would effectuate the policies of the Act. Of course the discharge of strikers engaged in non-Section 7 activities often may be for cause, or their reinstatement may not effectuate the policies of the Act, but in certain circumstances it may. The point is that where collective action is precipitated by an unfair labor practice, a finding that that action is not protected under § 7 does not, *ipso facto,* preclude an order reinstating employees who have been discharged because of their participation in the unprotected activity.[62]

The Board has often judged the conduct of strikers where their employer has denied them reinstatement. When employee misconduct is obviously extreme, the Board will often determine that the offending employee has forfeited his or her protection under the Act and should not be returned to the job. For example, employers have been held to have lawfully refused to reinstate workers who have engaged in aggravated violence and property destruction,[63] misconduct on the picket line,[64] or even the disparagement of the employer's products.[65]

---

[62] NLRB v. H.N. Thayer Co., 213 F.2d 748, 757, 34 L.R.R.M. 2250, 2253 (1st Cir. 1954). On remand, the Board indicated disagreement with the Court's rationale, 115 N.L.R.B. 1591, 38 L.R.R.M. 1142 (1956). However, in Blades Mfg. Corp., 144 N.L.R.B. 561, 54 L.R.R.M. 1087 (1963), *enforcement denied,* 344 F.2d. 988, 59 L.R.R.M. 2210 (8th Cir. 1965), the Board said it would follow *Thayer.*

[63] NLRB v. Mt. Clemens Pottery Co., 147 F.2d 262, 16 L.R.R.M. 501 (6th Cir. 1945); Standard Lime and Stone Co. v. NLRB, 97 F.2d 531, 2 L.R.R.M. 674 (4th Cir. 1938) (employee convicted for assault and battery upon fellow employee); Revere Metal Art Co., 127 N.L.R.B. 1028, 46 L.R.R.M. 1448 (1960), *enforced,* 287 F.2d 632, 47 L.R.R.M. 2635 (2d Cir. 1961) (beating nonstriker); Farah Mfg. Co., 202 N.L.R.B. 666, 82 L.R.R.M. 1623 (1973) (assault on supervisor); Ohio Power Co., 215 N.L.R.B. 165, 88 L.R.R.M. 1007 (1974) (assault on supervisor).

[64] NLRB v. Perfect Circle Co., 162 F.2d 566, 20 L.R.R.M. 2558 (7th Cir. 1947) (barring supervisor entrance to plant); Talladega Foundry & Mach. Co., 122 N.L.R.B. 125, 43 L.R.R.M. 1073 (1958) (preventing loading and unloading operations by threat of physical presence of strikers).

[65] NLRB v. Local 1229, IBEW (Jefferson Std. Broadcasting Co.), 346 U.S. 464, 33 L.R.R.M. 2183 (1953), *aff'g* 94 N.L.R.B. 1507, 28 L.R.R.M. 1215 (1951). *See also,* Boeing Airplane Co. v. NLRB, 238 F.2d 188, 38 L.R.R.M. 2276 (9th Cir. 1956); Hoover Co. v. NLRB, 191 F.2d 380, 28 L.R.R.M. 2353 (6th Cir. 1951); Patterson-Sargent Co., 115 N.L.R.B. 1627, 38 L.R.R.M. 1134 (1956).

In *Milk Wagon Driver's Union v. Meadowmoor Dairies,*[66] the Supreme Court held that a striker's use of unseemly language on the picket line "in a moment of animal exuberance" does not deprive the striker of the right to reinstatement.[67] In *Montgomery Ward & Co. v. NLRB,*[68] the Tenth Circuit refused to enforce the Board's reinstatement order of an employee who had cursed at a customer crossing the picket line. The court reasoned that although name calling has generally been excused when directed at nonstrikers and members of management, the striking employee must exercise a greater degree of self-control with regard to the employer's customers and other members of the general public.[69] This decision reflects the principle of the *Fansteel* case which held that the benefits of the Act extended only to protected activities guaranteed by the Act.

Coronet Casual *and the* Clear Pine Mouldings *Test*

Before 1973, a threat of violence by an employee operated to lose his or her statutory protection.[70] In *Coronet Casuals, Inc.,*[71] however, the Board fashioned a rule that threats, not accompanied by any physical acts or gestures that would underscore the message, would not disqualify a striker from reinstatement. In cases that followed, the Board held that verbal threats unaccompanied by physical acts or gestures did not constitute serious strike misconduct warranting an employer's refusal to reinstate, but this line of cases had only limited success before the circuit courts.[72]

---

[66] 312 U.S. 287, 7 L.R.R.M. 310 (1941).

[67] *Id.* at 293, 7 L.R.R.M. at 312. *Cf.* Longview Furniture Co., 110 N.L.R.B. 1734, 35 L.R.R.M. 1254 (1954).

[68] 374 F.2d 606, 64 L.R.R.M. 2712 (10th Cir. 1967).

[69] *Id.* at 608, 64 L.R.R.M. at 2713. *Cf.* Rock Road Trailer Parts and Sales, 204 N.L.R.B. 1136, 83 L.R.R.M. 1467 (1973) (loud and belligerent remarks that threaten to put employer out of business and are made in front of customers are not protected).

[70] *See, e.g.,* Brookville Glove Co., 114 N.L.R.B. 213, 36 L.R.R.M. 1548 (1955), *enforced sub nom.,* NLRB v. Leach, 234 F.2d 400, 38 L.R.R.M. 2252 (3d Cir. 1956); Socony Vacuum Oil Co., 78 N.L.R.B. 1185, 22 L.R.R.M. 1321 (1948). In both cases, striking employees had threatened nonstrikers with bodily harm should they enter or attempt to enter the struck plant. There were no accompanying gestures or acts.

[71] 207 N.L.R.B. 304, 84 L.R.R.M. 1441 (1973).

[72] W.C. McQuaide, Inc., 220 N.L.R.B. 593, 594, 90 L.R.R.M. 1345 (1975), *enforcement denied,* 552 F.2d 519, 94 L.R.R.M. 2950 (3d Cir. 1977); *See also* A. Duie Pyle, Inc., 263 N.L.R.B. 744, 111 L.R.R.M. 1140 (1982); Georgia Kraft Co., 258 N.L.R.B. 908, 912, 108 L.R.R.M. 1223 (1981), *enforced,* 696 F.2d 931, 112 L.R.R.M. 2824 (11th Cir. 1983), *remanded to Board upon Clear Pines Moulding,* 115 L.R.R.M. 3296 (1984); Arrow Indus. 245 N.L.R.B. 1376, 102 L.R.R.M. 1525 (1979); M.P. Indus., 227 N.L.R.B. 1709, 94 L.R.R.M. 1608 (1972); Associated Grocers of New England v. NLRB, 562 F.2d 1333, 1336, 96 L.R.R.M. 2630 (1st Cir. 1977), *denying enforcement to* 227 N.L.R.B. 1200, 95 L.R.R.M. 1031.

In *Clear Pine Mouldings*[73] the Board disavowed *Coronet Casual*
and announced that it would return to its earlier standard for
judging strike misconduct. The Board acknowledged that it agreed
with criticism of *Coronet Casual* by the First[74] and Third[75] Circuits.
And in such cases the Board adopted the Third Circuit test, i.e.,
whether the misconduct is such that, under the circumstances existing, it may reasonably tend to coerce and intimidate employees
in the exercise of rights protected under the Act.[76] In reviewing the
Taft-Hartley Act, the Board found no evidence of a Congressional
intent to condone violence, and stated:

> We believe it is appropriate, at this point to state our view that the
> existence of a strike in which some employees elect to voluntarily
> withhold their services does not in any way privilege those employees
> to engage in other than peaceful picketing and persuasion. They have
> no right, for example, to threaten those employees who, for whatever
> reason, have decided to work during the strike, to block access to the
> employer's premises, and certainly no right to carry or use weapons
> or other objects of intimidation. As we view the statute, the only
> activity the statute privileges in this context, other than peaceful
> patrolling, is the nonthreatening expression of opinion, verbally or
> through signs and pamphleting similar to that found in Section 8(c).[77]

Clear Pine Mouldings may have cleared the differences between
the Board and the courts on this subject. Under its prior rulings
the Board often appeared to condone flagrant picket line misconduct. For example, in *Georgia Kraft Co.* the Board condoned obscene
gestures by drunken strikers to pregnant women. The Supreme
Court granted *certiorari*, but remanded to the Board upon the *Clear
Pine Mouldings* decision,[78] a step that can be seen as approval of
the Board's direction in this area. How *Clear Pine Mouldings* will
evolve is conjectural; it does appear to signal a tougher, more direct
posture.[79]

---

[73] 268 N.L.R.B. 1044, 115 L.R.R.M. 1113 (1984).

[74] Associated Grocers of New England v. NLRB, 562 F.2d 1333, 1336, 96 L.R.R.M.
2630 (1st Cir. 1977) *denying enforcement to* 227 N.L.R.B. 1200, 95 L.R.R.M. 1031 ("a
serious threat may draw its credibility from the surrounding circumstances and not
the physical gesture of the speaker").

[75] NLRB v. McQuaide, Inc., 552 F.2d 519, 94 L.R.R.M. 2950 (3d Cir. 1977): "[An
employer] need not countenance conduct that amounts to intimidation and threats
of bodily harm."

[76] 268 N.L.R.B. at 1046, 115 L.R.R.M. at 1115.

[77] *Id.* at 1047, 115 L.R.R.M. at 1116–7.

[78] 258 N.L.R.B. 908, 912, 108 L.R.R.M. 1223 (1981), *enforced,* 696 F.2d 931, 112
L.R.R.M. 2824 (11th Cir. 1983), *remanded,* 115 L.R.R.M. 3296 (1984).

[79] Earlier Board decisions might have come out differently under the *Clear Pine
Mouldings* test. *See, e.g.,* NLRB v. Thor Power Tool Co., 351 F.2d 584, 587, 60 L.R.R.M.
2237 (7th Cir. 1965) (obscene remark to supervisor); NLRB v. Hartmann Luggage
Co., 453 F.2d 178, 79 L.R.R.M. 2139, 2142 (6th Cir. 1971) (threat to "kill" a strike

CONDITIONS GOVERNING REINSTATEMENT V. JUSTIFIED DISMISSAL

Past decisions nevertheless will still provide the answers for individual cases. The Board has offered various justifications for ordering the reinstatement of an employee who has misbehaved. For example, the Board may find that the employee engaged in similar misconduct at an earlier time without having been punished, or that the misconduct was minor or momentary and not serious enough to justify discharge. In vindicating the use of threats, the Board has found that those threats should not have been taken seriously when they were not intended to be carried out, were obviously incredible, or occurred in an otherwise casual conversation.

In *NLRB v. Burnup and Sims*,[80] the Supreme Court held that an employer's good faith belief is no defense to a discharge of a striker for misconduct that did not in fact occur. The Court observed that "[u]nion activity often engenders strong emotions and gives rise to active rumors. A protected activity acquires a precarious status if innocent employers can be discharged while engaging in it, even though the employer acts in good faith."[81] Accordingly, the Court

---

breaker); NLRB v. Wichita Television Corp., 277 F.2d 579, 585, 45 L.R.R.M. 3096, 3100 (10th Cir. 1960) (strikers carried large obstructive umbrellas on picket line, heckled nonstrikers, and obstructed doorway); NLRB v. Brookside Indus., Inc., 308 F.2d 224, 227, 51 L.R.R.M. 2148 (4th Cir. 1962) (threats of physical harm); NLRB v. Zelrich Co., 334 F.2d 1011, 1014, 59 L.R.R.M. 2225 (5th Cir. 1965) (threats); NLRB v. Big Ben Dept. Stores, Inc., 396 F.2d 78, 81, 68 L.R.R.M. 2311 (2d Cir. 1968) (obnoxious and overbearing employee found to have been discharged because of his union activities, and not his shortcomings); NLRB v. Terry Coach Indus., Inc., 411 F.2d 612, 71 L.R.R.M. 2287, 2288 (9th Cir. 1969), *enforcing* 166 N.L.R.B. 560, 65 L.R.R.M. 1583 (1967) (blocked entrance to plant with truck and directed profanity toward nonstriking employees); Richlands Textile Inc., 220 N.L.R.B. 615, 90 L.R.R.M. 1391 (1975) (threat to burn down employee's house if he did not join the union); Asplundh Tree Expert Co., 220 N.L.R.B. 352, 90 L.R.R.M. 1425 (1975) (alleged threat to supervisor where there was nothing to suggest that the employee intended to engage in violence); Advance Indus. Div., Overhead Door Corp., 220 N.L.R.B. 431, 90 L.R.R.M. 1257 (1975) (individual instances of strikers aiming a gun at employer's light pole, throwing gravel at nonstriking employee's car, pounding on nonstriker's car, and shaking employer's snowplow).

[80] 379 U.S. 21, 23, 57 L.R.R.M. 2385 (1964).

[81] *Id.*, 57 L.R.R.M. at 2386. *Accord*, General Elec. Co., Battery Prod., Capacitor Dept. v. NLRB, 400 F.2d 713, 721, 69 L.R.R.M. 2081 (5th Cir. 1968), *cert. denied*, 394 U.S. 904, 70 L.R.R.M. 2828 (1969); NLRB v. Laney & Duke Storage Warehouse Co. 369 F.2d 859, 866, 63 L.R.R.M. 2552 (5th Cir. 1966); Rubin Bros. Footwear, Inc., 99 N.L.R.B. 610, 30 L.R.R.M. 1109 (1952), *set aside on other grounds*, 203 F.2d 486, 31 L.R.R.M. 2614 (5th Cir. 1953). *But cf.*, NLRB v. Community Motor Bus Co., 439 F.2d 965, 76 L.R.R.M. 2844 (4th Cir. 1971) (It was undisputed that the employees engaged in misconduct); Pullman Inc., Trailmobile Div., 407 F.2d 1006, 70 L.R.R.M. 2849, 2855–2856 (5th Cir. 1969) (court disbelieved the employer's alleged "honest belief" that misconduct had occurred).

stated the rule that "§ 8(a)(1) is violated if it is shown that the discharged employee was at the time engaged in a protected activity, that the employer knew it was such, that the basis of the discharge was an alleged act of misconduct in the course of that activity, and that the employee was not, in fact, guilty of that misconduct."[82] Pursuant to *Burnup and Sims,* the burden initially is on the employer to prove his good-faith belief that the employee committed the alleged acts. Thereafter, the burden shifts to the General Counsel to prove the employee was innocent of strike misconduct.[83]

Furthermore, an employer may not be able to discharge an employee for strike misconduct if he fails to act promptly, but takes action which may be construed as condonation.[84] An employer whose employees engage in unprotected activity therefore has a choice: terminating their employment because of the misconduct, or instead condoning the breach by demonstrating a "willingness to forgive the improper aspect of concerted action, to 'wipe the slate clean.'"[85] Yet, as the Sixth Circuit stated in *Plasti-Line Inc. v. NLRB:*

> [C]ondonation may not be lightly presumed from mere silence or equivocal statements, but must clearly appear from some positive act by an employer indicating forgiveness and an intention of treating the guilty employees as if their conduct had not occurred.[86]

Thus, the failure of an employer to state that it would not reemploy an individual engaged in misconduct does not support a presumption that the employer did, in fact, intend to reinstate the employee. Nor, for example, does mere silence,[87] an equivocal statement,[88] the

---

[82] 57 L.R.R.M. at 2386

[83] Auto Workers (Udylite Corp.) v. NLRB, 455 F.2d 1357, 79 L.R.R.M. 2031, 2039 (D.C. Cir. 1971); Dallas Gen. Drivers v. NLRB, 389 F.2d 553, 67 L.R.R.M. 2370, 2371 (D.C. Cir. 1968); NLRB v. Plastic Applicators, Inc., 369 F.2d 495, 63 L.R.R.M. 2510, 2511–2512 (5th Cir. 1966); Rubin Bros. Footwear, Inc., 99 N.L.R.B. 610, 611, 30 L.R.R.M. 1109 (1952). *Cf.* Kayser-Roth Hosiery Co. v. NLRB, 447 F.2d 396, 78 L.R.R.M. 2130, 2133 (6th Cir. 1971).

[84] *E.g.,* Quality Limestone Prods. Inc., 153 N.L.R.B. 1009, 59 L.R.R.M. 1589 (1965).

[85] Confectionary & Tobacco Drivers Union, Local 805 v. NLRB, 312 F.2d 108, 113, 52 L.R.R.M. 2163 (2d Cir. 1963). *See also,* Stewart Die Casting Corp. v. NLRB, 114 F.2d 849, 855–856, 6 L.R.R.M. 907 (7th Cir. 1940), *cert. denied,* 312 U.S. 680, 7 L.R.R.M. 326 (1941); NLRB v. Marshall Car Wheel & Foundry Co., 218 F.2d 409, 413, 35 L.R.R.M. 2320 (5th Cir. 1955); Packers Hide Ass'n v. NLRB, 360 F.2d 59, 62, 62 L.R.R.M. 2115 (8th Cir. 1966); NLRB v. Wallick & Schwalm Co., 198 F.2d 477, 484 (3d Cir. 1952); NLRB v. Community Motor Bus Co., 439 F.2d 965, 76 L.R.R.M. 2844, 2847 (4th Cir. 1971); NLRB v. Cast Optics Corp., 458 F.2d 398, 79 L.R.R.M. 3093, 3097 (3d Cir. 1972).

[86] 278 F.2d 482, 487, 46 L.R.R.M. 2291, 2294 (6th Cir. 1960), quoting from NLRB v. Marshall Car Wheel & Foundry Co., 218 F.2d 409, 414, 35 L.R.R.M. 2320 (5th Cir. 1955).

[87] Packers Hide Ass'n v. NLRB, 360 F.2d 59, 62 L.R.R.M. 2115 (8th Cir. 1966).

[88] NLRB v. Marshall Car Wheel & Foundry Co., 218 F.2d 409, 35 L.R.R.M. 2320 (5th Cir. 1955).

shrugging of shoulders,[89] or a reply littered with generalities, constitute the equivalent of an affirmative act of forgiveness sufficient to involve a finding of condonation.[90] Thus, in *NLRB v. Colonial Press*,[91] the court rejected the Board's condonation finding where company representatives solicited striking employees to come in and talk about reemployment, saying "the door is always open." The court construed the company statements as only preliminary invitations to negotiate reemployment and not as condonation or unconditional offers of reinstatement.

Once the employer has condoned the unprotected aspects of concerted employee conduct, the customary protections of the Act prevail. The employer may not thereafter rely upon such activity as grounds for reprisal. As the Second Circuit explained, the condonation principle rests upon "a clear public interest in the prompt settlement of labor disputes."[92] Having once waived its privilege to discharge or otherwise to take action against the employees for striking, the employer is bound to that decision. If, however, subsequent to the condonation, the employee repeats the very activity which had been condoned, this action may constitute a breach of the "condonation agreement." The employer may once again be entitled to discharge or discipline the employee.[93]

---

[89] Merck & Co., 110 N.L.R.B. 67, 34 L.R.R.M. 1603 (1954).

[90] *Cf.* NLRB v. Dorsey Trailers Inc., 179 F.2d 589, 25 L.R.R.M. 2333 (5th Cir. 1950).

[91] 509 F.2d 850, 88 L.R.R.M. 2337 (8th Cir. 1975), *rev'g* 207 N.L.R.B. 673, 84 L.R.R.M. 1596 (1973).

[92] Confectionary & Tobacco Drivers, 312 F.2d 108, 113, 52 L.R.R.M. at 2167.

[93] Poloron Products of Indiana, 177 N.L.R.B. No. 54, 71 L.R.R.M. 1577 (1969). In this same vein, the court in Marshall Car Wheel & Foundry Co. observed that condonation entails "the resumption of the *former* relationship between the strikers and respondent. . . . " *See* 218 F.2d 409, 414, 35 L.R.R.M. 2320, 2323 (5th Cir. 1955) (emphasis added).

CHAPTER XI

Remedies Designed to Restore the Union's Representational Integrity

Section 8(a)(2) of the National Labor Relations Act makes it unlawful for an employer to "dominate or interfere with the formation or administration of any labor organization or contribute financial or other support to it."[1] The purpose of the provision is twofold; it is designed both to force the employer to "refrain from any action which will place him on both sides of the bargaining table,"[2] and to ensure the employees that those who represent them will not become so subject to employer influence that they are unable to devote themselves to the interests of the group they purport to represent.[3] The Act, however, was also intended to increase industrial stability by encouraging a more productive spirit between labor and management, and it does not prohibit certain forms of employer cooperation.[4] In order to accommodate these varied ends, the Board has not looked upon domination, interference, support, or partiality as comparable, but instead has viewed these violations as differing in degree of unlawful activity and therefore necessitating different remedies.

---

[1] 29 U.S.C. § 158(a)(2).

[2] NLRB v. Mt. Clemens Metal Prods. Co., 287 F.2d 790, 791, 47 L.R.R.M. 2771, 2772 (6th Cir. 1961); see also Nassau and Suffolk Contractors Ass'n, 118 N.L.R.B. 174, 40 L.R.R.M. 1146 (1957).

[3] Holland Mfg. Co., 129 N.L.R.B. 776, 47 L.R.R.M. 1067 (1960). See also Bisso Towboat Co., 192 N.L.R.B. 885, 78 L.R.R.M. 1230 (1971); Pangles Master Mkts., Inc., 190 N.L.R.B. 332, 77 L.R.R.M. 1596 (1971); Brescombe Distributor Corp., 179 N.L.R.B. 787, 72 L.R.R.M. 1590 (1969), enforced sub nom. Liquor Salesmen Local 195 v. NLRB, 452 F.2d 1312, 78 L.R.R.M. 2641 (D.C. Cir. 1971). In each of these cases, the Board found a violation where the presence of a supervisory employee on the union negotiating team cast doubt on the independence of the labor organization.

[4] See NLRB v. Magic Slacks, Inc., 314 F.2d 844, 52 L.R.R.M. 2641 (7th Cir. 1963). The Board and the courts have struggled to distinguish between permitted cooperation and proscribed domination; the line drawn is often a fine one. See, e.g., NLRB v. Cabot Carbon Co. 360 U.S. 203 (1959); NLRB v. Streamway Div. of Scott & Fetzer Co., 691 F.2d 288 (6th Cir. 1982) Hertzka & Knowles v. NLRB, 503 F.2d 625, 87 L.R.R.M. 2503 (9th Cir. 1974), denying enforcement to 206 N.L.R.B. 191, 84 L.R.R.M. 1556 (1973); NLRB v. Clapper's Mfg. Inc., 458 F.2d 414 (3d. Cir. 1972); NLRB v. Ampex Corp., 442 F.2d 82 (7th Cir. 1971).

CRITERIA DETERMINING DEGREES OF EMPLOYER INTERFERENCE

Because the statute does not define a dominated labor organization, the Board, through adjudication, has fashioned a test identifying certain characteristics which, when present, confirm the existence of domination. In its most classic form, domination occurs where the employer creates, administers, and finances a labor organization.[5] Similarly, the Board has found domination in cases in which, for example, the employer controlled the meetings of the organization, either directly by presiding over and participating in the decisions of the group, or indirectly through funding, dictation of the agenda, assuming responsibility for preparing a report of the meeting for the employees, or choosing the employee representatives.[6] The mere existence of one or more of these conditions will not necessarily result in a finding of a *per se* violation of section 8(a)(2); instead, the Board will apply a subjective test and look at all the circumstances in order to determine

> whether the organization exists as the result of a choice freely made by the employees, in their own interests, and without regard to the desires of their employer, or whether the employees formed and supported the organization, rather than some other, because they knew their employer desired it, and feared the consequences if they did not.[7]

The Board has often found a violation in the employer's *potential* to control a labor organization.[8] The courts of appeals, on the other hand, require a showing of *actual* dominance or control.[9]

---

[5] Wahlgreen Magnetics, 132 N.L.R.B. 1613, 48 L.R.R.M. 1542 (1961); Bisso Towboat Co., 192 N.L.R.B. 885, 78 L.R.R.M. 1230 (1971). An enumeration of the factors commonly weighed by the Board can be found in Spiegel Trucking Co., 225 N.L.R.B. 178, 92 L.R.R.M. 1604 (1976).

[6] *See e.g.,* Lawson Co. v. NLRB, 753 F.2d 471, 118 L.R.R.M. 2505 (6th Cir. 1985); Jet Spray Corp., 271 N.L.R.B. No. 32, 116 L.R.R.M. 1379 (1984); Kux Mfg. Co., 233 N.L.R.B. 317, 97 L.R.R.M. 1052 (1977); STR, Inc., 221 N.L.R.B. 496, 90 L.R.R.M. 1591 (1975).

[7] NLRB v. Wemyss, 212 F.2d 465, 34 L.R.R.M. 2124 (9th Cir. 1954). *See also* Newport News Shipbuilding & Dry Dock Co. v. NLRB, 308 U.S. 241, 5 L.R.R.M. 665 (1939) (employer may not exercise such control as to deprive employees of the "complete freedom of action guaranteed to them by the Act").

[8] *See, e.g.,* Stephens Institute, 241 N.L.R.B. 454, 100 L.R.R.M. 1603 (1979); Northeastern Univ., 235 N.L.R.B. 858, 98 L.R.R.M. 1347 (1978).

[9] *See* NLRB v. Homemaker Shops, Inc., 724 F.2d 535, 115 L.R.R.M. 2321 (6th Cir. 1984); NLRB v. Northeastern Univ., 601 F.2d 1208, 101 L.R.R.M. 2767 (1st Cir. 1979); Hertzka & Knowles v. NLRB, 502 F.2d 625, 630, 87 L.R.R.M. 2503, 2506–07 (9th Cir. 1974); Chicago Rawhide Mfg. Co. v. NLRB, 221 F.2d 165, 167, 35 L.R.R.M. 2665 (7th Cir. 1955).

The extent of the employer's involvement in the affairs of the union differentiates interference from domination; interference implies that the involvement is not so great as to subject the labor organization to the will of the employer.[10] Interference violations usually involve employer intrusion upon the administration and maintenance of the labor union, not upon its formation. For example, the Board has found that an employer interfered with the union when company executives and supervisors had retained their union memberships and participated in union affairs despite their promotions from the rank and file.[11] Conversely, however, the Board has found evidence of employer interference in the formation of a union even though the employer was subsequently unable to dominate it.[12]

Section 8(a)(2) of the Act also prohibits an employer from contributing "financial or other support" to a labor organization. Support or assistance has been found in cases in which an employer has granted a union favors such as access to company meeting rooms,[13] or arranged to defray the costs associated with union administrative and organizational work.[14] However, the Board eschews a mechanistic test for improper assistance, looking instead to the totality of facts and often applying a *de minimis* rule.[15]

Finally, the Board has held that the Act also prohibits an employer from demonstrating partiality to one of a number of rival unions competing for the employees' allegiance.[16] The Board has struggled to balance the notion of employer impartiality against the section 8(a)(5) principle of recognition as bargaining representative of any labor organization that enjoys an uncoerced majority among employees. In *Midwest Piping and Supply Co., Inc.,*[17] the Board held that an employer faced with conflicting representation claims of two or more rival unions violates section 8(a)(2) if it recognizes or enters into a contract with one of those unions before its

---

[10] *See, e.g.,* Liquor Salesmen Local 195 v. NLRB (Brescombe Distributors Corp.), 452 F.2d 1312, 78 L.R.R.M. 2641 (D.C. Cir. 1971); Duquesne Univ., 198 N.L.R.B. 891, 81 L.R.R.M. 1091, 1093–94 (1972).

[11] Nassau and Suffolk Contractors Ass'n, 118 N.L.R.B. 174, 40 L.R.R.M. 1146 (1957).

[12] Spiegel Trucking Co., 225 N.L.R.B. 178, 92 L.R.R.M. 1604 (1976).

[13] *See, e.g.,* General Instruments Corp., 262 N.L.R.B. 1178, 111 L.R.R.M. 1017 (1982); Tuschak-Jacobsen, Inc., 223 N.L.R.B. 1298, 92 L.R.R.M. 1280 (1976).

[14] *See, e.g.,* Farmers Energy Corp., 266 N.L.R.B. 722, 113 L.R.R.M. 1037 (1983); Easy-Heat Wirekraft, 238 N.L.R.B. 1695, 99 L.R.R.M. 1681 (1978).

[15] *See* Coamo Knitting Mills, Inc., 150 N.L.R.B. 579, 58 L.R.R.M. 1116 (1964).

[16] *See, e.g.,* Schlabach Coal Co. v. NLRB, 611 F.2d 1161, 104 L.R.R.M. 2593 (6th Cir. 1979); MGR Equip. Corp., 272 N.L.R.B. No. 67, 117 L.R.R.M. 1302 (1984); Hartz Mountain Corp., 228 N.L.R.B. 492, 96 L.R.R.M. 1589 (1977); Penn Bldg. Maintenance Corp., 195 N.L.R.B. 183, 79 L.R.R.M. 1416 (1972).

[17] 63 N.L.R.B. 1060, 17 L.R.R.M. 40 (1945).

majority status has been determined by means of a Board election. In *Shea Chemical Corp.,*[18] the Board extended this neutrality doctrine to those situations where an incumbent union is faced with a timely challenge by a rival labor organization; in these circumstances, the Board held, *Midwest Piping* dictated that the employer refrain from negotiating a renewal labor agreement with the incumbent union until such time as a Board-conducted election has settled the representation issue.

Midwest Piping, and particularly its extension in *Shea Chemical,* received a decidedly negative reaction in the courts of appeals,[19] and in two companion cases decided in 1982, the Board reexamined these precedents. In *Bruckner Nursing Home,*[20] the Board addressed an employer's conduct when faced with rival unions seeking initially to represent its unorganized employees. The Board held that, prior to the filing of a valid election petition by one of these unions, the employer is free to recognize another union that represents an "uncoerced, unassisted majority;" but once an employer is notified of a valid petition, it must refrain from recognizing any of the rivals. And in *RCA Del Caribe,*[21] the Board, overruling *Shea Chemical,* held that an employer does not violate section 8(a)(2) merely by negotiating or executing a contract with an incumbent union even if a second union has filed a representation petition reasoning that "preservation of the status quo through an employer's continued bargaining with an incumbent is the better way to approximate employer neutrality."[22]

DISESTABLISHMENT AND WITHDRAWAL OF RECOGNITION REMEDIES

In order to effectuate the purposes of section 8(a)(2) and restore the status quo appropriately, the Board has adopted remedies in addition to the normal cease-and-desist orders that directly relate to the seriousness of the violation. If the employer's unlawful practices are proven to be so extensive that they constitute domination of a labor organization, the Board will issue an order directing the

---

[18] 121 N.L.R.B. 1027, 42 L.R.R.M. 1486 (1958).

[19] *See, e.g.,* NLRB v. Wintex Knitting Mills, Inc., 610 F.2d 430, 104 L.R.R.M. 2529 (6th Cir. 1979); NLRB v. Suburban Transit Corp., 499 F.2d 78, 86 L.R.R.M. 2626 (3d Cir. 1974); Playskool, Inc. v. NLRB, 477 F.2d 66, 82 L.R.R.M. 2916 (7th Cir. 1973).

[20] 262 N.L.R.B. 955, 110 L.R.R.M. 1374 (1982). The Third Circuit has upheld the Board's *Bruckner* rule in Haddon House Food Prods. v. NLRB, 764 F.2d 182, 119 L.R.R.M. 3021 (3d Cir. 1985).

[21] 262 N.L.R.B. 963, 110 L.R.R.M. 1369 (1982).

[22] *Id.* at 965, 110 L.R.R.M. at 1371.

disestablishment of the dominated union.[23] Compliance with this remedy may require, in Judge Learned Hand's phrase, "absolute and public cleavage" between the dominated organization and any successor to it,[24] and that the employer publicly announce its intention to cease bargaining with the union. When the misconduct involves either widespread interference or support but falls short of actual domination, the Board typically orders the employer to withdraw recognition unless or until the union has been certified by the Board[25] and to rescind and cease effectuating any contract with the union if the violation has tainted the contract.[26]

When *Midwest Piping* and *Brucker Nursing Home* violations have occurred, the Board usually orders the employer to cease recognizing the union until it is certified by the Board.[27] However, if the employer's support of one labor organization is accompanied by other unfair labor practices that undermine majority support of the rival union, the Board may issue a *Gissel* bargaining order.[28]

MONETARY AND REIMBURSEMENT REMEDIES

When the Board finds, in the context of a section 8(a)(2) violation, that the employees have paid to the tainted union initiation fees, dues, or other financial obligations related to union membership,

[23] *See, e.g.,* Comet Corp., 261 N.L.R.B. 1414, 110 L.R.R.M. 1276 (1982); Fry Foods, Inc., 241 N.L.R.B. 76, 100 L.R.R.M. 1513 (1979); Metropolitan Alloys Corp., 233 N.L.R.B. 966, 97 L.R.R.M. 1220 (1977); Glover Packing Co., 191 N.L.R.B. 547, 77 L.R.R.M. 1695 (1971); Dade Drydock Corp., 58 N.L.R.B. 833, 15 L.R.R.M. 67 (1944).

[24] Western Union Tel. Co. v. NLRB, 113 F.2d 992, 996, 6 L.R.R.M. 753, 757 (2d Cir. 1940). *See also* NLRB v. Tappan Stove Co., 174 F.2d 1007, 24 L.R.R.M. 2125 (6th Cir. 1949)

[25] *See, e.g.,* Mallouk Realty Corp., 265 N.L.R.B. 1225, 112 L.R.R.M. 1236 (1982); Flex Plastics, Inc., 262 N.L.R.B. 651, 110 L.R.R.M. 1365 (1982), *enforced,* 726 F.2d 272, 115 L.R.R.M. 3036 (6th Cir. 1984). If, however, the employer's improper support or assistance does not affect the union's majority status, a cease-and-desist order, standing alone, may be the appropriate remedy. *See* True Temper Corp., 217 N.L.R.B. 1120, 89 L.R.R.M. 1228 (1975).

[26] *See* NLRB v. Hunter Outdoor Prods., Inc., 440 F.2d 876, 76 L.R.R.M. 2969 (1st Cir. 1971). The distinction between the remedies of disestablishment and withdrawal of recognition was first advanced by the Board in Carpenter Steel Co., 76 N.L.R.B. 670, 21 L.R.R.M.1232 (1948), as a direct response to the Taft-Hartley amendments of § 10(c), 29 U.S.C. § 160(c).

[27] *See* Signal Transformer Co., 265 N.L.R.B. 272, 111 L.R.R.M. 1556 (1982) (even where incumbent union has lost majority status, employer may not recognize rival union where incumbent has not abandoned its claim of representation).

[28] *See* NLRB v. Cas Walker's Cash Stores, 659 F.2d 79, 108 L.R.R.M. 3007 (6th Cir. 1981); *also* Kurz-Kasch, Inc., 239 N.L.R.B. 1044, 100 L.R.R.M. 1118 (1978). The Second Circuit has expressed some reservation concerning the Board's use of bargaining orders as remedies for § 8(a)(2) violations; *see* Coating Prods., Inc. v. NLRB, 648 F.2d 108, 107 L.R.R.M. 2337 (2d Cir. 1981). For a fuller discussion of *Gissel* bargaining orders, see Chapter XII.

it will usually order that the employer reimburse the employees for such payments.[29]

The situation normally arises where the employees have been subject to an illegal union security agreement with a check-off clause, and have been forced to support and contribute to the supported union to retain their jobs.[30] In *Virginia Electric & Power Co. v. NLRB,*[31] the Supreme Court upheld such a reimbursement remedy against employer claims that the remedy was punitive. Where, however, employees are not bound by any mandatory union membership clause and willingly consent to pay their union dues, the Board and courts have refused to order reimbursement;[32] in those situations, the payments have not been "coerced," and coercion is a predicate of any nonpunitive remedy for a violation of section 8(a)(2).[33] At least one court has ruled that reimbursement of illegally checked-off dues would not be ordered where the Board has subsequently certified the union as the employees' representative.[34]

REMEDIES FOR UNION UNFAIR LABOR PRACTICES

Although a union's representational integrity is most often compromised by an employer's violation of section 8(a)(2), it may also be deemed tainted by findings that the union itself has restrained or coerced employees in violation of section 8(b)(1)(A)[35] of the Act, or has violated section 8(b)(2)[36] by causing or attempting to cause an employer to discriminate against an employee for that employee's union activity (or lack thereof). Where the Board finds a vio-

---

[29] *See, e.g.,* Farmers Energy Corp. v. NLRB, 730 F.2d 1098, 115 L.R.R.M. 3469 (7th Cir. 1984); R.J.E. Leasing Corp., 262 N.L.R.B. 373, 110 L.R.R.M. 1313 (1982); Presbyterian Community Hosp., 230 N.L.R.B. 599, 95 L.R.R.M. 1610 (1977). Reimbursement of dues is also an appropriate remedy where an employer has executed a collective bargaining agreement with one of a number of rival unions in violation of *Bruckner Nursing Home. See* Haddon House Food Prods. v. NLRB, 764 F.2d 182, 119 L.R.R.M. 3021 (3d Cir. 1985). Moreover, if the supported union is a party to the proceedings and is found itself to have committed acts of coercion, the union and employer may be held jointly and severally liable for the reimbursement. *See, e.g.,* National Maritime Union v. NLRB (Monfort of Colorado, Inc.), 683 F.2d 305, 111 L.R.R.M. 2286 (9th Cir. 1982); Rainey Security Agency, 274 N.L.R.B. No. 41, 119 L.R.R.M. 1043 (1985); Baine Serv. Sys., Inc., 248 N.L.R.B. 563, 103 L.R.R.M. 1518 (1980); Desco Vitro-Glaze, Inc., 230 N.L.R.B. 379, 96 L.R.R.M. 1467 (1977).

[30] *See, e.g.,* R.J.E. Leasing Corp., 262 N.L.R.B. 373, 110 L.R.R.M. 1313 (1982); Presbyterian Community Hosp., 230 N.L.R.B. 599, 95 L.R.R.M. 1610 (1977).

[31] 319 U.S. 533, 12 L.R.R.M. 739 (1943).

[32] *See, e.g.,* Al Pfister Truck Serv., 236 N.L.R.B. 217, 99 L.R.R.M. 1024 (1978); Acme Wire Works, Inc., 229 N.L.R.B. 333, 96 L.R.R.M. 1603 (1977).

[33] Carpenters Local 60 v. NLRB, 365 U.S. 651, 47 L.R.R.M. 2900 (1961).

[34] NLRB v. Englander Co., 237 F.2d 599, 38 L.R.R.M. 2765 (3d Cir. 1956).

[35] 29 U.S.C. § 158 (b)(1)(A).

[36] 29 U.S.C. § 158 (b)(2).

lation of section 8(b)(1)(A) or 8(b)(2), it normally issues a cease-and-desist order and directs such further affirmative relief as may be necessary to undo the specific act of restraint, coercion, or discrimination.[37]

Administrative law judges have also recommended that the Board mandate an additional remedy that would prohibit a union with an extensive history of sections 8(b)(2) and (1)(A) violations from representing any employee not already represented by it for a period of three years, unless and until it is certified by the Board. A further recommendation is that the union be required to cease from soliciting membership application cards unless the cards contain statements acknowledging the union's former violation of employees' statutory rights.[38] The Board, however, has refused to grant the expanded remedies recommended in those cases. Thus, in *Amalgamated Local Union 355 (Russell Motors, Inc.)*,[39] the Board, with court approval, ruled that such remedies were punitive, exceeding the purely remedial nature of proper Board remedies in that their provisions were not designed solely to remedy the particular unfair labor practices committed in the instant case. In this case, the Board was found to have contemplated future violations of the Act by including among its remedies a broad order to Local 355 not to cause any employer to restrain or coerce any employee in the exercise of his or her section 7 rights. Under the broad order, future violations would be subject to contempt of court proceedings and make available powerful judicial remedies which are beyond the purely remedial nature of Board orders.

---

[37] *See* Chapter IV, *supra.*

[38] *See* Raymond Buick, Inc., 173 N.L.R.B. 1292, 70 L.R.R.M. 1106 (1968), *as modified,* 182 N.L.R.B. 504, 74 L.R.R.M. 1137 (1970); Vanella Buick Opel, Inc., 194 N.L.R.B. 744, 79 L.R.R.M. 1090 (1971); Amalgamated Local Union 355 (Russell Motors, Inc.), 198 N.L.R.B. 351, 80 L.R.R.M. 1757 (1972).

[39] 198 N.L.R.B. 351, 80 L.R.R.M. 1757 (1972), *enforced,* 481 F.2d 966, 83 L.R.R.M. 2849 (2d Cir. 1973).

CHAPTER XII

Bargaining Orders to Remedy Employer Unfair Labor Practices: The Gissel Decision

In *NLRB v. Gissel Packing Co.*,[1] the Supreme Court affirmed the Board's issuance of a bargaining order based upon authorization cards signed by a majority of the employees as a remedy in instances where the employer's unfair labor practices had undermined the union's majority status and made a fair election improbable. *Gissel* also confirmed that the duty of an employer to bargain can arise without a Board election, and that union authorization cards, when obtained from a majority of employees without misrepresentation or coercion, are sufficiently reliable to provide the union with an alternate route to becoming the collective bargaining representative. *Gissel* established Board criteria for determining the appropriateness of the bargaining order based upon an analysis of the impact of the various unfair labor practices on the election process and the "laboratory conditions" sought by the Board for representation elections.[2]

The *Gissel* bargaining order is one of the least understood remedies in the labor law. The courts of appeals in the various circuits have been critical of the Board's approach in regard to lack of predictability and supporting analysis. The predictability factor has, of course, been exacerbated by the turnover in Board membership.

Gissel has been under fire since its inception. Some of its critics today would impose a *Gissel* bargaining order upon a collective bargaining unit where less than a majority of the employees have joined the union. This suggestion is not only inconsistent with the intent of the statutory background and with the *Gissel* decision itself, it is also unworkable. The legal arena is not necessarily the place to remedy unions' problems today which may be more effec-

---

[1] 395 U.S. 575, 71 L.R.R.M. 2481 (1969).
[2] General Shoe Corp., 77 N.L.R.B. 124, 21 L.R.R.M. 1337 (1948).

tively addressed by the unions themselves by reviewing economic and social trends and the way that they conduct their own business. In any event, remedies should not be inconsistent with the key tenets of our democratic society.

This chapter will evaluate the use of the *Gissel* order. Specific considerations will include: 1) the issuance of a card-based bargaining order; 2) the Board's analysis of the causal relationship between the misconduct and the election process; 3) review of bargaining orders by the courts of appeals; 4) interim bargaining orders (by injunction); and 5) retroactive effect of bargaining orders.

ESTABLISHING A BARGAINING RELATIONSHIP ABSENT EMPLOYER UNFAIR LABOR PRACTICES

Several options exist for an employer when a union demands recognition in its efforts to organize a particular unit of employees. The employer may extend voluntary recognition to the union on the basis of majority strength shown by signed authorization cards,[3] polling of employee sentiment,[4] or other evidence. In such situations, it is not necessary to proceed through NLRB's representation procedure. The parties are free to engage in collective bargaining and sign a contract, and the union would be the collective bargaining representative (albeit uncertified) of the employees.

In the event that the employer does not wish voluntarily to recognize the union, either party may petition the NLRB for a representation election.[5] The NLRB election process, deeply rooted in the foundations of our democratic society, has been the preferred certification process since 1939.[6] It allows both the union and the employer to campaign for the votes of the employees. The employees' freedom of choice is protected by the secrecy of the ballot box with a government representative present. If the union receives a majority of the votes cast, it is certified as the collective bargaining representative.[7]

---

[3] Extending recognition to a union that, in fact, lacks majority status is likely to constitute a violation of §§ 8(a)(1) and 8(a)(2) of the Act. *See, e.g.,* International Ladies Garment Workers v. NLRB, 366 U.S. 731, 48 L.R.R.M. 2251 (1961). For discussion of illegal dominations or assistance to a union, see Chapter XI, *supra.*

[4] Struksnes Constr. Co., 165 N.L.R.B. 1062, 65 L.R.R.M. 1385 (1967).

[5] *See* 29 U.S.C. §§ 159(c)(1)(A) and (B).

[6] Cudahy Packing Co., 13 N.L.R.B. 526, 4 L.R.R.M. 321 (1939).

[7] *See* General Box Co., 82 N.L.R.B. 678, 23 L.R.R.M. 1589 (1949). A certified union is protected for a reasonable period of time, usually one year, from the claim that it no longer represents a majority of the employees. Brooks v. NLRB, 348 U.S. 96, 35 L.R.R.M. 2158 (1954). The Act further protects a certified union against recognitional or organizational picketing by another union, 29 U.S.C. § 158(b)(7)(B). Note,

GISSEL *BARGAINING ORDERS TO ESTABLISH*
BARGAINING RELATIONSHIPS

A history of the evolution of the *Gissel* bargaining order is instructive. Under the Wagner Act, the Board relied extensively upon card checks in representation cases until *Cudahy Packing Co.*[8] in 1939, when it noted its preference for secret elections:

> Although in the past we have certified representatives without an election upon a showing of the sort here made, we are persuaded by our experience that the policies of the Act will best be effectuated if the question of representation which has arisen is reached in an election by secret ballot.[9]

However, in *Joy Silk Mills*,[10] the Board noted an exception; it ordered the employer to bargain with the union, where its denial of the union's request for recognition based upon authorization cards was not based upon a good-faith doubt of the union's majority status. As noted by the Court of Appeals for the District of Columbia in enforcing *Joy Silk Mills:*

> An employer may refuse recognition to a union when motivated by a good-faith doubt as to that union's majority status. . . . When, however, such refusal is due to a desire to gain time and to take action to dissipate the union's majority, the refusal is no longer justifiable and constitutes a violation of the duty to bargain set forth in Section 8(a)(5) of the Act.[11]

Initially, the Board allowed a union to have two chances. If unsuccessful in an election, the union could seek a bargaining order if it could show the employer had refused to recognize an authorization card majority and had engaged in unfair labor practices.[12] However, in *Aiello Dairy Farms Co.*,[13] the Board held that once a union chose the election route, it waived its opportunity subsequently to seek the bargaining order. This created a "Hobson's

---

29 U.S.C.A § 158(b)(7)(A) extends similar protection to a noncertified union lawfully recognized by an employer. A certified union, under § 8(b)(4)(D), is free from certain restrictions placed on concerted activity during work assignment disputes. The Act also provides what has become known as the "election bar" doctrine which will not allow another election to be held within one year of a prior, valid election. 29 U.S.C. § 159(c)(3). Once the union is either voluntarily recognized or certified by the NLRB, the employer is required to bargain with it in good faith. Failure to do so could result in a violation of § 8(a)(5) of the Act.

[8] 13 N.L.R.B. 526, 4 L.R.R.M. 321 (1939).

[9] 13 N.L.R.B. at 531–32.

[10] 85 N.L.R.B. 1263, 24 L.R.R.M. 1548 (1949), *enforced as modified,* 185 F.2d 732, 27 L.R.R.M. 2012 (D.C. Cir. 1950), *cert. denied,* 341 U.S. 914, 27 L.R.R.M. 2633 (1951).

[11] 185 F.2d at 741.

[12] Davidson Co., 94 N.L.R.B. 142, 28 L.R.R.M. 1026 (1951).

[13] 110 N.L.R.B. 1365, 35 L.R.R.M. 1235 (1954).

choice," that itself was reversed ten years later in *Bernel Foam Products Co.*[14]

> [T]he so-called 'choice' which the union is forced to make under Aiello between going to an election or filing an 8(a)(5) charge is at best a Hobson's choice. Although an election is a relatively swift and inexpensive way for the union to put the force of law behind its majority status, the procedure is highly uncertain entailing the real possibility that because of conduct by the employer no fair election will be held.[15]

In *Aaron Brothers*,[16] the Board modified the *Joy Silk* doctrine to provide that the NLRB's General Counsel had the burden of proving employer bad faith. Evidence of bad faith consisted of the commission of unfair labor practices which led to a diminution of the union's majority status. Absent that bad faith, the employer did not have to provide a reason for rejecting the union's claim to majority status, and he "will not be held to have violated his bargaining obligations . . . simply because he refuses to rely upon cards, rather than an election, as the method for determining the union's majority."[17]

The *Aaron Brothers* "bad faith" approach formed the basis of the NLRB's brief to the Supreme Court in *Gissel* seeking to affirm the issuance of bargaining orders.[18] (See Appendix for summary of the *Gissel* case history.) But at the oral argument before the Court, counsel for the NLRB announced that the Board had abandoned the *Joy Silk* doctrine, and that it was now of the view that an employer's good faith was largely "irrelevant." The Board suggested that the "key to the issuance of a bargaining order is the commission of serious unfair labor practices that interfere with the election processes and tend to preclude the holding of a fair election."[19] The Supreme Court agreed, and in its opinion formulated criteria for issuing bargaining orders which vary according to the scope and degree of the employer's unlawful conduct and its impact upon the employees.[20]

---

[14] 146 N.L.R.B. 1277, 56 L.R.R.M. 1039 (1964).
[15] 146 N.L.R.B. at 1280.
[16] 158 N.L.R.B. 1077, 62 L.R.R.M. 1160 (1966).
[17] *Id.* at 1078, 62 L.R.R.M. at 1161.
[18] 395 U.S. at 594, 71 L.R.R.M. at 2488.
[19] *Id.*
[20] The Court dealt with two other significant issues. It upheld the Board's *Cumberland Shoe* authorization card doctrine, noting that elections will continue to be held in the vast majority of cases and ". . . employees should be bound by the clear language of what they sign, unless that language is deliberately and clearly cancelled by a union adherent with words calculated to direct the signer to disregard and forget the language above his signature." 395 U.S. at 606, 71 L.R.R.M. at 2493. It also held (interpreting § 8(c) of the Act) that ". . . an employer is free to communicate to his employees any of his general views about unionism or any of his specific views

First, the Court discussed the "exceptional" case, where an employer had committed such "outrageous" and "pervasive" unfair labor practices that a bargaining order might issue without inquiry into majority status. The Court observed:

> Despite our reversal of the Fourth Circuit [in three of the four consolidated cases comprising *Gissel*] on all major issues, the actual area of disagreement between our position here and that of the Fourth Circuit is not large as a practical matter. [T]he Fourth Circuit . . . left open the possibility of imposing a bargaining order, *without need of inquiry into majority status* on the basis of cards or otherwise, in "exceptional" cases marked by "outrageous" and "pervasive" unfair labor practices.[21]

Such a bargaining order would be appropriate, the Court stated, for misconduct so coercive of employee rights that its effects could not be hoped to be dissipated by application of traditional remedies (e.g., an order to cease and desist).[22] Of course, this language was *dicta*,[23] as the unions involved in all the cases considered in *Gissel* had achieved card majorities. Nevertheless, the Court's language appeared to be an invitation to the Board to issue minority bargaining orders in extreme cases to prevent an employer from benefiting from extraordinarily coercive conduct. In two subsequent cases the Board has issued minority bargaining orders.[24] The question of whether the Board has the authority to do so led to a split in the courts of appeals,[25] and ultimately to the Dotson Board's rejection of such authority, as we shall discuss below.

As to the second category where the Court approved the Board's authority to issue a bargaining order (known as *Gissel II*), the Court stated:

---

about a particular union, so long as the communications do not contain a 'threat of reprisal or force or promise of benefit.' " *Id.* at 618, 71 L.R.R.M. at 2497.

[21] *Gissel*, 395 U.S. at 613, 71 L.R.R.M. at 2495 (emphasis added).

[22] *Id.* at 614, 71 L.R.R.M. at 2495.

[23] It was actually *"dicta* upon *dicta,"* for the Fourth Circuit case cited by the Court in reference to minority bargaining orders itself contained only *dicta* upon this point. *Id.* at 613, 71 L.R.R.M. at 2495, *citing* NLRB v. Logan Packing Co., 386 F.2d 562, 570, 66 L.R.R.M. 2596, 2603 (4th Cir. 1967).

[24] United Dairy Farmers Coop. Ass'n, 257 N.L.R.B. 772, 107 L.R.R.M. 1577 (1981) (United Dairy Farmers II), *on remand from* 633 F.2d 1054, 105 L.R.R.M. 3034 (3rd Cir. 1980); Conair Corp., 261 N.L.R.B. 1189, 110 L.R.R.M. 1161 (1982), *enforcement denied,* Conair Corp. v. NLRB, 751 F.2d 1355, 114 L.R.R.M. 3169 (D.C. Cir. 1983).

[25] United Dairy Farmers Coop. Ass'n v. NLRB, 633 F.2d 1054, 105 L.R.R.M. 3034 (3d Cir. 1980); J.P. Stevens Co. v. NLRB, 441 F.2d 514, 76 L.R.R.M. 2817 (5th Cir. 1971) (approving of minority bargaining orders) (*dicta;* union had majority at one point); NLRB v. Montgomery Ward & Co., 554 F.2d 996, 95 L.R.R.M. 2433 (10th Cir. 1977) (*dicta;* union majority was present); Ona Corp. v. NLRB, 729 F.2d 713, 714 n.4, 115 L.R.R.M. 3665 n.4 (11th Cir. 1984) (*dicta;* Board decision found the unfair practices were not "outrageous" and hence not in the *Gissel I* category); *but see* Conair Corp. v. NLRB, 721 F.2d 1355, 114 L.R.R.M. 3169 (D.C. Cir. 1983).

The only effect of our holding here is to approve the Board's use of the bargaining order in less extraordinary cases marked by less pervasive practices which nonetheless still have the tendency to undermine majority strength and impede the election processes. The Board's authority to issue such an order on a lesser showing of employer misconduct is appropriate, we should re-emphasize, where there is also a showing that at one point the union had a majority; in such a case, of course, effectuating ascertainable employee free choice becomes as important a goal as deterring employer misbehavior. In fashioning a remedy in the exercise of its discretion, then, the Board can properly take into consideration the extensiveness of an employer's unfair labor practices in terms of their past effect on election conditions and the likelihood of their recurrence in the future. If the Board finds that the possibility of erasing the effects of past practices and of ensuring a fair election (or a fair rerun) by the use of traditional remedies, though present, is slight and that employee sentiment once expressed through cards would, on balance, be better protected by a bargaining order, then such order should issue.[26]

The *Gissel II* category, then, involves less serious cases, but nonetheless cases marked by "pervasive practices" which have the tendency to undermine majority strength and to make a fair election difficult. This situation requires proof that, at some point in time, the union possessed majority status. The Court stated that the Board has the authority to issue the bargaining order without proof that the union has been able to maintain its majority status,[27] and even where it is clear that the union, having earlier achieved majority status, represents only a minority when the order is entered.[28] In this case the Board must find the possibility of erasing the effects of the employer's past practices and of having a fair election to be slight.

The third category addressed by the Court (known as *Gissel III* cases) are those characterized by "minor or less extensive unfair labor practices, which, because of their minimal impact on the election machinery, will *not* sustain a bargaining order" [29]

APPLICATION OF GISSEL *CRITERIA* IN DETERMINING IMPACT OF EMPLOYER MISCONDUCT ON THE ELECTION ATMOSPHERE

The *Gissel* Court ruled that employer unfair labor practices do not *per se* justify the issuance of a bargaining order; [30] only those

---

[26] *Gissel*, 395 U.S. at 614, 615.
[27] *Id.* at 610, 71 L.R.R.M. at 2495.
[28] *Id.*
[29] *Id.* at 615, 71 L.R.R.M. at 2496 (emphasis added).
[30] *Id.* at 613–15, 71 L.R.R.M. at 2495–96.

that make the possibility of holding a fair election unlikely provide such justification. Thus, the Court affirmed that the bargaining order was to be an extraordinary remedy, with Board elections continuing to be the favored method of determining union majority status.[31] The Court left to the Board the determination of which types of unfair labor practices, under all the circumstances, foreclose or make unlikely the possibility of holding a fair election in a noncoercive atmosphere, and hence justify a *Gissel II* bargaining order.[32]

Application of the criteria has varied and evolved over the years.[33] The distinctions between the categories, especially between *Gissel II* and *Gissel III*, have been at times confusing, and the Board has often been unable to show why, in a given case, a fair election could not be possible. This has produced a situation where the application of the *Gissel* principles is in any given case quite unpredictable. The Board decisions, developed on a case-by-case basis, have resulted in a general state of confusion, which has been harshly criticized by the courts of appeal.[34] Indeed, Board Member Dennis recently spoke of the Board's "proclivity for issuing or not issuing bargaining orders 'without rhyme, reason or differentiating factors other than . . . conclusory statements.' "[35]

---

[31] *Id.* at 602–03, 615, 71 L.R.R.M. at 2491, 2496. The Court clearly put the burden on the party seeking the bargaining order to show why a fair election could not be held, by emphasizing that unfair practices which do not interfere with the election machinery cannot be used to justify issuance of a bargaining order.

[32] *Id.* at 614, 71 L.R.R.M. at 2495–96.

[33] *Gissel* left unresolved questions. For example, it was not until six years later, in Linden Lumber v. NLRB, 419 U.S. 301, 87 L.R.R.M. 3236 (1974), that the Supreme Court held that " . . . unless an employer has engaged in an unfair labor practice that impairs the election process, a union with authorization cards purporting to represent a majority of the employees which is refused recognition has the burden of taking the next step in involving the Board's procedure." 419 U.S. at 310.

The union is not under this burden if the employer has breached an agreement with the union to verify majority status. Snow and Sons, 134 N.L.R.B. 709, 49 L.R.R.M. 1228 (1961), *enforced*, 308 F.2d 687, 51 L.R.R.M. 2199 (9th Cir. 1962). Further, the employer may relieve the union of this task if the employer has independent knowledge of the union's strength. Sullivan Elec. Co., 199 N.L.R.B. 809, 81 L.R.R.M. 1313 (1972), *enforced*, Sullivan Elec. Co. v. NLRB, 479 F.2d 1270, 83 L.R.R.M. 2513 (6th Cir. 1973). *See also* Tennessee Shell Co., 212 N.L.R.B. 193, 86 L.R.R.M. 1704 (1974), *petition for review denied*, 515 F.2d 1018, 90 L.R.R.M. 2844 (D.C. Cir. 1975).

[34] Since the 1969 *Gissel* case, the Supreme Court has been content to allow the lower courts and the Board to wrestle with the unresolved issues, choosing not to clarify any aspect of *Gissel*. *See* John Cuneo, Inc. v. NLRB 459 U.S. 1178, 1178–1181 (1983) (Rehnquist, J., dissenting from denial of certiorari and urging that the Court review the current application of the *Gissel* decision by circuit courts).

[35] Regency Manor Nursing Home, 275 N.L.R.B. No. 271, DAILY LAB. REP. E-1, E-2 (July 31, 1985) (Member Dennis, concurring).

Gissel "Category One" Conduct: Minority Bargaining Orders

Perhaps the most controversial Board decisions have been those involving the category one offenses leading to the so-called minority bargaining order. In *United Dairy Farmers II,* a three-member panel of the Board ordered an employer who had committed a variety of unfair labor practices [36] to bargain with a union which had lost the election and was not supported by a majority of the signed authorization cards. *United Dairy Farmers II* was before the Board on remand from the Third Circuit, after that court had considered the *Gissel dicta* and held that the Board possessed the authority to issue minority bargaining orders.[37] The court's remand instructed the Board to consider the employer's practices in light of this holding, and decide if it wished to use this occasion to issue a minority bargaining order.[38]

The Conair *and* Gourmet Foods *Orders.* In its initial decision in this case, the Board had not issued such an order, as Member Penello denied that the Board held such authority,[39] while Members Truesdale and Murphy reserved the question for a later case.[40] The two remaining members, Chairman Fanning and Member Jenkins, argued that the Board had such power,[41] and their views prevailed in *United Dairy Farmers II,* a decision rendered by a three-member Board panel consisting of Fanning, Jenkins, and Donald A. Zimmerman. The decision was unanimous, with the third participating member, the newly appointed Zimmerman, holding that the Third Circuit's decision was binding upon the Board for the particular case before it.[42] Zimmerman thus reserved for the future whether he would support his two colleagues to form a Board majority on this issue.

This occurred one year later. In *Conair Corporation,*[43] Zimmerman joined Fanning and Jenkins to issue a bargaining order on the basis of the employer's serious, repeated, and illegal acts absent a showing of majority. Chairman Van de Water and Member Hunter dissented.

---

[36] These included discharging union supporters, threatening plant closure should the union be voted in, granting illegal benefits, and changing work conditions. United Dairy Farmers II, 257 N.L.R.B. 772, 773, 107 L.R.R.M. 1577, 1578–79.

[37] United Dairy Farmers Coop. Ass'n v. NLRB (United Dairy Farmers I), 633 F.2d 1054, 1069, 105 L.R.R.M. 3034, 3045 (3d Cir. 1980).

[38] *Id.* at 1069–70, 105 L.R.R.M. at 3045.

[39] United Dairy Farmers Coop. Ass'n (United Dairy Farmers I), 242 N.L.R.B. 1026, 1038, 101 L.R.R.M. 1278, 1289 (1979).

[40] *Id.* at 1027, n.5, 101 L.R.R.M. at 1280 n.5.

[41] *Id.* at 1032–33, 101 L.R.R.M. at 1283.

[42] 257 N.L.R.B. at 772 n.8, 107 L.R.R.M. at 1578 n.8.

[43] 261 N.L.R.B. 1189, 110 L.R.R.M. 1161 (1982) (involving threats of plant closure and discharges, actual discharges, promises of benefits, interrogations, surveillance).

The Board's order in *Conair Corporation* thus marked the first time a full Board issued a minority bargaining order. The majority rationalized the risk of imposing a minority union on an unwilling majority by stating:

> [W]e find that the risk of imposing a minority union on employees for an interim period is greatly outweighed by the risk that, without a bargaining order, all employees would be indefinitely denied their statutory right to make a fair determination whether they desire union representation.[44]

The majority, quoting the Supreme Court, noted that if the employees so desired, they could file a decertification petition later.[45]

The majority's approach balanced the right of employees to the opportunity for union representation against the risk of imposing a minority union on an unwilling majority. However, this approach was rejected by the District of Columbia Court of Appeals, which refused to enforce the Board's bargaining order, noting that the *Gissel* Supreme Court opinion was *dicta*, and not dispositive.[46] The court held that the Act did not grant the Board the power to issue minority bargaining orders.[47]

The *Conair* court of appeals was especially concerned about imposing a union on unwilling employees without a clear congressional mandate:

> Absent a union election victory or some other concrete manifestation of majority assent to union representation, it is impossible to project the employees choice reliably; imposition of a bargaining order in these circumstances runs a high risk of opposing the majority's will . . . . Without a clear direction from Congress, we are not prepared to recognize administrative authority, or arrogate power to ourselves, to remedy one possible injustice by taking the substantial chance of imposing another.[48]

After its rebuff in *Conair,* the Board issued no further minority bargaining orders. Indeed, in 1984, in *Gourmet Foods, Inc.,*[49] a reconstituted Board repudiated its *Conair* decision. In *Gourmet Foods,* the union never achieved a majority. Two members of the Board took the opportunity to issue a comprehensive opinion on the issue of minority bargaining orders, even though that issue was not raised

---

[44] *Id.* at 1194, 110 L.R.R.M. at 1166.

[45] *Id., quoting Gissel,* 395 U.S. at 613, 71 L.R.R.M. at 2495.

[46] Conair Corp. v. NLRB, 721 F.2d 1355, 1381, 114 L.R.R.M. 3169, 3187 (D.C. Cir. 1983).

[47] *Id.* at 1383–84, 114 L.R.R.M. at 3189–90.

[48] *Id.* at 1383, 114 L.R.R.M. at 3189.

[49] 270 N.L.R.B. No. 113, 116 L.R.R.M. 1105 (1984).

by the General Counsel before the administrative law judge.[50] Chairman Dotson and Member Hunter (with Member Dennis concurring in a separate opinion) conducted a thorough review of the legislative history of the NLRB, the *Gissel* decision, and the circuit court and Board decisions both before and following *Gissel* before concluding that the principle of majority rule was so fundamental to the Act that the Board had no statutory power to violate it.[51] Member Zimmerman dissented.[52] *Gourmet Foods* has been the final word of the Board to date concerning minority *Gissel* orders.

Arguments in the Debate. Although both sides to the debate over minority bargaining orders speak of the importance of employee free choice, the focus of their respective concerns, in fact, differs. The *Gourmet Foods* decision provides a clear summary of both sides' perspectives and supporting arguments.

Champions of minority bargaining order tend to focus primarily on employer misconduct and the need to deter the employer from illegal practices. Thus, in *Gourmet Foods*, dissenting Member Zimmerman scores the majority for "rendering the Board powerless to provide full *deterrence* of unfair labor practices and full restitution of employee rights in cases of the most egregious misconduct . . . ,"[53] and proceeds to stress the legitimacy of remedies aimed at changing employer conduct (although he acknowledges that the Board cannot issue punitive orders).[54] The tone of his dissent, expressing outrage at the majority's unwillingness to wield the club of the minority bargaining order as employer, reveals that his true concern centers on punishing the employer:

> The plurality opinion presents only one other possible reason for not issuing nonmajority bargaining orders . . . that the orders will not be effective in restoring free choice. How do my colleagues know this? the Board has issued only two [such] . . . orders in its history. . . . This fleeting experiment . . . hardly seems sufficient basis for an informed opinion. Nonmajority bargaining orders *may* have the desired restitutional value, and surely *will* have an extra deterrent value, where other remedies surely will not.[55]

Opponents of minority bargaining orders, by contrast, focus on the rights of employees, emphasize the majority rule principle, and stress employee free choice, unfettered by governmental intrusion:

---

[50] *Id.*, slip op. at 4–5, 116 L.R.R.M. at 1107.
[51] *Id.*, slip op. at 7–26, 116 L.R.R.M. at 1107–1114.
[52] *Id.*, slip op. at 32–47, 116 L.R.R.M. at 1117–1126.
[53] *Id.*, slip op. at 43, 116 L.R.R.M. at 1121 (emphasis added).
[54] *Id.*, slip op. at 44 n.31, 116 L.R.R.M. at 1121 n.31 (citations omitted).
[55] *Id.*, slip op. at 46, 116 L.R.R.M. at 1122 (emphasis in original) (footnote omitted).

[T]he majority rule principle is such an integral part of the Act's current substance and procedure that it must be adhered to in fashioning a remedy, even in the most "exceptional" cases ... for it is the culmination of choice *by a majority of employees* that leads to the process of collective bargaining; the choice by a majority gives legitimacy and effectiveness to a union's role as exclusive bargaining representative....[56]

One court has expressed concern over majority choice even more emphatically. In discussing the need for the Board to carefully explain its reasons for issuing any bargaining order, Judge Adams of the Third Circuit forcefully stated, in a case where the union *had* in fact achieved a majority:

The *Gissel* bargaining order, like judicial review itself, is potentially antidemocratic: the order arises from an adversarial union-employer proceeding in which the employees have no choice, and imposes a union on a majority of employees who may oppose it.[57]

Judge Adams pointed out that in the case of *Gissel* orders, only the union and the employer are heard before the Board. The employees' desires are not represented unless one is willing to presume, without a secret-ballot election, that the union is already favored by an employee majority.

Opponents of minority orders also emphasize that, as a practical matter, imposing such orders cannot put in place a strong union where the employees are either too cowed or indifferent to support it. In their view, a *Gissel* order merely imposes the structure of a union in the workplace without inquiry into whether that union has employee support behind it.[58]

Proponents of *Gissel* orders see vindication of employee free choice (which free choice is equated with the insertion of a union into the workplace) as a good in itself, regardless of whether the union thus imposed is successful in negotiating a contract.[59] In this view, vindication of employees' rights, coupled with the desire to deter (if

---

[56] *Id.*, slip op. at 16, 18–19, 117 L.R.R.M. at 1111, 1112 (emphasis in original).

[57] NLRB v. Atlas Microfilming Div. of Sertafilm, Inc., 753 F.2d 313, 320, 118 L.R.R.M. 2628, 2634 (3rd Cir. 1985); *see also* NLRB v. K & K Gourmet Meats, Inc., 640 F.2d 460, 469, 470, 106 L.R.R.M. 2448, 2455 (3rd Cir. 1981) (because the bargaining order "disenfranchises" workers, it must be used only in the most "exceptional" cases).

[58] Gourmet Foods, 270 N.L.R.B. No. 113, slip op. at 25, 116 L.R.R.M. at 1114; *see also* Weiler, *Promises to Keep: Securing Workers' Rights to Self-Organization Under the NLRA,* 96 HARV. L. REV. 1769, 1795 n.94 (1983) (discussing a study showing that in 90 percent of the surveyed cases *Gissel* orders had not led to more than an initial collective bargaining contract, which was then not renewed, or had produced no contract at all).

[59] *See* Gourmet Foods, 270 N.L.R.B. No. 113, slip op. at. 46 n.34, 116 L.R.R.M. at 1122 n.34.

not punished) offending employers in the future, tips the balance in favor of the minority bargaining order, even if such an order is not effective in more practical terms.

Gissel *"Category Two"*: The Search for a Standard

The Supreme Court clearly endorsed the use of bargaining orders in "cases marked by less pervasive practices which nonetheless still have the tendency to undermine majority strength and impede the election process." [60] Imposing this *Gissel II* bargaining order, however, requires that the union establish that at one point it enjoyed majority support.[61] Furthermore, the Board must justify its issuance of a *Gissel II* order by explaining which practices undermined the union's strength, and why they so poisoned the campaign atmosphere as to make a fair election unlikely.[62]

The Court gave guidance to the Board by suggesting the following analytical framework:

> In fashioning a remedy in the exercise of its discretion, then, the Board can properly take into consideration the extensiveness of an employer's unfair labor practices in terms of their past effect on election conditions and the likelihood of their recurrence in the future. If the Board finds that the possibility of erasing the effects of past practices and of ensuring a fair election (or a fair rerun) by the use of traditional remedies, though present, is slight and that employee sentiment once expressed through cards would, on balance, be better protected by a bargaining order, then such an order should issue.[63]

The Supreme Court test, as thus established, stresses the *effects* of an employer's unfair labor practices, rather than the practices *per se*. It requires that the Board do more than list the illegal activities; it must perform the task of analyzing, on a case-by-case basis, the impact of the activities on the election atmosphere.

Throughout the 1970s the Board did not apply this test in a consistent manner. In many cases the Board's decisions stressed the severity of employer's actions, without explaining how those actions influenced the employees. The Board has attempted to persuade the courts to accept the theory that certain extremely severe unfair labor practices should automatically result in a *Gissel II* order. It is a theory which the courts for the most part have resisted, insisting

---

[60] *Gissel,* 395 U.S. at 614, 71 L.R.R.M. at 2495.
[61] *Id.*
[62] *Id.*
[63] *Id.* at 614–15, 71 L.R.R.M. at 2496.

instead that the Board undertake the more detailed analysis of employee sentiment, as influenced by the employer violations.[64]

FACTORS LEADING TO ISSUANCE
OF A GISSEL II ORDER

The present discussion will focus on the Board's view of what types of conduct allegedly justify the issuance of a *Gissel II* order. Although the particular case-by-case approach utilized by the Board has impaired predictability in this area,[65] a review of the Board's *Gissel* decisions provides guidance sufficient to justify the following comments.

"Hallmark" Unfair Labor Practices

Despite paying lip service to the requirement that it show the impact of employer misconduct on the possibility of holding a fair election, the Board has shown a tendency to issue bargaining orders based solely on the types of illegal acts performed by an employer. References, therefore, to certain so-called hallmark unfair labor practices [66] are often made by the Board as if their mere existence *per se* justifies the issuance of a bargaining order.[67]

---

[64] *E.g.*, NLRB v. K & K Gourmet Meats, 640 F.2d at 470, 106 L.R.R.M. at 2455, where the court stated:

> No room is left [by *Gissel*] for automatic formulae under which, for example, one threat, two coerced interrogations and a promise of a wage increase will result in an order [to bargain] while another combination will not.

[65] The Board has justified the general case-by-case approach by echoing the *Gourmet Meats* warning, stating:

> Determination of the appropriateness of a bargaining order is not based on "automatic formulae" involving any set combination or type of unfair labor practices. Rather, the impact on employees' choice and the election process is what is critical.

PBA, Inc., 270 N.L.R.B. No. 143, 116 L.R.R.M. 1162 (1984). In practice, however, Board inconsistency has been the Board's hallmark.

[66] *E.g.*, Horizon Air Serv., Inc., 272 N.L.R.B. No. 33, 117 L.R.R.M. 1312 (discussing types of hallmark violations), *enforced*, NLRB v. Horizon Air Serv., Inc., 761 F.2d 22, 119 L.R.R.M. 2203 (1st Cir. 1985); *compare* Sidex Furniture Corp., 270 N.L.R.B. No. 89, 116 L.R.R.M. 1140 (1984) (interrogations not enough to justify bargaining order); L.M. Berry & Co., 266 N.L.R.B. 47, 112 L.R.R.M. 1246 (1983) (promises of benefits not of significant magnitude to justify order).

[67] J. Coty Messenger Serv., Inc., 272 N.L.R.B. No. 42, 117 L.R.R.M. 1280, *enforcement denied in part*, NLRB v. J. Coty Messenger Serv., Inc., 763 F.2d 92, 119 L.R.R.M. 2779 (2d Cir. 1985) (Board refers to the Second Circuit's hallmark violations language); Pace Oldsmobile, Inc., 256 N.L.R.B. 1001, 107 L.R.R.M. 1414, *enforced in part, vacated in part*, 681 F.2d 99, 110 L.R.R.M. 2646 (2d Cir. 1982), *on remand*, 265 N.L.R.B. 1527, 112 L.R.R.M. 1186, *enforcement denied*, 739 F.2d 108, 116 L.R.R.M. 3137 (2d Cir. 1984).

Although this tendency to overemphasize the illegal acts themselves, without analysis of their impact upon the employees, has led to numerous enforcement denials in the circuits, the seriousness of employer misconduct is by no means deemed irrelevant. To the contrary, it is the first and most important factor to be considered by the Board in assessing whether to issue a bargaining order. The Second Circuit has provided a list of the most egregious, or hallmark, illegal acts:

> "Hallmark violations" include: such employer misbehavior as the closing of a plant or threats of a plant closure or loss of employment, the grant of benefits to employees or the reassignment, demotion or discharge of union adherents in violation of § 8(a)(3) of the Act.[68]

The common denominator of these violations (with the exception of threatening to close the plant) is that all represent completed actions. Lesser threats or promises normally will not be deemed sufficient to justify a bargaining order.[69] If an employer's acts do not fall within the hallmark category, they will normally not be sufficient to justify a bargaining order, unless repeated or coupled with some factor intensifying their effect.[70]

---

[68] NLRB v. Jamaica Towing, Inc., 632 F.2d 208, 212–13, 105 L.R.R.M. 2959, 2962 (2d Cir. 1980).

[69] Regency Manor Nursing Home, 275 N.L.R.B. No. 271, DAILY LAB REP. (July 31, 1985) at E-2 (Member Dennis, concurring). In her concurrence, Member Dennis proposes a framework for Gissel order analyses, taking into account the nature of the violations, their pervasiveness, and, in some cases, mitigating factors. She also stated that threats alone, not constituting completed action, normally should not justify a bargaining order. See also Horizon Air Serv., Inc., 272 N.L.R.B. No. 33, 117 L.R.R.M. 1312 (discussing hallmark violations); see L.M. Berry & Co., 266 N.L.R.B. 47, 112 L.R.R.M. 1246 (1983); but see Hedstrom Co. v. NLRB, 629 F.2d 305, 105 L.R.R.M. 2183 (3d Cir. 1980), cert. denied, 450 U.S. 996, 106 L.R.R.M. 2817 (1981) (threat to stop expansion plans, coupled with other illegal actions, supports a bargaining order); Ona, Div. of Ona Corp., 261 N.L.R.B. 1378, 110 L.R.R.M. 1271 (threat not to invest more in plant would be sufficient to support a bargaining order) (administrative judge's opinion; dicta) (subsequent history omitted).

[70] Regency Manor, DAILY LAB REP. (July 31, 1985) at E-3 citing Jamaica Towing, 632 F.2d at 213, 105 L.R.R.M. at 2963 (Member Dennis, concurring). It is difficult to state with certainty if the mere promise of additional future benefits, by itself, would justify a bargaining order, but apparently it would not be sufficient. The leading Jamaica Towing case did not include promises (as opposed to an actual grant) of benefits in its list of hallmark violations. Some Board decisions appear to consider promises as hallmark violations, but other cases take the opposite position. L.M. Berry & Co., 266 N.L.R.B. 47, 112 L.R.R.M. 1246 (1983); House of Cycle, Inc., 264 N.L.R.B. 1030, 112 L.R.R.M. 1075 (1982); Alco Venetian Blind Co., 253 N.L.R.B. 1216, 106 L.R.R.M. 1117 (1981). One reason that it is difficult to make this determination is that promises of benefits are almost always coupled with other illegal actions. E.g., Daniels Cadillac, 270 N.L.R.B. No. 86, 117 L.R.R.M. 1110 (1984) (interrogations, promises, solicitation of grievances, and withdrawal of signed union cards; held, no bargaining order justified); see DeQueen Gen. Hosp. v. NLRB, 744 F.2d 612, 117 L.R.R.M. 2534, (8th Cir. 1984), enforcing 264 N.L.R.B. 480, 112 L.R.R.M. 1106 (despite numerous unfair labor practices, firings were key to issuance of bargaining order).

A second factor considered by the Board in weighing the gravity of the employer's action is the identity of the employer's management personnel who performed the unlawful acts. This factor is reasonable, for it can be presumed that a threat made, or action taken, by a high-level supervisory employee will be believed by employees to be employer policy, rather than the opinion of a lower-level functionary who cannot back up his threats.[71]

A third factor, and one relating to the impact of the misconduct upon the employees, is whether employees are aware of the employer's unlawful actions. Employer misconduct will not count toward the decisions to issue a *Gissel* order unless the employees know of that misconduct.[72] In this connection, the Board has considered that employee knowledge is likely to be more thoroughly disseminated in smaller units.[73]

Impact Inquiry Concerning Effects of Employer Misconduct

While the Board presumes employee knowledge of employer misconduct is equivalent to a finding of coercive impact, this presumption is not in itself sufficient to justify a bargaining order. It does not relieve the Board of its duty of making an independent inquiry into how, in fact, the particular unit of employees was affected by employer misconduct. Under *Gissel,* the Board is supposed to protect employee free choice by issuing a bargaining order only when it finds and concludes that the employees cannot be expected to participate in an election without experiencing fears generated from past employer coercion. How well the Board performs this impact inquiry determines the receptiveness of the courts to any resulting bargaining order. The courts have accused the

---

[71] *Compare* J & D Wall Baking Co., 272 N.L.R.B. No. 157, 117 L.R.R.M. 1402 (1984) (general manager performed illegal acts; bargaining order issued) *and* J. Coty, 272 N.L.R.B. No. 42, 117 L.R.R.M. 1280 (1984) (top company executives involved) *with* Delta Hosiery, Inc., 259 N.L.R.B. 1005, 109 L.R.R.M. 1063 (1982) (threats by lower-level supervisor presumed ignored by employees).

[72] J.J. Newberry Co. v. NLRB, 645 F.2d 148, 107 L.R.R.M. 2018 (2d Cir. 1981) (employee knowledge of employer misconduct will not be assumed); *but see* Frank Black Mech. Servs., Inc., 271 N.L.R.B. No. 201, 117 L.R.R.M. 1183 (1984) (because of small size of unit—thirty persons—and extent of unlawful activity, Board presumes all employees know of such); *see also* Devon Gables Nursing Home, 237 N.L.R.B. 775, 99 L.R.R.M. 1071, *enforced,* NLRB v. Tischler, 615 F.2d 509, 103 L.R.R.M. 3033 (9th Cir. 1980).

[73] The Board has repeatedly emphasized the magnified effect of unfair labor practices on small units. Horizon Air Servs., Inc., 272 N.L.R.B. No. 33, 117 L.R.R.M. 1312, *enforced,* NLRB v. Horizon Air Servs., Inc., 761 F.2d 22, 119 L.R.R.M. 2203 (1st Cir. 1985); Bremal Elec., Inc., 271 N.L.R.B. No. 231, 117 L.R.R.M. 1247 (1984); Frank Black Mech. Servs., Inc., 271 N.L.R.B. No. 201, 117 L.R.R.M. 1183 (1984).

Board of turning *Gissel* on its head by the Board's unwillingness to perform the task of justifying its freely issued bargaining orders.[74]

Despite this appellate court criticism, however, the Board has performed the requisite impact analysis in a sufficient number of cases to draw conclusions as to what shape that analysis will take, when made. The mere fact that the union lost an election after successfully collecting a card majority is not proof that, between the period of card majority and the day of election, the employer's unlawful activities dissipated the union's support. The election loss could simply mean that employees signed cards without committing themselves to finally voting for the union, or that they simply changed their minds for reasons unrelated to the employer's actions. Consequently, the Board looks for evidence that the employees have been intimidated or cowed by the employer.[75] At first glance, one might imagine that this is a subjective inquiry, difficult to perform, which is perhaps why the Board at times appears loath to perform it, and instead adopts analytical short-cuts.

Of course, the *Gissel* impact inquiry is not necessarily or wholly subjective, for it is possible for the Board to simply examine the coercive actions allegedly practiced by the employer, and deduce what effect those actions would have on the normal employees. Is the normal employee intimidated when union leaders are fired and the employer threatens to close the plant? Presumably so; hence, a *Gissel* order would result.

In this connection, the Board often appears committed to supporting a presumption that the existence of hallmark violations *per se* will have a lasting effect on employees,[76] merely supporting that presumption with any additional evidence available bearing on the

---

[74] *E.g.,* in NLRB v. Marion Rohr, 714 F.2d 228, 231, 114 L.R.R.M. 2126, 2129 (2d Cir. 1983) the court spoke disparagingly of the Board's "well-established preference for issuing a bargaining order," *citing* United States v. Kopper Co., 652 F.2d 290, 292 n.5 (2d Cir.), *cert. denied,* 454 U.S. 1083 (1981); Red Oaks Nursing Home, Inc. v. NLRB, 633 F.2d 503 (7th Cir. 1980).

[75] Ironically, if the employer can prove that the employees ignored its unlawful actions, it may prevail on the *Gissel* order issue. NLRB v. American Spring Bed Mfg. Co., 670 F.2d 1236, 109 L.R.R.M. 2875 (1st Cir. 1982); Oil, Chemical, and Atomic Workers Int'l Union, 269 N.L.R.B. 129, 116 L.R.R.M. 1428 (1984); PBA, Inc., 270 N.L.R.B. No. 143, 116 L.R.R.M. 1162 (1984); House of Cycle, Inc., 264 N.L.R.B. 1030, 112 L.R.R.M. 1075 (1982) (employees unaware of illegal conduct; no bargaining order); *cf.* Delta Hosiery, Inc., 259 N.L.R.B. 1005, 109 L.R.R.M. 1063 (1982) (employees knew of threats but were presumed not to have given credence to lower-level supervisor).

[76] *E.g.,* Horizon Air Servs., Inc., 272 N.L.R.B. No. 33, 117 L.R.R.M. 1312, *enforced,* NLRB v. Horizon Air Servs., Inc., 761 F.2d 22, 119 L.R.R.M. 2203 (1st Cir. 1985); Bremal Elec. Inc., 271 N.L.R.B. No. 231, 117 L.R.R.M. 1247 (1984); DeQueen Gen. Hosp., 264 N.L.R.B. 480, 112 L.R.R.M. 1106 (administrative law judge's opinion).

attitudes of the affected employees.[77] The Board has also noted the source of the misconduct (high- versus low-level management) and the size of the unit, however, in attempts to prove to the satisfaction of an appellate court that the requisite detailed analysis has been performed.

The Board also considers the timing and the extent of the unfair practices, plus any history of anti-union animus on the part of the employer. The timing-extent factor is not susceptible to much predictability because of Board inconsistency; the decisions lead in opposite directions. The Board has issued bargaining orders both because the employer misconduct was continuous throughout a lengthy campaign period,[78] and again because the illegal conduct was concentrated in a three-day period, then was not repeated for the remaining weeks before an election.[79]

For example, in *Air Products,* the Board spoke of the employer's conduct as being "not sporadic, but continuous in nature, lasting up until the day of the election," and this "steady unlawful pressure" convinced the Board to issue a bargaining order.[80] The Board appeared impressed by the message that the consistency of illegal effort sent to employees. By contrast, in *Piggly Wiggly,* the Board emphasized an employer's *short-lived* "blitz" of unfair practices over a three-day period in issuing an order,[81] not requiring the steady and continuous pressure that it would deem critical in *Air Products,* thus illustrating that the timing issue is one that can be applied in a variety of manners to achieve any desired result. The Board might just as easily have found in *Piggly Wiggly* that the employer's halt of its illegal practices after only three days was a mitigating factor; however, it found just the opposite.

Finally, some courts have directed the Board to consider the labor history of the employer prior to the current unfair labor practice charges.[82] This is consistent with the *Gissel* mandate that consid-

---

[77] Greyhound Food Mgt., Inc., 258 N.L.R.B. 1293, 108 L.R.R.M. 1318, *enforced without written opinion,* NLRB v. Greyhound Food Mgt., Inc., 709 F.2d 1506, 113 L.R.R.M. 3816 (6th Cir. 1983) (the young age of the employees at issue is a relevant factor in considering the coercive effect of unfair labor practices).

[78] *E.g.,* Frank Black Mech. Servs., Inc., 271 N.L.R.B. No. 201, 117 L.R.R.M. 1183 (1984); Air Prods. & Chems., Inc., 263 N.L.R.B. 341, 111 L.R.R.M. 1024, *enforced,* NLRB v. Air Prods. & Chems., Inc., 717 F.2d 141, 114 L.R.R.M. 2397 (4th Cir. 1983).

[79] Piggly Wiggly Tuscaloosa Div., 258 N.L.R.B. 1081, 108 L.R.R.M. 1323, *enforced,* Piggly Wiggly v. NLRB, 705 F.2d 1537, 113 L.R.R.M. 2810 (11th Cir. 1983) (employer "blitzes"); *but see* PBA, Inc., 270 N.L.R.B. No. 143, 116 L.R.R.M. 1162 (1984) (bargaining order not issued, in part, because threats to fire union supporters were confined to short period of time).

[80] Air Prods., 263 N.L.R.B. at 341, 111 L.R.R.M. at 1025.

[81] Piggly Wiggly, 258 N.L.R.B. at 1082, 108 L.R.R.M. at 1325.

[82] *E.g.,* NLRB v. Marion Rohr Corp., 714 F.2d 228, 114 L.R.R.M. 2126 (2d Cir. 1983).

eration be given to the likelihood of future repetition of an employer's misconduct when considering a bargaining order.[83] Presumably, one should not judge an employer's actions in isolation from its general policies and actions regarding unions. An employer may be given the opportunity to exhibit its willingness to cooperate in holding a fair rerun election, by an examination of its conduct after the first allegations of misconduct have been brought.[84] By the same token, the employer's history of anti-union animus before the current dispute is relevant to the consideration of whether any alleged misconduct will be repeated if a new election is ordered.[85]

The type of misconduct engaged in by the employer is by far the most important factor examined by the Board in a *Gissel* impact inquiry.[86] If the misconduct is not considered sufficiently egregious, the Board inquiry ends and no analysis of the actual effect of that misconduct on the employees' free choice is made. Closely linked with the act of misconduct is its source, i.e., the management level of the employer representative. Third, the Board considers the extent to which the employer's actions have permeated the bargaining unit, with emphasis on the size of the unit and employee knowledge of the illegalities. The Board also considers the timing and extent of the practices, as well as the history of the employer involved.

Taking all of the above factors together, the Board deduces their effect on the employees before deciding to issue a bargaining order. That exercise, in theory, should produce an order that any court of appeals will enforce if the Board actually follows that analytical exercise. In practice, however, the courts have found much to complain of when it comes to reviewing the Board's issuance of *Gissel* orders.

ENFORCEMENT OF GISSEL ORDERS IN THE COURTS OF APPEALS

Three aspects of appellate court enforcement of *Gissel* orders are worthy of comment. First, and most important, is the fact that since

---

[83] *Gissel*, 395 U.S. at 614, 71 L.R.R.M. at 2496.

[84] *Jamaica Towing*, 632 F.2d at 214, 105 L.R.R.M. at 2964 (discussing the need of the Board to consider events subsequent to the initial certification election) (citations omitted).

[85] *Marion Rohr*, 714 F.2d at 231, 114 L.R.R.M. at 2128 (citations omitted).

[86] Union misconduct has also been a factor; union violence has been a defense to a bargaining order. Laura Modes Co., 144 N.L.R.B. 1592, 54 L.R.R.M. 1299 (1963). This is true especially where the violent conduct demonstrated a plan of intimidation against the employer. United Mineral and Chem. Corp., 155 N.L.R.B. 1390, 60 L.R.R.M. 1537 (1965). *Cf.* Top Form Mills, 273 N.L.R.B. No. 158, 118 L.R.R.M. 1460 (1984).

the 1970s, the enforcement of *Gissel* orders has become one of the most contentious battlegrounds between the Board and its reviewing courts, leading to relatively harsh criticism directed from the latter to the former. Second, some conflict has developed among the circuits themselves on the issue of the proper effect to be accorded the long delays experienced by litigants appearing before the Board on *Gissel* orders (i.e. should "subsequent events" be considered?). Third, the *Gissel* problem is beginning to force the appeals courts to address the issue, created by the Board during the late 1970s, of the role of administrative law judges (ALJs), and the extent to which the Board may be allowed to adopt an ALJ's findings and conclusions *in toto,* without issuing an opinion independently of the ALJ.[87]

The Supreme Court held in *Gissel* that if the Board determines that a free and uncoerced election has been rendered unlikely by an employer's illegal practices, a bargaining order may (but not *must*) issue. The courts thus require the Board to make such a determination.[88] The courts have required the Board to make clear factual findings in support of its bargaining orders, as one one court explained:

> [B]y "specific findings" in this regard we hardly mean that the Board must determine how many employees actually were caused to abandon the Union. We mean only that it estimate the impact, taking into account the factors in the particular case which are indicative of actual effect or which plausibly in light of existing knowledge, would contribute to or detract from an actual impact. This is, after all, what the courts which have made their own analysis have done. Similarly the "detailed analysis" of the likelihood of recurring misconduct and of the potential curative effect of ordinary remedies only requires an appraisal of those factors which might reasonably have a bearing, such as whether the employer has a history of anti-union animus and Labor Act violations, whether the employer has taken

---

[87] In a sense, *Gissel* has produced a host of questions related to how the Board currently operates, its historical preference for a case-by-case and, therefore, potentially inconsistent adjudication of its caseload, the possibility of increasing reliance on ALJs and the consequences for administrative law developments, and the impact on the Board's current backlog of cases on the appropriate nature of the remedy. Of course the Dotson Board could defuse the ALJ issue by refusing to follow the lead of the prior Board, but the Dotson Board has not yet been heard on this issue.

Until 1977, invidious discrimination based on race, alienage, or national origin could prevent a union's certification. Bekins Moving and Storage Co., 211 N.L.R.B. 138, 86 L.R.R.M. 1323 (1974). Sex discrimination did not count. Bell & Howell, 213 N.L.R.B. 407, 87 L.R.R.M. 1172 (1974). In 1977, the Board held that issues relating to race, alienage, or national origin discrimination would not be considered prior to certification, but would be considered through the unfair labor practice route. Handy Andy, 228 N.L.R.B. 447, 94 L.R.R.M. 1354 (1977). This was similarly extended to discrimination based upon sex. Bell & Howell Co., 230 N.L.R.B. 420, 95 L.R.R.M. 1333 (1977), *enforced,* 598 F.2d 136, 100 L.R.R.M. 2192 (D.C. Cir. 1979).

[88] *Gissel,* 395 U.S. at 614, 71 L.R.R.M. at 2496.

affirmative rectifying measures or otherwise indicated his cooperativeness in assuring a fair election etc.[89]

Earlier we discussed the Board's failure consistently to perform an analysis of the impact of an employer's unfair labor practices on the employees. As a result, many courts have refused to enforce bargaining orders when the Board has failed to make appropriate detailed findings of fact. Time and again the courts have scored the Board for merely

> listing [the] unfair labor practices followed by the conclusory statement that a fair election is no longer possible . . . [T]his does not satisfy the Board's responsibility to analyze the attending circumstances.[90]

In *NLRB v. Apple Tree Chevrolet, Inc.*, for example, the Fourth Circuit's frustration with the Board was clear:

> [W]e remanded this case to permit the Board a second opportunity to make findings sufficient to establish the dissipation of [the union's] majority, the continuing effects of the employer's misconduct, and the ineffectiveness of the usual remedies. The Board has failed to make such findings. Implicit in our earlier opinion was the need for the Board to gather additional . . . evidence to substantiate what were and continued to be only conclusory statements clothed with little more than transparent factual generalities.[91]

The court refused to remand a second time, and instead simply denied the Board's petition for enforcement. In *Windsor Industries*, the Second Circuit stated, "[W]e reiterate what we have said repeatedly, that the Board must make a particularly thorough analysis of the need for a bargaining order," [92] this especially where a twenty-two month time lag and employee turnover were not considered as factors by the Board.

Finally, as already noted, the Second Circuit has spoken disparagingly of the Board's obvious "preference" for bargaining orders.[93]

---

[89] First Lakewood Associates v. NLRB, 582 F.2d 416, 423, 99 L.R.R.M. 2192, 2197 (7th Cir. 1978), *quoting* Peerless of America, Inc., v. NLRB, 484 F.2d 1108, 1118 n.16, 83 L.R.R.M. at 3008 n.16 (7th Cir. 1973).

[90] *Marion Rohr Corp.*, 714 F.2d at 231, 114 L.R.R.M. at 2128 (citations omitted). *See also* NLRB v. Windsor Indus., Inc., 730 F.2d 860, 865, 115 L.R.R.M. 3649, 3653 (2d Cir. 1984) ("we reiterate what we have said repeatedly . . . " [about the need for a proper analysis]); K & K Gourmet Meats, 640 F.2d 460, 106 L.R.R.M. 2448; NLRB v. Apple Tree Chevrolet, Inc., 671 F.2d 838, 109 L.R.R.M. 2946 (4th Cir. 1982) (refusing, for a second time, to enforce a Board bargaining order for failure to provide sufficient analysis and findings of fact); NLRB v. Retair, Inc., 646 F.2d 249, 107 L.R.R.M. 3081 (6th Cir. 1981); *Red Oaks Nursing Home*, 633 F.2d at 503, 105 L.R.R.M. at 3028.

[91] *Apple Tree Chevrolet*, 671 F.2d at 841, 109 L.R.R.M. at 2948.

[92] *Windsor Indus.*, 730 F.2d at 865, 115 L.R.R.M. at 3653 (other citations omitted).

[93] *Marion Rohr Corp.*, 714 F.2d at 231, 114 L.R.R.M. at 2128 (other citations omitted).

Observing that one member of the Board panel dissented from the issuance of the bargaining order, this circuit in *Marion Rohr Corp.* said that the other two members should have been especially careful to state the reasons why they believed no fair election was possible, and concluded:

> Instead of doing so [stating their analysis], the panel majority without adequate explanation, indulged in the Board's by now well-established preference for issuing a bargaining order.[94]

The court also refused to remand the case to the Board, citing the four-year lapse of time between the filing of the original charges and "the Board's *continuing failure to comply with our request for reasoned analysis....* "[95]

The Court of Appeals for the Third Circuit has been even more blunt in its reaction to the Board's traditional *Gissel* policy:

> The dissent faults us for carrying on "guerrilla warfare" against the Supreme Court's *Gissel* decision. To the contrary, our view is that the Board has ignored *Gissel's* limitations and has issued bargaining orders in cases where such action was clearly not warranted. In so doing, the Board has failed to carry out the declared policy of the National Labor Relations Act of "protecting the exercise by workers of full freedom of association." . . . We do not believe that the court's function is to rubber stamp administrative actions that are arbitrary or contrary to law.[96]

The courts' dispute with the Board over *Gissel* has complicated the issue of Board bargaining orders. The refusal to remand in reaction to the stubbornness of the Board is worth special note, for it illustrates the serious nature of the growing impatience of the courts with the Board's treatment of *Gissel*. Refusals to remand also mean that the courts, not the Board, are making the final decisions, even though it is the Board that should have the "expertise" to answer labor relations questions. Refusals to remand in the procedural posture of denying a petition for enforcement hardly constitute the type of justice envisioned by the framers of the Act or by the employees who seek its protection.

In *Marion Rohr Corp.*, for example, the employer dismissed a new hire for possessing a blank union card, threatened to discharge other employees for supporting the union, interrogated other employees, and threatened loss of benefits and more onerous working condi-

---

[94] *Id.*

[95] *Id.* at 232, 114 L.R.R.M. at 2129 (emphasis added).

[96] NLRB v. Keystone Pretzel Bakery, 674 F.2d 197, 109 L.R.R.M. 3277, 3280 n.3. (3d Cir. 1982) (citation omitted), *withdrawn and rereported,* 696 F.2d 257, 112 L.R.R.M. 2349 (3d Cir. 1982).

tions. In *Windsor Industries*, the employer laid off two of the most active union supporters, and made implied promises of benefits at a "gripe" meeting of twelve of the fifteen unit employees. And in *Apple Tree Chevrolet*, the employer granted several new benefits involving the pension fund and vacation pay, solicited grievances by having a psychologist interview small groups of employees, warned employees not to get on the "wrong list," and undertook coercive interrogation. Yet because of deficiencies in the Board's analyses, none of its bargaining orders were upheld in these cases, all of which clearly involved serious illegal conduct.

The Board's task is to prove that a fair election is not a realistic possibility by either establishing that the past misconduct of the employer will have a "lingering" effect on the employees, or by proving that it is likely that the employer will repeat its misconduct during a new election campaign, if ordered.[97] The inquiry into the likelihood of the repetition of misconduct could also be satisfied by a finding that the employer has a history of anti-union animus.[98] The circuits' disputes with the Board over its performance of this analysis has not made this task any less of a requirement.

Some circuits further require that the Board take into account the need for a bargaining order as of the time that order is issued, allowing "changed circumstances" to modify the remedy imposed.[99] Employee turnover is the most common "changed circumstance" that must be considered in these circuits. Other factors, such as the replacement of the manager responsible for the illegal conduct, may also be relevant, however.[100]

In *Marion Rohr Corp.*, the court stated:

> [T]he Board may not, as it has done here, simply disregard factors that militate against enforced bargaining. For example, we have consistently held that events subsequent to the employer's violations, such as the passage of time and the substantial turnover of employees, are relevant and important factors which must be considered.[101]

---

[97] Apple Tree Chevrolet, 251 N.L.R.B. 666, 667–78 105 L.R.R.M. 1220 (1980).

[98] *See Gissel*, 395 U.S. at 614–15, 71 L.R.R.M. at 2495–96; *Atlas Microfilming*, 753 F.2d at 319, 1918 L.R.R.M. at 2633 (3d Cir. 1985) (discussing the continuing impact of a threat to close the plant if the union won) (citations omitted); *see* St. Francis Hosp. v. NLRB, 729 F.2d 844, 115 L.R.R.M. 3352 (D.C. Cir. 1984) (court takes into account the fact that the unfair labor practices continued even after the union lost the election).

[99] *Marion Rohr Corp.*, 714 F.2d at 228, 114 L.R.R.M. at 2128; *First Lakewood Associates*, 582 F.2d at 423, 99 L.R.R.M. at 2197 (7th Cir. 1978) (citation omitted).

[100] *First Lakewood Associates*, 582 F.2d at 424, 99 L.R.R.M. at 2198.

[101] 714 F.2d at 228, 114 L.R.R.M. at 2128 (citations omitted).

In this case, 35 percent of the employees had left in the seventeen-month period between the commencement of the unfair labor practices and the Board hearing.[102]

In *First Lakewood Associates,* the court mandated the Board's consideration of the fact that the supervisor who had been responsible for coercive anti-union conduct had been replaced, albeit for reasons unrelated to his illegal activities, noting:

> The lingering effects of coercive conduct are less likely to be sustained with much vigor if the person responsible for such conduct has long departed. . . .[103]

Arrayed in opposition to these circuit decisions are those circuits which hold that to force an examination of changed circumstances only rewards an employer who continues lengthy litigation.[104]

The weight of authority allows the Board to establish the lingering effect of unfair labor practices without forcing "changed circumstances" (usually meaning employee turnover) to automatically forestall bargaining orders.

In response to its difficulty with the circuits regarding the lack of detailed findings and analysis, the Board began a new tactic in the late 1970s, basing bargaining orders almost exclusively upon the findings and analysis of an ALJ, whose findings and analysis the Board simply adopts as its own. This short-cut initially has been allowed by at least two circuits.[105] However, there already has been some uneasiness expressed about the practice, which might grow if the Dotson Board continues the use of this method.[106]

In *Atlas Microfilming,* although not rejecting the use of the ALJ's opinion in that case involving a union with a majority of the employees' support, Judge Adams sounded a warning for the future:

---

[102] *Id.* at 228, 114 L.R.R.M. at 2128; *see also, Red Oaks Nursing Home,* 633 F.2d at 510, 105 L.R.R.M. at 3032 (employee turnover must be considered).

[103] *First Lakewood Assocs.,* 582 F.2d at 424, 99 L.R.R.M. at 2198.

[104] *Hedstrom Co.,* 629 F.2d 305, 105 L.R.R.M. 2183 (3d Cir. 1980) (subsequent history omitted); Chromalloy Mining and Minerals v. NLRB, 620 F.2d 1120, 104 L.R.R.M. 2987 (5th Cir. 1980) (Board must consider, but is not bound by, employee turnover); L.B. Foster Co. v. NLRB, 418 F.2d 1, 72 L.R.R.M. 2736 (9th Cir. 1969); St. Francis Fed. of Nurses and Health Professionals v. NLRB, 729 F.2d 844, 115 L.R.R.M. 3352 (D.C. Cir. 1984) (Board need not consider employer turnover, passage of time or supervisors' replacement); Coil-A.C.C., Inc. v. NLRB, 712 F.2d 1074, 113 L.R.R.M. 3783 (6th Cir. 1983); Piggly Wiggly v. NLRB, 705 F.2d 1081, 113 L.R.R.M. 1323; NLRB v. Wilhow Corp., 666 F.2d 1294, 109 L.R.R.M. 2116 (10th Cir. 1981) (Board is permitted to disregard the fact that six of twelve unit members signed a letter to withdraw their support of the union).

[105] Windsor Indus., Inc., 730 F.2d at 866, 115 L.R.R.M. at 3653–54; Kenworth Trucks of Philadelphia, Inc., v. NLRB, 580 F.2d 55, 98 L.R.R.M. 2263 (3rd Cir. 1978).

[106] Atlas Microfilming, 753 F.2d at 320–21, 118 L.R.R.M. at 2634 (concurring opinion of Adams, Jr.).

[E]ven though it is not legally required to do so, the Board would be well-advised to undertake some independent consideration and to articulate, at least briefly, its reasons. . . . While the Board may have given this matter [careful] consideration we cannot determine whether in fact it did so since it merely adopted the ALJ's findings. Therefore, while I concur because the Board did all that was required under the state of the law in this Circuit, I write to urge the Board and Congress to reconsider this policy.[107]

INTERIM BARGAINING ORDERS

The Board has, on occasion, sought the even more extraordinary remedy of an interim bargaining order. Pursuant to section 10(j) of the Act, the Board can petition a district court for appropriate relief or a restraining order. The district court can grant such relief as it deems just and proper. The Board has on occasion sought the district court to order an employer to bargain prior to any election, certification, or bargaining order on an interim basis pending resolution of the unfair labor practice. Such an order, if granted by the court, is potentially of enormous impact.

The interim bargaining order could bring a union into existence where none had existed theretofore, and could place a court's imprimatur upon a unit that had not been found to be an appropriate unit by the Board. It is a remedy that, if abused, could set the collective bargaining system on its head. Bargaining, pursuant to a court's injunction, while awaiting the outcome of additional potentially prolonged litigation, is not likely to be stable. The potential harm to both employer and the employees that could result from interim, mandatory bargaining if subsequently the charges are dismissed or are not all upheld is virtually incalculable. It is an area where the Board has and should continue to exercise extreme restraint.

The circuit courts have split on the issuance of this injunction. The basis of their disagreement is the question of what status quo the court is attempting to maintain with the injunctive relief (pending the Board's resolution, which is subject to court review).

In *Kaynard v. MMIC, Inc.*,[108] the Court of Appeals for the Second Circuit, in upholding the district court's entry of injunctive relief, summarized the facts in the case: four of the five employees signed cards and gave them to a union representative, who was threatened with a lead pipe and chased from the employer's premises with at least one employee watching. The employer told another employee

---

[107] *Id.*
[108] 734 F.2d 950, 116 L.R.R.M. 2465 (2d Cir. 1984).

about the event and questioned that employee about his involvement with the union. When the employer received a telegram for recognition sent by the union, he assembled the employees and threatened to close the shop. Two employees were subsequently told either to sign letters renouncing the union or be fired. Employees were promised both wage and benefit increases. One employee was visited at home by the employer, who said another employee, the union organizer, would be fired in the morning; he was. The list goes on.[109] The election was inconclusive, as three of the five ballots were challenged.[110] Then the litigation began.

The Second Circuit noted two tests for the entry of an interim bargaining order: first, whether there was reasonable cause to believe the unfair labor practices had been committed; second, whether the relief sought was just and proper.[111] Subjecting the facts of the case to the first test, the court declared:

> Indeed, in terms of the number, variety, and malevolence of the unfair labor practices here involved, the company's course of conduct strikes us as an extraordinary example of unlawful interference with organizational rights.[112]

Focusing on the issue of whether the injunctive relief sought was just and proper, the court noted that the bargaining restores the status quo to the point where, prior to the unfair labor practices, the employer had received signed authorization cards from four of the five employees. The court further noted that the employer had engaged in such egregious and coercive unfair labor practices as to make a fair election virtually impossible.[113] The court stated, referring to *Gissel,* that extensive analysis of other factors is not required when a case falls within the *Gissel I* category, which the case at hand did. The court also ordered the additional remedy of double costs and $1,000 damages against the employer because of the frivolous appeal.[114]

In *Levine v. C&W Mining Co.,*[115] the Sixth Circuit agreed with the Second Circuit that the status quo to be protected was the

---

[109] *Id.* at 952, 116 L.R.R.M. at 2466.

[110] *Id.*

[111] *Id.* at 953, 116 L.R.R.M. at 2467; Kaynard v. Palby Lingerie, Inc. 625 F.2d 1047, 104 L.R.R.M. 2897 (2d Cir. 1980); Seeler v. Trading Port, Inc., 517 F.2d 33, 89 L.R.R.M. 2513 (2d Cir. 1975).

[112] 734 F.2d at 953–54, 116 L.R.R.M. at 2467.

[113] *Id.*

[114] *Id.* at 954–55, 116 L.R.R.M. at 2468. *See* discussion at chapter XV, *infra*, concerning these remedies. It is worth noting that the court, in a circuit that has traditionally been critical of how the Board handles *Gissel* orders, stated: "The Board does not take lightly the commencement of a § 10(j) action."

[115] 610 F.2d 432, 102 L.R.R.M. 3093 (6th Cir. 1979).

situation in existence prior to the commission of the unfair labor practices (which would give benefit to the union card sign-up period).[116]

The opposite result was reached by the Fifth Circuit in *Boire v. Pilot Freight Carriers.*[117] There, the circuit court, affirming the district court, noted that the status quo to be preserved was "the last uncontested status which preceded the pending controversy." [118] That period was prior to the union activity and, thus, an interim bargaining order would materially alter the status quo and create, by judicial fiat, a relationship that never existed.[119] The Fifth Circuit concluded that the interim bargaining injunction was simply too large a step to take to preserve issues for ultimate determination by the Board.[120]

This is perhaps the key point, and one of the obvious reasons for Board restraint in seeking an interim bargaining order: in such situations, there has not been a Board adjudication. If the Board has been experiencing problems with enforcement of its bargaining order after Board adjudication, one can easily imagine the enormity of the problem in the pre-adjudication period.

There also exists the lurking problem of whether the unit is appropriate. In *Taylor v. Cisco Resorts,*[121] the district court declined to issue an interim order because the appropriate bargaining unit had not been determined.

RETROACTIVE APPLICABILITY OF THE BARGAINING ORDER: TRADING PORT

Gissel bargaining order cases involve a union's demand for recognition and an employer who undermines the union's majority status by the commission of one or more unfair labor practices. The process of adjudication of these issues, from the hearing before an administrative law judge, to an appeal before the NLRB or circuit court, can take years from the union's initial demand for recognition or filing of a representation petition. Assuming the union's position is ultimately upheld and a bargaining order issues, the question is when the duty to bargain takes effect.

---

[116] *Id.* at 437, 102 L.R.R.M. at 3097.
[117] 515 F.2d 1185, 89 L.R.R.M. 2908 (5th Cir. 1975); *reh'g denied,* 521 F.2d 795, 90 L.R.R.M. 3055 (1975).
[118] 515 F.2d at 1194, 89 L.R.R.M. at 2914 (citation omitted).
[119] *Id.* (citation omitted).
[120] *Id.*
[121] 458 F. Supp. 152, 99 L.R.R.M. 3446 (D. Nev. 1978).

For the last ten years, the NLRB has held the bargaining order to have retroactive effect. In 1975, the NLRB held in *Trading Port, Inc.*: [122]

> We find that an employer's obligation under a bargaining order remedy should commence as of the time the employer has embarked on a clear course of unlawful conduct or has engaged in sufficient unfair labor practices to undermine the union's majority status. Such a position eliminates the possible ill effects of dating a bargaining order as of the issuance of the Board's decision, which has resulted in unremedied unfair labor practices, while at the same time assuring, as the Supreme Court stressed in *Gissel*, that bargaining orders, by remedying all of an employer's unfair labor practices, will 'reestablish the conditions as they existed before the employer's unlawful campaign' and not place a union in a disadvantaged position. Moreover, it seems to accord most closely with what actually happened. An employer, as the Supreme Court has held, has a right to an election so long as he does not fatally impede the election process. Once he has so impeded the process, he has forfeited his right to a Board election, and must bargain with the union on the basis of other clear indications of employees' desires. It is at that point, we believe, the employer's unlawful refusal to bargain has taken place. [123]

In the earlier *Steel-Fab* decision, the three-to-two majority (Chairman Miller and Members Kennedy and Penello) held that the seriousness of the employer's misconduct and its impact upon a fair election were the relevant considerations in deciding to issue a bargaining order. The majority also felt no need to find additionally that the employer had also violated section 8(a)(5). [124] The dissenting minority (Members Fanning and Jenkins) argued that the section 8(a)(5) finding was necessary to give retroactive effect to the bargaining order. [125]

A similar case came to the Board subsequently in *Elm Hill Meats*, [126] where the employer rejected the union's demand for recognition. The union petitioned for an election and, subsequently, filed unfair labor practice charges. During the period between the

---

[122] 219 N.L.R.B. 298, 89 L.R.R.M. 1565 (1975), *reversing* Steel Fab, Inc., 212 N.L.R.B. 363, 86 L.R.R.M. 1474 (1974).

[123] *Id.* at 301, 89 L.R.R.M. at 1569. *See also* American Map Co., 219 N.L.R.B. No. 186, 90 L.R.R.M. 1242 (1975); Baker Mach. & Gear, Inc., 220 N.L.R.B. No. 40, 90 L.R.R.M. 1454 (1975); Independent Sprinkler & Fire Protection Co., 220 N.L.R.B. No. 140, 90 L.R.R.M. 1564 (1975); Ann Lee Sportswear, Inc. 220 N.L.R.B. No. 153, 90 L.R.R.M. 1352 (1975); Donelson Packing Co. and Riegel Provision Co., 220 N.L.R.B. No. 159, 90 L.R.R.M. 1549 (1975).

[124] Steel-Fab, Inc., 212 N.L.R.B. 363, 86 L.R.R.M. 1474 at 1476. *See also* Chairman Miller's dissent in United Packing Co., 187 N.L.R.B. 878, 880, 76 L.R.R.M. 1156, 1158 (1971).

[125] Steel–Fab, at 367–69, 86 L.R.R.M. at 1479–1483.

[126] Elm Hill Meats of Owensboro, 213 N.L.R.B. 874, 87 L.R.R.M. 1227 (1974).

issuance of the ALJ's decision and the Board's decision, the employer closed the plant for economic reasons. Based upon the *Steel-Fab* precedent and the fact that the closing took place two months before the Board's decision and order were entered, the bargaining obligation was not applied to the decision to close or its effects.[127]

Trading Port reconsidered the *Steel-Fab/Elm Hill* rationale and held that a retroactive bargaining order was appropriate, in that in those cases an employer who committed serious unfair labor practices could be rewarded by the long delay before the remedy was ordered. Additionally, the delay could provide a substantial period of time during which the employer could make unilateral changes after the union had established majority status.[128]

Thus, in accordance with *Trading Port,* an independent section 8(a)(5) violation need not be found to support a bargaining order, and that bargaining order will date from when "the employer has embarked on a clear course of unlawful conduct or has engaged in sufficient unfair labor practices to undermine the union's majority status." [129] This same issue was reargued in *Beasley Energy, Inc.* wherein, the majority reiterated the *Trading Port* holding, despite the dissent of Member Walther as to the appropriateness of the bargaining order's application in the absence of a specific section 8(a)(5) violation.[130]

Some question remains as to precisely when the bargaining order becomes retroactively effective. If the employer has committed sufficient unfair labor practices to warrant a bargaining order and the union has never demanded recognition, the bargaining order will be retroactive to the date the union attained majority status.[131] If the union has demanded recognition, the bargaining order will be retroactive to that date (which may be somewhat later than the date the union achieved majority status).[132] Note that in both of these instances, the employer committed the unfair labor practices prior to the union's achievement of majority status.

Where the employer commits the unfair labor practices after the union has achieved majority status, the bargaining order will be retroactive only to when the employer embarked on the clear course

---

[127] *Id.* at 874–75, 87 L.R.R.M. at 1229.

[128] Trading Port, Inc., 89 L.R.R.M. at 1569.

[129] *Id.*

[130] Beasley Energy, Inc., 228 N.L.R.B. 93, 94 L.R.R.M. 1563 (1977).

[131] Shenanigans, 264 N.L.R.B. 908, 112 L.R.R.M. 1096 (1982), *enforced as modified,* 723 F.2d 1360, 115 L.R.R.M. 2297 (7th Cir. 1983); Permanent Label Corp., 248 N.L.R.B. 118, 103 L.R.R.M. 1513 (1980).

[132] Albertson Mfg. Co., 236 N.L.R.B. 663, 98 L.R.R.M. 1402 (1978).

of unlawful conduct.[133] And, in *Chromalloy Mining and Minerals,*[134] where the achievement of majority status, demand for recognition, and embarkation on a clear course of unlawful conduct all took place more than six months prior to the filing of the unfair labor practice charges, the bargaining order was made retroactive to the first day of the six-month statute of limitations set forth in section 10(b) of the Act.

Other union-endorsed retroactive theories have not been successful. In *Clothing & Textile Workers v. NLRB,*[135] the Board, upheld by the Court of Appeals for the District of Columbia in a case where the employer litigated its election objections to the circuit court and lost, held that the union's requested retroactive "make-whole" remedies be denied.[136] Noting the Board's great discretion in the area of remedies, the court supported the Board's findings that retroactive bargaining orders apply only in the case where the employer has committed unfair labor practices; that the Board acts reasonably in denying attorney fees and litigation expenses unless the employer has acted in bad faith in asserting nondebatable defenses to drag out proceedings; and that the union's requested "interim" grievance procedure outside of a collective bargaining contract was unnecessary "or perhaps even undesirable" to advance the purposes of the Act.[137]

In *Local 669 v. NLRB,*[138] the Court of Appeals for the District of Columbia joined the Third, Eighth and Tenth Circuits [139] in approving the issuance of retroactive bargaining orders. *Local 669* is of interest for the following reasons, all of which were addressed in Justice Rehnquist's dissent to the Supreme Court's denial of certiorari.[140] The appeals court did uphold the retroactive bargaining order, citing *Trading Port.* The order was made retroactive to

---

[133] Jasta Mfg. Co., 246 N.L.R.B. 48, 102 L.R.R.M. 1610 (1979).

[134] 238 N.L.R.B. 688, 99 L.R.R.M. 1642 (1978).

[135] 264 N.L.R.B. No. 14, 111 L.R.R.M. 1456 (1982), *enforced,* 736 F.2d 1559, 117 L.R.R.M. 2453 (D.C. Cir. 1984).

[136] *Id.* at 1570, 117 L.R.R.M. at 2461–62.

[137] *Id.,* 117 L.R.R.M. at 2462. *See* East Bay Chevrolet, 262 N.L.R.B. No. 85, 110 L.R.R.M. 1329 (1982) where, on remand from the Court of Appeals for the Ninth Circuit [659 F.2d 1006, 108 L.R.R.M. 2846 (1981)], the Board amended its prior bargaining order, consistent with the Circuit Court's opinion to delete the portion requiring any agreement resulting from the bargaining to be effective from a specific, earlier date.

[138] 681 F.2d 11, 110 L.R.R.M. 2845 (D.C. Cir. 1982), *cert. denied,* 459 U.S. 1178 (1983).

[139] Hedstrom Co., v. NLRB, 629 F.2d 305, 105 L.R.R.M. 2183 (3d Cir. 1980) (*en banc*), *cert. denied,* 450 U.S. 996, 106 L.R.R.M. 2817 (1981); Alumbaugh Coal Corp. v. NLRB, 635 F.2d 1380, 106 L.R.R.M. 2001 (9th Cir. 1980); Ann Lee Sportswear, Inc. v. NLRB, 543 F.2d 739, 93 L.R.R.M. 2653 (10th Cir. 1976).

[140] Local 669 v. NLRB, 459 U.S. at 1178–83. (Justice Powell joined in the dissent.)

the date on which the union attained majority support, demanded recognition, and on which the company both rejected the demand and embarked on its course of unlawful conduct.[141] *Local 669* also adopted the NLRB's *Drug Package*[142] doctrine, which considers employees striking for recognition to be unfair labor practice strikers where, as in *Local 669*, the employer engaged in widespread illegal conduct designed to frustrate the statutory scheme set forth for representation elections.[143]

Needless to say, the criticisms of the *Gissel* bargaining order are intensified by the retroactive concept of *Trading Port*. The interim time period can be years between the date of the union's obtaining majority support and the employer embarking on the course of illegal conduct and enforcement of the Board's bargaining order in a court of appeals. Assuming retroactivity, interim management decisions affecting the wages, hours, and working conditions of the employees could be (and have been) subject to a bargaining obligation with the collective bargaining representative of those employees.[144] But an interim attempt to bargain with the union absent a Board order (although unlikely in most of these cases) runs the risk of a violation of section 8(a)(2) of the Act if the union does not, in fact, represent a majority of the employees in an appropriate unit.

The real issue that emerges from all these cases is predictability. To the extent that *Gissel* orders—especially in category II—have not been very predictable, retroactivity aggravates the wound.

CONCLUDING REMARKS: WHITHER GISSEL?

Predictability is the issue that needs to be resolved first, and it is within the power and expertise of the Board to solve it. Critics

---

[141] 681 F.2d at 25, 110 L.R.R.M. at 2855.

[142] Drug Package Inc. v. NLRB, 570 F.2d 1340, 97 L.R.R.M. 2851 (8th Cir. 1978), *enforcing in part*, 228 N.L.R.B. 108, 94 L.R.R.M. 1570 (1977).

[143] 681 F.2d at 27, 110 L.R.R.M. 2856–57.

[144] In Hedstrom Co. the Board's first bargaining order was vacated by the Third Circuit because the Board failed to make "specific findings" regarding the immediate and residual effect of the unfair labor practices and a "detailed analysis" assessing the likelihood of holding a fair rerun election. On remand, NLRB reinstated its bargaining order which was subsequently upheld by the circuit court. The organizational activity began in 1974; the second opinion of the circuit court was issued six years later. The employer issued certain work rules in 1976 which the union said were subject to collective bargaining (in addition the rules were alleged and found to have been promulgated to undermine the union). The employer defended by noting the bargaining order in effect at the time was subsequently vacated. However, on remand the Board held and the circuit court enforced the second bargaining order retroactive to a date prior to the promulgation of the work rules, thereby finding a further § 8(a)(5) violation. Hedstrom Co. v. NLRB, 629 F.2d 305, 105 L.R.R.M. 2188 (3rd Cir. 1980).

have suggested revisiting the Supreme Court or having the Board issue regulations for bargaining orders, but these alternatives are unnecessary. The Board can accomplish the desired goal with a consistent case-by-case analysis. It must break free from the result-oriented history of the past. If the Supreme Court has to reenter this arena, it will be a result of the Board's default.

There should not be minority-based bargaining orders. *Gourmet Foods* is correct. Neither *Gissel,* nor the statute and the policies underlying the statute, support this undemocratic remedy, and in any event, it is an ineffective remedy. If the union does not have the support of a majority of the employees, it is not likely to have the strength to survive in the collective bargaining arena. The statute allows employees the right to organize or not to organize. It also recognizes that it is the economic strength of the parties that should resolve issues in the bargaining process and establish the terms of the collective bargaining agreement.

Furthermore (although admittedly there is no hard data to support this thesis), one of the current trends in representation elections in the historically unionized northeastern sector of our country is to identify a significant number of employees in the voting unit that have had bad prior experiences with unions and who, as a result, are vocal and effective campaigners against the union. This is a situation that only the unions can correct for themselves. A *Gissel* order will not give long-term support to a bargaining unit under these circumstances. Even Professor Weiler, who has been very critical of the representation process under the Act, stated in his 1983 article:

> Given an unfavorable conjunction of social and economic conditions, no union field organizer will have much chance of signing up a particular group of employees, whatever the legal setting.[145]

The Board must unravel the confusion between employer conduct resulting in a *Gissel II* finding and conduct resulting in a *Gissel III* finding. The Supreme Court has given sufficient guidance, and the case-by-case method of adjudication is well-suited to the job. This is where, from a practitioner's standpoint, the problem really lies. Few employers enter into the waters of *Gissel I.* A significant number, however, can get into situations where the predictable difference between a *Gissel II* and a *Gissel III* is quite important. This is where most of the cases fall and, therefore, this is where most of the dissatisfaction rests.

The conflicts with the circuit courts are unnecessary and dysfunctional. The reputation and credibility of the Board as the agency

---

[145] Weiler, *supra* n.58, at 1820.

of administrative expertise in the area of labor relations has taken an unfortunate beating. And this fallout affects other areas, not merely the *Gissel* remedy.

The current Board has an enormous task ahead of it in this area. On the one hand, the business community has not rejoined the ranks of the Board supporters because of still lingering dissatisfaction with the not-so-distant result-oriented days. On the other hand, the union community is threatening to ignore both the Board and the Act because of labor's inability to be as effective as it currently desires. It will take steady hands at the tiller to navigate a course that both sides will respect, but it can be done. Based upon our knowledge of the current Board membership, there probably has not been a better time to undertake the task.

CHAPTER XIII

Remedying Breaches of the Bargaining Obligation

Sections 8(a)(5) [1] and 8(b)(3) [2] make it an unfair labor practice for employers and unions to refuse to bargain collectively. Section 8(d) in defining the obligation to bargain collectively requires in part that the employer and union "confer in *good faith* with respect to wages, hours, and other terms and conditions of employment. . . ." [3] We will now examine the remedies available to the Board when either the employer or the union fails to fulfill its bargaining obligations. The usual remedy consists of an order to cease and desist from refusing to bargain, to bargain collectively with the other party, if requested, and to post notices of compliance with the Act. [4]

IMPROPER WITHDRAWAL OF RECOGNITION

In the absence of unusual circumstances, a union's majority is presumed irrebuttable for a reasonable period, normally one year, after the certification of the union as the bargaining representative. [5] The bargaining obligation is that there be at least one year of actual bargaining between the parties. [6] Thus, where the refusal to bargain

---

[1] 29 U.S.C. § 158(a)(5).

[2] 29 U.S.C. § 158(b)(3).

[3] 29 U.S.C. § 158(d) (emphasis added). The section provides in relevant part that:

> For the purposes of this section, to bargain collectively is the performance of the mutual obligation of the employer and the representative of the employees to meet at reasonable times and confer in good faith with respect to wages, hours, and other terms and conditions of employment or the negotiation of an agreement, or any question arising thereunder, and the execution of a written contract incorporating any agreement reached if requested by either party, but such obligation does not compel either party to agree to a proposal or require the making of a concession.

[4] NLRB v. Leatherwood Drilling, 513 F.2d 270, 89 L.R.R.M. 2460 (5th Cir. 1975).

[5] Brooks v. NLRB, 348 U.S. 96, 98, 35 L.R.R.M. 2158 (1954); Air Express Int'l v. NLRB, 659 F.2d 614, 108 L.R.R.M. 2795 (5th Cir. 1981); Armco Drainage & Metal Prods., 116 N.L.R.B. 1260, 38 L.R.R.M. 1457 (1956).

[6] Mar-Jac Poultry Co., 136 N.L.R.B. 785, 49 L.R.R.M. 1854 (1962). *Cf.* Groendyke Transport Inc., 207 N.L.R.B. 381, 84 L.R.R.M. 1458 (1973).

occurs during this initial one-year period, the Board generally will order bargaining for one year less the time, if any, during which the employer had bargained in good faith.[7] If the employer's refusal to bargain is regarded as egregious, the Board may prescribe no set-off of time.[8]

After the initial year, the presumption of the union's majority status continues, but may be rebutted by a showing that the union no longer commands a majority, or by objective evidence of the employer's good faith doubt of the union's majority status.[9] To justify withdrawal of union recognition in the light of its presumptive representative status, the employer affirmatively must show either "that the union in fact no longer enjoyed majority support on the date of the refusal to bargain, or that the refusal to bargain was predicated upon a reasonably grounded good-faith doubt of majority support."[10] Where, however, the union's loss of majority or the employer's doubt of majority is caused by employer unfair labor practices, the employer is precluded from asserting the union's changed status as a defense to a refusal-to-bargain charge.[11] Where the Board finds an employer has violated the Act by improperly withdrawing recognition from the union, the Board generally will order the employer to "cease and desist" from refusing to bargain and from committing further similar violations. The Board will also order the employer to recognize and bargain with the union upon request and to post the appropriate notices.[12]

If an employer who illegally withdraws recognition from the union also abrogates a collective bargaining agreement, the Board can "enforce" the agreement by ordering the employer to reactivate

---

[7] Canton Health Care Ctr., 269 N.L.R.B. 289, 115 L.R.R.M. 1279 (1984); Mar-Jac Poultry Co., 136 N.L.R.B. 785, 49 L.R.R.M. 1854 (1962).

[8] Glomac Plastics, Inc., 234 N.L.R.B. 1309, 97 L.R.R.M. 1441 (1978), enforced, 592 F.2d 94, 100 L.R.R.M. 2508 (2d Cir. 1979).

[9] NLRB v. Carmichael Constr. Co., 728 F.2d 1139, 115 L.R.R.M. 3041 (8th Cir. 1984); NLRB v. Little Rock Downtowner, 414 F.2d 1084, 1091, 72 L.R.R.M. 2044 (8th Cir. 1969); Celanese Corp. of Am., 95 N.L.R.B. 664, 672, 28 L.R.R.M. 1362 (1951), cited with approval in NLRB v. Burns Sec. Servs., 406 U.S. 272, 279, n.3, 80 L.R.R.M. 2225 (1972); NLRB v. Cayuga Crushed Stone, Inc., 474 F.2d 1380, 1383, 82 L.R.R.M. 2951 (2d Cir. 1973).

[10] Terrell Mach. Co. v. NLRB, 427 F.2d 1088, 1090, 73 L.R.R.M. 2381 (4th Cir. 1970), cert. denied, 398 U.S. 929, 74 L.R.R.M. 2440 (1970).

[11] Franks Bros. Co. v. NLRB, 321 U.S. 702, 14 L.R.R.M. 591 (1944); NLRB v. Sky Wolf Sales, 470 F.2d 827, 830, 82 L.R.R.M. 2050 (9th Cir. 1972); C & C Plywood Corp., 163 N.L.R.B. 1022, 64 L.R.R.M. 2065 (1967), enforced, 413 F.2d 112, 71 L.R.R.M. 2796 (9th Cir. 1969); NLRB v. Parma Water Lifter Co., 211 F.2d 258, 33 L.R.R.M. 2810 (1954) (9th Cir. 1954), cert. denied 348 U.S. 829, 34 L.R.R.M. 2898 (1954).

[12] See, e.g., NLRB v. Leatherwood Drilling, 513 F.2d 270, 89 L.R.R.M. 2460 (5th Cir. 1975) and cases there cited.

and abide by it, and to pay, with interest, wages and other monetary benefits lost by the employees.[13]

SUBJECTS OF BARGAINING

There has never been a statutory definition or listing of those subjects of collective bargaining that are required by the Act. Therefore, over the years the Board, and to a lesser extent the courts, have defined those subjects of bargaining which are compulsory or mandatory as well as other subjects of bargaining which the Board and the courts have deemed to be "permissive" or "illegal." [14] Both the Board and the courts have been quite liberal in construing almost all subjects involving in any way wages, hours, and other terms and conditions of employment as mandatory subjects of bargaining.

In *NLRB v. Wooster Division of the Borg-Warner Corp.,*[15] the Supreme Court discussed the difference between mandatory and permissive bargaining subjects.[16] The Court, in holding that the employer's insistence on the inclusion of permissive bargaining subjects in the agreement was a refusal to bargain in good faith, stated:

> The Company's good faith has met the requirements of the statute as to the subjects of mandatory bargaining. But that good faith does not license the employer to refuse to enter into agreements on the ground that they do not include some proposal which is not a mandatory subject of bargaining. We agree with the Board that such conduct is, in substance, a refusal to bargain about the subjects that are within the scope of mandatory bargaining. This does not mean that bargaining is to be confined to the statutory subjects. Each of the two controversial clauses is lawful in itself. Each would be enforceable if agreed to by the Unions. But it does not follow that because the Company may propose these clauses, it can lawfully insist upon them as a condition to any agreement.[17]

---

[13] NLRB v. George E. Light Boat Storage, Inc., 373 F.2d 762, 64 L.R.R.M. 2457 (5th Cir. 1967), *modified,* 382 F.2d 577, 66 L.R.R.M. 2384 (5th Cir. 1967); NLRB v. Huttig Sash & Door Co., 362 F.2d 217, 62 L.R.R.M. 2271 (4th Cir. 1966).

[14] Singer Mfg. Co., 24 N.L.R.B. 444, 6 L.R.R.M. 405 (1940), *modified on other grounds and enforced,* 119 F.2d 131, 8 L.R.R.M. 740 (7th Cir. 1941), *cert. denied,* 313 U.S. 595, 8 L.R.R.M. 458 (1941); NLRB v. Bachelder, 120 F.2d 574, 8 L.R.R.M. 723 (7th Cir. 1941); Inland Steel Co., 77 N.L.R.B. 1, 21 L.R.R.M. 1310 (1948), *enforced,* 170 F.2d 247, 22 L.R.R.M. 2506 (7th Cir., 1948), *cert. denied,* 336 U.S. 960, 24 L.R.R.M. 2019 (1949), NLRB v. Wooster Division of the Borg-Warner Corp., 356 U.S. 342, 42 L.R.R.M. 2034 (1958) and Meat Cutters Local 421 (Great Atlantic & Pacific Tea Co.), 81 N.L.R.B. 1052, 23 L.R.R.M. 1464 (1949). Cox & Dunlop, *Regulation of Collective Bargaining by the National Labor Relations Board,* 63 HARV. L. REV. 389 (1950).

[15] 356 U.S. 342, 42 L.R.R.M. 2034 (1958).

[16] 356 U.S. 342, 349, 42 L.R.R.M. 2034 (1958).

[17] *Id.*

Examples of permissive subjects of bargaining include performance
bond [18] and legal-liability clauses,[19] interest arbitration,[20] industry
promotion funds,[21] bargaining unit definitions,[22] and collective bargaining provisions concerning employees who are not covered by
the Act, such as supervisors [23] and agricultural laborers.[24]

To summarize, an employer or union has a statutory obligation
pursuant to section 8(a)(5) or 8(b)(3) to bargain only with regard to
mandatory subjects of bargaining and is not required to bargain
with respect to permissive subjects of bargaining. If a party insists
on bargaining to impasse over a permissive bargaining subject, this
constitutes a violation of section 8(a)(5) or 8(b)(3). In addition, a
unilateral change of a subject of mandatory bargaining normally
will violate section 8(a)(5),[25] whereas a unilateral change of a subject
of permissive bargaining may not violate section 8(a)(5).[26]

Illegal subjects of bargaining include closed shop provisions,[27] hot
cargo clauses that violate section 8(e),[28] as well as contract provisions
which would discriminate among employees based on race, religion,
sex, or national origin.[29] Although bargaining may take place with
respect to illegal subjects, neither party may require that the other
agree to such provisions and they are never properly included in a
contract.[30]

A union may waive its right to be consulted before an employer
unilaterally changes a mandatory subject of bargaining so long as

---

[18] NLRB v. American Compress Warehouse, 350 F.2d 365, 59 L.R.R.M. 2739 (5th
Cir. 1965), cert. denied, 382 U.S. 982, 61 L.R.R.M. 2147 (1966).
[19] Radiator Specialty Co., 143 N.L.R.B. 350, 53 L.R.R.M. 1319 (1963), enforced in
part, 336 F.2d 495, 57 L.R.R.M. 2097 (4th Cir. 1964).
[20] Plumbers Local 387 (Mech. Contractors Ass'n of Iowa, Inc.), 266 N.L.R.B. 129,
112 L.R.R.M. 1365 (1983).
[21] Big D Serv. Co., 267 N.L.R.B. No. 25, 113 L.R.R.M. 1144 (1983); Carpenters Local
2265 (Mill Floor Covering, Inc.), 136 N.L.R.B. 769, 49 L.R.R.M. 1842 (1962), enforced,
317 F.2d 269, 53 L.R.R.M. 2311 (6th Cir. 1983).
[22] Canterbury Gardens, 238 N.L.R.B. 864, 99 L.R.R.M. 1279 (1978).
[23] Southern Cal. Pipe Trades Dist. Council 16 (Aero Plumbing Co.), 167 N.L.R.B.
1004, 66 L.R.R.M. 1233 (1967), enforced, 449 F.2d 668, 78 L.R.R.M. 2260 (9th Cir.
1971).
[24] District 50, Mine Workers (Central Soya Co.), 142 N.L.R.B. 930, 53 L.R.R.M.
1178 (1963).
[25] NLRB v. Katz, 369 U.S. 736, 50 L.R.R.M. 2177 (1962).
[26] Allied Chem. & Alkaline Workers Local 1 v. Pittsburgh Plate Glass Co., 404
U.S. 157, 78 L.R.R.M. 2974 (1971).
[27] Penello v. Mine Workers, 88 F.Supp. 935, 25 L.R.R.M. 2368 (D.D.C. 1950).
[28] Lithographers Local 17 (Graphic Arts Employers Ass'n), 130 N.L.R.B. 985, 47
L.R.R.M. 1374 (1961), aff'd, 309 F.2d 31, 51 L.R.R.M. 2093 (9th Cir. 1962), cert. denied,
372 U.S. 943, 52 L.R.R.M. 2673 (1963).
[29] Metal Workers (Hughes Tool Co.), 147 N.L.R.B. 1573, 56 L.R.R.M. 1289 (1964).
[30] Honolulu Star-Bulletin, Ltd., 123 N.L.R.B. 395, 43 L.R.R.M. 1449 (1959), enforcement denied on other grounds, 274 F.2d 567, 45 L.R.R.M. 2184 (D.C. Cir. 1959).

the waiver is clear and unmistakable.[31] Thus, an employer who has bargained for and won the right to make particular and specific types of unilateral changes in wages, hours, or working conditions need not bargain again during the life of a contract in order to exercise those rights.[32]

SURFACE BARGAINING

Section 8(d) requires that the employer and union "meet at reasonable times and confer in good faith with respect to . . . the negotiation of an agreement."[33] In *NLRB v. Montgomery Ward & Co.*[34] the Ninth Circuit defined the duty to bargain in good faith as an:

> obligation . . . to participate actively in the deliberations so as to indicate a present intention to find a basis for agreement . . . an open mind and a sincere desire to reach an agreement . . . a sincere effort . . . to reach a common ground.[35]

The Board and the courts now review the quality of negotiations by making a detailed examination of the facts and looking at the "totality of conduct" of the parties.[36] In connection with examining the totality of conduct of the bargaining, the Board and the courts look to see whether there has been "real" or "surface" bargaining.[37] Thus, there will be a finding of a refusal to bargain in good faith if it is concluded that an employer or union is merely going through the motions of bargaining.[38]

In cases where there has been a finding of bad-faith surface bargaining, the Board will enter a cease and desist order and an affirmative bargaining order.[39] In addition, in egregious cases, the

---

[31] NLRB v. Perkins Mach. Co., 326 F.2d 488, 55 L.R.R.M. 2204 (1st Cir. 1964), *accord* NLRB v. C & C Plywood Corp., 385 U.S. 421, 430–431, 64 L.R.R.M. 2065 (1967), *affirming*, 148 N.L.R.B. 414 (1967); Timken Roller Bearing Co. v. NLRB, 325 F.2d 746, 751, 54 L.R.R.M. 2785 (6th Cir. 1963), *cert. denied*, 376 U.S. 971, 55 L.R.R.M. 2878 (1964); Beacon Journal Pub. Co. v. NLRB, 401 F.2d 366, 367–368, 69 L.R.R.M. 2232 (6th Cir. 1968); NLRB v. Item Co., 220 F.2d 956, 35 L.R.R.M. 2709 (5th Cir. 1955) *cert. denied*, 350 U.S. 836, 36 L.R.R.M. 2716 (1955).

[32] *See, e.g.*, Ador Corp., 150 N.L.R.B. 1658, 1660, 58 L.R.R.M. 1280, 1281 (1965).

[33] 29 U.S.C. § 158(d).

[34] 133 F.2d 676, 12 L.R.R.M. 508 (9th Cir. 1943).

[35] *Id.* at 686, 12 L.R.R.M. at 517.

[36] B.F. Diamond Constr. Co., 163 N.L.R.B. 161, 64 L.R.R.M. 1333 (1966), *enforced per curiam*, 410 F.2d 462, 71 L.R.R.M. 2112 (5th Cir. 1969), *cert. denied* 396 U.S. 895, 72 L.R.R.M. 2432 (1969).

[37] Joy Silk Mills, Inc. v. NLRB, 185 F.2d 732, 27 L.R.R.M. 2012 (D.C. Cir. 1950).

[38] Greensboro News Co., 222 N.L.R.B. 893, 91 L.R.R.M. 1308 (1976), *enforced per curiam*, 549 F.2d 308, 94 L.R.R.M. 2752 (4th Cir. 1977).

[39] Irvington Motors, Inc., 147 N.L.R.B. 565, 56 L.R.R.M. 1257 (1964), *enforced per curiam*, 343 F.2d 759, 58 L.R.R.M. 2816 (3d Cir. 1965).

Board has ordered an employer to reimburse the employee-members of the union negotiating committee for wages lost because of attendance at negotiating sessions [40] and has even ordered the employer to reimburse the union for its bargaining expenses.[41]

UNILATERAL CHANGES

The employer's bargaining obligation continues during the life of the contract and as long thereafter as the union retains its majority status. While the contract is in effect, the employer must bargain not only over questions arising from alleged breaches of the contract,[42] but also over other mandatory bargaining subjects not included in the existing contract.[43] In short, absent waiver, section 8(a)(5) does not permit the employer to make unilateral changes in employment conditions—whether or not established by contract—unless he consults first with his employees' bargaining representative.[44]

In order to determine whether an employer's unilateral action constitutes a breach of its statutory bargaining obligation, and to decide upon the appropriate remedy for such violation, "the particular facts of a particular case must be examined." [45] A few representative cases will illustrate typical Board remedies to cure unilateral refusals to bargain.

An employer who unilaterally implements changes in rates of pay, wages, hours, or other terms or conditions of employment will be ordered to reimburse employees for lost wages or other benefits which occurred because of the changes.[46] For example, employers who have discontinued unilaterally the payment of regularly sched-

---

[40] M.F.A. Milling Co., 170 N.L.R.B. 1186, 68 L.R.R.M. 1077 (1968),

[41] Harowe Servo Controls, Inc., 250 N.L.R.B. 958, 105 L.R.R.M. 1147 (1980).

[42] See Timken Roller Bearing Co. v. NLRB, 325 F.2d 746, 753, 54 L.R.R.M. 2785 (6th Cir. 1963), cert. denied, 376 U.S. 971, 55 L.R.R.M. 2878; NLRB v. Goodyear Aerospace Corp., 388 F.2d 673, 674, 67 L.R.R.M. 2447 (6th Cir. 1968).

[43] NLRB v. Jacobs Mfg. Co., 196 F.2d 680, 683–684, 30 L.R.R.M. 2098, (2d Cir. 1952); Local Union No. 9735, United Mine Workers v. NLRB, 258 F.2d 146, 149, 42 L.R.R.M. 2320 (D.C. Cir. 1958).

[44] NLRB v. C & C Plywood, 385 U.S. 421, 425, 64 L.R.R.M. 2065 (1967); NLRB v. Katz, 369 U.S. 736, 743, 50 L.R.R.M. 2177, 2180 (1962); NLRB v. Huttig Sash & Door Co., 377 F.2d 964, 65 L.R.R.M. 2431 (8th Cir. 1967); International Woodworkers of America, Local 3-10 v. NLRB, 380 F.2d 628, 630, 65 L.R.R.M. 2633 (D.C. Cir. 1967).

[45] NLRB v. American Nat'l Ins. Co., 343 U.S. 395, 400, 30 L.R.R.M. 2147 (1952); NLRB v. Denton, 217 F.2d 567, 570, 35 L.R.R.M. 2217 (5th Cir. 1954), cert. denied, 348 U.S. 981, 35 L.R.R.M. 2709 (1955).

[46] See, e.g. Overnite Transp. Co. v. NLRB, 372 F.2d 765, 770, 64 L.R.R.M. 2359 (4th Cir. 1967), cert. denied, 389 U.S. 838, 66 L.R.R.M. 2307; Leeds & Northrup Co. v. NLRB, 391 F.2d 874, 879–880, 67 L.R.R.M. 2793 (3d Cir. 1968); NLRB v. Frontier Homes Corp., 371 F.2d 974, 981, 64 L.R.R.M. 2320 (8th Cir. 1967).

uled bonuses will be ordered to pay bonuses as in the past and to bargain in the future about such changes.[47] Where an employer was found to have violated the Act by reducing unilaterally employees' hours of work, the employees were reimbursed for the monetary value of the hours of work lost.[48] Similarly, an employer who unilaterally changed work schedules and lunch periods, and who eliminated free coffee, was ordered to reinstate the previous schedules, reinstate the coffee program, and pay employees their lost wages.[49] In like manner, deviation of an employer from past practice of recalling laid-off employees in order of seniority prompted the Board to order the affected employees made whole for monetary losses which they incurred as a result of not being recalled.[50] Reimbursement also will be ordered to remedy unilateral elimination of overtime work, if there is a "practical way to measure how much overtime would have been available or which employees would have availed themselves of overtime opportunities had they been offered." [51]

In addition to monetary remedies, the Board will attempt to restore the status quo ante with respect to in-plant conditions.[52] The fact that certain employees may have benefited from the employer's violation does not alter the Board's power to restore previolation conditions, "for it is public and not private rights that are being vindicated." [53] For example, an employer who improperly changed job classifications to exclude some employees from the bargaining unit was ordered to rescind the change and restore the classifica-

---

[47] *See* NLRB v. Marland One-Way Clutch Co., 520 F.2d 586, 89 L.R.R.M. 2721 (7th Cir. 1975); Gas Machinery Co., 221 N.L.R.B. 129, 90 L.R.R.M. 1730 (1975) (unilateral withholding of Christmas bonuses); *but cf.* Century Elec. Motor Co. v. NLRB, 447 F.2d 10, 78 L.R.R.M. 2042 (8th Cir. 1971) (no violation in elimination of Christmas bonus).

[48] Amoco Chems. Corp., 211 N.L.R.B. 618, 86 L.R.R.M. 1483 (1974).

[49] *See* Missourian Publ. Co., 216 N.L.R.B. 175, 88 L.R.R.M. 1647 (1975). *But compare* Ladish Co., 219 N.L.R.B. 354, 89 L.R.R.M. 1653 (1975). Although the employer there had violated the Act by refusing to honor the union's request to bargain about vending machine food prices, the employer was not ordered to bargain about every proposed price change, but rather to bargain on price changes only after they were effectuated unilaterally, and upon request by the union. *See also* E.I. duPont de Nemours & Co., 269 N.L.R.B. 24, 115 L.R.R.M. 1192 (1984).

[50] Hamilton Elecs. Co., 203 N.L.R.B. 206, 83 L.R.R.M. 1097 (1973).

[51] Chemvet Labs. Inc., 204 N.L.R.B. No. 40, 83 L.R.R.M. 1405 (1973), *enforced in pertinent part,* Chemvet Labs. Inc. v. NLRB, 497 F.2d 445, 86 L.R.R.M. 2262 (8th Cir. 1974).

[52] *See* Fibreboard Paper Prods. Corp. v. NLRB, 379 U.S. 203, 57 L.R.R.M. 2609 (1964).

[53] *See* Office & Professional Employees v. NLRB, 419 F.2d 314, 70 L.R.R.M. 3047, 3053 (D.C. Cir. 1969); Virginia Elec. and Power Co. v. NLRB, 391 U.S. 533, 540, 12 L.R.R.M. 739 (1943).

tions.[54] Where appropriate, however, the Board may require that the employees express a desire for the former conditions before ordering a restoration of the status quo ante. If they accept the new conditions, no make-whole order is warranted. Only if the employees desire a restoration of the earlier conditions will they be reimbursed for losses resulting from the violation.[55]

UNILATERAL DECISIONS TO CLOSE, RELOCATE, SUBCONTRACT, OR OTHERWISE CHANGE UNIT OPERATIONS

In the *Darlington* case, the Supreme Court ruled that an employer has the right to terminate its entire business completely for whatever reason it chooses.[56] Such a decision does not free it from its bargaining obligations, however. At the very least the employer is required to bargain over the effects of its decision.[57] Thus, the employer must give notice to the union so that it has an opportunity to bargain over its members' employment status with respect to such items as pensions, seniority, and severance pay.[58] Where an employer is found to have violated this bargaining obligation, the Board will order it to bargain with the union over the effects of the closing.[59]

The employer's bargaining obligation is much broader, however, when its decision involves less than a complete closing and affects its employees' working conditions. Examples of this may include transferring work to a new plant, partially closing operations, or subcontracting.[60] Thus, in *Fibreboard Paper Products Corp. v. NLRB*,[61] the Supreme Court held that section 8(a)(5) had been violated when an employer failed to bargain with the union about its

---

[54] Office & Professional Employees v. NLRB, 419 F.2d 314, 70 L.R.R.M. 3047 (D.C. Cir. 1969). *See also* Abingdon Nursing Center, 197 N.L.R.B. No. 781, 80 L.R.R.M. 1470 (1972) (employer ordered to reinstate old hours for kitchen employees and reinstitute a hot lunch program); Federal Mogul Corp., 209 N.L.R.B. 343, 85 L.R.R.M. 1353 (1974).

[55] Johnson's Indus. Caterers, Inc., 197 N.L.R.B. 352, 80 L.R.R.M. 134 (1972), *enforced per curiam*, NLRB v. Johnson's Indus. Caterers, 478 F.2d 1208, 83 L.R.R.M. 2847 (6th Cir. 1973).

[56] Textile Workers v. Darlington Mfg. Co., 380 U.S. 263, 58 L.R.R.M. 2657 (1965). Under *Darlington*, a partial closing to chill unionism would violate the Act.

[57] NLRB v. Royal Plating & Polishing Co., 350 F.2d 191, 196, 60 L.R.R.M. 2033 (3d Cir. 1965).

[58] NLRB v. Rapid Bindery Inc., 293 F.2d 170, 48 L.R.R.M. 2658 (2d Cir. 1961); Morrison Cafeterias Inc. v. NLRB, 431 F.2d 254, 74 L.R.R.M. 304 (8th Cir. 1970).

[59] NLRB v. Summit Tooling Co., 474 F.2d 1352, 83 L.R.R.M. 2044 (7th Cir. 1973).

[60] *See* Textile Workers v. Darlington Mfg. Co., 380 U.S. 263, 58 L.R.R.M. 2657 (1965).

[61] 379 U.S. 203, 57 L.R.R.M. 2609 (1964).

decision to subcontract unit work, although the decision merely involved replacing employees in the existing bargaining unit with others who would do the same work in the same plant.[62] The order, unlike that in *Darlington,* required the employer in *Fibreboard* to resume the discontinued operations, although legitimate business reasons were involved in the decision to discontinue. The Court ordered also that former employees be reinstated with back pay. Rejecting employer arguments that the employees had been discharged "for cause," the Court did not find that section 10(c) [63] barred reinstatement. This statutory provision, the Court held, was designed to prevent the NLRB from reinstating an individual who had been discharged because of misconduct, and was not intended to curtail the Board's broad power to fashion remedies when the loss of employment "stems directly from an unfair labor practice." [64]

The Supreme Court in *Darlington* left open the question of whether and when an employer must bargain an economic decision to close part of its business.[65] The Court recognized that a partial

---

[62] In a sense, *Darlington* and *Fibreboard* illustrate markedly different employer decisions to change operations. The former involved a complete closure; the latter a mere replacement of employees in a continuing unit. Between these extremes fall almost unlimited types of decisions, and there has been continual litigation attempting to determine whether the employer is required to bargain over the operational decision itself, or merely over its effects. *Compare, e.g.,* NLRB v. Adams Dairy, Inc., 350 F.2d 108, 113, 60 L.R.R.M. 2084 (8th Cir. 1965), *cert. denied,* 382 U.S. 1011, 61 L.R.R.M. 2192 (1966), *with* International Ladies' Garment Workers' Union (McLoughlin Mfg. Corp.) v. NLRB, 463 F.2d 907, 916–917, 919, 80 L.R.R.M. 2716 (D.C. Cir. 1972). Remedies for violations in this area are rather straightforward, and will generally include bargaining, monetary reimbursement, reinstatement, and notice-posting orders. Questions regarding substantive violations with respect to these management decisions are quite complex, however, and to discuss them more fully here is beyond the scope of this study. The issues concerning employer decisions to subcontract, automate, relocate, or completely or partially to close operations are fully discussed and analyzed in MISCIMARRA, THE NLRB AND MANAGERIAL DISCRETION: PLANT CLOSINGS, RELOCATIONS, SUBCONTRACTING AND AUTOMATION, Lab. Rel. Pub. Pol Ser. No. 24 (1983).

[63] 29 U.S.C. § 160(c)(1970), provides in part that "no order of the Board shall require the reinstatement of any individual as an employee who has been suspended or discharged or the payment to him of any backpay, if such individual was suspended or discharged *for cause. . . .* " (emphasis added).

[64] 379 U.S. at 217, 57 L.R.R.M. at 2614. *See also* Florida-Texas Freight, Inc., 203 N.L.R.B. 529, 83 L.R.R.M. 1093 (1973), *enforced sub nom.* NLRB v. Florida-Texas Freight, Inc., 489 F.2d 1275, 85 L.R.R.M. 2845 (6th Cir. 1974), in which the employer was ordered to set aside the subcontract, reinstate employees, and reimburse them for any loss of pay and bargain with the union; *and* Arnold Graphic Indus. v. NLRB, 505 F.2d 257, 87 L.R.R.M. 2753 (6th Cir. 1974), where the employer was ordered to return transferred equipment to its first location, and to reinstate employees. Backpay was denied in view of employer's history of harmonious labor relations with the union, the absence of anti-union animus in unilateral change, the economic hardship on the employer, and the employer's willingness to recognize the union.

[65] Textile Workers v. Darlington Mfg. Co., 380 U.S. 263, 58 L.R.R.M. 2657 (1965).

closing could "chill unionism" thereby resulting in a violation of section 8(a)(3).[66] In *First National Maintenance Corp. v. NLRB,*[67] the Supreme Court held that a decision to close part of a business purely for economic reasons is not a refusal to bargain, although there must be bargaining concerning the effects of such a decision. In reaching its decision, the Court said:

> We conclude that the harm likely to be done to an employer's right to operate freely in deciding whether to shut down part of its business purely for economic reasons outweighs the incremental benefit that might be gained through the Union's participation in making the decision, and we hold that the decision itself is *not* part of 8(d)'s "terms and conditions" over which Congress has mandated bargaining.[68]

The Court further said:

> Management must be free from the constraints of the bargaining process to the extent essential for the running of a profitable business. It also must have some degree of certainty beforehand as to when it may proceed to reach decisions without fear of later evaluations labeling its conduct an unfair labor practice.[69]

Still left open after *First National Maintenance Corp.* were questions such as whether decision bargaining is required for a plant relocation. The Board first announced that it would interpret *First National Maintenance* restrictively[70] and would require decision bargaining if a closing resulted in work being moved elsewhere.[71] A more recently constituted Board overruled this decision and held rather that whereas it would respect contractually agreed-upon prohibitions against work relocation during the term of an agreement, it would not give a union bargaining rights which it had not secured at the bargaining table and placed in the agreement. Therefore, it held that no decision bargaining was required concerning decisions to partially move the business from one plant to another so long as there were no specific restrictions concerning such moves within the collective bargaining agreement.[72]

In addition, the Board has indicated that a number of management decisions affecting the "direction of the business" such as sales, subcontracting, automation, restructuring, and consolidation

---

[66] *Id.* at 275, 58 L.R.R.M. at 2661.

[67] 452 U.S. 666, 107 L.R.R.M. 2705 (1981).

[68] *Id.* at 686, 107 L.R.R.M. at 2713.

[69] *Id.* at 678–679, 107 L.R.R.M. at 2710.

[70] General Counsel Memorandum No. 81–57, November 30, 1981.

[71] Milwaukee Spring Div. of Illinois Coil Spring Co., 265 N.L.R.B. 206, 111 L.R.R.M. 1486 (1982).

[72] Milwaukee Spring Div. of Illinois Coil Spring Co., 268 N.L.R.B. 601, 115 L.R.R.M. 1065 (1984), *affirmed* 765 F.2d 175, 119 L.R.R.M. 2801 (1985).

of operations are bargainable only if the decision involved "turns upon" labor costs. If it does not, there is no obligation to bargain.[73]

In restoring the status quo ante, employers have been ordered to return work to facilities from which it had been removed when these facilities were still in operation, and in some cases when the facilities had been closed.[74] The Board will listen to extenuating circumstances, however, which may justify not restoring the discontinued operation. Examples of such circumstances are where the decision to discontinue was motivated by compelling economic considerations,[75] where the employer had sold its assets,[76] where a lease had or would soon run out[77] or where the employer had purchased new facilities at a new location.[78] The Board will order restoration unless it is convinced that doing so will place an unjustified burden on the employer.[79]

In any event, the Board will order bargaining and, if applicable, back pay. In cases where decision bargaining is ordered, back pay, if also ordered, will run from the date of termination of the employees until the earliest of the following conditions: (1) the union's failure to request bargaining or its failure to bargain, (2) the union's bad-faith bargaining[80] (3) an agreement; or (4) a bona fide impasse. Where effects bargaining is ordered, back pay will begin to run from five days after the date of the Board's decision and order, until one of the conditions listed above is met.[81] If the employer can prove that the operation would have been discontinued at some definite point in time, back pay will be terminated as of that time.[82]

---

[73] Otis Elevator Co., 269 N.L.R.B. 891, 115 L.R.R.M. 1281 (1984); Pennsylvania Energy Corp., 274 N.L.R.B. No. 174, 119 L.R.R.M. 2183 (1984); Kroger Co., 273 N.L.R.B. No.70, 118 L.R.R.M. 1172 (1983); Gar Wood-Detroit Truck Equip. Inc., 274 N.L.R.B. No. 23, 118 L.R.R.M. 1417 (1983); Nurminco, 274 N.L.R.B. No. 112, 119 L.R.R.M. 1059 (1984); Fraser Shipyards Inc., 272 N.L.R.B. No. 80, 117 L.R.R.M. 1328 (1984); Columbia City Freight Lines, Inc., 271 N.L.R.B. No. 5, 116 L.R.R.M. 1311 (1985).

[74] Stone & Thomas, 221 N.L.R.B. 573, 90 L.R.R.M. 1570 (1975); Syufy Enters., 220 N.L.R.B. 738, 90 L.R.R.M. 1289 (1975).

[75] Kosher Kitchens, 190 N.L.R.B. 465, 77 L.R.R.M. 1339 (1971).

[76] Avila Group, Inc., 218 N.L.R.B. 633, 89 L.R.R.M. 1364 (1975); Burroughs Corp., 214 N.L.R.B. 571, 88 L.R.R.M. 1115 (1974).

[77] 218 N.L.R.B. 633, 89 L.R.R.M. 1364 (1975).

[78] Royal Norton Mfg. Co., 189 N.L.R.B. 489, 77 L.R.R.M. 102 (1971).

[79] NLRB v. American Mfg. Co. of Tex., 351 F.2d 74 (5th Cir. 1965), *enforced as modified*, 139 N.L.R.B. 815, 51 L.R.R.M. 1392 (1962); Drapery Mfg. Co., 170 N.L.R.B. 1706, 68 L.R.R.M. 1027 (1968).

[80] National Family Opinion, 246 N.L.R.B. 521, 102 L.R.R.M. 1641 (1979).

[81] National Car Rental, 252 N.L.R.B. 159, 105 L.R.R.M. 1263 (1981); Royal Plating & Polishing, 160 N.L.R.B. 990, 63 L.R.R.M. 1045 (1966); Walter Pape, Inc., 205 N.L.R.B. 719, 84 L.R.R.M. 1055 (1973).

[82] Brockway Motor Trucks, 251 N.L.R.B. 29, 104 L.R.R.M. 1515 (1980); National Family Opinion, Inc., 246 N.L.R.B. 521, 102 L.R.R.M. 1641 (1979).

ALTER EGO EMPLOYERS

In several industries, and particularly in the construction industry, unionized employers have in recent years created nonunion
entities to help them compete in the marketplace. The success of
an employer in doing this depends upon its sophistication and in
particular upon the degree of separation between the unionized
entity and the new nonunion entity.[83] The Board, when faced with
a refusal-to-bargain charge in this context, will examine in detail
the relationships between the union and nonunion entities.[84] If it
finds that there are two actually separate employers it will not find
a section 8(a)(5) violation.[85] When the required separation is not
present, however, the Board will find that the nonunion employer
is really in effect the alter ego of the unionized employer.[86] In such
cases, the Board may find that the union represents the employees
of the nonunion employer and order that the nonunion employer
be bound by the terms of the union's agreement with the union
employer.[87] In addition, orders may issue requiring that employees
be paid for wages they would have received under the union contract, that they be reimbursed for any medical or dental bills they
may have paid directly to health care providers, as well as any
premiums they may have paid to third party insurance companies,
and requiring the applicable contributions to union-management
trust funds.[88]

ORDERS TO PROVIDE BARGAINING INFORMATION

One party in collective bargaining may gain an unfair advantage
if allowed to justify its bargaining positions with data and information not made available to the other side. As the Second Circuit
summarized in *Prudential Insurance Co. v. NLRB:*

> It is now beyond question that the duty to bargain in good faith
> imposed upon the employer by § 8(a)(5) includes an obligation to pro-

---

[83] Kiewit Sons' Co., 231 N.L.R.B. 76, 95 L.R.R.M. 1510 (1977), aff'd, 595 F.2d 844,
100 L.R.R.M. 2792 (D.C. Cir. 1979); Western Union Corp., 224 N.L.R.B. 274, 92
L.R.R.M. 1443 (1976), aff'd sub. nom. Telegraph Workers v. NLRB, 571 F.2d 665, 97
L.R.R.M. 2962 (D.C. Cir.), cert. denied, 439 U.S. 827, 99 L.R.R.M. 2600 (1978); United
Constructors & Goodwin Constr. Co., 233 N.L.R.B. 904, 97 L.R.R.M. 1409 (1977).

[84] Id.

[85] Id.

[86] Ellsworth Sheet Metal, Inc., 235 N.L.R.B. 1273, 98 L.R.R.M. 1274 (1978), enforced,
603 F.2d 214, 103 L.R.R.M. 2603 (2d Cir. 1979).

[87] Plumbers Local 519 v. Service Plumbing Co., 401 F.Supp. 1008, 90 L.R.R.M. 3127
(S.D.Fla. 1975).

[88] Ellsworth Sheet Metal, Inc., 235 N.L.R.B. 1273, 98 L.R.R.M. 1274 (1978), enforced,
603 F.2d 214, 103 L.R.R.M. 2603 (2d Cir. 1979).

vide the employees' statutory bargaining representative with information that is necessary and relevant to the proper performance of its duties. E.g., *N.L.R.B. v. Acme Industrial Co.*, 385 U.S. 432, 64 LRRM 2069 (1967); *N.L.R.B. v. Truitt Mfg. Co.*, 351 U.S. 149, 38 LRRM 2042 (1956); *Fafnir Bearing Co. v. N.L.R.B.*, 362 F.2d 716, 62 LRRM 2415 (2d Cir. 1966). And this obligation applies with as much force to information needed by the Union for the effective administration of a collective bargaining agreement already in force as to information relevant in the negotiation of a new contract. *N.L.R.B. v. Acme Industrial Co.*, *supra; Fafnir Bearing Co. v. N.L.R.B., supra.*[89]

In ascertaining whether certain information must be supplied under the statute, the Board will act "upon the probability that the desired information was relevant, and that it would be of use to the union in carrying out its statutory duties and responsibilities."[90] When the Board finds that such requested information has been illegally withheld, the offending party will be required to provide the information.[91]

As stated by the Supreme Court in *Detroit Edison Co. v. NLRB*,[92] employers are entitled, where appropriate, to have safeguards placed on information provided to a union. In that case the employer had refused to furnish the union with copies of employee aptitude

---

[89] 412 F.2d 77, 81, 71 L.R.R.M. 2254, 2257 (2d Cir. 1969).

[90] NLRB v. Rockwell-Standard Corp., 410 F.2d 953, 957, 71 L.R.R.M. 2328, 2331 (6th Cir. 1969), *quoting from*, NLRB v. Acme Indus. Co., 385 U.S. 432, 437, 64 L.R.R.M. 2069 (1967).

[91] *See, e.g.,* Prudential Ins. Co. v. NLRB, 412 F.2d 77, 71 L.R.R.M. 2254 (2d Cir. 1969) (names and addresses of insurance agents who do not belong to union); Stanley Bldg. Specialties Co., 166 N.L.R.B. 984, 65 L.R.R.M. 1684 (1967), *enforced sub nom.* Steelworkers v. NLRB, 401 F.2d 434, 69 L.R.R.M. 2196 (D.C. Cir. 1968), *cert. denied,* 395 U.S. 946, 71 L.R.R.M. 2426 (1969) (financial data); NLRB v. Western Wirebound Box Co., 356 F.2d 88, 61 L.R.R.M. 2218 (9th Cir. 1966) (records relevant to wage increase demands); Tex Tan Welhausen Co. v. NLRB, 419 F.2d 1265, 72 L.R.R.M. 2885 (5th Cir. 1969) (time study information); NLRB v. Rockwell-Standard Corp., 410 F.2d 953, 71 L.R.R.M. 2328 (6th Cir. 1969) (information on job classifications and wage rates of nonunit employees); NLRB v. Twin City Lines, Inc., 425 F.2d 164, 74 L.R.R.M. 2024 (8th Cir. 1970) (information concerning employees' claims filed pursuant to an arbitration award necessary for the union to evaluate the merits of grievances); NLRB v. Marland One-Way Clutch Co., 520 F.2d 856, 89 L.R.R.M. 2721 (7th Cir. 1975) (information on past methods of computing Christmas bonus); Hawkins Constr. Co., 210 N.L.R.B. No. 152, 86 L.R.R.M. 1549 (1974) (information concerning employer's refusal to hire members referred by union). *But compare* the following cases in which employer violations did not result in an order requiring it to furnish the information: C-B Buick, Inc. v. NLRB, 506 F.2d 1086, 87 L.R.R.M. 2878 (3d Cir. 1974) (information denied because of its diluted relevance to negotiations and the administration of the contract caused by passage of time and execution of a new contract); General Elec. Co., 188 N.L.R.B. No. 105, 76 L.R.R.M. 1433 (1971) (order requiring employer to correlate wage information data with specific companies involved in survey is limited to disclosure of only such data the employer has in its possession); Fawcett Printing Corp., 201 N.L.R.B. No. 139 (1973) (because of the confidential nature of the information, certain portions need not be furnished, and union access to other portions is limited.)

[92] 440 U.S. 301, 100 L.R.R.M. 2728 (1979).

test questions, answer sheets, and test scores. The Board's order granting the union the right to this information was overruled by the Supreme Court, which decided that the order did not provide the necessary protections for the employer's interest in the security of the tests.

In *Electrical Workers (IUE) v. NLRB*,[93] a case involving the issue of confidentiality, the D.C. Circuit approved requiring employers to provide the union with a compilation of numbers, types, dates, and alleged bases of discrimination; but *not* copies of entire affirmative action files or individualized information contained in employment discrimination complaints filed with governmental agencies by unit employees. In the court's view, this limited disclosure enabled the union to determine amounts of discrimination, without jeopardizing the confidentiality of employee complaints and "the desirability of confidential, frank self-analysis on the part of the employer."[94]

THE H.K. PORTER DECISIONS

In *H.K. Porter Co. v. NLRB*,[95] the Supreme Court held that even though the NLRB has the power "to require employers and employees to negotiate, it is without power to compel a company or a union to agree to any substantive contractual provision of a collective bargaining agreement."[96] The Court observed that even when agreement between the parties is impossible, "it was never intended that the Government would in such cases step in, become a party to the negotiations and impose its own views of a desirable settlement."[97] The Supreme Court reaffirmed its previous decision, which had held that the Board may not, either directly or indirectly, compel concessions or otherwise sit in judgment upon the substantive terms of collective bargaining agreements,[98] and that section 8(d) was an attempt by Congress to prevent the Board from controlling the terms of a contract.[99]

This case began its route to the Supreme Court with a Board finding that the employer's refusal to agree to check-off was not made in good faith but was done solely to frustrate collective bar-

---

[93] 648 F.2d 18, 105 L.R.R.M. 3337 (D.C. Cir. 1980) *enforcing as modified* Westinghouse Elec. Corp., 239 N.L.R.B. 106, 99 L.R.R.M. 1482 (1978) and General Motors Corp., 243 N.L.R.B. 186, 101 L.R.R.M. 1461 (1979).
[94] 648 F.2d at 28, 105 L.R.R.M. at 3344.
[95] 397 U.S. 99, 73 L.R.R.M. 2561 (1970).
[96] *Id.* at 102, 73 L.R.R.M. at 2562.
[97] *Id.* at 103–104, 73 L.R.R.M. at 2562.
[98] NLRB v. American Ins. Co., 343 U.S. 395, 404, 30 L.R.R.M. 2147 (1952).
[99] NLRB v. Insurance Agents, 361 U.S. 477, 45 L.R.R.M. 2704 (1960).

gaining negotiations. The District of Columbia Circuit granted enforcement of a conventional bargaining order.[100] During negotiations following the court's decision, the union insisted that the court's order required the employer to agree to check-off; the employer refused. Clarification of the court's opinion was requested by the union. The court declared that it was permissible for the Board to order the employer to grant a check-off, and that "a check-off in return for a reasonable concession by the union may be the only effective remedy in this case."[101] The Board then ordered H.K. Porter to grant check-off without requiring a "reasonable concession" in return.[102] The circuit court affirmed the order.

In reversing the decision of the circuit court, the Supreme Court held that the Board's remedial powers, although broad, are limited to carrying out the policies of the Act itself.[103] Thus, allowing the Board to compel agreement would violate the fundamental premise of the Act — to protect "private bargaining under governmental supervision of the procedure alone, without any official compulsion over the actual terms of the contract."[104] The Supreme Court concluded its opinion by holding that if the Board's power is insufficiently broad, it is a matter for Congress, and not the courts, to decide and correct:

> In reaching its decision the Court of Appeals relied extensively on the equally important policy of the Act that workers' rights to collective bargaining are to be secured. In this case the Court apparently felt that the employer was trying effectively to destroy the union by refusing to agree to what the union may have considered its most important demand. Perhaps the court, fearing that the parties might resort to economic combat, was also trying to maintain the industrial peace which the Act is designed to further. But the Act as presently drawn does not contemplate that unions will always be secure and able to achieve agreement even when their economic position is weak, nor that strikes and lockouts will never result from a bargaining to impasse. It cannot be said that the Act forbids an employer or a union to rely ultimately on its economic strength to try to secure what it cannot obtain through bargaining. It may well be true, as the Court of Appeals felt, that the present remedial powers of the Board are insufficiently broad to cope with important labor problems. But it is the job of Congress, not the Board or the courts, to decide when and if it is necessary to allow governmental review of proposals for collective bargaining agreements and compulsory submission to

---

[100] 363 F.2d 272, 62 L.R.R.M. 2204 (D.C. Cir. 1966), *cert. denied,* 385 U.S. 851, 63 L.R.R.M. 2236 (1966).

[101] Steelworkers v. NLRB, 389 F.2d 295, 302, 66 L.R.R.M. 2761 (D.C. Cir. 1967).

[102] 172 N.L.R.B. 966, 68 L.R.R.M. 1337 (1968).

[103] 397 U.S. at 108, 73 L.R.R.M. at 2564 (1970).

[104] *Id.*

one side's demands. The present Act does not envision such a process. . . ."[105]

COMPELLING THE SIGNING OF A NEGOTIATED CONTRACT

Although *H.K. Porter* holds that the NLRB may not compel the parties to agree to specific contract terms, once a contract has been negotiated and concluded, the Board may require the parties to sign and acknowledge the existence of the contract and to make whole the employees who may have suffered losses as a result of the failure of the employer to abide by the terms of the contract. For example, in *NLRB v. Strong Roofing & Insulating Co.,*[106] the employer was found to have withdrawn from a multi-employer bargaining unit too late to escape the contract negotiated on his behalf. The Supreme Court approved the Board's remedial order which required the employer to sign the contract,[107] and reimburse the employees for the fringe benefits which would have been paid had the employer initially signed the contract and abided by its terms. The Court rejected the employer's argument that the Board had improperly inserted itself into the enforcement of the contract, contrary to the policy and scheme of the Act. The Court held that, although the Board has no plenary authority to administer and enforce collective bargaining contracts, it "is not trespassing on forbidden territory when it inquires whether negotiations have produced a bargain which the employer has refused to sign and honor. . . . To this extent the collective contract is the Board's affair, and an effective remedy for refusal to sign is its proper business."[108]

---

[105] *Id.* at 107–109, 73 L.R.R.M. at 2564, 2565. *Accord* Moore of Bedford v. NLRB, 451 F.2d 406, 78 L.R.R.M. 2769, 2772 (4th Cir. 1971); NLRB v. Tex Tan Welhausen Co., 434 F.2d 405, 75 L.R.R.M. 2554 (5th Cir. 1970), *on remand* (following *H.K. Porter*) 397 U.S. 819, 74 L.R.R.M. 2064 (1970), *vacating and remanding,* 419 F.2d 1265, 72 L.R.R.M. 2885 (5th Cir. 1969); Ameri-Crete Ready Mix Corp., 207 N.L.R.B. No. 509, 84 L.R.R.M. 1623 (1973). *But see* Hinson v. NLRB, 428 F.2d 133, 74 L.R.R.M. 2194 (8th Cir. 1970), (*H.K. Porter* is no bar to a Board order requiring employer to pay health, welfare, and retirement benefit contributions, where § 8(a)(5) violation was predicated on the employer's unilateral termination of such payments upon expiration of existing contract).

[106] 393 U.S. 357, 70 L.R.R.M. 2100 (1969).

[107] *See also,* H.J. Heinz Co. v. NLRB, 311 U.S. 514, 524–526, 7 L.R.R.M. 291 (1941); NLRB v. Ogle Protection Serv., Inc., 375 F.2d 497, 64 L.R.R.M. 2792 (6th Cir. 1967), *cert. denied,* 389 U.S. 843, 66 L.R.R.M. 2308 (1967).

[108] Strong Roofing & Insulation Co., 393 U.S. at 361, 70 L.R.R.M. at 2101–2102 (1969). *And see* NLRB v. K & H Specialties Co., 407 F.2d 820, 70 L.R.R.M. 2880 (6th Cir. 1969) which applied *Strong Roofing,* and held that the Board has jurisdiction to determine the amount of back pay due employees. The court rejected employer arguments that under the terms of the contract, the amount of back pay should have been determined by arbitration. For other cases applying the principles set forth in *Strong Roofing,* see Crimptex, Inc., 221 N.L.R.B. No. 54, 90 L.R.R.M. 1508

Although an employer or union may have violated section 8(a)(5) in its bargaining conduct, it will not be ordered to sign a collective bargaining agreement unless it can be shown that there has been a "complete meeting of the minds as to all of the terms to be incorporated in a final contract."[109] Thus, where the employer and union have not resolved their differences, and "were still at loggerheads"[110] over important issues, the *Strong Roofing* rationale will not apply. And even where the Board had found that the parties "had reached agreement in principle as to the substantive terms of a collective-bargaining agreement," the employer was not ordered to execute the document when "there was no agreement as to the language to go into the contract. . . ."[111] In cases where an order to sign is deemed inappropriate, the Board has simply required the employer to bargain in good faith upon the union's request, and if an understanding is reached, to embody it in a signed contract. Furthermore, in order to provide the union sufficient time to bargain for such an agreement, the Board has extended the union's certification for a period of up to one year from the commencement of the employer's good faith bargaining.[112]

In cases where the contract has expired prior to the date of the Board's decision, at the union's option the employer is ordered to execute the agreement, which is to be effective from the date when agreement was reached. Alternatively, the union can choose to

(1975) (NLRB order directing employer to sign contract is clarified to require that the contract be effective as of the date on which the agreement would have been executed had it not been for the employer's unlawful conduct); NLRB v. Raven Indus., Inc., 508 F.2d 1289, 88 L.R.R.M. 2103 (8th Cir. 1974) (employer ordered to give retroactive effect to contract, but not to pay sick leave, since evidence failed to show this agreement on this term); NLRB v. Crimptex, Inc., 517 F.2d 501, 89 L.R.R.M. 2465, 2468 (1st Cir. 1975); NLRB v. Summit Tooling Co., 474 F.2d 1352, 83 L.R.R.M. 2044 (7th Cir. 1973); NLRB v. Tex Tan Welhausen Co., 434 F.2d 405, 75 L.R.R.M. 2554 (5th Cir. 1970); NLRB v. Stafford Trucking, Inc., 77 L.R.R.M. 2465 (7th Cir. 1971) (employer who refused to sign agreement ordered to pay lost wages and benefits with interest); Southland Dodge, 205 N.L.R.B. No. 54, 84 L.R.R.M. 1231 (1973), *enforced,* 492 F.2d 1238, 85 L.R.R.M. 2768 (3d Cir. 1974) (employer ordered to sign contract, give it retroactive effect, and make employees whole for any loss suffered. The Board refused a request for lost union dues, since the employees had not executed check-off authorization); Coletti Color Prints, 204 N.L.R.B. No. 96, 83 L.R.R.M. 1598 (1973) (order to execute contract and make employees whole). *Accord* NLRB v. Mayes Bros., Inc., 383 F.2d 242, 66 L.R.R.M. 2031 (5th Cir. 1967); NLRB v. M & M Oldsmobile, 377 F.2d 712, 65 L.R.R.M. 2149 (2d Cir. 1967).

[109] Orion Tool, Die & Mach. Co., 195 N.L.R.B. 1080, 79 L.R.R.M. 1636, 1638 (1972).
[110] *Id.*
[111] Zenith Radio Corp., 187 N.L.R.B. 785, 76 L.R.R.M. 1115, 1116 (1971), *enforced per curiam,* 489 F.2d 773, 80 L.R.R.M. 2768 (7th Cir. 1972); J.W. Praught Co., 212 N.L.R.B. 482, 87 L.R.R.M. 1507 (1974) (evidence did not establish that the employer had orally agreed to contract terms). *Cf.* Retail Clerks v. NLRB (Montgomery Ward & Co.), 373 F.2d 655, 64 L.R.R.M. 2108 (D.C. Cir. 1967).
[112] *See* Zenith Radio Corp., 187 N.L.R.B. 785, 76 L.R.R.M. 1115, 1116 (1971); Orion Tool, Die, and Mach. Co., 195 N.L.R.B. 1080, 79 L.R.R.M. 1636, 1638 (1972).

forego the contract and the employer must commence bargaining immediately for a new contract.[113] If the union determines that the employer should sign the contract, then employees will be made whole for the loss of benefits which would have accrued to them, including interest, as a result of the employer's refusal to sign.[114] The courts have enforced this type of Board order.[115]

If the unsigned contract does not contain a dues-deduction clause and if employees have not signed check-off authorizations, the Board will not require an employer to pay a union the dues it would have collected even though the contract contains a union security clause.[116] Payment will be ordered, however, if the contract contains a dues-deduction clause and if the employees have signed check-off authorizations.[117]

THE EX-CELL-O *DECISION*

When an employer has been found to have violated section 8(a)(5) by a refusal to bargain in good faith, unions have often requested that such employer be ordered to make the employees whole for the wages and other fringe benefits which might have been gained had the employer bargained in good faith with the union. This highly controversial remedy is fully discussed in Chapter XIV. To summarize, the NLRB's position announced in *Ex-Cell-O Corp.*[118]

---

[113] Worrell Newspapers, 232 N.L.R.B. 402, 97 L.R.R.M. 1029 (1977).

[114] Ogle Protection Serv., Inc., 149 N.L.R.B. 545, 57 L.R.R.M. 1337 (1964).

[115] *See* NLRB v. New England Die Casting Co., 242 F.2d 759, 49 L.R.R.M. 2616 (2d Cir. 1957), *enforcing,* 116 N.L.R.B. 1, 38 L.R.R.M. 1175 (1956). *But see* NLRB v. Huttig Sash & Door, Inc., 362 F.2d 217, 62 L.R.R.M. 2271 (4th Cir. 1966), where the Board ordered that if the union decided the contract was no longer satisfactory, the contract would not be enforced retroactively against the employer. Rather, the union would be given the option of bargaining for a new agreement. The Fourth Circuit rejected this order as inconsistent with the major basis of the Board's decision that the parties had already entered into an agreement. Subsequent decisions have limited *Huttig Sash & Door* to its particular circumstances, noting that the relevant issues were not briefed or argued to the Fourth Circuit and that the decision was "academic" since the old contract had expired and the parties were required to bargain anyway. *See* NLRB v. M & M Oldsmobile, 377 F.2d 712, 718, 65 L.R.R.M. 2149, 2154 (2d Cir. 1967); NLRB v. Beverage-Air Co., 402 F.2d 411, 416–417, 69 L.R.R.M. 2369, 2373 (4th Cir. 1968). In both of these cases, the union was given the option of bargaining for a new contract or putting the old contract into effect retroactively with the employees receiving reimbursement for lost benefits. *Accord* General Asbestos & Rubber Div., Raybesto Manhattan, Inc., 183 N.L.R.B. 213, 74 L.R.R.M. 1649 (1970); Schill Steel Prods. Inc., 161 N.L.R.B. 939, 63 L.R.R.M. 1388 (1966); NLRB v. Schill Steel Prods., 480 F.2d 586, 83 L.R.R.M. 2369, 2386 (5th Cir. 1972).

[116] Hickory Farms of Ohio, 222 N.L.R.B. 418, 92 L.R.R.M. 1177 (1977), *enforced,* 558 F.2d 526, 95 L.R.R.M. 3096 (9th Cir. 1977); Monument Printing Co., 231 N.L.R.B. 1215, 96 L.R.R.M. 1177 (1977).

[117] Stackpole Components Co., 232 N.L.R.B. 723, 96 L.R.R.M. 1324 (1977).

[118] Ex-Cell-O Corp., 185 N.L.R.B. 107, 74 L.R.R.M. 1740 (1970).

has been that it does not have the statutory power under the no-concession language of section 10(a) to award such a remedy. The District of Columbia Circuit, on the other hand, has held that the Board enjoys this authority.[119] To date, this remedy has not been ordered by the Board, which has continued to follow its position in *Ex-Cell-O.*

A UNION'S REFUSAL TO BARGAIN IN GOOD FAITH

When the Board finds that a union has refused to bargain, it provides the usual remedy of an order to cease and desist from refusing to bargain and to bargain if requested by the employer.[120] A union will also be required to sign an agreed-upon contract.[121] However, a union will not be ordered to make the employees whole for wages lost as a result of its failure to sign a contract.[122] Unions have been ordered to cease and desist from using the grievance and arbitration procedures in a collective bargaining agreement or during the collective bargaining process as a means of expanding "its established collective bargaining relationship beyond the bounds of the [certified] unit."[123]

The Board has devised special remedies in cases involving massive union violations of section 8(b)(3). Thus in *Teamsters Local 705 (Gasoline Retailers Ass'n)*[124] the Board found extensive unlawful activities carried out by Local 705:

> (1) Local 705 induced gasoline station dealers to sign agreements recognizing Local 705 as the exclusive collective-bargaining representative of a majority of station employees, although Local 705 did

---

[119] *See* Electrical Workers (IUE) (Tiidee Prods., Inc.) v. NLRB, 426 F.2d 1243, 73 L.R.R.M. 2870 (D.C. Cir. 1970), *reh'g denied,* 431 F.2d 1206, 75 L.R.R.M. 2350 (1970), *cert. denied,* 400 U.S. 950, 75 L.R.R.M. 2752 (1970), *on remand,* 194 N.L.R.B. 1234, 79 L.R.R.M. 1175 (1972); Ex-Cell-O Corp. v. NLRB, 449 F.2d 1058, 77 L.R.R.M. 2547 (D.C. Cir. 1971); Retail Clerks Local 1401 v. NLRB (Zinke's Foods, Inc.), 463 F.2d 816, 79 L.R.R.M. 2984 (D.C. Cir. 1972); Steelworkers v. NLRB (Quality Rubber Co.), 430 F.2d 519, 74 L.R.R.M. 2747 (D.C. Cir. 1970).

[120] American Radio Ass'n, 82 N.L.R.B. 1344, 24 L.R.R.M.1006 (1949); Meat Cutters Local 421 (Great Atlantic & Pacific Tea Co.), 81 N.L.R.B. 1052, 23 L.R.R.M. 1464 (1949).

[121] Sheet Metal Workers Local 65 (Inland Steel Prods. Co.), 120 N.L.R.B. 1678, 42 L.R.R.M. 1231 (1958); Local 1464, IBEW (Kansas City Power and Light Co.), 275 N.L.R.B. No. 80, 119 L.R.R.M. 1147 (1985) (where union failed to sign because, contrary to the agreement of the parties, the final printed version of the contract did not contain a union "bug" indicating that it had been printed by union workers).

[122] *See* Graphic Arts Union Local 280 (James H. Barry Co.), 235 N.L.R.B. 1084, 98 L.R.R.M. 1188 (1978), *enforced,* 596 F.2d 904, 101 L.R.R.M. 2664 (9th Cir. 1979).

[123] Electrical Workers (IUE) Local 445, 216 N.L.R.B. 173, 88 L.R.R.M. 1234 (1975).

[124] Teamsters Local 705 (Gasoline Retailers Ass'n), 210 N.L.R.B. 210, 86 L.R.R.M. 1011 (1974).

not really represent those employees; (2) Local 705 required employers to put station employees into the union and to pay initiation fees and dues although the employees were not properly members of Local 705 at all; (3) Local 705 coerced employers and station managers to be members of Local 705—and in certain stations to be the only members of Local 705; (4) Local 705 did not negotiate with station dealers about their employees' pay or other terms and conditions of their employment, although Local 705 pretended to be their representative and although it collected their dues; (5) Local 705 did not see to it that they were paid the wages required by its contracts, nor did Local 705 even inquire what wages you were being paid; (6) Local 705 coerced station dealers to pay dues on and take in as station union members people who were not even employed at the station; and (7) Local 705 told the employers that they do not have to pay their employees the wages required by its contracts with the employers.[125]

The Board order required Local 705 to publish a notice stating in part:

We will stop doing these things and we will not do them again. Furthermore:

We will stop giving effect to such contracts.

We will stop collecting union dues, assessments, health and welfare payments, or other payments under such contracts or on dues checkoff or other wage withholding or payment authorizations signed by employees under or in relation to such contracts.

We will promptly refund to employees of the 82 employers involved in the National Labor Relations Board proceeding, with interest, payments of union initiation fees, dues, assessments, health and welfare payments, and other payments made by those employees or on their behalf under or in relation to such contracts, to the extent required by the National Labor Relations Board Order.

We will not act or pretend to act for you when we do not really represent you.[126]

---

[125] 210 N.L.R.B. at 213.
[126] *Id.*

CHAPTER XIV

Extraordinary Remedies

Respondents generally comply with the traditional NLRB unfair labor practice remedies detailed in the preceding chapters. Fortunately, there are only a few respondents who engage in persistent violations of the Act, who flagrantly disregard employees' section 7 rights, or who delay the implementation of NLRB orders by frivolous litigation. In cases where such conduct does occur, however, the Board (with the support of the courts, for the most part) requires remedial or other measures which are unnecessary in the vast majority of cases. The Board reasons that only additional steps on the part of the offending party will suffice to undo the pernicious effects of particularly egregious unfair labor practices. The remaining chapters deal with Board and court sanctions available in these extraordinary situations.

JUSTIFICATION FOR EXTRAORDINARY REMEDIES

The Board has indicated that generally it will order extraordinary remedies only in those situations where, because of the severity of the unfair labor practice in question or because of repeated unfair labor practice violations extending to other plants of the same employer, the usual Board remedies are not sufficient to undo the effects of the respondent's illegal activities. The remedies discussed in this chapter may be ordered in conjunction with a *Gissel* bargaining order,[1] although typically they are ordered where a union's attempt at organization has fallen short of attaining the majority status generally required to support a bargaining order. In these cases the Board fashions these extraordinary remedies with a view toward guaranteeing that employees be able to exercise their free choice in deciding whether to have union representation.

As is true in connection with all remedies fashioned by the Board, the courts have generally deferred to the Board's choice of extraordinary remedies. They have been guided by the Supreme Court's

---

[1] *See* NLRB v. Gissel Packing Co., 395 U.S. 575, 71 L.R.R.M. 2481 (1969). This case is discussed in detail in Chapter XII, *supra*.

admonishment in *Virginia Electric & Power Co. v. NLRB* [2] that the selection of remedies made by the Board must stand "unless it can be shown that the order is a patent attempt to achieve ends other than those which can fairly be said to effectuate the policies of the Act." [3] But while generally deferring to the administrative expertise of the NLRB, the courts have recognized that there are certain limits to the Board's exercise of discretion.

First, it is clear that the NLRB's choice of an extraordinary remedy must not be punitive. No matter how many violations a party has committed, the remedy must not be designed as a punishment but rather should operate to recreate the status quo. Although the distinction between what is "punitive" and what is "remedial" is often semantic, [4] there is a real tension between the two poles in the reported cases. Thus, the District of Columbia Circuit has indicated that, in determining an appropriate remedy, the NLRB has an obligation to take into account a party's history of recalcitrance; [5] but the same court has cautioned that the mere citation by the Board of a history of violations by a party is insufficient in and of itself to justify an extraordinary remedy. [6]

This points to a second factor—the necessity that the remedy be tailored to the specific violations that have been found. The remedy must not be premised upon speculation by the Board that it will be in the best interest of affected employees. Instead, a court will require that the NLRB (or an administrative law judge who is affirmed by the NLRB) provide specific factual findings in support of the necessity of going beyond the Board's traditional remedies for unfair labor practices. [7]

EXTRAORDINARY NOTICE AND POSTING REQUIREMENTS

As part of a remedy for less serious unfair labor practice violations, the Board will require an employer to post a copy of the official NLRB notice in conspicuous places on its premises. Ordi-

---

[2] 819 U.S. 533, 12 L.R.R.M. 739 (1943). *See also* general discussion at Chs. II and III, *supra.*

[3] 819 U.S. at 540, 12 L.R.R.M. at 742.

[4] *See* NLRB v. Seven-Up Bottling Co., 344 U.S. 344, 348, 31 L.R.R.M. 2237, 2239 (1953); Steelworkers v. NLRB (Florida Steel Corp.), 646 F.2d 618, 630, 106 L.R.R.M. 2578, 2583 (D.C. Cir. 1981). *See also* discussion at Ch. II *supra*, n.23 and accompanying text.

[5] Textile Workers Union v. NLRB, 475 F.2d 973, 976, 82 L.R.R.M. 2471 (D.C. Cir. 1973).

[6] Florida Steel Corp. v. NLRB, 713 F.2d 823, 113 L.R.R.M. 3625 (D.C. Cir. 1983).

[7] Steelworkers v. NLRB (Florida Steel Corp.), 646 F.2d 618, 630, 106 L.R.R.M. 2578, 2583 (D.C. Cir. 1981); *see also* Florida Steel Corp. v. NLRB, 713 F.2d 823, 118 L.R.R.M. 3625 (D.C. Cir. 1983) (NLRB's supporting findings inadequate).

narily, such posting of an official NLRB form is considered sufficient to dissipate the impact of the employer's unlawful acts.

In cases such as those described above involving more serious or repeated violations, however, the Board has often concluded that the mere posting of its notice is an insufficient remedy. In these cases, the Board typically will require that an employer take one or more of the following additional steps of notification: publishing a copy of the NLRB notice in a company publication; mailing a copy of the notice to the homes of affected employees; publishing the notice in local newspapers; having a company official sign the notice; or having a company official (particularly the company official responsible for the violations) read the notice to a group of employees. One or more of these extraordinary notice and posting requirements have been applied in numerous cases.[8]

By and large, the decisions of the courts of appeals have supported the Board's authority to apply these remedies in appropriate circumstances.[9] There has been some debate among the courts, however, over Board-imposed requirements that a company president or other official read the notice to employees in person. In *Teamsters Local 115 v. NLRB (Haddon House Food Products)*,[10] the District of Columbia Circuit refused to enforce a decision of the Board compelling a company president personally to read a notice to employees; the court cited the president's lack of personal involvement in the unfair labor practice as indicating a "lack of particularized need for such an *ad hominem* remedy."[11] In its later ruling in *Conair Corp. v. NLRB*,[12] the same circuit did enforce another Board order requiring that a company official read a notice to affected employees, but this time, the court concluded that adequate factual findings

---

[8] *See, e.g.,* Gourmet Foods, Inc., 270 N.L.R.B. No. 113, 116 L.R.R.M. 1105 (1984); Conair Corp., 261 N.L.R.B. 1189, 110 L.R.R.M. 1161 (1982); J.P. Stevens & Co., 239 N.L.R.B. 738, 100 L.R.R.M. 1052 (1978); Florida Steel Corp. 231 N.L.R.B. 651, 96 L.R.R.M. 1070 (1977); United Supermkts., Inc., 261 N.L.R.B. 1291, 110 L.R.R.M. 1173 (1982); Sambo's Rest., Inc., 247 N.L.R.B. 777, 103 L.R.R.M. 1181 (1980). When the Board has concluded that a respondent has engaged in serious or repeated violations, it will typically order a number of the extraordinary remedies referred to in the text. But the remedy in each case should be tailored to the specific facts of each case; and, in many instances, the Board will find that one of the "usual" extraordinary posting requirements is inappropriate. *See, e.g.,* F.W.I.L. Lundy Bros., 248 N.L.R.B. 415, 103 L.R.R.M. 1520 (1980) (no necessity for publishing order in local newspaper because of "possibly unduly harsh effect on Respondent's business"). See parallel discussion in Ch. VII, *supra,* text accompanying n.18 *et seq.*

[9] *See, e.g.,* NLRB v. Union Nacional de Trabajadores, 540 F.2d 1, 12, 92 L.R.R.M. 3425, 3432–83 (1st Cir. 1976); J.P. Stevens & Co. v. NLRB, 880 F.2d 292, 304, 65 L.R.R.M. 2829, 2837–39 (2d Cir. 1967); NLRB v. Weirton Steel Co., 183 F.2d 584, 26 L.R.R.M. 2442 (3rd Cir. 1950).

[10] 640 F.2d 392, 106 L.R.R.M. 2462 (D.C. Cir. 1981).

[11] *Id.* at 403, 106 L.R.R.M. at 2471.

[12] 721 F.2d 1355, 114 L.R.R.M. 3168 (D.C. Cir. 1983).

were presented in the NLRB opinion to support the official's personal involvement. In a dissent to the majority's holding on this issue, however, Judge Ginsburg, citing a previous decision of the District of Columbia Circuit in *International Union of Electrical, Radio & Machine Workers v. NLRB (Scott's Inc.)*,[13] referred to such a requirement as a "humiliation . . . incompatible with the democratic principles of the dignity of man."[14]

EXTRAORDINARY ACCESS REQUIREMENTS

The majority of instances of egregious violations necessitating extraordinary remedial provisions occur in the course of a union's attempt to organize workers at a particular location of the targeted employer. With reference to these organizing attempts, the Board and the courts have fashioned a series of guidelines which define a union's right of access to an employer's property and its opportunities to address employees. In general, nonemployee union organizers have no right of direct access to an employer's premises for the purpose of distributing pamphlets or making speeches absent the union's inability to reach the employees in other ways; this has been the broad teaching of Supreme Court opinions beginning with *NLRB v. Babcock & Wilcox Co.*[15] An employer also may ordinarily limit the right of union adherents among its employees to speak to other employees to nonworking time,[16] and it has the right to make "captive audience" speeches or to otherwise address employees on company time and premises with no "captive audience" right of rebuttal by a union or by other employees.[17]

In a number of cases involving flagrant and repeated violations, however, which indicate a resistance to employee self-determination, the NLRB, as a remedial measure, has granted extraordinary access rights to union representatives. In appropriate cases, these rights have included: direct access to company property; access to

---

[13] 383 F.2d 230, 66 L.R.R.M. 2081 (D.C. Cir. 1967).

[14] 721 F.2d at 1401, 114 L.R.R.M. at 3204, (Ginsburg, J., dissenting).

[15] 351 U.S. 105, 38 L.R.R.M. 2001 (1956). The Supreme Court itself has noted that "the balance struck by the Board and the Courts under the Babcock accommodation principle has rarely been in favor of trespassing organizational activity"; Sears, Roebuck & Co. v. San Diego County District Council of Carpenters, 436 U.S. 180, 205, 98 L.R.R.M. 2282, 2292 (1978).

[16] *See* Our Way, Inc., 268 N.L.R.B. 384, 115 L.R.R.M. 1009 (1983).

[17] *See* Livingston Shirt Corp., 107 N.L.R.B. 400, 33 L.R.R.M. 1156 (1956); *but see* May Dept. Stores Co., 136 N.L.R.B. 797, 49 L.R.R.M. 1862 (1962) (employer "captive audience" speech without union right of response unlawful where employer had imposed broad, but valid, no-solicitation rules for nonworking time). The Sixth Circuit denied enforcement of the Board's decision in May Dept. Stores Co. v. NLRB, 316 F.2d 797, 53 L.R.R.M. 2172 (6th Cir. 1963).

company bulletin boards; equal time to respond to the employer's speeches; access to employees on nonworking time; and the furnishing of a name and address list of employees.[18] In cases where an employer's flagrant unfair labor practices are found to have an effect on employee activity at other of the employer's plants, the Board will order union access to those other plants, including their bulletin boards. This is particularly true where the unfair practices form part of a company-wide policy.[19] These extraordinary access rights have been premised on the fact that a mere cease-and-desist order is insufficient to restore the status quo and to give the union an adequate opportunity to pursue its attempts at organization free of the taint of previous unfair labor practices.

While the courts of appeals have for the most part enforced such remedies in appropriate situations,[20] some Board remedies have not met with success. In *Florida Steel Corp. v. NLRB*,[21] for example, the Fifth Circuit refused to enforce an NLRB order granting access to a union at the company's unorganized plants, finding that such access would cease to be remedial in the context of a charge relating to failure to bargain at the organized plants.

In addition, the specter of the Supreme Court's decision in *Babcock & Wilcox* casts a shadow over these remedies. In a number of decisions, the Board itself, on the authority of *Babcock & Wilcox*, has refused to grant extraordinary access remedies when alterna-

---

[18] *See, e.g.,* United Farmers Coop. Ass'n, 242 N.L.R.B. 1026, 101 L.R.R.M. 1278 (1979); Haddon House Food Prods., Inc., 242 N.L.R.B. 1057, 101 L.R.R.M. 1294 (1979); Sambo's Rest., Inc., 247 N.L.R.B. 777, 103 L.R.R.M. 1181 (1980); F.W.I.L. Lundy Bros., 248 N.L.R.B. 415, 103 L.R.R.M. 1520 (1980); Conair Corp., 721 F.2d 1355, 114 L.R.R.M. 3168 (D.C. Cir. 1983). The granting of direct access to an employer's property as a remedial measure will still be denied, however, if such access is not viewed as necessary for the union to undo the respondent's unfair labor practices; *see* Greenfield Mfg. Co., 199 N.L.R.B. 756, 82 L.R.R.M. 1015 (1972). In another case the Board denied a union's request for access on the ground that the Board might be viewed as supporting one particular union at the expense of another; Malrite of Wisconsin, Inc., 213 N.L.R.B. 830, 87 L.R.R.M. 1676 (1974).

[19] *See* J.P. Stevens & Co., 239 N.L.R.B. 738, 100 L.R.R.M. 1052 (1978); J.P. Stevens & Co., 240 N.L.R.B. 33, 100 L.R.R.M. 1342 (1979); Florida Steel Corp., 244 N.L.R.B. 385, 102 L.R.R.M. 1181 (1979); Florida Steel Corp., 262 N.L.R.B. 1460, 110 L.R.R.M. 1472 (1982).

[20] *See, e.g.,* J.P. Stevens & Co. v. NLRB, 388 F.2d 896, 67 L.R.R.M. 2055 (2d Cir. 1967); NLRB v. Koval Press, Inc., 622 F.2d 579, 106 L.R.R.M. 2603 (3d Cir. 1980); J.P. Stevens & Co. v. NLRB, 623 F.2d 322, 104 L.R.R.M. 2573 (4th Cir. 1980); Steelworkers v. NLRB (Florida Steel Corp.), 646 F.2d 616, 106 L.R.R.M. 2573 (D.C. Cir. 1981).

[21] 620 F.2d 79, 104 L.R.R.M. 2833 (5th Cir. 1980). *See also* NLRB v. H.W. Elson Bottling Co., 379 F.2d 223, 227, 65 L.R.R.M. 2673, 2675 (6th Cir. 1967) (refusing to enforce that part of Board order granting union the right to hold in-plant meetings on company time since "no problem of union access to or communication with employees").

tive methods were available.[22] This position contrasted with an earlier decision by the Sixth Circuit in *Decaturville Sportswear Co. v. NLRB*,[23] where the court stated that the propriety of access as an organizational tool and the propriety of access as a remedial measure present two separate questions and that the latter issue is not addressed by *Babcock & Wilcox*. In an exhaustive and well-reasoned opinion by Judge Edwards, the District of Columbia Circuit agreed in large part with the Sixth Circuit and held that access to one of a company's plants can in fact be premised upon violations which occurred at another plant.[24] But recognizing that *Babcock & Wilcox* has some relevance in the remedial area, the court explained that:

> [A]ccess may be awarded as a remedial measure if necessary to offset the direct consequences or effects of an employer's unlawful conduct . . . . Absent the necessity to counter these harmful consequences, access cannot be justified as a remedial measure and instead may directly affront the principles announced in *Babcock* . . . . In granting access as a remedial measure, therefore, a burden lies upon the Board to substantiate its conclusion that access is necessary to offset the consequences of unlawful employer conduct.[25]

The court remanded the case to the Board, however, to consider and make findings on the seriousness of the violation, the knowledge of this violation at other plants, the distance between plants, the existence of union organizing activity at other plants, and the effect of the passage of time between violations.[26]

REIMBURSEMENTS TO THE UNION

The National Labor Relations Act on its face is consistent with the usual "American Rule"[27] in requiring that each party bear its own cost of litigation and expenses, but in certain circumstances the Board and the courts have fashioned exceptions.

---

[22] *See* Greenfield Mfg. Co., 189 N.L.R.B. 756, 82 L.R.R.M. 1015 (1972); Heck's, Inc., 191 N.L.R.B. 886, 77 L.R.R.M. 1513 (1971); Winn-Dixie Stores, Inc., 224 N.L.R.B. 1418, 92 L.R.R.M. 1625 (1976), *enforced in relevant part*, 567 F.2d 1343, 97 L.R.R.M. 2866 (5th Cir. 1978).

[23] 406 F.2d 886, 70 L.R.R.M. 2472 (6th Cir. 1969).

[24] Steelworkers v. NLRB (Florida Steel Corp.), 646 F.2d 616, 106 L.R.R.M. 2573 (D.C. Cir. 1981).

[25] *Id.* at 638, 106 L.R.R.M. at 2590.

[26] When this case again reached the District of Columbia Circuit after remand, that court refused to enforce significant portions of the notice and access orders on the ground that the Board had failed to articulate anything other than the respondent's past conduct in support of the order. Florida Steel Corp. v. NLRB, 718 F.2d 823, 113 L.R.R.M. 3625 (D.C. Cir. 1983).

[27] *See, e.g.,* Alyeska Pipeline Serv. Co. v. Wilderness Soc., 421 U.S. 240 (1975).

The Tiidee Products *Exception*

In *Tiidee Products, Inc.,*[28] the Board made an exception to the American Rule and indicated that it would order payment of litigation fees and expenses by a respondent when that respondent's defense is "frivolous." The Board stated:

> Accordingly, in order to discourage future frivolous litigation, to effectuate the policies of the Act, and to serve the public interest, we find that it would be just and proper to order respondent to reimburse the Board and the Union for their expenses incurred in the investigation, preparation, presentation and conduct of these cases, including the following costs and expenses incurred in both the Board and Court proceedings: reasonable counsel fees, salaries, witness fees, transcript and record costs, printing costs, travel expenses and per diem, and other reasonable costs and expenses.[29]

Under the rationale of *Tiidee,* a "frivolous" defense is one which obviously lacks merit or is not debatable, but is not one which fails simply upon the administrative law judge's resolutions of conflicting testimony. The NLRB policy set forth in *Tiidee* was approved by the Supreme Court in *NLRB v. Food Store Employees Local 347 (Heck's, Inc.)*[30] On remand in *Heck's,* the Board explained its attorneys' fees and litigation expense policy as evincing an

> intent to refrain from assessing litigation expenses against a respondent notwithstanding that the respondent may have been found to have engaged in clearly aggravated and pervasive misconduct or in the flagrant repetition of conduct previously found unlawful, where the defenses raised by that respondent are debatable rather than frivolous.[31]

The Board has regarded the payment of attorneys' fees by a respondent as a truly extraordinary expense. When such reimbursement has been requested, the Board for the most part has found either that the unfair labor practices were not flagrant or that the asserted defenses were not frivolous.[32] Accordingly, the requested remedy has not often been granted. In *J.P. Stevens Co.,*[33] however, the Board expanded its holding in *Tiidee* to cover what the Fourth Circuit termed a "narrow new category of cases"; it

---

[28] 194 N.L.R.B. 1234, 79 L.R.R.M. 1175 (1972).

[29] *Id.* at 1236–37, 79 L.R.R.M. at 1799.

[30] 417 U.S. 1, 86 L.R.R.M. 2209 (1974).

[31] 215 N.L.R.B. 765, 767, 88 L.R.R.M. 1049, 1051–52 (1974).

[32] *See, e.g.,* Kings Terrace Nursing Home, 227 N.L.R.B. 251, 94 L.R.R.M. 1081 (1976); East Bay Chevrolet, 242 N.L.R.B. 625 (1979), *enforced in relevant part,* 659 F.2d 1006, 1011, 108 L.R.R.M. 2846, 2849–50 (9th Cir. 1981); Vitek Elec., Inc., 268 N.L.R.B. 522, 115 L.R.R.M. 1075 (1984), *enforced in relevant part,* 763 F.2d 561, 572 n.15, 119 L.R.R.M. 2699, 2708–09 (3d Cir. 1985).

[33] 244 N.L.R.B. 407, 102 L.R.R.M. 1039 (1979).

required payment of litigation expenses by an employer that had pursued litigation which in itself had not been found frivolous but which was part of a pattern of disobedience and a policy of intransigence.[34] This decision was enforced by the Fourth Circuit, which found that the Board had sufficiently articulated its rationale for this expansion to a situation characterized by "flagrant, aggravated, persistent, and pervasive employer misconduct."[35] The decision of the Fourth Circuit was vacated by the Supreme Court,[36] however, and remanded for further consideration in light of *Summit Valley Industries, Inc. v. Carpenters.*[37] Because of the settlement between the Board and J.P. Stevens of all outstanding charges, neither the Fourth Circuit nor the Board had occasion to address the issue anew.[38] In a case decided after the Supreme Court's remand in *J.P. Stevens,* however, the Board directed that a respondent reimburse the Board for costs and expenses incurred in connection with the litigation, characterizing the respondent's asserted defenses as "patently frivolous" and noting its "long history of intransigence."[39]

Reimbursement for Organizing Expenses

In cases involving flagrant or persistent unfair labor practices, the Board has also been asked to require the offending employer to reimburse the union for losses in organizing expenses and dues. The litigation history of this remedy parallels that of requests for reimbursement of legal expenses. As a threshold matter, the Board normally will not order payment of organizing expenses and dues absent a showing that a respondent's defenses to unfair labor practice charges were frivolous and nondebatable.[40] But the Board will require a further showing that a nexus exists between the employer's unlawful conduct and the additional organizing expenses or

---

[34] *Id.* at 458–59.
[35] J.P. Stevens & Co. v. NLRB, 668 F.2d 767, 777, 109 L.R.R.M. 2345, 2352 (4th Cir. 1980).
[36] 458 U.S. 1118, 110 L.R.R.M. 2896 (1982).
[37] 456 U.S. 717, 110 L.R.R.M. 2441 (1982).
[38] *See* J.P. Stevens & Co., 268 N.L.R.B. 8, 114 L.R.R.M. 1241 (1983).
[39] Autoprod, Inc., 265 N.L.R.B. 331, 332, 111 L.R.R.M. 1521, 1522 (1982).
[40] *See, e.g.,* Hartz Mountain Corp., 228 N.L.R.B. 492, 96 L.R.R.M. 1589 (1977), *enforced sub nom.* District 65, Distributive Workers v. NLRB, 593 F.2d 1155, 99 L.R.R.M. 2640 (D.C. Cir. 1978); Ameri-Crete Ready Mix Corp., 207 N.L.R.B. 509, 84 L.R.R.M. 1628 (1978). Consistent with its treatment of litigation expenses, however, the Board has ordered an employer to pay union organizing expenses without a finding of nonfrivolous litigation. J.P. Stevens & Co., Inc., 244 N.L.R.B. 407, 102 L.R.R.M. 1039 (1979). The Fourth Circuit enforced this expansion of the Board's position with regard to organizing expenses in J.P. Stevens & Co. v. NLRB, 668 F.2d 767, 109 L.R.R.M. 2345 (4th Cir. 1980), but the opinion of the Court of Appeals was vacated by the Supreme Court. *See* n.36 *supra,* and accompanying text.

loss of dues to the union.[41] In practice, such a nexus may be difficult to establish and may prove too speculative to support an order.[42] Furthermore, when a union wins an election despite an employer's flagrant unfair labor practices, the Board (with court approval) has denied requests for organizing expenses and union dues and fees.[43]

Make-Whole Remedies

In cases where employers are found to have violated section 8(a)(5) by improperly refusing to bargain, unions often have requested that the Board provide a remedy which would make its members whole for the wages and other fringe benefits that might have accrued from the bargaining process had the employer bargained in good faith. In *Ex-Cell-O Corp.*,[44] the Board took the position that it does not have the statutory power to order such a remedy. In reaching this conclusion, the Board relied heavily on the Supreme Court's decision in *H.K. Porter Co. v. NLRB*,[45] where the Court held that, although the Board had the power to require the parties to negotiate, it was without power to compel a company or a union to agree to any substantive contractual provision. In *Ex-Cell-O*, the Board concluded that to order the monetary damages sought by the union, it would be required to speculate on how much the employer was prepared to give and how little the union was willing to take, and then to assume that a contract favorable to the union's members would result from the negotiations.

The District of Columbia Circuit has disagreed with the Board's holding in *Ex-Cell-O*.[46] In a series of cases, . . . it has held that the Board does possess the statutory authority to grant this make-whole remedy. But the court has never ordered the Board to implement this remedy, finding instead in all cases presented to it that the remedy was not appropriate because the employer's violation was debatable and not a "clear and flagrant" refusal to bargain for "patently frivolous" reasons.[47]

---

[41] Tiidee Prods., Inc., 194 N.L.R.B. 1284, 79 L.R.R.M. 1175 (1975).

[42] *See* Winn-Dixie Stores v. NLRB, 567 F.2d 1343, 97 L.R.R.M. 2866 (5th Cir. 1978), *enforcing,* 224 N.L.R.B. 190, 92 L.R.R.M. 1625 (1976).

[43] Electrical Workers (IUE) v. NLRB (Tiidee Prods., Inc.), 502 F.2d 349, 86 L.R.R.M. 2093 (D.C. Cir. 1974).

[44] 185 N.L.R.B. 107, 74 L.R.R.M. 1740 (1970).

[45] 397 U.S. 99, 73 L.R.R.M. 2561 (1970).

[46] International Union of Elec., Radio, and Mach. Workers v. NLRB (Tiidee Prods., Inc.), 426 F.2d 1243, 73 L.R.R.M. 2870 (D.C. Cir. 1970).

[47] *See* Ex-Cell-O Corp. v. NLRB, 449 F.2d 1058, 1064–65, 77 L.R.R.M. 2547, 2552 (D.C. Cir. 1971); Retail Clerks Local 1401 v. NLRB (Zinke's Foods, Inc.), 463 F.2d 816, 79 L.R.R.M. 2984, 2990 (D.C. Cir. 1972); Steelworkers v. NLRB (Quality Rubber Co.), 430 F.2d 519, 512–22, 74 L.R.R.M. 2747, 2749 (D.C. Cir. 1970).

The question of the statutory authority of the Board to fashion a make-whole remedy for an employer's illegal refusal to bargain has not been resolved by the Supreme Court. In *Lipman Motors Inc. v. NLRB*,[48] the Second Circuit refused to order this type of monetary relief, stating that the Board should not

> undertake the speculative adventure of fixing damages by 'determining' whether the parties would have reached an agreement if they had bargained in good faith and what the terms of that hypothetical agreement would have been.[49]

Other circuits have considered such make-whole remedies but have avoided ruling on the NLRB's statutory authority. In *Steelworkers v. NLRB (Metco, Inc.)*,[50] a majority of the Fifth Circuit found no need to consider the Board's statutory authority since the employer's objections to the union's certification were not frivolous and its litigation was not undertaken to delay collective bargaining. The Ninth Circuit has followed the same course in several cases.[51]

The Board has never accepted that it has the statutory authority to order this make-whole remedy. Thus, despite indications to the contrary from the District of Columbia Circuit in the early 1970s, the issue has largely remained dormant since that time.

---

[48] 451 F.2d 823, 78 L.R.R.M. 2808 (2d Cir. 1971).

[49] *Id.* at 829, 78 L.R.R.M. at 2813. The Supreme Court's disapproval of a court of appeals' "speculative" expansion of a Board-ordered remedy in Sure-Tan, Inc. v. NLRB, __ U.S. __, 116 L.R.R.M. 2857 (1984), lends support to the *Lipman Motors* analysis.

[50] 495 F.2d 1342, 86 L.R.R.M. 2984 (5th Cir. 1974).

[51] East Bay Chevrolet v. NLRB, 659 F.2d 1006, 1010, 108 L.R.R.M. 2846, 2849 (9th Cir. 1981).

CHAPTER XV

Penalties for Frivolous Appeals, Court Contempt, and Injunction Proceedings

The focus of this chapter is court proceedings and sanctions that supplement the Board's remedial powers. In it, we consider the use of penalties by the appellate courts to discourage frivolous appeals of NLRB orders. We also examine the contempt of court sanctions available for use against respondents who defy court-enforced Board orders. Further, we consider injunctions against certain union violations which Congress has designated so serious as to require the General Counsel of the Board to seek injunctive relief under section 10(1) of the Act if there is "reasonable cause to believe" that one of these violations is occurring. Next we discuss the increasingly used injunctions under section 10(j) of the Act, under which the Board may seek to preserve the status quo, protect the efficacy of its order, or to prevent harmful impact upon the public interest or the frustration of the purposes of the Act. Finally we discuss injunction under sections 10(e) and 10(f) of the Act.

THE SMITH AND WESSON PENALTY
FOR FRIVOLOUS APPEALS

The courts of appeal have indicated irritation at frivolous appeals on Board orders and have shown a willingness to attach penalties to such conduct. In *NLRB v. Smith & Wesson,*[1] the First Circuit held that the Board's findings were clearly supported by substantial evidence of record, and that the employer's resistance to its order was frivolous. It stated, "some penalty should attach to taking up our time with such a meritless contention." The court not only

---

[1] 424 F.2d 1072, 1073, 74 L.R.R.M. 2173, 2174 (1st Cir. 1970).

awarded the Board its regular costs, but added the sum of $250 for expenses.[2] The Fifth Circuit in *Monroe Auto Equipment Co. v. NLRB*[3] held that where the law was clearly contrary to the employer's position, it was appropriate under Rule 38 of the Federal Rules of Appellate Procedure[4] to direct the assessment of double costs and a reasonable award of attorneys' fees.

While the Seventh Circuit has recognized the availablity of such a penalty, it refused to award it where the outcome turned on credibility resolutions, and because the court did not want to chill the assertion of rights which were held in good faith.[5] The Ninth Circuit originally declined to assess the penalty but reserved the right to do so on appropriate future circumstances.[6] Approximately seven months later, it assessed double costs against the employer in *NLRB v. Catalina Yachts.*[7] The Eighth Circuit, in *Royal Typewriter Co. v. NLRB,*[8] sustained the propriety of such penalties but refused to upset the Board's denial of legal expenses and costs to the union, ruling that it was in the discretion of the Board as to whether to award such penalties for frivolous litigation on the part of the employer, and that it would not overrule the exercise of Board discretion in that situation unless the litigation was so frivolous as to enable the reviewing court to find an abuse of discretion.

The Supreme Court's 1982 decision in *J.P. Stevens,*[9] however, casts some doubt on the validity of these decisions. In *J.P. Stevens,* the Fourth Circuit had characterized the employer's litigation matter as "meritless but arguably non-frivolous." Nonetheless it sustained the Board's order of litigation and organizational expenses to the union and costs of appeals litigation to the Board, finding such expenses were justified in cases of "flagrant, aggravated, persistent,

---

[2] *Accord,* NLRB v. United Shoe Mach. Corp., 445 F.2d 633, 635, 77 L.R.R.M 2719 (1st Cir. 1971); General Tire & Rubber Co. v. NLRB, 451 F.2d 257, 259, 78 L.R.R.M. 2836 (1st Cir. 1971); NLRB v. Ramada Inns, Inc., 190 N.L.R.B. 450, 77 L.R.R.M. 1681, 1971, *enforced,* 79 L.R.R.M. 2927, 2928 (1st Cir. 1972); NLRB v. Hijos de Ricardo Vela, Inc., 475 F.2d 58, 82 L.R.R.M. 2967, 2970 (1st Cir. 1973); NLRB v. Bedford Discounters, Inc., 484 F.2d 923, 84 L.R.R.M. 2332 (1st Cir. 1973); Hedison Mfg. Co. v. NLRB, 643 F.2d 32, 106 L.R.R.M. 2897 (1st Cir. 1981).

[3] 511 F.2d 611, 89 L.R.R.M. 2104, 2106 (5th Cir. 1975).

[4] Rule 38 of the Federal Rules of Appellate Procedure provides that: "If a court of appeals shall determine that an appeal is frivolous, it may award just damages and single or double costs to the appellee."

[5] NLRB v. F & F Labs., Inc., 517 F.2d 551, 89 L.R.R.M. 2549 (7th Cir. 1975).

[6] NLRB v. Sauk Valley Mfg. Co., 486 F.2d 1127, 84 L.R.R.M. 2679 (9th Cir. 1973); East Wind Enters. v. NLRB, 664 F.2d 754, 109, L.R.R.M. 2974 (9th Cir. 1981).

[7] 679 F.2d 180, 110 L.R.R.M. 2843 (9th Cir 1982).

[8] 533 F.2d 1030, 92 L.R.R.M. 2013 (8th Cir. 1976).

[9] J.P. Stevens & Co. v. NLRB, 458 U.S. 1118, 110 L.R.R.M. 2896 (1982).

and pervasive employer misconduct."[10] The Supreme Court upon certiorari, however, vacated and remanded to the court, directing it to reconsider the case under its recent *Summit Valley Industries v. Local 112*[11] decision.

The *Summit Valley* case involved a claim for attorneys' fees for prior Board cases in a section 303 action. In that decision, the Supreme Court ruled that the "American Rule" be applied in the labor situation. The court noted that under the American Rule, attorneys' fees were not considered "damages" and were only collected under a few limited exceptions, where specifically authorized by Congress, or as provided under contract between the parties. The court noted that absent statutory authority or an enforceable contract provision, the only exceptions to such awarding of attorneys' fees were in situations of bad faith or of willful disobedience of a court order. Since the remand in the *J.P. Stevens* case, no court has specifically dealt with or analyzed the question of the awarding of attorneys' fees for frivolous appeal, and the real meaning or effect of the Supreme Court decision is unknown. The Fourth Circuit will never have the opportunity to issue an explanation upon remand of the *J.P. Stevens* case, since that case was part of the settlement of all outstanding charges entered into between the NLRB and J.P. Stevens.[12] As part of the settlement, J.P. Stevens did agree to pay one million dollars to the charging party union over a two-year period, apparently to cover litigation and organizational costs resulting from the unfair labor practice charges in all of the cases settled.

CONTEMPT OF COURT PROCEEDINGS

Once a court enforces an order of the Board, that order becomes a lawful decree of a court which has the inherent power to enforce compliance through the civil contempt sanction, upon request of the Board.[13] Thus, if a respondent either refuses to comply with affirmative requirement of a particular order or commits a violation of its terms he may be subject to contempt of court proceedings.

---

[10] J.P. Stevens & Co. v. NLRB, 668 F.2d 767, 109 L.R.R.M. 2345 (4th Cir. 1982).
[11] 456 U.S. 717, 110 L.R.R.M. 2441 (1982).
[12] J.P. Stevens & Co., 268 N.L.R.B. 8, 114 L.R.R.M. 1241 (1983).
[13] *See, e.g.,* NLRB v. Sheet Metal Workers, Local No. 80, 491 F.2d 1017, 85 L.R.R.M. 2490 (6th Cir. 1974) (violation of a consent judgment ordering union to cease running a hiring hall in a discriminatory manner); Teamsters, Local 745 (Farmers Co-op. Gin Ass'n) v. NLRB, 500 F.2d 768, 86 L.R.R.M. 2110 (D.C. Cir. 1974) (employer violation of a bargaining order); NLRB v. J.P. Stevens & Co., 464 F.2d 1326, 80 L.R.R.M. 3126 (2d Cir. 1972); NLRB v. J.P. Stevens & Co., 81 L.R.R.M. 2285 (2d Cir. 1972); NLRB v. Mooney Aircraft, Inc., 366 F.2d 809, 61 L.R.R.M. 2163 (5th Cir. 1966).

This makes available powerful sanctions beyond the purely remedial power of the Board.

"In a civil contempt proceeding, the company's intent or willfulness is not at issue, but the only issue is whether there has been, in fact, compliance with a court's order."[14] The employer's willingness to comply and a lack of any flagrance of violation are factors to be considered in fashioning the appropriate remedy for the contempt, which must be proved by clear and convincing evidence, but not beyond a reasonable doubt.[15]

It is well established that the courts "should impose whatever sanctions are necessary under the circumstances to grant full remedial relief, to coerce the contemnor into compliance with [the] court's order, and to fully compensate the complainant for losses sustained."[16] Thus, in NLRB-related civil contempt proceedings, the courts will routinely order respondents to pay the Board all fees, costs, and expenditures incurred during the contempt proceedings. These include counsel fees incurred in investigation, preparation, presentation, and final disposition of the contempt case.[17] Further, in order to ensure that the respondent complies with the terms of the decree, the courts consistently order a fine for any further violation plus a fine for each day each violation continues. For example, in *NLRB v. Amalgamated Local Union 355 (Robin Ford)*,[18] the court anticipated future violations and ordered compliance fines of $10,000 from the union and $2,000 from each of its officers. Also in that case, if such future violations were of a continuing nature, the union and its officers would have been required to pay fines of $1,000 and $200 per day, respectively.[19] Another illustration is found in *NLRB v. Johnson Mfg. Co.*,[20] where an employer who had refused to bargain in good faith with the union was fined $50,000, to be

---

[14] Florida Steel Corp. v. NLRB, 648 F.2d 233, 107 L.R.R.M. 3043 (5th Cir. 1981).

[15] NLRB v. John Zinc Co., 551 F.2d 799, 94 L.R.R.M. 3067 (10th Cir. 1977).

[16] NLRB v. Union Nacional de Trabajadores, 611 F.2d 926; 103 L.R.R.M. 2176 (1st Cir. 1979); Florida Steel Corp. v. NLRB, 648 F.2d 233, 107 L.R.R.M. 3043 (5th Cir. 1981); NLRB v. Vander Wal, 316 F.2d 631, 52 L.R.R.M. 2761, 2763 (9th Cir. 1963), *accord*, United States v. United Mine Workers, 330 U.S. 258, 19 L.R.R.M. 2346 (1947).

[17] NLRB v. Union Nacional de Trabajadores, 611 F.2d 926, 103 L.R.R.M. 2176 (1st Cir. 1979); Florida Steel Corp. v. NLRB, 648 F.2d 233, 107 L.R.R.M. 3043 (5th Cir. 1981). *See, e.g.,* NLRB v. Nickey Chevrolet Sales, Inc., 76 L.R.R.M. 2849, 2853 (7th Cir. 1971); NLRB v. J.P. Stevens & Co., 464 F.2d 1326, 80 L.R.R.M. 3126 (2d Cir. 1972); NLRB v. Clinton Packing Co., 527 F.2d 560, 91 L.R.R.M. 2560 (8th Cir. 1976).

[18] 77 L.R.R.M. 2989 (E.D.N.Y. 1971).

[19] *See also* NLRB v. Schill Steel Prods., Inc., 480 F.2d 586, 83 L.R.R.M. 2669, 2672 (5th Cir. 1973); NLRB v. Sheet Metal Workers Local No. 80, 491 F.2d 1017, 85 L.R.R.M. 2490 (6th Cir. 1974); NLRB v. Ambrose Distrib. Co., 382 F.2d 92, 65 L.R.R.M. 3057 (9th Cir. 1967).

[20] 511 F.2d 153, 88 L.R.R.M. 3553 (5th Cir. 1975).

returned if the employer presented satisfactory evidence of compliance with the new court order within sixty days. Similarly, in *NLRB v. F.M. Reeves & Sons*,[21] the court enforced a fine of $1,000 for the employer's past acts of contempt.

In a case involving an "unusually intransigent" union found guilty of civil contempt of the Board order, the court accepted the recommendation of a Special Master appointed to hear evidence not only to assess attorneys' fees and costs to the NLRB, but also to impose prospective compliance fines on the union to deter future violations.[22] It is interesting to note that in this case the union attempted to claim that there was no contempt since it had entered into a private settlement with the charging party company. The court, however, noted that a private settlement between a union and a company would not moot the Board's contempt charges against the union.

In contempt proceedings involving employer refusals to bargain, the Fifth Circuit has devised remedies which surpass those employed by the Board in similar violations. In *NLRB v. Schill Steel Products, Inc.*,[23] the court ordered the employer to bargain until full agreement or bona fide impasse was reached. The existence of such impasse was to be decided by the court, and a failure to find such an impasse was to be considered a failure to bargain in good faith. Such a failure would subject the employer to compliance fines of $5,000 for the violation, plus a fine of $1,000 for each day the violation continued. In addition, the employer was not permitted to refuse to meet with the union at reasonable times, or to withdraw recognition from the union until further order of the court. Bargaining sessions were to be held at least fifteen hours per week, unless the union gave written permission otherwise. Sworn reports signed both by the employer and the union were to be filed with the court clerk and the Board every thirty days detailing the nature and course of the bargaining. If the Board determined that the employer was not bargaining in good faith, it was required to submit a report and supporting brief to the court and propose appropriate sanctions. If the employer was found to have engaged in bad faith bargaining, the compliance fines would then be imposed.

A further alternative available to the court in dealing with the recalcitrant violator is to issue a writ of body attachment under

---

[21] 273 F.2d 710, 47 L.R.R.M. 2480 (10th Cir. 1961).

[22] NLRB v.Union Nacional de Trabajadores, 611 F.2d 926, 103 L.R.R.M. 2176 (1st Cir. 1979).

[23] 480 F.2d 586, 83 L.R.R.M. 2669, 2670–2671 (5th Cir. 1973). *See also* NLRB v. Johnson Mfg. Co., 511 F.2d 153, 88 L.R.R.M. 3553 (5th Cir. 1975); NLRB v. J.P. Stevens & Co., Inc. 563 F.2d 8, 96 L.R.R.M. 2150 (2d Cir. 1977).

which the appropriate officer or agent of the offending respondent will be confined to jail until the court's decree is obeyed.[24] Finally, if it can be shown that the respondent "knowingly, willfully and intentionally" violated the court's decree, the Board may petition the court to find the respondent criminally liable for his conduct.[25] Sentences for criminal contempt include monetary fines and imprisonment. Contempt of court proceedings therefore provide powerful sanctions to use when employers and unions violate Board orders which have been enforced by the courts of appeals.[26]

SECTION 10(1) INJUNCTIONS

The National Labor Relations Act provides certain exemptions to the Norris-LaGuardia Act's[27] general prohibition of injunctions in labor disputes.[28] Section 10(1) describes various conditions under which the regional office or attorney, on behalf of the Board, may apply to the appropriate United States District Court for injunctive relief. Injunctions issued under this section are by no means designed to provide a final and fair labor practice remedy; rather they are designed to give provisional relief which expires upon the issuance of a final Board order.[29] The provisional nature of these injunctions consummates the intent of Congress to give the Board the primary authority to remedy unfair labor practices. Even though these injunctions do not constitute remedies of the Board

---

[24] *See* NLRB v. Savoy Laundry, Inc., 354 F.2d 78, 61 L.R.R.M. 2021, 2023 (2d Cir. 1965); and NLRB v. Schill Steel Prods., Inc., 480 F.2d 586, 83 L.R.R.M. 2669, 2672 (5th Cir. 1973).

[25] *See, e.g.,* Winn-Dixie Stores, Inc., 386 F.2d 309, 66 L.R.R.M. 2427 (5th Cir. 1967); NLRB v. Star Metal Mfg. Co., 187 F.2d 856, 27 L.R.R.M. 2437 (3rd Cir. 1951).

[26] A description of the NLRA contempt process and an analysis of its effectiveness can be found in Bartosic & Lanoff, *Escalating the Struggle Against Taft-Hartley Contemnors,* 39 U. CHI. L. REV. 255 (1972).

[27] 47 Stat. 70 (1932), 29 U.S.C. §§ 101–105 (1976).

[28] *See generally* § 10(h) of the NLRA [29 U.S.C. § 160(h)] which provides that:

> When granting appropriate temporary relief or a restraining order, or making and entering a decree enforcing, modifying, and enforcing as so modified, or setting aside in whole or in part an order of the Board, as provided in this section, the jurisdiction of courts sitting in equity shall not be limited by the Act entitled "An Act to amend the Judicial Code and to define and limit the jurisdiction of courts sitting in equity, and for other purposes," approved March 23, 1932 (U.S.C., Supp. VII, tit. 29, §§ 101–115).

[29] Section 10(1) permits the court to enter appropriate injunctive relief "pending final adjudication of the Board with respect to such matter." *See also* Sears, Roebuck & Co. v. Painters, Local 419, 397 U.S. 655, 658–659, 74 L.R.R.M. 2001, 2002–2003 (1970). *Cf.* Building & Constr. Trades Council of Philadelphia v. Samoff, 414 U.S. 808, 84 L.R.R.M. 2421 (1973); Vincent v. Teamsters, Local 294, 424 F.2d 124, 73 L.R.R.M. 2983 (2d Cir. 1970).

itself, it is appropriate to mention them here because their use may preserve the status quo and thus complement the Board's remedial authority. Section 10(1) provides in part that:

> Whenever it is charged that any person has engaged in an unfair labor practice within the meaning of paragraph (4)(A), (B), or (C) of section 8(b), or section 8(e) or section 8(b)(7), the preliminary investigation of such charge shall be made forthwith and given priority over all other cases except cases of like character in the office where it is filed or to which it is referred. If, after such investigation, the officer or regional attorney to whom the matter may be referred has reasonable cause to believe such charge is true and that a complaint should issue, *he shall,* on behalf of the Board, petition any district court of the United States (including the district court of the United States for the District of Columbia) within any district where the unfair labor practice in question has occurred, is alleged to have occurred, or wherein such person resides or transacts business, for appropriate injunctive relief pending the final adjudication of the Board with respect to such matter. Upon the filing of any such petition the district court shall have jurisdiction to grant such injunctive relief or temporary restraining order as it deems just and proper, notwithstanding any other provision of law: *Provided further,* That no temporary restraining order shall be issued without notice unless a petition alleges that substantial irreparable injury to the charging party will be unavoidable and such temporary restraining order shall be effective for no longer than five days and will become void at the expiration of such period. . . .[30]

Thus, section 10(1)[31] sets forth situations in which the NLRB regional officer is required to seek injunctive relief.[32] The Board must allege the following: (1) an unfair labor practice charge has been filed;[33] (2) a preliminary investigation of the charge has been undertaken;[34] (3) there is reasonable cause to believe that one of

---

[30] 29 U.S.C. § 160(8) (emphasis added).

[31] In fiscal year 1984, the NLRB's General Counsel sought 95 section 10(1) injunctions. This compares with 233 sought in 1974. *See* 39 NLRB ANN. REP. 241 (1974).

[32] Schauffler v. Highway Truck Drivers, 196 F. Supp. 471, 47 L.R.R.M. 2400 (E.D. Pa. 1960) is the only case on the issue of who exercises the ultimate responsibility for making the reasonable cause determination. It is generally assumed that the right or the power to petition for an injunction under § 10(1) rests in the General Counsel. It is clear that the Board itself plays no part whatsoever in that determination. In that case the court ruled that the responsibility for that determination, and for filing under § 10(1), rests in the regional officer (in that case, the designated Regional Director), not the General Counsel.

[33] *See* LeBaron v. Los Angeles Bldg. & Constr. Trades Council, 84 F. Supp. 629, 24 L.R.R.M. 2131 (S.D. Cal. 1949), *aff'd mem.*, 185 F.2d 405, 27 L.R.R.M. 2184 (9th Cir. 1950), *vacated on other grounds,* 342 U.S. 802, 28 L.R.R.M. 2625 (1951).

[34] Since a preliminary investigation is a prerequisite to injunctive relief under § 10(1), LeBaron v. Kern County Farm Labor Union, Local 218, 80 F. Supp. 156, 23 L.R.R.M. 2077 (S.D. Cal. 1948), the Board must comply with its own procedures and requirements or face dismissal of its suit. *See* Madden v. Masters, Mates & Pilots, Local 3, 259 F.2d 297, 42 L.R.R.M. 2792 (7th Cir. 1978). Nevertheless, neither the

the specified violations has occurred; (4) the evidence warrants granting relief; (5) the court has jurisdiction; and (6) the parties are subject to the Act.

Although the Board must establish a prima facie case, this may be done merely by producing evidence sufficient to lead a reasonable person to believe that an unfair labor practice has occured.[35] Nevertheless, it must be remembered that section 10(1) injunctive remedies have been statutorily defined to apply to certain specified unfair labor practices. Consequently, any request for relief must clearly reflect evidence of those illegal acts to avoid the possibility of enjoining lawful conduct.[36]

The regional director need not establish that there was, in fact, a violation, or absolute validity to his legal theory; he need only demonstrate a reasonable cause to believe that the elements of an unfair labor practice are present.[37] Further, a court may even direct the issuance of a section 10(1) injunction if it finds "significant

---

failure of the Board to allege that a preliminary investigation had been conducted, McLeod v. Local 239, Teamsters, 180 F. Supp. 679, 45 L.R.R.M. 2302 (E.D.N.Y. 1959) (technical defect in Board's petition which could be readily cured), nor proof as to the sufficiency of the investigation, see Building & Constr. Trades Council of Metro District v. Alpert, 302 F.2d 594, 50 L.R.R.M. 2154 (1st Cir. 1962) (allegations as to the scope, nature and extent of the investigation not required); Madden v. Hod Carriers, Local 41, 277 F.2d 688, 46 L.R.R.M. 2181 (7th Cir. 1960), cert. denied, 364 U.S. 863, 46 L.R.R.M. 3091 (1960) (union request for production of files and records pertaining to an investigation denied), may be raised by a respondent union as a defense.

[35] See, e.g., Hull v. Teamsters, Local 24, 148 F. Supp. 145, 39 L.R.R.M. 2370 (N.D. Ohio 1957); LeBaron v. Los Angeles Bldg. & Constr. Trades Council, 84 F. Supp. 629, 24 L.R.R.M. 2131 (S.D. Cal. 1949); Styles v. Local 760, Elec. Workers, 80 F. Supp. 119, 22 L.R.R.M. 2446 (E.D. Tenn. 1948).

[36] See Potter v. Houston Gulf Coast Bldg. Trades Council, 482 F.2d 837, 841, 83 L.R.R.M. 3042, 3044 (5th Cir. 1973), wherein the Fifth Circuit stated that "whenever possible, a grant of equitable relief should be carefully tailored so as to permit the continuation of primary activities while stamping out the illegal secondary conduct and its deleterious impact." This view is exemplified by the district court decision in Kaynard v. Local 707, Teamsters, 73 L.R.R.M. 2575 (E.D.N.Y. 1969). In that case, the court enjoined union-sponsored picketing where one of its primary purposes was recognitional, despite the claim that it was in support of discharged employees to gain reinstatement. The court, however, refused to grant a blanket injunction against picketing, noting that the discharged employees retained the right to picket on their own behalf in order to gain reemployment.

On the other hand, when union activity has both an unlawful, as well as lawful, objective, it will be enjoined. See Greene v. Bangor Bldg. Trades Union, 165 F. Supp. 902, 42 L.R.R.M. 2713 (D. Me. 1958); Getreu v. Teamsters, Local 327, 37 L.R.R.M. 2133 (N.D. Tenn. 1955).

[37] Hirsch v. Bldg. & Constr. Trades Council of Philadelphia, 530 F.2d 298, 91 L.R.R.M. 2438 (3d Cir. 1976); Squillacote v. International Brotherhood of Teamsters, Local 34, 561 F.2d 31, 95 L.R.R.M. 2977 (7th Cir. 1977), holding that the legal theory underlying the unfair labor practice should be substantial and not frivolous.

possibility" that the picketing will violate the Act,[38] or that it cannot be said "that there is not a reasonable basis upon which the NLRB would be able to sustain its charge before the Board." [39]

The "reasonable cause to believe" standard of section 10(1) is applicable only to the unfair labor practices charged.[40] Factual proof of all other matters, such as jurisdiction over the parties sought to be restrained, is required.[41] For example, although an international union may be made a proper party to the suit,[42] it cannot be made responsible for a local's misconduct without evidence that the international participated, authorized, ratified, or engaged in the unlawful conduct.[43] Finally, relief will be granted where the court

---

[38] Bennett v. Local 456, Teamsters, 459 F. Supp. 223, 99 L.R.R.M. 3109 (S.D.N.Y. 1978).

[39] Hendricks v. Amalgamated Meat Cutters, 555 F.2d 175, 95 L.R.R.M. 2095 (8th Cir. 1977); Humphrey v. International Longshoremen's Ass'n, 548 F.2d 494, 94 L.R.R.M. 2374 (4th Cir. 1977).

[40] In mandatory suits pursuant to § 10(1), the "reasonable cause to believe" standard is limited to questions concerning the alleged unfair labor practice and whether a party should be enjoined; it is an insufficient standard to establish whether such a party is subject to the Act. LeBaron v. Kern County Farm Labor Union, 80 F. Supp. 156, 23 L.R.R.M. 2077 (S.D. Cal. 1948). On the other hand, the standard has been applied to questions as to whether a group of employees who engaged in secondary activities was a labor organization within the meaning of the Act. *Compare* Madden v. Masters, Mates, & Pilots, Local 28, 166 F. Supp. 862, 42 L.R.R.M. 2793, (N.D. Ill. 1958) (no reasonable cause to believe that organization composed exclusively of supervisory personnel was subject to the Act), *with* Madden v. Masters, Mates, & Pilots, Local 47, 259 F.2d 297, 42 L.R.R.M. 2742 (7th Cir. 1958) (reasonable cause to believe employee organization subject to the Act where its members were employed to give technical advice and assistance).

[41] A court's jurisdiction in § 10(1) proceedings is not dependent upon the dollar volume of commerce affected, IBEW, Local 501 v. NLRB, 341 U.S. 694, 28 L.R.R.M. 2115 (1951); but rather is based upon the question of whether interstate commerce is affected by the allegedly unlawful activities in question. Kaynard v. Nassau and Suffolk Bldg. & Constr. Trades Council, 61 L.R.R.M. 2674 (E.D.N.Y. 1966); *cf.* Local 74 Carpenters v. NLRB, 341 U.S. 947, 28 L.R.R.M 2121 (1951). *But see* Madden v. Teamsters, Local 364, 40 L.R.R.M. 2595 (N.D. Ind. 1957) (injunction denied where court doubted Board would assert jurisdiction under current monetary standards). *Compare* McLeod v. Local 1199, Drug and Hosp. Union (666 Cosmetics, Inc.), 80 L.R.R.M. 2503 (S.D.N.Y. 1972), *with* McLeod v. Building Service Employees Union, Local 32E, 227 F. Supp. 242, 55 L.R.R.M. 2380 (S.D.N.Y. 1964).

[42] Brown v. Oil & Chem. Workers, 80 F. Supp. 708, 23 L.R.R.M. 2016 (N.D. Cal. 1948). *Compare* Matson Navigation Co. v. Seafarers Union, 100 F. Supp. 730, 29 L.R.R.M. 2364 (D. Md. 1951) (supervisors' union, ordinarily outside the jurisdiction of the Act, will be enjoined where it is acting as a "front" for a national labor federation which is subject to the Act), *with* Humphrey v. Local 639, Teamsters, 369 F. Supp. 730, 86 L.R.R.M. 2968 (D. Md. 1974) (fact that mixed unit composed of guards and other employees is noncertifiable does not render it immune to injunction). *See also* Alpert v. International Typographical Union, 161 F. Supp. 427, 41 L.R.R.M. 2704 (D. Mass. 1958), discussed at note 53, *infra*, for an explanation of the rationale for making internationals responsible for the acts of their locals.

[43] Sperry v. Operating Engineers, Local 6-6A-6B, 43 L.R.R.M. 2167 (W.D. Mo. 1958).

deems it "just and proper" [44] and where its denial may result in irreparable injury [45] either to the charging party [46] or to the public interest. [47]

While the district court, under section 10(1), may prohibit further strikes or picketing to protect the status quo, it is improper for a court to issue a further order allocating work among competing groups since that is not necessary to preserve the status quo, and the authority to assign work under the Act is the responsibility of the Board, not of the Court. [48]

SECTION 10(j) INJUNCTIONS

Unlike section 10(1), the provisions of section 10(j) are not mandatory, but rather grant the Board the discretionary power to apply to a district court "for appropriate temporary relief," and authorize the court to grant such relief "as it deems just and proper." [49]

---

[44] Douds v. Local 24368, Wire & Metal Lathers, 86 F. Supp. 542, 24 L.R.R.M. 2487 (S.D.N.Y. 1949).

[45] *E.g.,* Goldfarb v. Rochester State Bd. of the Amalgamated Clothing Workers, 85 L.R.R.M. 2622 (W.D.N.Y. 1974). In *Goldfarb,* unlawful picketing by the clothing workers, who were engaged in a bitter organizational struggle at Farah Mfg. Co., directed at a retailer, subjected the neutral to "irreparable damage" by interference with its business "and by damage to its good name [*i.e.,* good will], a critical element to a major retailer."
See also Douds v. ILGWU, Local 66, 124 F. Supp. 919, 34 L.R.R.M. 2540 (S.D.N.Y. 1954); and Getreu v. District 50, Mine Workers, 30 L.R.R.M. 2048 (E.D. Tenn. 1952). In both of these cases, the court determined that a union seeking to force an employer to recognize it, by engaging in work stoppages or picketing, despite the valid certification of a rival union, causes the employer irreparable harm.

[46] *See* Douds v. Milk Drivers & Dairy Employees, Local 584, 154 F. Supp. 222, 40 L.R.R.M. 2669 (2d Cir. 1957), *stay denied,* 154 F. Supp. 222, 40 L.R.R.M. 2673 (2d Cir. 1957), wherein the Second Circuit denied the union's request for a stay of a district court injunction where such a request, if granted, would have compelled the charging employers either to yield to the union's demands or to go out of business.

[47] Cosentino v. Longshoremen (ILA), 107 F. Supp. 235, 30 L.R.R.M. 2683 (D.P.R. 1952) (economic life of Puerto Rico threatened by Longshoremen's attempt to obtain control of all organized labor on island); Brown v. Roofers, Local 40, 86 F. Supp. 50, 24 L.R.R.M. 2472 (N.D. Cal. 1949) (jurisdictional strike involving rights of six craftsmen properly enjoined to permit four to five hundred other employees to remain on job to complete public housing project).

[48] Cunard v. Local 282, Int'l Brotherhood, 576 F.2d 471, 98 L.R.R.M. 2569 (2d Cir. 1978).

[49] The provisions of § 10(j) [29 U.S.C. § 160(j)] are as follows:

> The Board shall have power, upon issuance of a complaint as provided in subsection (b) charging that any person has engaged in or is engaging in an unfair labor practice, to petition any district court of the United States (including the District Court of the United States in the District of Columbia), within any district wherein the unfair labor practice in question is alleged to have occurred or wherein such person resides or transacts business, for approriate temporary relief or restraining order. Upon the filing of any such

Under section 10(j) the Board's petition must allege that the following conditions exist; (1) an unfair labor practice charge has been filed; [50] (2) a complaint has been issued, [51] (3) the facts presented support the charge; (4) there is a likelihood that the unfair labor practice will continue unless restrained; (5) the district court has jurisdiction; [52] and (6) the persons sought to be restrained are subject to the Act. [53] Of course, the primary prerequisites are whether the unlawful conduct, as a matter of law, constitutes an unfair labor practice and whether the record shows a reasonable probability that the acts alleged were in fact committed. As a matter of proof, the General Counsel must first establish reasonable cause to believe that the statute has been violated. [54] As the Eighth Circuit indicated

---

petition the court shall cause notice thereof to be served upon such person, and thereupon shall have jurisdiction to grant to the Board such temporary relief or restraining order as it deems just and proper.

The Board sought § 10(j) injunctions on eighteen occasions in fiscal year 1974. *See* 39 NLRB ANN. REP. 341 (1974). In 1982, 1983, and 1984, the Board sought § 10(j) injunctions on 53, 83, and 30 occasions, respectively. A thorough review of the use of the § 10(j) injunction during the terms of former General Counsel Peter G. Nash can be found in the *Report of the NLRB General Counsel on Section 10(j) Injunction Proceedings under Taft-Hartley Act in Period from August 1971 to July 1975.* 90 L.R.R.M. 12–37 (1975); DAILY LAB. REP. No. 161 (BNA, 1975).

[50] *Cf.* Douds v. Longshoremen, ILA, 147 F. Supp. 103, 39 L.R.R.M. 2110 (S.D.N.Y. 1956), *aff'd*, 241 F.2d 278, 39 L.R.R.M. 2388 (2d Cir. 1957). A union contention that a complaint based on a defective charge precluded the granting of jurisdiction was rejected on the grounds that the initial defect, admittedly a technicality, was cured by subsequent events.

[51] *See, e.g.,* Kaynard v. Bagel Bakers Council of Greater N.Y., 68 L.R.R.M. 2140 (E.D.N.Y. 1968); Reynolds v. Marlene Indus. Corp., 250 F. Supp. 722, 61 L.R.R.M. 2342 (S.D.N.Y. 1966); Evans v. Typographical Union, 76 F. Supp. 881, 21 L.R.R.M. 2375 (S.D. Ind. 1948).

[52] The courts have been rather lenient in terms of the requisite notice which is afforded to charged parties under the terms of the Act. *Compare* Reynolds v. Marlene Indus. Corp., 250 F. Supp. 724, 63 L.R.R.M. 2097 (S.D.N.Y. 1966) (service of process upon president of subsidiaries sufficient to bind loosely integrated company), *with* Douds v. Anheuser-Busch, 28 L.R.R.M. 2277 (D.N.J. 1951) (sufficient notice given where Board agent rather than federal marshall served process on respondent employer).

[53] *See* Kaynard v. Bagel Bakers Council of Greater N.Y., 68 L.R.R.M. 2140 (E.D.N.Y. 1968) (injunction issued against employer association properly extended to include successor member); Alpert v. International Typographical Union, 161 F. Supp. 427, 41 L.R.R.M. 2704 (D. Mass. 1958) (international union, which approved unlawful strike by member local union, was proper party defendent in injunction suit). The *Alpert* case is particularly important because it prevents an international union, which has supported illegal practices by one of its locals, from escaping all liability for its misconduct. In effect, the international is made a surety for the observance of the injunction by the local, which may be virtually judgment-proof in any subsequent contempt proceedings.

[54] Squillacote v. Local 248, 534 F.2d 734, 92 L.R.R.M. 2089 (7th Cir. 1976); Eisenberg v. Wellington Hall Nursing Home, 651 F.2d 902, 107 L.R.R.M. 2958 (3d Cir. 1981);

in *Minnesota Mining & Manufacturing Co. v. Meter*,[55] when both of these questions have been answered in the affirmative, a district court may properly assume jurisdiction to entertain a request for injunctive relief.[56]

It is now well established that once a complaint is issued, the regional director is entitled to injunctive relief even though the matter is shortly to go to trial before an administrative law judge.[57] Where the court is persuaded it is just and proper, it can issue a temporary restraining order [58] without a full hearing on the issues. However, even though the court has issued a preliminary restraining order without a full hearing at a prior occasion, it will not follow with a temporary injunction if after hearing it finds that there is no reasonable cause to believe that the respondent had, in fact, violated the Act.[59]

Once the Board has established that there is reasonable cause to believe that the Act has been violated, it must then demonstrate that an injunction would be "just and proper" under the circumstances. Pursuant to this criteria, injunctions have been issued on various grounds: to prevent the frustration of the purposes of the Act; [60] to preserve or restore the status quo pending final adjudication by the Board; [61] to probe the efficacy of the Board's final

---

Kaynard v. Palby Lingerie, 625 F.2d 1047, 104 L.R.R.M. 2897 (2d Cir. 1980); Boive v. Pilot Freight, 515 F.2d 1185, 89 L.R.R.M. 2908 (5th Cir. 1975), *cert. denied* 426 U.S. 934, 92 L.R.R.M. 2768 (1976); Angle v. Sachs, 382 F.2d 655 (10th Cir. 1967).

[55] 385 F.2d 265, 269, 66 L.R.R.M. 2444, 2447 (8th Cir. 1967).

[56] *See also* McLeod v. Constr. Workers, Local 147, 292 F.2d 358, 48 L.R.R.M. 2655 (2d Cir. 1961); Elliott v. Dubois Chemicals, Inc., 201 F. Supp. 1, 50 L.R.R.M. 2279 (N.D. Tex. 1962); Jaffee v. Newspaper and Mail Deliverers Union of N.Y., 97 F. Supp. 443, 27 L.R.R.M. 2583 (S.D.N.Y. 1951).

[57] Fuchs v. Hood Indus., Inc., 590 F.2d 395, 100 L.R.R.M. 2547 (1st Cir. 1979).

[58] Squillacote v. Local 248, 534 F.2d 734, 92 L.R.R.M. 2089 (7th Cir. 1976).

[59] Hendrix v. American Stores Packing Co., 113 L.R.R.M. 2036 (D. Neb. 1983). In the *American Stores* case, the district court judge was, in fact, so upset that in his decision denying the temporary injunction he specifically found that in his opinion it was the charging party union that had refused to bargain in good faith over the plant closure, concluding that the union members had been misled and that it was the bargaining committee of the union that had placed the company in a position where it could not continue to operate and "brought the certain result of the union members at Lincoln going jobless."

[60] Angle v. Sachs, 382 F.2d 655, 659, 66 L.R.R.M. 2111, 2114 (10th Cir. 1967); Minnesota Mining and Mfg. Co. v. Meter, 385 F.2d 265, 272, 66 L.R.R.M. 2444 (8th Cir. 1967); Jaffee v. Henry Heide, Inc., 115 F. Supp. 52, 58, 31 L.R.R.M. 2634 (S.D.N.Y. 1953).

[61] *See* the cases cited *supra*, footnote 60, and Johnston v. J.A. Hackney & Sons, Inc., 300 F. Supp. 375 (E.D.N.C. 1969); McLeod v. General Elec. Co., 366 F.2d 847, 849, 63 L.R.R.M. 2065 (2d Cir. 1966); Johnston v. J.P. Stevens & Co., 341 F.2d 891, 892, 58 L.R.R.M. 2457 (4th Cir. 1965).

order, which might be nullified if the injunction does not issue; [62] or to prevent harmful impact on the public interest.[63]

The courts have found that the section 10(j) injunction is not "just and proper" in situations where the alleged violation involved a novel Board theory seeking to prevent picketing inside a privately owned office building,[64] or where the court felt that reinstatement could be properly remedied by back pay, and there was no evidence that the refusal to reinstate would have undercut the union's bargaining authority.[65] On the other hand, the Third Circuit did order reinstatement in a section 10(j) decision in which it found that the employer's discharge of a member of the union bargaining committee made reinstatement essential to maintaining the integrity of the collective bargaining relationship.[66]

The Board has experienced difficulty in obtaining bargaining orders under section 10(j). It was successful in *Kaynard v. MMIC*[67] and a few prior cases. In cases in which a bargaining relationship had not existed, however, the courts have just as often found that establishment of the status quo does not require a bargaining order.[68]

The courts have recognized that section 10(j) provides for an "extraordinary remedy,"[69] and that the injunction under section 10(j)

---

[62] Angle v. Sachs, 382 F.2d 655, 66 L.R.R.M. 2111 (10th Cir. 1967); Minnesota Mining and Mfg., 385 F.2d 265, 66 L.R.R.M. 2444 (8th Cir. 1967); Lebus v. Manning, Maxwell and Moore Inc., 218 F. Supp. 702, 705–706, 54 L.R.R.M. 2122 (D. La. 1963); Reynolds v. Curley Printing Co., 247 F. Supp. 317, 323–324, 60 L.R.R.M. 2413 (D. Tenn. 1965).

[63] *See* Penello v. United Mine Workers, 88 F. Supp. 935, 942, 25 L.R.R.M. 2368 (D.D.C. 1950); McLeod v. General Elec. Co., 257 F. Supp. 690, 708, 62 L.R.R.M. 2809 (S.D.N.Y. 1966), *rev'd*, 366 F.2d 847, 63 L.R.R.M. 2065 (2d Cir. 1966).

[64] Silverman v. 40–41 Reality Assocs., Inc., 668 F.2d 678, 109 L.R.R.M. 2542 (2d Cir. 1982).

[65] Kobell v. Suburban Lines, Inc., 731 F.2d 1076, 115 L.R.R.M. 3297 (3d Cir. Mar. 20, 1984); Eisenberg v. Hartz Mountain Corp., 519 F.2d 138, L.R.R.M. 2707 (3d Cir. 1975).

[66] Eisenberg v. Wellington Hall Nursing Home, 651 F.2d 902, 107 L.R.R.M. 2958 (3d Cir. 1981).

[67] 734 F.2d 950, 116 L.R.R.M. 2465 (2d Cir. 1984); Kaynard v. Palby Lingerie Inc., 625 F.2d 1047, 104 L.R.R.M. 2897 (2d Cir. 1980); Hirsch v. Trim Lean Meat Prods., 479 F. Supp. 1351, 102 L.R.R.M. 2950 (D.C. Del. 1979); Levin v. C & W Mining Co., 610 F.2d 432, 102 L.R.R.M. 3039 (6th Cir. 1979); *see* Sealer v. Trading Post, Inc., 517 F.2d 33, 89 L.R.R.M. 2513 (2d Cir. 1975) for Second Circuit standards for § 10(j) bargaining orders.

[68] NLRB v. Windsor Indus., Inc., 730 F.2d 860, 115 L.R.R.M. 3649 (2d Cir. 1984); Boyer v. Pilot Freight Carriers, Inc., 515 F.2d 1185, 89 L.R.R.M. 2908 (5th Cir. 1975); Taylor v. Circo Resorts, Inc., 458 F. Supp. 152 (D. Nev. 1978); Hendrix v. S.S. Kresge Co., 440 F. Supp. 1335, 97 L.R.R.M. 2987 (D. Kan. 1977)

[69] Boyer v. Pilot Freight Carriers, Inc., 515 F.2d 1185, 89 L.R.R.M. 2908 (5th Cir. 1975).

is moot once the Board rules on the underlying charges.[70] Some courts have instituted specific time limits for the duration of the section 10(j) injunction, to pressure the Board to prevent delay under the extraordinary injunctive relief. The Third Circuit in *Eisenberg v. Hartz Mountain Corp.*[71] set a specific six-month limitation on the restraints it imposed under section 10(j). The Eighth Circuit later accepted the advisability of such time limits on injunctions granted in order to encourage expedited handling by the Board.[72] The Seventh Circuit, however, has refused to impose a six-month limitation on section 10(j) injunctions.[73]

Other courts have ruled that a delay on the part of the Board between the time of the violation and the petitioning of the court for temporary injunction is also a factor that should be considered when deciding whether the granting of the relief is just and proper.[74] This, however, has not presented any major impediment to the Board in obtaining section 10(j) relief.

SECTION 10(e) AND 10(f) INJUNCTIONS

Sections 10(e) and 10(f) of the Act [75] authorize the U.S. Court of Appeals to "grant such temporary relief or restraining order as it deems just and proper" pending the outcome of proceedings pursuant to the Board's application for enforcement of an unfair labor practice order.[76] The legal standard applicable to NLRB requests for such relief were set forth by the Fourth Circuit in *NLRB v. Aerovox,*[77] as follows:

> As the first prerequisite for relief pending appeal, the Board must establish reasonable cause to believe the Act had been violated. This alone, however, is insufficient to show why the normal processes of

---

[70] Barber v. Central Cartage, Inc., 583 F.2d 335, 99 L.R.R.M. 2252 (7th Cir. 1978).

[71] 519 F.2d 138, 89 L.R.R.M. 2705 (3rd Cir. 1975).

[72] Davidoff v. Minneapolis Bldg. & Constr. Trades Council, 550 F.2d 407, 99 L.R.R.M. 2801 (8th Cir. 1977).

[73] Squillacote v. Graphic Arts Int'l Union, 540 F.2d 853, 93 L.R.R.M. 2257 (7th Cir. 1976).

[74] Boyer v. Pilot Freight Carriers, Inc., 515 F.2d 1185, 89 L.R.R.M. 2908 (5th Cir. 1975); Solien v. Merchants Home Delivery Serv., 557 F.2d 622, 95 L.R.R.M. 2596 (8th Cir. 1977).

[75] 29 U.S.C. §§ 160(e), 160(f).

[76] NLRB orders are not self-enforcing. Hence they become legally binding upon respondents only upon enforcement by the appropriate court of appeals.

[77] 389 F.2d 475, 67 L.R.R.M. 2158 (4th Cir. 1967). *See also* International Union, UAW v. NLRB (Ex-Cell-O Corp.), 449 F.2d 1046, 76 L.R.R.M. 2753, 2756, n.29 (D.C. Cir. 1971).

court enforcement should not be followed. A second test should be applied. It must appear from the circumstances of the case that the remedial purposes of the Act will be frustrated unless relief pendente lite is granted. These standards, we believe, will generally satisfy the Act's requirement that temporary relief be just and proper.[78]

It should be emphasized that section 10(e) and 10(f) relief is requested sparingly by the Board and is not generally available in enforcement proceedings.[79]

---

[78] 67 L.R.R.M. at 2159.

[79] Further explication of the requirements for § 10(e) relief can be found in Minnesota Mining & Mfg. v. Meter, 385 F.2d 265, 270–271, 273, 66 L.R.R.M. 2444 (8th Cir. 1967); McLeod v. Compressed Air Workers, 292 F.2d 358, 48 L.R.R.M. 2655 (2d Cir. 1961); Firestone Synthetic Rubber & Latex Co. v. Potter, 400 F.2d 897, 69 L.R.R.M. 2415 (5th Cir. 1968); Angle v. Sachs, 382 F.2d 655, 66 L.R.R.M. 2111, 2114 (10th Cir. 1967); Sears, Roebuck and Co. v. Carpet Layers Local No. 419, AFL-CIO, 397 U.S. 655, 659 (1970); NLRB v. Beverage Air Co., 391 F.2d 255, 257, 67 L.R.R.M. 2763 (4th Cir. 1968); NLRB v. ILGWU, 274 F.2d 376, 44 L.R.R.M. 2003 (3rd Cir. 1959); and Sachs v. Davis & Hemphill, Inc., 295 F. Supp. 142, 71 L.R.R.M. 2126 (4th Cir. 1969), applying § 10(j) standards to § 10(e).

CHAPTER XVI

Conclusion

Of the many thoughts that have passed through our minds during the more than two years in which this book was being written, one stands out: the Act has stood the test of time and has worked well, probably far better than the drafters envisioned over fifty years ago.

The Wagner Act of 1935 protected the rights of employees who chose to engage in collective bargaining, and the Taft-Hartley amendments of 1947 expressly extended the protection to employees who chose to refrain from collective bargaining. The Act was intended to prevent or restrain certain prohibited activities. Underlying our labor legislation has been the assumption that it is in the best long-range interests of all of the parties to have their disputes and collective bargaining relationships governed by their respective economic strengths, and not by government or by statutory regulation.

Although there have been problems from time to time, the fact is that the statutory system and our industrial economy are working more effectively than virtually any other model known to the world. Nonetheless, recently some strong attacks have been made against the Board and its processes. Lane Kirkland, president of the AFL-CIO, has recently said:

> The trade union movement of America was not created by the National Labor Relations Board—and this yellow dog Board cannot stop the trade union movement in America. We are going to outlast the bastards and sign up their undertakers on our way forward into the future.[1]

Kirkland has also referred to the need to deregulate labor law and return to "the law of the jungle."[2]

Similar sentiments have also been heard from William Wynn, president of the United Food and Commercial Workers:

---

[1] *President's Policies Eroding Job Opportunities, Kirkland Declares*, 209 DAILY LAB. REP. A-11 (October 29, 1985).

[2] Hoerr, *Collective Bargaining Is In Danger Without Labor-Law Reform*, BUS. WK. 29 (July 16, 1984).

[B]ecause the UFCW cannot rely on the NLRB for justice, we'll get
it ourselves. We'll get it in the streets if necessary.[3]

These attacks are unwarranted. Unions today are facing myriad
problems, some of their own making and some not. But the union
movement will better represent its members and their long-range
interests by focusing on solving these problems rather than attempting to intimidate the Board with irresponsible verbal attacks
or attempting to change enforcement of the statute. Although these
issues are essentially outside of the scope of this work, they at least
must be mentioned here.

Unions with currently depleted memberships view a new employee as a potential member. The new employee is younger and
better educated than ever before, and also is more likely to be female
and / or from a minority group than ever before. These are groups
that traditionally have neither been union members nor actively
solicited to be union members. Although the union movement has
talked about the need to organize these workers, there is a paucity
of evidence of successful attempts or results. Newspaper headlines
concerning union corruption and racketeering do little to encourage
new members, nor do the increasing lawsuits alleging unions' failures to represent their members. Changes in the Act or its enforcement will not solve these problems.

In general, public support for the union movement has eroded.
Although there exists a recognition of the labor movement's con-
tribution to the industrial history of the United States, there is a
public sense of being fed up with unnecessary strikes, intransigent
bargaining positions, violence, corruption, abuse of power, and self-
dealing. The lack of public support has affected the unions' ability
to organize new members, conduct consumer boycotts, enforce
picket lines, and enjoy the political support to which the union
movement had become accustomed.

The United States economy has undergone a number of profound
structural changes in the last two decades. Until just recently,
unpredicted and significant increases in energy costs affected both
the methods of production and the ultimate cost of the commodities
produced. The emergence of a highly competitive world market has
dramatically affected the commodities that U.S. industries can produce domestically and market effectively. As a result of these factors

---

[3] *Hearings Before the Subcomm. on Labor-Mgmt. Relations of the House Comm.
on Education and Labor and the Subcomm. on Manpower and Housing of the House
Comm. on Govt. Operations,* 98th Cong. 2d Sess. (1984) (statement of William H.
Wynn, President, United Food and Commercial Workers Int'l Union), *reprinted in*
123 DAILY LAB. REP. F-1 (June 26, 1984).

and a number of others, the U.S. industrial economy continues its transformation from a manufacturing to a service emphasis.

The recent recessionary economy also exacted a considerable toll from the union movement. While it might be too simplistic to point at unions as the sole culprits behind cost-push inflation, clearly their members and other observers saw the relative inability, and sometimes refusal, of their leadership to deal effectively with the downturn in the economy and the resultant loss of jobs. The traditional organizing cry of "we'll get you more" seemed empty; the traditional confrontational "adversary atmosphere" in the workplace seemed dysfunctional.[4]

Deregulation of certain major industries, such as trucking and the airlines, has provided increased competition—much of it union free—in these industries. The loss of the unions' almost monopolistic hold on these workforces has cost the unions not only members but also positions of power in these and other industries.

Without ending a legal monograph by making economic conclusions, suffice it to say that the unions' problems have predominantly economic and social underpinnings and do not call for legal correction, at least not in terms of the Act. Many of the recommended changes to the Act or its enforcement today would artificially provide additional economic strength to the unions' positions. Questions are being asked about the unions' ability to negotiate first contracts, if the employer is resolved to bargain hard.[5] Some of the recommendations would likely provide short-term relief for the unions. For example, one suggestion is to do away with the right to replace strikers during first-contract negotiations. Another is to do away with the prohibition against secondary boycotts.[6] These changes almost certainly would provide immediate respite for the unions by providing considerably more economic power, but they would not be in the best interests of the economy. The immediate advantage to the unions could well lead to excesses which could severely cripple the industries on the receiving end of this new power.

---

[4] Although the authors do not necessarily agree with many of his conclusions, Professor Paul C. Weiler is one of the more thoughtful commentators about labor law and the labor movement today. Even Weiler notes: "What is also needed is some profound self-reflection and self-renewal by the union movement itself." *Speech by Paul C. Weiler before National Academy of Arbitrators,* 112 DAILY LAB. REP. E-10 (June 11, 1985).

[5] Cooke, *The Failure to Negotiate First Contracts: Determinations and Policy Implications,* 38 INDUS. & LAB. REL. REV. 163 (1985).

[6] Note the forum discussion between Mark A. DeBernardo, Labor Law Manager, U.S. Chamber of Commerce, and Laurence Gold, General Counsel, AFL-CIO. 7–10 *NLRB at 50: Labor Board at the Crossroads,* BNA Special Report (1985). See also *Speech by Paul C. Weiler before National Academy of Arbitrators, supra* note 4.

At the same time, we give warning to those employers who are celebrating the demise of the union movement. Although not necessarily democratic internally, the union movement has participated as a traditional political force in our democratic society. For the most part, the labor movement in the United States has not fallen into the trap into which labor movements in other countries have stepped. Employers bent on taking advantage of their economic power today should not attempt to bargain unions out of existence; inevitably, something else will fill that void. During this century an enormous amount of federal legislation has been passed (much of it imitated on the state level) which regulates the employment environment: the Fair Labor Standards Act, the Civil Rights Act, the Age Discrimination in Employment Act, OSHA, and ERISA, to name a few. Unions have generally supported this legislation, which ironically has taken away some of their traditional functions. In addition, the courts currently seem very willing to involve themselves in regulating the employer-employee relationship. As unions decline, will the erosion of the at-will doctrine accelerate? Will legislation enter the at-will arena? Would we be better off replacing the union movement with increased governmental regulation? We reiterate our warning to employers who are bent on hearing the unions' death rattle, regardless of the cost.

There are, at the same time, certain changes that would be beneficial. There is little argument that the Board's procedures should move as quickly as possible and that long delays in adjudication, or large caseload backlogs, do not lead to justice for anyone. Edward B. Miller, former chairman of the NLRB, noted correctly in 1977 that

> [p]romptness clearly benefits the charging party. Justice delayed is justice denied. But promptness also frequently benefits the charged party, who should not have to be under a cloud of uncertainty and face possible litigation over a long period of time. If the accused is innocent, he has a right to be declared innocent at the earliest possible date.[7]

Chairman Miller's comments are equally appropriate and accurate today. Before experimenting with new remedies, it would be far more advantageous to see that the old remedies are working expeditiously. The certainty of quick justice and a quick remedy is the surest deterrent of all. No one can defend the delays that have characterized recent Board decisionmaking. Delays only encourage

---

[7] Miller, *An Administrative Appraisal of the NLRB*, Labor Relations and Public Policy Series No. 16 at p. 46, University of Pennsylvania, The Wharton School, Industrial Research Unit (rev. ed. 1980) (emphasis in original).

abuse of the system by all parties, thereby producing further delay and a concomitant loss of respect for the system.

Regarding specific remedies, the *Gissel* area particularly is long overdue for attention. As noted in detail in Chapter XII, *supra,* this does not mean that there should be an undemocratic remedy such as a minority bargaining order. First, such a bargaining order ignores employee free choice. Second, the union would not have the support of the collective bargaining unit and thus would lack the economic strength necessary to bargain effectively. In most circumstances, the union's early demise would be inevitable. At the same time, the lack of predictability as to what conduct will or will not lead to a majority bargaining order must be corrected and clarified. The Board conflicts with the Court of Appeals concerning *Gissel* orders have affected far more than just the enforcement of these orders and must be minimized.

In some instances, traditional remedies may work too slowly in the midst of a union organizational campaign. Reinstatement (if desired) and backpay (offset by interim earnings) are little consolation to a discharged union organizer or to a union long after the representation election is lost. The calculated use of this delaying tactic could be offset by the increased use of the section 10(j) injunction power. This traditional remedy could be more effective in such instances if used more frequently. This is not to say, however, that discharges during organizational campaigns automatically fit into this category. To the contrary, most will probably not. The Act at section 10(c) protects discharge for cause. An increased use of the section 10(j) injunction brings with it the increased burden of careful evaluation by both the General Counsel and the Board before unleashing this powerful weapon. This burden is consistent with the fact that, above all, respect for the law and for the Act must be encouraged. This will require fair and consistent case adjudication. It will require predictability in well-enunciated, straightforward, clearly written decisions.

Unfortunately, while the unions are currently talking about ignoring the statute because it does not solve their problems as they would like, management's confidence in the Act, lost during the recent result-oriented years, has not returned. The current Board must continue to bring all of the parties back to the table and restore their confidence in the Act. As the Board begins its second fifty years, this is its most important task.

APPENDICES

Appendix A

THE *GISSEL* RULING

Gissel is actually a consolidation of four cases: three from the Fourth Circuit, *Gissel Packing Co., Heck's Inc.*, and *General Steel Products, Inc.;* and one from the First Circuit, *Sinclair Company.* All of the cases involved union organizational campaigns that resulted in the union obtaining authorization cards from a majority of the employees. In each case, the employer refused to bargain with the union based upon the card majority and embarked upon, or continued, vigorous anti-union campaigns that gave rise to multiple unfair labor practice charges.

In *Gissel*, the union did not seek an election, but merely filed unfair labor practice charges. The facts included a company vice-president telling two employees, who were later discharged, that if caught talking to union men "You God-damned things will go"; interrogation of employees about union activities; promises of better benefits; warnings that if the union got in the vice-president would take his money and let the union run the shop, and that the union would not get in and would have to fight the company first; and sending an agent to a union meeting to identify union adherents (which led to the discharge of two employees). The Board found violations of section 8(a)(1), specifically, coercive interrogation, threats of discharge, and promise of benefits; and violations of section 8(a)(3), specifically, discharge of employees for union activities.

In *Heck's*, the election was blocked because of the unfair labor practices. Among the facts were an employee singled out of an assembled group by the company president to ask if he had signed a union card; the leading union supporter being terminated; an employee interrogated about his union activities, encouraged to withdraw his authorization, and warned that a union victory would lead to reduced hours, fewer raises, and withdrawal of bonuses; and two union supporters offered higher-paying jobs if they would use their influence to "break up the union." The Board found violations of section 8(a)(1), specifically coercive interrogations, threat of reprisals, creation of appearance of surveillance, and offering benefits to oppose a union; and a violation of section 8(a)(3), specifically, discharge of employee for union activities.

The *General Steel* election was lost by the union and set aside because of the unfair labor practices. In *General Steel*, throughout the six-month union campaign, the company's foremen and supervisors interrogated employees about union involvement; threatened employees with discharge for union activities or voting for the union; suggested that the union might hurt business or make new jobs harder to obtain, warned that strikes and other dire economic consequences would result; and asserted that, although the company would have to negotiate, it could negotiate endlessly and not have to sign anything. The Board found violations of section 8(a)(1), specifically, coercive interrogations, and threats of reprisals, including discharge.

In each of the above three cases, the Board, finding that the unions had obtained cards from a majority of the employees in the unit, ordered the employers to bargain with the unions. The Fourth Circuit denied enforcement of the bargaining order in all three cases.

In *Sinclair Company,* the factual pattern was quite similar to those in the other three cases. The employer committed multiple unfair labor practices, the union lost the election, and the Board, finding that the union held a valid card majority, ordered the company to bargain. In *Sinclair Company,* the company president told all of the employees about a past strike that almost put the company out of business; declared that the company was still on thin ice and a strike could lead to closing, as the parent company had ample facilities elsewhere; said that the employees, because of their age and skills, would have a tough time finding jobs and, if the employees did not believe him, to look around town and see the other closed plants. The last statement was subsequently reemphasized in a letter to the employees. A pamphlet referring to the prior strike and the fact that the union was strike-happy followed; another pamphlet was distributed, listing area companies that had gone out of business because of union demands, which included a cartoon showing a grave being prepared for Sinclair. The day before the election, the president again told the employees of the precarious financial condition of the company, that a strike could jeopardize continued operation, and the age and education level of the employees would make reemployment difficult. The Board found section 8(a)(1) violations, specifically, that under the totality of the circumstances, the president's communications tended to convey the belief or impression that selection of the union could lead to a plant closing, or to transfer of production, with a resultant loss of jobs. The Board found that these activities tended to foreclose the possibility of holding a fair election. The First Circuit, disavowing the Fourth Circuit's approach, enforced the bargaining order. The Supreme Court granted certiorari to resolve, among other issues, this conflict among the circuits. 395 U.S. 575, 579–590, 71 L.R.R.M. 2481, 2482–2486.

Appendix B

DEFENSES TO *GISSEL:*
ABSENCE OF A CARD MAJORITY

In that a card majority is essential to a *Gissel II* order, the lack thereof is likely to be a defense. Effective defenses include:
(1) Lack of a card majority. Ona Corp. v. NLRB, 261 N.L.R.B. No. 187, 110 L.R.R.M. 1271 (1982), *enforced in part, denied in part,* 729 F.2d 713, 115 L.R.R.M. 3665 (11th Cir. 1984) (cards not authenticated; General Counsel has burden of proving majority status); NLRB v. Marion Rohr, 714 F.2d 228, 114 L.R.R.M. 2126 (2nd Cir. 1983) (cards not obtained from majority of employees); Fuchs v. Jet Spray Corp., 560 F. Supp. 1147, 114 L.R.R.M. 3493 (D. Mass. 1983), *affirmed,* 725 F.2d 664, 116 L.R.R.M. 2191 (1st Cir. 1983) (Board not entitled to injunction requiring employer to bargain with union as union lacked majority support in appropriate unit); Grismac Corp., 205 N.L.R.B. 1108, 84 L.R.R.M. 1256 (1973), *enforced,* 492 F.2d 1247, 86 L.R.R.M. 2152 (7th Cir. 1974); Trend Corp. and G.E. Corp., 263 N.L.R.B. 295, 111 L.R.R.M. 1111 (1982) (changes in composition of unit caused union to lose majority status before unfair labor practices committed); *but see* Pinter Brothers, 227 N.L.R.B. 921, 94 L.R.R.M. 1284 (1977) (majority status established by adding signed cards of nonvoters to union votes in an election that had been set aside).
(2) Card majority revoked. Struthers-Dunn, Inc., 228 N.L.R.B. 49, 95 L.R.R.M. 1204 (1977), *enforcement denied,* 574 F.2d 796, 98 L.R.R.M. 2385 (3d Cir. 1978) (cards revoked prior to unfair labor practices); *cf.* NLRB v. Flex Plastics, 726 F.2d 272, 115 L.R.R.M. 3036 (6th Cir. 1984) (Board warranted in ordering employer to bargain with union that lost decertification elections; unfair labor practices committed by employer undermined union's majority strength); NLRB v. Air Prods. and Chems., 717 F.2d 141, 114 L.R.R.M. 2397 (4th Cir. 1983) (revocation of previous card majority discounted because it occurred after employer unfair labor practices.)
(3) Cards forged. Imco Container Co., 148 N.L.R.B. 312, 56 L.R.R.M. 1497 (1964).
(4) Nature of the card misrepresented. Cumberland Shoe Corp., 144 N.L.R.B. 1268, 54 L.R.R.M. 1233 (1963), *enforced,* 351 F.2d 917, 60 L.R.R.M. 2305 (6th Cir. 1965) (cards clearly setting forth the

union as the signer's bargaining representative will be invalidated for misrepresentation only if the signer is told the cards' only purpose is to obtain a secret ballot election). *See also* NLRB v. Horizon Air Services, 761 F.2d 22, 119 L.R.R.M. 2203 (1st Cir. 1985). DeQueen Gen. Hosp. v. NLRB, 744 F.2d 612, 117 L.R.R.M. 2534 (8th Cir. 1984); NLRB v. Ed Chandler Ford, Inc., 718 F.2d 892, 115 L.R.R.M. 2543 (9th Cir. 1983); Burlington Indus. v. NLRB, 680 F.2d 974, 110 L.R.R.M. 2649 (4th Cir. 1982).

(5) Coercion. NLRB v. Savair Mfg. Co., 414 U.S. 270, 84 L.R.R.M. 2929 (1973) (offer by union to waive initiation fee for employees signing cards prior to election constitutes interference and grounds for setting aside election; use of cards obtained in this manner to support a *Gissel* order disapproved).

(6) Supervisory interference. Neuman Nursing Home, 270 N.L.R.B. No. 96, 116 L.R.R.M. 1447 (1984) (authorization cards directly solicited by supervisor shall not be counted for purpose of determining union's majority status); Stewart Sandwich Serv., 260 N.L.R.B. 805, 109 L.R.R.M. 1235 (1982) (fact that two low-level supervisors were present and spoke at two union meetings and signed cards does not taint authorization cards signed by other employees); Melba Theatre, 260 N.L.R.B. 18, 109 L.R.R.M. 1151 (1982), *citing* El Rancho Market, 235 N.L.R.B. 468 (1978), *enforced,* 603 F.2d 223 (9th Cir. 1979); (supervisory involvement in union organizational activities will taint a union's card majority where [1] supervisor's activity implied to employees that employer favored the union, or [2] employees were coercively induced to sign authorization cards because of fear of supervisory retaliation), *but see* UAW v. I.T.T. Lighting Fixtures, Inc., 104 S. Ct. 2361 (1984) (White, J., dissenting from denial of certiorari) (urging that the Court review an apparent "per se" rule used by the Second Circuit in condemning supervisory pro-union activities during election campaigns).

Index of Cases

STUDIES OF NEGRO EMPLOYMENT

Order from University Microfilms, Inc.
Attn: Books Editorial Department
300 North Zeeb Road
Ann Arbor, Michigan 48106

*Order this book from the Industrial Research Unit, The Wharton School, University of Pennsylvania, Philadelphia, Pennsylvania 19104

Racial Policies of American Industry Series

Order from: Kraus Reprint Co., Route 100, Millwood, New York 10546